CW01673889

a secret garden

a secret garden

Indian Paintings from the Porret Collection

B.N. Goswamy, Jeremiah P. Losty and John Seyller

museum rietberg Scheidegger & Spiess

Un petit jardin pour se promener, et l'immensité pour rêver.
À ses pieds ce qu'on peut cultiver et cueillir; sur sa tête ce qu'on peut étudier et méditer; quelques fleurs sur la terre et toutes les étoiles dans le ciel.

Victor Hugo, *Les Misérables*

When Babur had his Garden of Fidelity (*Bagh-i-Wafa*) constructed at the beginning of the 16th century south of the fortress of Adinapur in present-day Afghanistan, he praised its plants, waterways and the central section of the garden. He furthermore took great delight in the change of colors in the clover meadow at the pool.

Danielle Porret, whose collection of Indian paintings is partially reproduced in this catalogue, has referred to her collection as being like *A Secret Garden* – a man-made place to linger and dwell in and to give inspiration and joy. Her garden, however, was never meant to be like Babur's *charbagh* – a preconceived and planned space. The collection just seems to have built up over time, with a steady trickle of works being added to it as years went by.

Danielle Porret's first encounter with the Far East took place in the sitting room of her family at a very young age. Her grandparents owned a Qing-dynasty *cloisonné* which bedazzled her eyes and drew her attention but was kept at safe distance. It did, however, spark her interest in the Far East. When she decided to attend university to become an interpreter, she felt the need to also nourish her interest in the Far East.

She eventually got to know the Orientalist Jean Herbert (1897–1980), who held the chair of Eastern Mythologies at Geneva University and taught classes mainly on the philosophical thoughts of Asia. Danielle Porret took great joy enroling in his classes as an extracurricular activity and as a chance to engage in a world not quite as technical as her profession in languages.

When she accepted her first position as interpreter at the International Coffee Organization in London, she had the chance to see an exhibition of the W.G. Archer collection. While she was hitherto mainly familiar with Persian paintings, the paintings from W.G. Archer were a true discovery for her. It led her to follow up on the artistic traditions of India.

London had – in comparison to Continental Europe – an active scene for the arts of the Indian Subcontinent. Great collections like the ones at the British Museum, the Victoria and Albert Museum and the British Library were easily accessible and Danielle Porret took advantage of the wide array of paintings that she could study firsthand.

When Danielle Porret returned to Geneva as a freelance interpreter, her first trip to India soon took place. She met, among other people, with Chotelal Bharany in 1972. Her profession allowed her to combine business travels with prolonged stays in India. There was even a period when she played with the thought of becoming a scholar in Indian art, abandoning her profession as interpreter. Robert Cran and Basil Gray, however, advised against that and urged her to keep on training her eye by handling as many paintings as possible.

As much as she liked the paintings brought to her attention, she also developed a wide network of scholars, specialists and collectors with whom she discussed her newly found field of interest. Don Baker, Edwin Binney, Toby Falk, Marc Zebrowski, Alvin O. Bellak, Stuart Cary Welch, W.G. Archer, Jagdish Mittal, Terence McInerney, Kumar Sangram Singh, Michael Spink, Michael Goedhuis and Francesca Galloway were among the people she discussed with. She would not seek advice from them for potential purchases, but rather liked to share her passion for Indian art with them. In her memory of the art scene in the mid 1970s, she also recollects how everybody was willing to share precious works with her – even if her budget would not allow for large acquisitions.

Besides her interest in subject matter, style and individual artists, a Deccani painting in the Heeramanek collection (cat. no. 14) she had purchased which needed urgent conservation treatment led to another field within Indian painting that she would actively engage in. Danielle Porret realized that restoration techniques were a highly intriguing field. She got in touch with a trained monk-palaeographer who was in charge of the library at the Convent des Cordeliers at Fribourg. He bluntly denied her wish to study the techniques of paper conservation with him. It was only through the course of several discussions that he realized that they both had much in common. Both were trained in professions that are highly technical and both felt that engaging in something quite different from their everyday activities was highly rewarding. The monk finally accepted her as a student and passed on his knowledge, which he had acquired in Rome at the Instituto Centrale di Patologia del Libro Alfonso Gallo. They spent several summers together, working on manuscripts and Danielle Porret was furthermore following up on the latest knowledge on conservation in the Netherlands and the United Kingdom.

The Indian paintings in the possession of Danielle Porret have been collected over the last forty years. When Danielle Porret was introduced to a curator at the Louvre by a common friend as a "collector," she would protest against such a designation. As the title of this publication suggests, the *Secret Garden* is not an assembly of representative works for public display, but rather a "personal adventure," as Porret calls it. The works were collected following a *coup de cœur* rather than a *coup de tête*. Danielle Porret keeps only a few favorites on the wall and the rest safely tucked away. It is important to her to live amidst her paintings and to find visual inspiration in them.

Coincidence led to the ties between her and the Museum Rietberg. In 1980, both Danielle Porret and the Museum Rietberg lent to a show at the Musée d'Ethnographie in Neuchâtel. It was the first time that she shared some of her works with a wider audience. Robert Cran wrote a small catalogue for this exhibition and some of the works of Danielle Porret were published there for the first time. At the opening of the exhibition, she got to know Eberhard Fischer, then director of the Museum Rietberg. From then on, they would discuss recent acquisitions and the developments on the art market and their contact became a real friendship. Danielle Porret once even demonstrated her skills as a conservator when she worked on a palm-leaf manuscript from Orissa in the collection of the Museum. Furthermore, she has generously lent to all major shows on Indian painting at the Rietberg, to *Wonders of a Golden Age* (1987), *Pahari Masters – Court Painters of Northern India* (1992), *Rama and Sita – The Ramayana in Indian Painting* (2008) and *The Way of the Master – The Great Artists of India, 1100–1900* (2011).

The Museum Rietberg is extremely happy that a group of works collected by Danielle Porret entered the collection in 2010, 2011 and 2013 and have found a permanent home among many other paintings.

A selection of the collection is published here by three eminent scholars on Indian art: B.N. Goswamy, Jeremiah Losty and John Seyller. We would like to thank all three for their outstanding work and their willingness to share their expertise and thoughts on the paintings that form part of the collection.

Albert Lutz, director of the Rietberg, has supported the department of Indian Painting generously in recent years and also made this publication possible. Elizabeth Hefti has demonstrated her experience in dealing with Indian Art, and we would like to thank her for the excellent design of this publication. Albert Walker has prepared all color separations with the necessary sensitivity. We are also indebted to Julie Pickard who thoroughly copy-edited all entries.

The authors of the entries would like to thank the following persons for their help and advice:

Milo Beach, Ainsley Cameron, Marina Chellini, Rosemary Crill, Jeevan Deol, Catherine Glynn, Navina Haidar, Shailka Mishra, Jagdish Mittal, Malini Roy, Gursharan Sidhu, Rupert Snell and Andrew Topsfield.

Above all, we are deeply obliged to Danielle Porret for her generosity and willingness to share her garden with us.

Eberhard Fischer and Jorrit Britschgi
| November 2013

catalogue

1 Bahram Gur with the Indian Princess in the Black Pavilion

2 Bahram Gur with the Tartar Princess in the Green Pavilion

Folio from the *Khamsa* of Nizami
Delhi or Western India, c. 1460–1475
Painting numbered 45 in the left margin
24.3 × 17.2 cm (folio), 20.2 × 12.5 cm (text area)

Folio from the *Khamsa* of Nizami
Delhi or Western India, c. 1460–1475
Painting numbered 4[8] in the left margin
24.2 × 17.2 cm (folio), 19 × 12.5 cm (text area)

These two paintings come from an intriguing copy of the *Khamsa* of Nizami produced in 15th-century India, presumably under Sultanate rule either at Delhi or in Western India. The manuscript was broken up sometime in the first half of the 20th century, when detached folios began to enter private collections; a large section of the manuscript appeared on the London art market in 2000.[1] Painting numbers written in the margins indicate that the manuscript once had seventy-two illustrations, about half of which are known.[2] The penultimate illustration (no. 71), which depicts a dying Iskandar, is twice the width of the others, taking as its lateral limits the span of the entire written surface rather than the usual two columns, but appearing across the center of a blank page that is ruled but not yet divided into four columns.[3] Together with some missing rubrics, this abnormal format suggests that work on the manuscript halted just short of completion.

The illustrations belong to the *Haft Paykar* (The Seven Beauties), a text completed by Nizami in 1197 and customarily situated as the fourth of the five *mathnawis* in the *Khamsa*. They are numbered 45 and 48, respectively, which means that since the final painting of the preceding book, *Layla wa Majnun*, is numbered 41, the *Haft Paykar* must have opened with two or three illustrations depicting heroic actions by Bahram Gur or his slave-girl Fitna.[4] Subsequent gaps in the series of painting numbers indicate that this *Haft Paykar* is illustrated both with the familiar septet of images of Bahram Gur with princesses of the seven climes in seven differently colored pavilions, but also with several paintings of the color-themed stories told in those pavilions.

The first folio here has two images: an exceptionally wide one depicting the seven pavilions arrayed together on three discrete platforms, and a typically small and square one showing Bahram Gur in the first pavilion, which is decorated in black and is presided over by an Indian princess dressed in that color. Although the intent of the upper painting is surely to represent the seven pavilions in which Bahram Gur is entertained on consecutive days of the week beginning with Saturday, the artist was not fastidious enough to match the colors to the order in which Nizami presents the pavilions, that is, black, yellow, green, red, blue, sandalwood and white. Thus, while the first pavilion on the right is properly black, the next is carelessly sandalwood or white. The Red and Yellow Pavilions are reversed in order, and the Green Pavilion that comes between them in the textual account of the week is omitted altogether in the introductory painting. Although the pavilions supposedly differ only in color, the artist has varied them slightly by adding several such minor embellishments as shuttered windows and scrollwork along the dome. Above the row of pavilions are four tricolored swags alternating between two concentric arcs of dark and light orange with an outer rim of white and two blue ones with similar gradations. This is the more dramatic of two conventions for sky and clouds seen throughout the manuscript, the other being two horizontal bands of light and dark blue, which are enhanced on occasion with two malformed Chinese-style clouds. The coexistence of the banded skies and Chinese-style clouds testifies to the commingling of styles originating in Mamluk Egypt and Shiraz. This same convergence of styles is apparent in the motif of a tree with enormous blossoms, oversized scrollwork designs on textiles, and round, Shirazi-style faces.

The smaller painting at the bottom of the page presents Bahram Gur in the Black Pavilion, where the enthroned king, clean-shaven on this Saturday, grasps a flower as he converses with the princess before a single female attendant holding a ewer. All three figures wear garments of black and gray, and have faces with slit-like eyes and tiny pupils drawn in black, along with noses, mouths, and double chins delineated in red. The chamber is supported by two adjacent slabs of different colors – a feature seen throughout the manuscript – and is otherwise empty but for a duck-headed aquamanile. A large tassel hangs from the center of the flattened scalloped arch, whose spandrels are ornamented with a blue shell-like quadrant rather than the loose curlicue designs found on some other buildings.

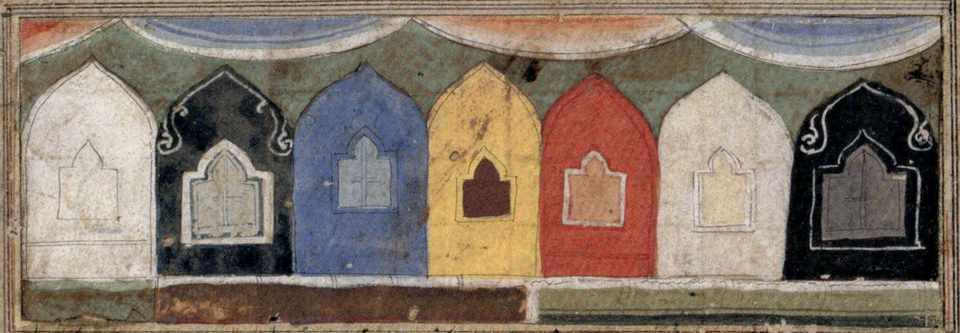

گنبدی کو ز قسم کیوان بود
در سیاهی چو مشک پنهان بود

وانکه بودش ز مشتری مایه
صندلی داشت رنگ پیرایه

وانکه مریخ بود بر کارش
گوهر سرخ بود در کارش

وانکه از آفتاب داد خبر
زرد بود او چو از حمایل زر

وانکه از زیب زهره یافت امید
بود درویش چو روی زهره سپید

وانکه بود از عطارد ش روزی
بود فیروزه گون ز فیروزی

وانکه مه کرد سوی برجش راه
داشت بر سبزهٔ چو طلعت ماه

برکشیده برین صفت پیکر
هفت گنبد بطبع هفت اختر

هفت پیکر تمام در عهدش
دختر هفت شاه در مهدش

کرده هر دختری برنگ و برای
گنبدی را بهفت گنبد جای

از نمودار خانه تا بنیش
کرده همرنگ روی گنبد خویش

روز تا روز شاه فرخ بخت
در سرای دگر نهادی تخت

شنبه آنجا که قسم شنبه بود
وان دگرها چنانکه زان بود

هر کجا جام باده نوشیدی
جامه همرنگ خانه پوشیدی

چون بنیروی رای فرزانه
مجلس آراسته بهر خانه

بانوی خانه پیش بنشستی
[illegible] آهستی بهر دستی

تا دل شاه را چگونه برد
شاه حلوای او چگونه خورد

گفتی افسانهای مهر انگیز
که کند گرم شهوت آتش تیز

گرچه زین گونه برکشید حصار
جان نبرد از اجل بآخر کار

ای نظامی ز گلشنی بگریز
که گلش خار گشت و خارش تیز

بزم بهرام روز شنبه بگنبد مشکین و افسانه شنیدن

با چنین ملک با دو روزه مقام
عاقبت بین چگونه شد بهرام

چونکه بهرام شد نشاط پرست
دیده در نقش هفت پیکر بست

روز شنبه ز دیر شماسی
خیمه زد در سواد عباسی

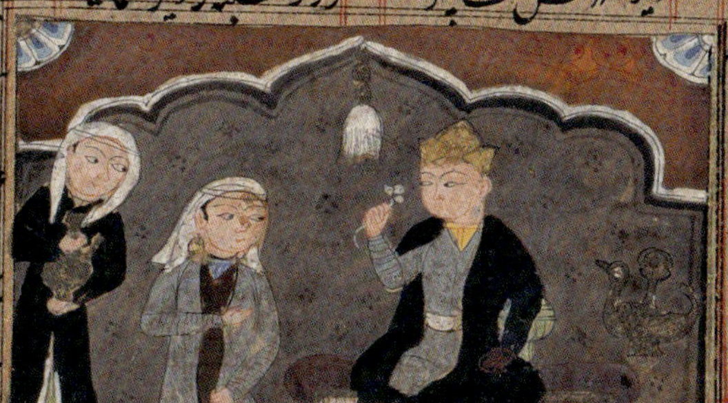

شد ز گنبد سرای غالیه فام
پیش بانوی هند شد بسلام

تا شب آنجا نشاط بازی کرد
عود سوزی و عطرسازی کرد

چون برافشاند شب [illegible] عاج
بر حریر سپید مشک سیاه

شاه ازان نوبهار کشمیری
خواست بوی چو باد شبگیری

45

When Bahram Gur visits the Green Pavilion two days later, he is unexpectedly shown with a heavy beard as well as with robes in two shades of the appropriate color. Seated on a low cushioned platform rather than a proper throne, he addresses the Tartar Princess while an attendant stands by with a platter heaped with food to complement the flask at the king's side. The arch and spandrels are decorated in the same manner as in the Black Pavilion, but the floor includes a strip of tilework with individual tiles divided diagonally into light and dark blue halves. Here, as elsewhere in the manuscript, the faces, crown, wimples, and bodies are thinly painted colored shapes that the artist delineates with cursorily drawn details in black or red.

While 15th-century Sultanate painting is notoriously uneven in style and quality, the general simplicity of these illustrations, their overall similarity to a dispersed manuscript of the *Khamsa* of Amir Khusraw, the modest, unpolished paper, and the use of Nasta'liq all point to non-royal patronage in the vicinity of one of the courts in Delhi or Western India about 1460–1475.[5] | JS

---

1 Fogg 2000, no. 28.

2 This tally differs from the number given in Fogg 2000, p. 74. A list of known pages is provided in Fogg 2000, p. 77.

3 San Diego Museum of Art 1990:253. The painting proper is published in Binney 1981, fig. 37. The usual process was to rule and write out the text first, as is demonstrated in painting number 58, which has an indented block intrusion at the bottom of the painting field where a correction had been made in the text.

4 Based on painting cycles found in other copies of the *Khamsa*, these illustrations would probably depict three of the following four episodes: Bahram Gur demonstrating his hunting prowess to Fitna by shooting an ass and a lion with a single arrow; Bahram Gur killing the dragon; Bahram Gur seizing the crown after shooting lions; and Fitna carrying an ox on her shoulders upstairs to Bahram Gur. This scenario assumes that the image of the seven pavilions was not included in the tally of paintings, as the absence of a painting number in the margin beside it suggests.

5 For the dispersed *Khamsa* of Amir Khusraw, see Brac de la Perrière 2008, pp. 263–270. On pp. 270–272, this author lists and discusses two little-known but very similar manuscripts, one tentatively identified as a *Shahnama* and the other a *Khamsa* of Nizami in Rome illustrated with thirty-two paintings.

آتشی از تو بود در دامن　پرده زن از میانه دور افکن　چون شدی شمع وار با من راست　دور دور افکن از میان برخاست

کآفتاب من از حمل شد شاد　کی ز برد العجوز آرم یاد　چند ازین داستان شاه نواز　گفت آن نازنین شنید بناز

چون چنان دید ترک توسن خوی　راه دادش بسرو سوسن بوی　بلبلی بر سریر غنچه نشست　غنچه بشکفت و گشت بلبل مست

طوطی دید پر شکر خانی　بی مگس ساخت شکر افشانی　ماهی را در آبگیر افکند　رطبی در میان شیر افکند

بود شیرین و خوبی عجبش　گرد شیرین حلاوت رطبش　شه چو آن نقش را پرند گشاد　قفل زرین ز درج بند گشاد

دید گنجینه بزر در خورد　گردش از زیبهای زرین خورد　زردست آنک شادمانی ازوست　ذوق حلوای زعفرانی ازوست

آنچه بینی که زعفران زردست　خنده بین زانک زعفران خوردست　نور شمع از نقاب زردی یافت　گاه موی بهار زردی یافت

زر که زردست مایه طربست　طین اصفر عزیز ازین سببست　شه که این داستان شنید تمام　در کنارش گرفت و خفت بکام

آمدن بهرام روز دوشنبه در گنبد سبز

چونک روز دوشنبه آمد شاه　چتر سرسبز برکشید بماه

شد برافراخت ...　سبز در سبز چون فرشته و باغ　رخت خود سوی سبز گنبد برد　دل بشادی و خرمی بسپرد

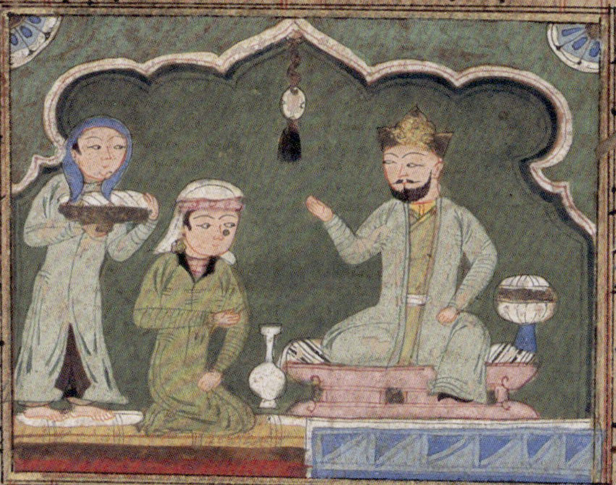

جون پر پسرزه ... وار　باغ انجم فشاند برگ بهار

زان خرامنده سرو سبز ...　خواست تا بر شکر گشاید تنگ

پری انکه که پرده بود نماز / شاد　بر سلیمان گشاده پرده راز

گفت ای جان من بجان تو شاد　همه جانها فدای جان تو باد

خانه دولتست خرگاهت　تاج و تخت آستان درگاهت

تاج را سربلندی از سر تست　تخت را پادشاهی از در تست

گوهرت عقد مملکت را تاج　همه عالم بدرگهت محتاج　چون دعا گفت بر سریر بلند　برگشاد از عقیق چشمه قند

افسانه گفتن دختر پری را در گنبد سیوم

گفت شخصی عزیز بد در روم　خوب و خوشدل چو انگبین در موم

هرچه باید زآدمی ز هنر　داشت آن جمله نیکویی بسر　تا جهان خوبی و خردمندی　بود میلش بپاک پیوندی

گرو مان بر نظر نشاندندش　بشر پرهیزکار خواندندش　میخ امید روزی از سر ناز　در رهی خالی از نشیب و فراز

بهر ریش عشق ترکتازی کرد　فتنه با عقل دست بازی کرد　پیکری دید در لفافه خام　چون در ابر سیاه ماه تمام

3 Prince Danyal

Attributed to Manohar
Mughal c. 1595–1600
23.2 × 15.2 cm (folio), 12.8 × 6.5 cm (painting)
Museum Rietberg, Collection Danielle Porret, 2011.385

The stout figure depicted here fingering his pearl and ruby necklace and gripping the end of his golden *patka* is Akbar's third son, Prince Danyal, who "sacrificed himself to wine" at the age of thirty-three in March 1605, when he collapsed after quaffing contaminated alcohol from a gun barrel. He can be identified on the basis of five other portraits ranging from childhood to adulthood, all but one by Manohar, son of the master artist Basawan and a particularly accomplished royal portraitist in his own right.[1] Danyal's most distinctive features are his aquiline nose, thick black mustache sweeping downward to a heavy jaw, and bull neck. He is dressed in a gossamer-sheer six-pointed *jama* – a garment worn by the prince in two other portraits as well – with delicate beading along the lower hem and raised floral designs along the neckline, upper arms, and cuffs. In accordance with Mughal pictorial convention, no anatomical feature of the prince's torso is visible through the diaphanous *jama*, which instead merely casts a whitish sheen over the covered parts of his ruddy body and accentuates the dark musk-scented marks at the armpits. Manohar habitually emphasizes this change in color saturation most conspicuously below the waist, where the *paijama*'s vibrant reddish orange yields to a lighter and less assertive color covering the figure's full buttocks and thighs.

Typical of Manohar's handiwork, too, are the prince's taut face and intense expression, the tie-dyed cloth of his low-slung turban, the squarish shape of the hands, the ornate geometric designs on the *patka*, and the rocking pose suggested by the undulating lines of the footwear. The surfaces of both the figure and the flat green background are less refined than those of another portrait on which Jahangir has identified the figure as his deceased brother Danyal.[2] This points to a date before 1600, when Manohar accompanied the rebellious Prince Salim to Allahabad.

On the reverse is a quatrain signed by Muhammad Husayn al-Kashmiri, one of the most eminent Mughal calligraphers of Akbar's reign (1556–1605) and honored with the title *Zarrin Qalam* (Golden Pen). The signature is evidently cropped, ending abruptly with the phrase "in the year one thousand and." The numeral 20 written in the very corner of the surrounding cloud suggests that the date was AH 1020, equivalent to 1611–1612 CE. A similar panel of calligraphy by Muhammad Husayn is found on the reverse of a double portrait of Princes Danyal and Murad.[3] The surrounding blue floral band and the border inscribed with fragmentary writing in Shikasta script and impressed with an illegible seal appear to be 18th-century additions. | JS

1 For a recent overview of Manohar's career, see Seyller 2011.
2 The Metropolitan Museum of Art 1955.55.121.10.32a, published in Welch et al. 1987, no. 18.
3 Losty 2011, no. 1.

Published: Goswamy and Fischer 1987, no. 64

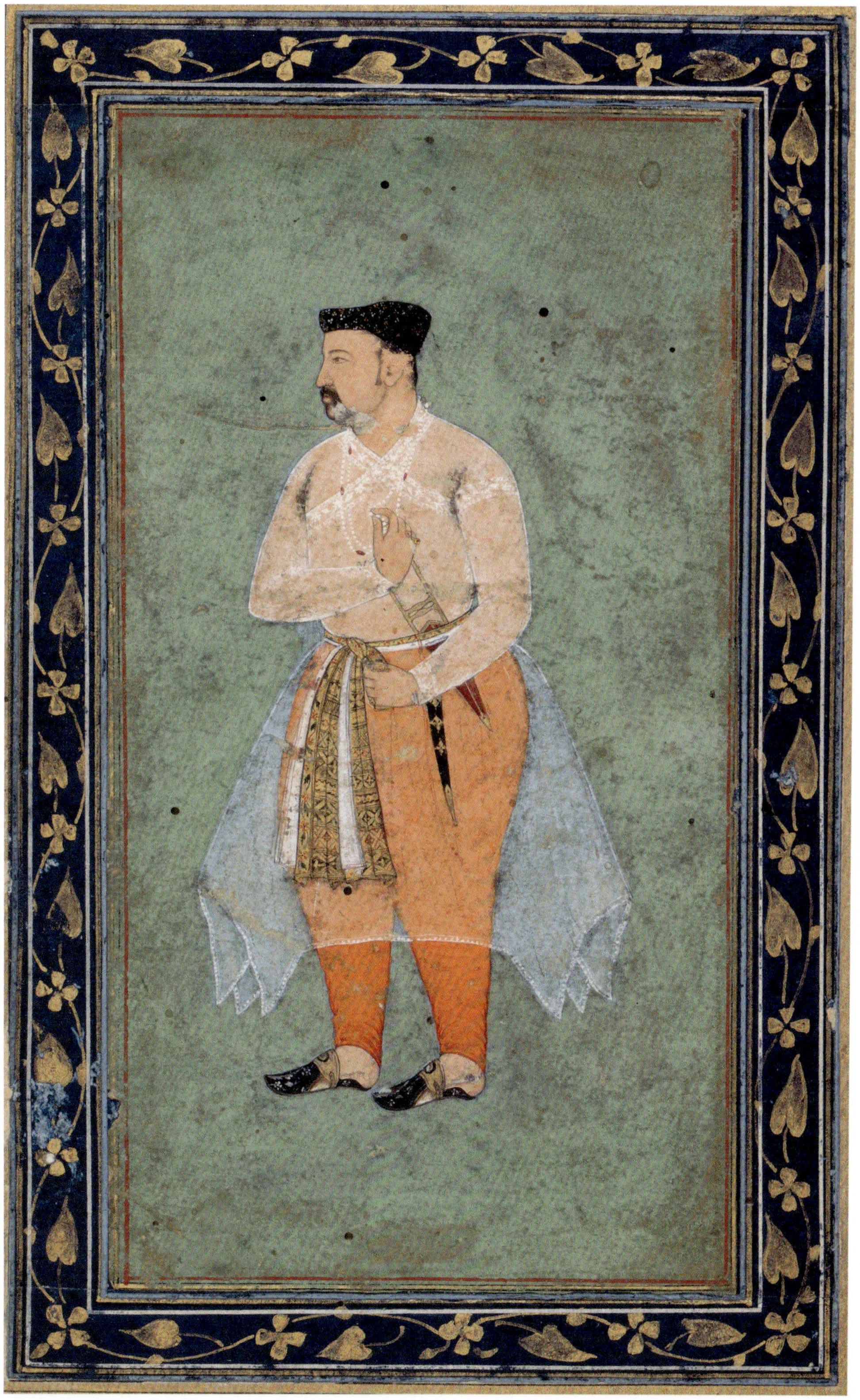

4 Bahram Gur with the Moorish Princess in the Yellow Pavilion

5 Bahram Gur with the Greek Princess in the White Pavilion

Folio from a *Khamsa* of Nizami (numbered page 389)
Popular Mughal style, c. 1600–1620
22.9 × 12.4 cm (folio), 20.2 × 9 cm (text area)
Museum Rietberg, Collection Danielle Porret, 2011.386

Folio from a *Khamsa* of Nizami (numbered page 429)
Popular Mughal style, c. 1600–1620
22.9 × 11.8 cm (folio), 18.8 × 9.3 cm (text area)
Museum Rietberg, Collection Danielle Porret, 2011.387

These two paintings belong to the *Haft Paykar* section of an otherwise unknown manuscript of the *Khamsa* of Nizami. They illustrate the second and seventh of the variously colored pavilions built for the pleasure of Bahram Gur, the Sasanian ruler, who as a prince chances upon a locked chamber in the palace at Khawarnaq adorned with a painting of seven princesses. Once Bahram Gur becomes king, he directs an architect to realize this unforgettable vision by building seven domed pavilions, each in the color associated with the planet governing the particular day of the week on which the king is to visit, and each occupied by a princess from one of the world's seven climes. The Yellow Pavilion is connected with the sun, and the White Pavilion with Venus.

Bahram Gur and the Moorish Princess sit together on an awkwardly rendered low *takht* with a golden throneback set asymmetrically behind only the king himself. The pavilion deviates from the typical imagery of such scenes, neither including a dome nor providing an interior space in which the two royal figures might be alone. Instead, the tête-à-tête is diffused by the presence of nine other females, none of whom brings refreshments or plays music. Two pairs of figures half-disappear behind an inexplicable feature rendered as a brown line with a kind of fringe. Save for the blue textile covering the *takht* and a smattering of trees and flowers, everything in the entire field is appropriately yellow or gold.

The illustration of Bahram Gur's visit to the White Pavilion naturally has similar imagery. The king and the Greek Princess are seated on a golden carpet within arm's reach of each other, once again with Bahram Gur alone amplified by a bolster and a golden throneback. This time there are five ancillary women, who once more are mere spectators rather than functioning servants. Behind the group is a quadripartite arcade with an unusual T-shaped form in the connecting spandrels. This portion of the pavilion, which again lacks a dome, opens onto a white ground filled with cypress and blossoming trees and a lone flower. Each figure wears a milky white garment.

The manuscript falls into the category known as the Popular Mughal style, a simplified, schematic version of the late 16th-century imperial Mughal style that is employed in numerous copies of the classics of Persian literature dating from 1601 to 1618.[1] This particular example does not exactly match any other in style, but is reasonably close in figure style and visual density to a *Shahnama* dated Muharram AH 1010/July 1601 CE.[2] Faces are rendered in both profile and three-quarter views, but are wholly formulaic and without modeling. Although the drawing is generally quite neat, the geometric *takht* and canopy are skewed far beyond what is found in contemporary imperial work, and the setting is merely a flat zone filled lightly with rudimentary vegetation. These qualities leave no doubt that the artist had at best a second-hand exposure to imperial painting. Other than Agra and Ahmedabad, no provenance is associated with this strain of Popular Mughal painting, which nonetheless remains distinct from another variant steeped more thoroughly in the indigenous Indian tradition. | JS

1 For an overview of this material, see Seyller 1999, pp. 32–38. A list of relevant manuscripts is given in note 52.
2 The Metropolitan Museum of Art, New York, 13.228.22.

نشستن بهرام گور روز شنبه در گنبد زرد و حکایت کردن دختر پادشاه اقلیم دوم

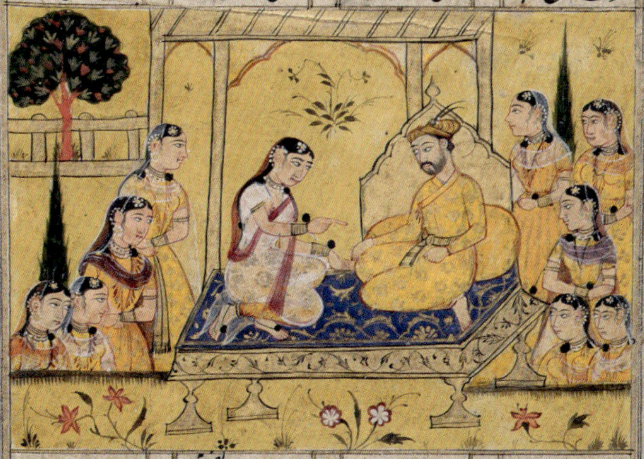

نشستن بهرام روز آدینه در گنبد سفید و حکایت کردن دختر ملک اقلیم هفتم

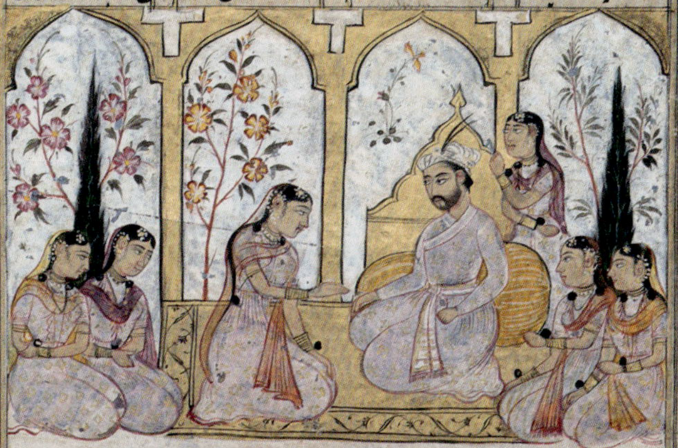

حکایت جوان پارسا با نور ... حکی

6 Two ascetics in a landscape

Attributed to Bichitr
Mughal, c. 1640–1650
34.3 × 22.4 cm (folio), 7.1 × 8.1 cm (painting)

This tiny painting of two ascetics understates most of the conventions normally used to represent Hindu holy men. The two sadhus engage in a usually wordless exchange, but neither is made dominant or subordinate enough by position or age to imply the familiar relationship of teacher and disciple. No kind of mat or ashram platform is laid down to suggest a scenario of host and visitor or indeed of any sense of a habitual dwelling, though the large tree behind the long-haired *sannyasi* confers on him greater visual weight and possibly spiritual authority. Apart from the meditation crutch in the left foreground, the ascetics' meager material possessions – a *mala* (string of beads), a saffron bag, a small dish, and a peacock-feather flywhisk – are muted and inconspicuous, and the vista beyond the barren patch of earth on which the figures sit is indistinct. Indeed, the painting is so spare and drab that we inevitably focus on the figures' faces, hands, and robes.

The most compelling of these elements is surely the older *sannyasi*'s face, which is rendered atypically in three-quarter view, with highlights on the eyelids framing the narrowed eyes and on the bridge and nostril of the thin nose. Long dreadlocks thickened with dung run through a flowing mane of loose hair, while the full dark beard is uniformly soft and frizzy. One well-articulated hand emerges unexpectedly from the mottled pale pink, cocoon-like robe, whose regular stitching runs in straight lines that are blithely unimpeded by the deep folds created by the underlying body and limbs. Distinguishing the second ascetic are the shorn head, raised eyes, and sharply delineated chin and jaw. His hands are elongated and well defined, and the dotted stitching of his robe again runs an uninterrupted course over many a fold.

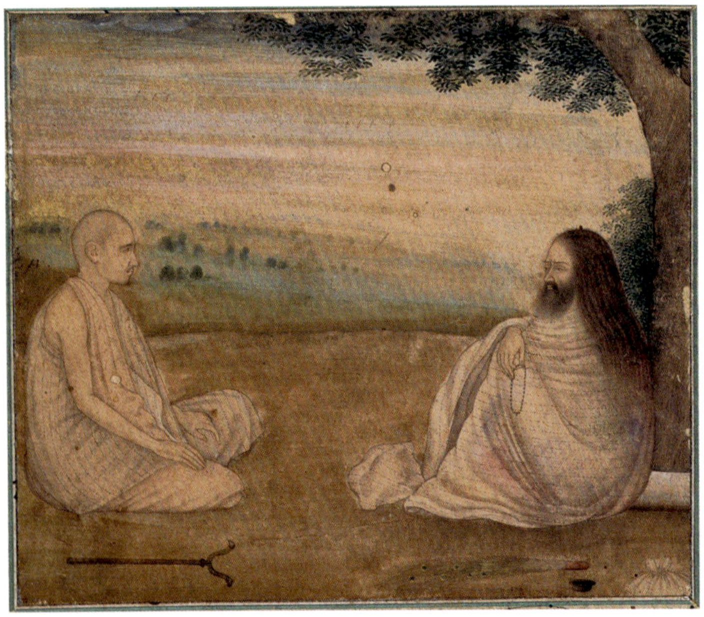

Some black marks behind this figure have been tentatively read as the name of Anup Chattar, a known Shahjahan-period artist; they are, however, too incongruously placed and written in too malformed a hand to be entertained as a credible ascription. Moreover, this very accomplished painting can be attributed to Bichitr (active c. 1610–1650), who painted sensitively characterized and exactly rendered Muslim holy men throughout his career. The elder ascetic's three-quarter-view face recalls that of Mu'in al-Din Chishti, in an ascribed portrait of c. 1610–1618,[1] as well as the imaginary likeness of Sa'di in a group scene of the 1640s.[2] The hands resemble those of Mulla Shah and his companions in another work from the Late Shah Jahan Album.[3] While several Mughal artists are capable of working in this meticulously drawn and lightly tinted manner, no one other than Bichitr combines it with a misty landscape dotted with trees rendered as blurry dabs of green.[4] Here, too, Bichitr returns to the modeling of the trunk and execution of the leaves used in the Sa'di composition. Once again he extends his interest in atmospheric effects to the sky, which has rough streaks of white and light blue brushed across a luminous zone of thinly painted gold. Amidst these streaky clouds are two faint strings of flying birds. A few European-inspired cumulus clouds loop along the painting's upper left edge.

At a later date the painting was set sideways and quite disharmoniously positioned within an illuminated opening page from a 16th-century Persian manuscript, on which vestiges of an effaced oval Persian seal can still be detected. | JS

1 Wright 2008, no. 36A.
2 Wright 2008, no. 63.
3 Leach 1995, vol. 1, no. 3.58.
4 Leach 1995, vol. 1, no. 3.58; and Okada and Richard 1986, no. 17.

Formerly in the Rothschild collection
Published: Colnaghi 1976, no. 105; Goswamy and Fischer 1987, no. 90

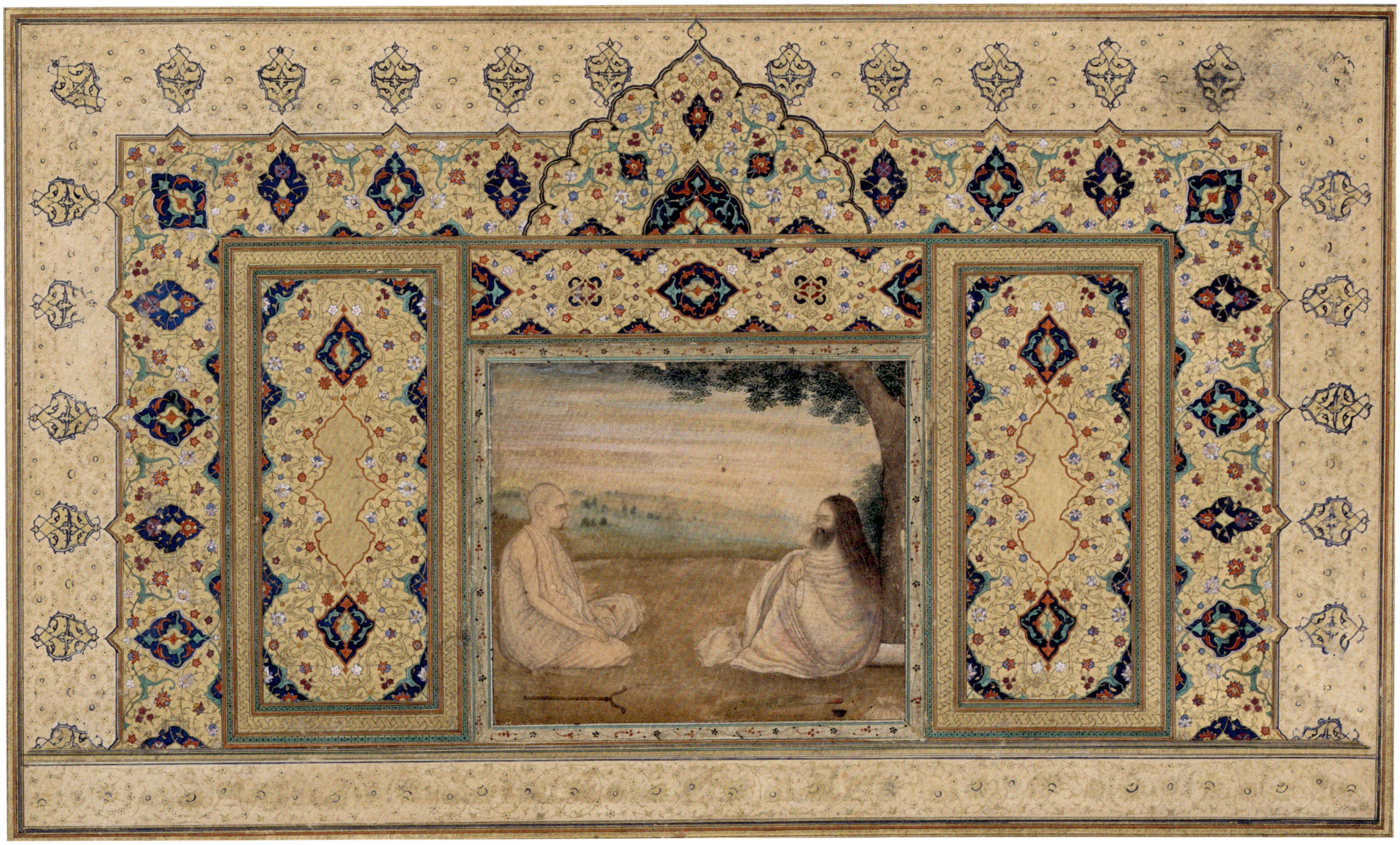

7 Naked ascetic

Mughal, c. 1650
19.1 × 13.3 cm (folio), 14.5 × 8.8 cm (painting)

A figure – ostensibly a renunciant of sorts – looks up as he sits naked before all the world, his physical estrangement from society accentuated by his isolation against a starkly barren ground. While ascetics habitually wear minimal loincloths and are accustomed to the negligible modesty they afford, this man is exposed without a stitch of cloth for cover. The artist makes him appear a bit self-conscious about this condition, posing him with one arm locked across his drawn-up and clenched legs and the other stuffed between them, as if to mitigate the figure's nakedness or at least to appease the viewer's sense of propriety. Thin rather than gaunt, the ascetic seems to have weathered well the hardships of his life. His finger- and toenails are neatly trimmed, his ribs do not protrude much, and his limbs have not yet acquired the sinewy quality induced by long periods of self-inflicted privation. His hair is close-cropped rather than shaggy or tonsured, and his heavy beard is more like an overgrown version of a courtly fashion than the unkempt stubble of most yogis.

Indeed, save for the exposed and somewhat misplaced ribs, the artist does not dwell on the figure's emaciated physique. Instead, he is interested in the figure's compact silhouette, which he strengthens with a dark, crisp outline, particularly around the nose, upper arms, and buttocks. This device emphasizes the curve of the haunches and the rhythmic lines of the calf and shin. The artist gives compositional prominence to the right hand, which forms a distinctively squared shape, and applies a network of texture strokes and highlights to the shoulders and arms.

He offers a remarkably detailed and poignant description of the naked figure's face, a trait unexpectedly more in keeping with Mughal portraiture than with genre studies. The beard, for example, is subtly streaked with gray, and the eyebrows are conspicuously thick and bushy, so much so that the further one is visible even beyond the profile. The eyes themselves are framed with a meticulously rendered eye socket and crow's feet, and contribute to a poignant expression of resignation.

The two inspection notes and a seal on the reverse provide invaluable documentation. The lower note, written in Persian, indicates that Fakhir Khan gave the painting to Iqbal Shah, a name bestowed upon Prince Dara Shikoh, the eldest son of Emperor Shahjahan (r. 1627–1658). Along with a valuation of thirty-two rupees, it also records that Muhibbullah, an imperial librarian, took custody of the painting on Rabi' I, regnal year 27 (January–February 1654), a phrase that provides a *terminus ante quem*. The work was one of many impressed with the seal of 'Alamgir's librarian, Sayyid 'Ali al-Husayni, dated regnal year one, AH 1069 (1658–1659 CE). Written in Devanagari script along the upper edge of the reverse are a familiar inspection note written in Amber in AH 1111 (1699–1700 CE), one scored-out Mewari inventory number (234) and another written in red (20/293) as well as a valuation of forty rupees. Together these notes indicate that Fakhir Khan, a noble who temporarily fell from grace at court for some improper acts, owned this painting and presented it to Dara Shikoh, who, not coincidentally, had intervened in regnal year 27 to have Fakhir Khan restored to favor. The work is one of some dozen Mughal paintings known to have made their way to the Amber court in 1699–1700. | JS

Published: Ehnbom and Topsfield 1987, no. 5; Sotheby's, London, 11 October 1991, lot 772

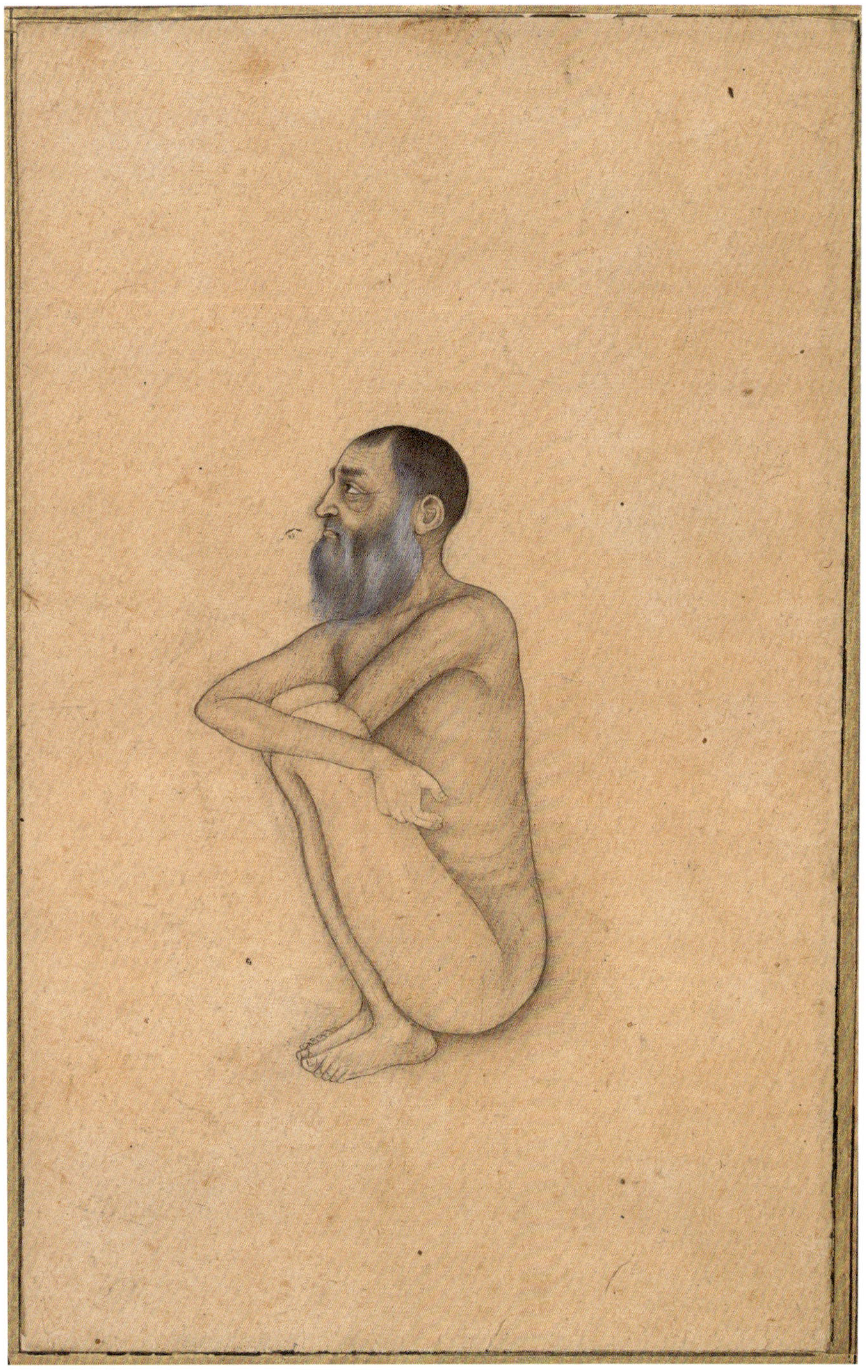

8 Prince Muhammad Akbar

Mughal, c. 1678
21.7 × 12.4 cm (painting, trimmed)
Museum Rietberg, Collection Danielle Porret, 2011.393

Notwithstanding the absence of a plume on his turban and costly jewelry about his neck, this adolescent figure is certainly a prince, since he is obviously important enough to merit an independent portrait, but still too young to have risen to a place of prominence among the Mughal nobility. And yet despite some seemingly distinctive features – a strongly curving brow, a conspicuously receding hairline, a moderate nose, and small ears – he eludes ready identification, a situation created by both the general paucity of imperial Mughal paintings in the last quarter of the 17th century and the even more acute dearth of inscribed portraits of 'Alamgir's sons and grandsons.[1]

The painting remains close enough stylistically to the highly refined manner of the waning days of Shahjahan's reign (1627–1658) to date the work to the 1670s. The face, for example, still exhibits credible modeling at the front of the eye even as the large iris and geometric eyelid show signs of the schematization that becomes more pronounced towards the end of the century. Similarly, both the wispy beard and surprisingly long hair above the ear retain a palpable sense of texture, and the figure's forest-green *jama* is at once pliant and broadly sculpted rather than being reduced to stiff flatness. There are relatively few royal figures that were of the appropriate age – about twenty years old – in the 1670s. The most likely is Prince Muhammad Akbar (b. 12 Zi'l-Hijja 1067/8 June 1657, d. 19 June 1707), the second son of Aurangzeb, the future Emperor 'Alamgir, who apparently enjoyed considerable favor for a time, and was appointed *subahdar* of the imperial province of Multan from 1676 to 1679. In 1680, however, his public punishment in the aftermath of failures in military campaigns in Rajasthan drove him into rebellion, which culminated when he rashly proclaimed himself emperor in 1681. He is tentatively identified as the young prince offering jewels to the enthroned 'Alamgir in a painting in the Chester Beatty Library,[2] and is the subject of a full-length portrait set into an elaborate and historically important mirror case.[3]

The artist introduces a few uncommon attributes into the royal portrait. He fronts the prince with an assertive black shield along with the usual sword and dagger, and has him tender a piece of fruit – apparently an apple guava (*psidium guajava*) – rather than the customary flower, *pan*, or jeweled ornament. He grounds the figure on a nondescript mound, to which he adds, quite gratuitously, a single flowering plant, which is described with sufficient botanical precision that it can be identified as an oxeye (*Heliopsis helianthoides*). And he caps off the composition with brilliantly colored and streaky clouds arranged in a rough arc above the prince, a feature which became fashionable in portraiture towards the end of the 17th century. | JS

1 One notable contemporary exception is a portrait of Prince Bedar Bakht, the grandson of Emperor 'Alamgir, bearing the *samvat* date VS 1738, equivalent to 1681–1682 CE. The painting is published in Topsfield 2004, no. 126.
2 The painting is discussed and reproduced in Leach 1995, vol. 1, no. 4.6.
3 See Seyller 2010, fig. 15.

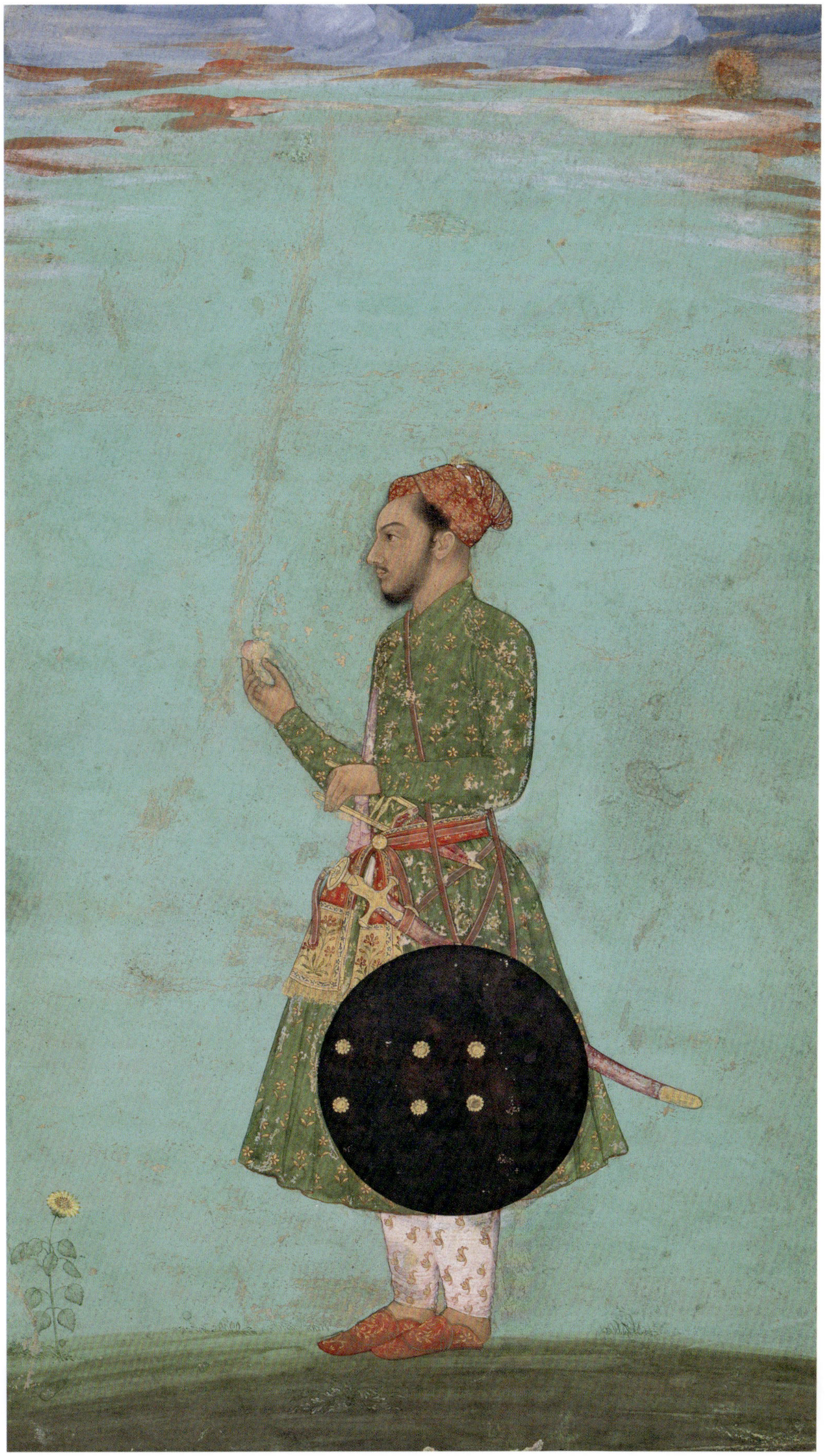

9 Standing youth

Ascribed to Muhammad Guhar
Mughal, dated AH 1103/1691–1692 CE
19.5 × 11 cm (folio)

One subject popular in Mughal painting from the beginning of the 17th century is the princely seeker, who, sensing the hollowness of extravagant palace life, turns to one holy man or another for spiritual succour. Images in this vein regularly show such a royal youth seated opposite a sage in either wordless communion or quiet discussion of a book that lies open between them. This lightly tinted drawing combines this familiar type with a less earnest and more sexually evocative conceit: an adolescent standing with an open oblong book of verses raised up just below his enticing, doe-eyed and downy-cheeked face.

Although the youth's conspicuous pearl drop earring and fashionable sidelock indicate that he has not shed all the trappings of privilege and vanity, he is nonetheless dressed in quite plain clothing. His long-sleeved, calf-length robe with optional openings for the arms sometimes appears among mid-century, Persian-inspired court apparel, as does the fur tippet thrown over his shoulders, though the latter is featured most often in combination with a gold brocade *kimkhab* or tunic-length coat. His floppy cap with a wide fur trim is, by contrast, a decidedly more unorthodox headgear, and generally worn by men of modest status and foreign origin. Both these items are commonplace by comparison to the youth's exotic wooden staff, which is comprised of two intertwined serpentine sticks terminating in large cobra hoods. Introduced into India around the time of Alexander the Great, the caduceus proper never seems to have enjoyed any symbolic currency among the subcontinent's religious orders, so this cobra-headed object must be a flamboyant meditation crutch intended to impart a wild flair to its owner.

Written near the figure's waist is a tiny ascription that provides the name of Muhammad Guhar, an otherwise undocumented artist, and the year 1103, a Hijra date equivalent to 1691–1692 CE. Given the elegant rendering of the youth's face and cap and the almost total absence of painting produced for 'Alamgir late in the puritanical emperor's reign, this information suggests that Muhammad Guhar was a well-trained artist who found a willing patron among the Mughal princes or nobility. | JS

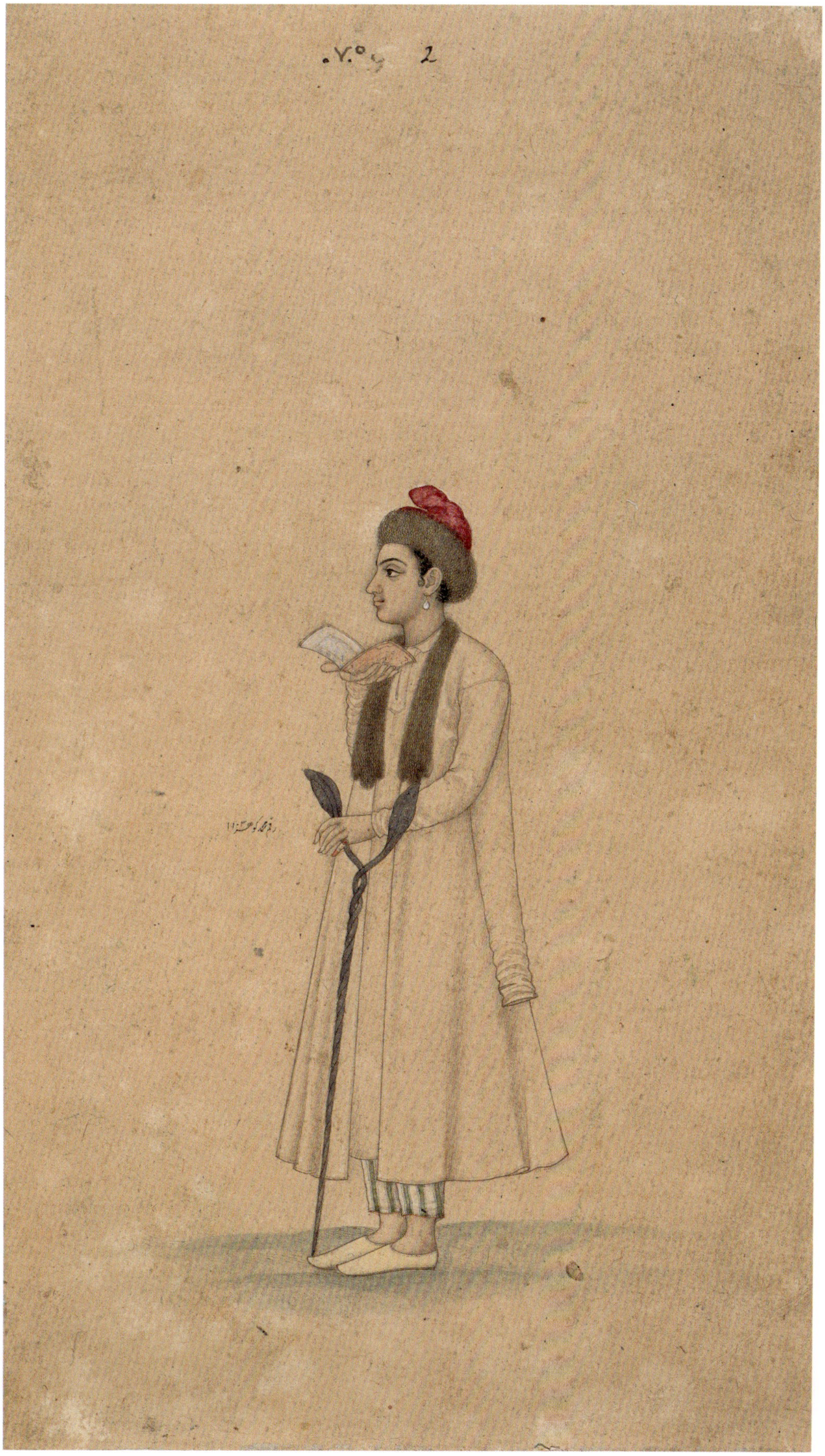
2

10 Demon leading a composite lion

Attributed to Dip Chand
Mughal style at Murshidabad or Patna, c. 1760–1765
27.2×34.7 cm (folio), 21.8×29.3 cm (painting)

Like many examples of this fantastic genre, this image of a demon leading a composite lion by a slack chain is at once fearsome and delightful. In this case, the demon himself contains no composite elements, but is made threatening by means of the traditional attributes of his species: enraged eyes, elephantine ears, bared fangs and teeth, and large curling horns. Yet bracketing his face are two rows of tightly coiled white hair, a frothy twist on demons' conventional hairiness. With this inventive detail and a jangling bell hung from his girdle at a suggestive spot, he assumes a demeanour more droll than menacing, taking on a whimsical quality that not even a dark body, clawed feet, hairy tail, and huge mace can dispel entirely.

The lion trailing behind his demonic master obviously does so of his own volition, for he turns his head outward in a confrontational stare, steps out in a cocky stride, and brandishes his tail like a whip. It is, however, the jumble of fully colored and aggressive animals cleverly contorted to flesh out every corner of every limb that makes this composite lion the consummate creature of the sorcerer's realm. Most striking are the symmetrically disposed green parrots, owls, ducks, and lions that splay out to form the face, which has as its axis a nose fashioned from a lone worm laid out tantalizingly in their midst. The lion's body consists of remarkably assorted beasts, which range from a nilgai, horse, leopard, rabbit, sheep, and bear to a monkey, tiger, camel, elephant, ibex, and fish, each looking about apprehensively as it nips, bites, or devours the creature before him. A tiger head and four red parrots comprise each clawed foot, and a cobra fanning his hood rises up as the tufted tail. Only one human – a full-faced, bareheaded man with a mustache and a leer – is subsumed into this predatory menagerie, and is relegated wittily to the beast's rump.

While similar composites were produced at courts all across India, this superb painting is distinguished by the imaginative variation in the animals' size, the inspired mix of profile, frontal, and inverted views, the controled draftsmanship, the high degree of contrast among juxtaposed forms, and the judicious inclusion of passages of rich or fanciful coloring. The thorough modeling of such beasts as the pouncing dog and curled-up tiger on the lion's left foreleg and more specifically of the demon's muscular body indicates that the painting is 18th-century Mughal work, a style also evident in the exaggerated color gradations of the demon's shorts.

The vast compositional space, which diffuses the focus on the intricate, puzzle-like image of the composite beast, is divided into two sharply delineated registers: a large, blue-gray lower zone and a small, icy blue upper one. Together, these zones unmistakably evoke a stark and deep landscape, an association furthered by pale striations that read as ridges and clouds. In its weighted proportions, cool hues, and smooth surfaces, this configuration of receding ground and hazy sky bears an uncanny resemblance to the backgrounds in paintings ascribed or attributed to Dip Chand (active c. 1760–1770),[1] a Murshidabad artist who moved to Patna in 1763 and is known from a series of portraits made there for William Fullerton.[2] It lacks, of course, the minuscule trees dotting the horizon that are seen in several of Dip Chand's portraits, but otherwise it is close enough to them to be plausibly regarded as part of the artist's œuvre at Murshidabad or Patna. This painting's association with a painter of Dip Chand's ability might also explain the extremely high level of accomplishment evident here, which surpasses several other composite scenes in comparable if slightly later 18th-century Mughal styles.[3] | JS

1 See Losty 2002, figs. 3–7, especially fig. 6. The paintings are published in color in Losty and Roy 2012, figs. 112–113.
2 Losty 2002, p. 42.
3 One comparable Murshidabad painting of demons driving and escorting a composite elephant is published in Del Bontà 1999, fig. 3. Another Murshidabad scene of demons urging on a fight of two composite elephants is published in Sotheby's, London, 10 October 1977, lot 22. Two slightly later paintings from Lucknow featuring a composite bull accompanied by angelic or human figures are apparently the work of the same artist. These unpublished paintings are preserved, respectively, in the collections of Ludwig Habighorst and Navin Kumar.

Formerly in the George P. Bickford collection

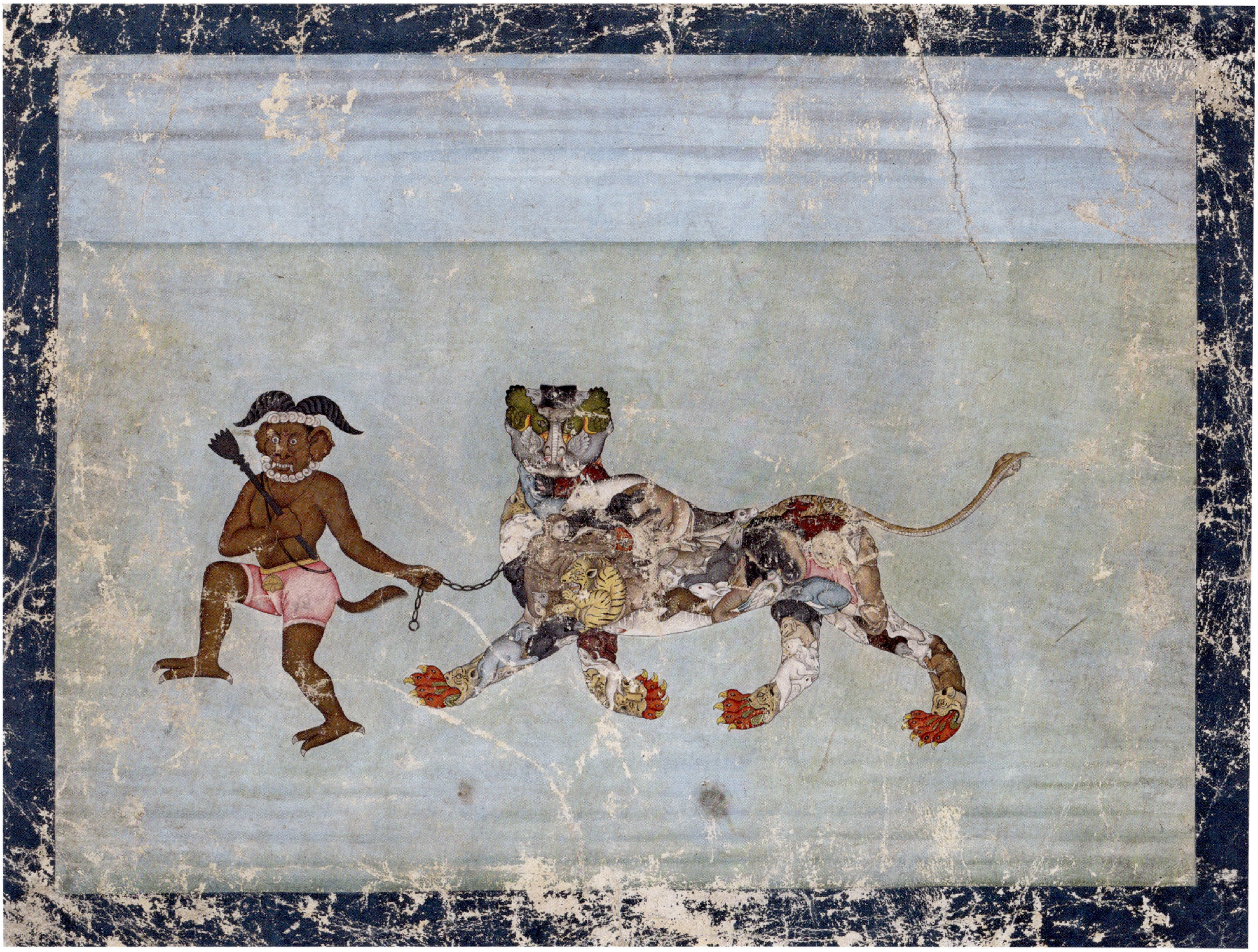

11 Portrait of Emperor Jahandar Shah

Attributed to 'Aqil Khan
Provincial Mughal style, probably at Lucknow, c. 1760
37.5 × 26.5 cm (folio), 18 × 11.7 cm (painting)

The identity of this nimbate ruler seated at a window is a surprisingly vexing matter. The figure's corpulence and the general mid 18th-century style of the portrait lead one to expect that it is Emperor Muhammad Shah, whose prolonged reign (1719–1748) provided ample opportunity for many a portrait.[1] That identification, however, can be ruled out because in exceedingly few of Muhammad Shah's portraits is he depicted with anything like this long, straight nose and full beard. There is a possibility that this unfinished work portrays Emperor Farrukhsiyar (r. 1713–1719), whose nose and eyebrow are in keeping with the features seen here, but whose thick, bushy beard is customarily depicted overspreading his upper cheeks rather than tidied up into the neatly sculpted shape seen here. Indeed, a few portraits of Farrukhsiyar of c. 1715 are reasonably close to this visage, which tellingly includes no gaps in the beard below the lips.[2] Yet the likelihood of this tenuous identification is diminished significantly by the existence of an unfinished portrait of Farrukhsiyar – this time with his canonical features – in the same format, size, and finish as this one,[3] making them, in effect, two distinct examples from a series of small and unfinished imperial portraits of emperors seated at a window. Hence, the subject appears to be the politically inconsequential and easily overlooked Jahandar Shah (1673–1713, r. 1712–1713), who eliminated his three brothers upon the death of their father, Bahadur Shah I, and seized the throne in March 1712, but suffered a gruesome end at the order of his nephew Farrukhsiyar less than a year later. In particular, the figure's profile and beard correspond closely to Jahandar Shah's features in an inscribed standing portrait and a contemporary dynastic scene.[4]

This painting is surely a posthumous likeness, for it is well outside the early 18th-century style of Jahandar Shah's reign. It is flat in nearly every aspect, most obviously in the rich fabrics of the turban, the exceedingly stiff collar, and the drily rendered fur tippet. The folds at armpits, elbows and wrists are schematically linear and the ear is somewhat disturbingly unarticulated. Indeed, this artist deviates from his penchant for flattened forms only in the jewelry, adding central daubs of white paint to the pearls and stronger rims of color to the rubies and emeralds in order to impart a modicum of three-dimensionality to them. Together with these features, the geometricized treatment of the eye supports an attribution to 'Aqil Khan, an artist whose several ascribed works are characterized by crisp patterns and eyes with a ring of white around the large iris, elegantly curved and darkly outlined eyelids, and an eye socket composed of well-defined complementary arcs.[5]

The unfinished state of the painting accounts for its jarringly unembellished setting and extraordinarily light coloring. The emperor's right hand, for example, lacks the sharp definition of the left, and the pale gray background stops inexplicably short of the space between the palm and fingers. Vestiges of the preliminary sketch of the inverted J-shaped form of a *sarpech* held between the forefinger and thumb can be discerned under high magnification. The bolster against which the emperor rests, the carpet draped over the low balustrade, and rolled-up blind – complete with protruding ends – above the window are all obviously left in a rudimentary state, though one can reconstruct their intended final appearance from very similar forms in 'Aqil Khan's portrait of Princess Zinat Afza Begam[6] and an unattributed portrait of Muhammad Shah.[7] The colors of the emperor's yellow-tinted and pale green garments undoubtedly were to be made stronger and opaque, and it is possible that the halo would eventually have been altered from a solid, pale yellow disc to a hollowed-out golden rim framing the head against an opaque blue-gray background.

On the reverse are four lines of Persian verse written in fine Nasta'liq script on gold-flecked paper. | JS

1 It was identified as such in Sotheby's, London, 10 October 1977, lot 32.
2 See, for example, Schmitz 2002, p. 3, fig. 2; Okada and Richard 1986, no. 50; Losty and Roy 2012, fig. 103; and Victoria and Albert Museum, Large Clive Album (I.S. 133–1964), f. 104b.
3 San Diego Museum of Art 1990:370.
4 Victoria and Albert Museum I.S. 149–1952; San Diego Museum of Art 1990:368, published in Dalrymple and Sharma 2012, no. 3.
5 See Losty and Leach 1998, no. 19; Leach 1986, no. 47; and Falk and Archer 1981, nos. 204–205. A painting published in Leach 1995, vol. 1, no. 4.39 can be attributed to him as well.
6 Losty and Leach 1998, no. 19, or Falk and Archer 1981, no. 203.
7 Losty and Roy 2012, fig. 107. It is possible that this work, too, should be associated with 'Aqil Khan.

Published: Sotheby's, London, 10 October 1977, lot 32

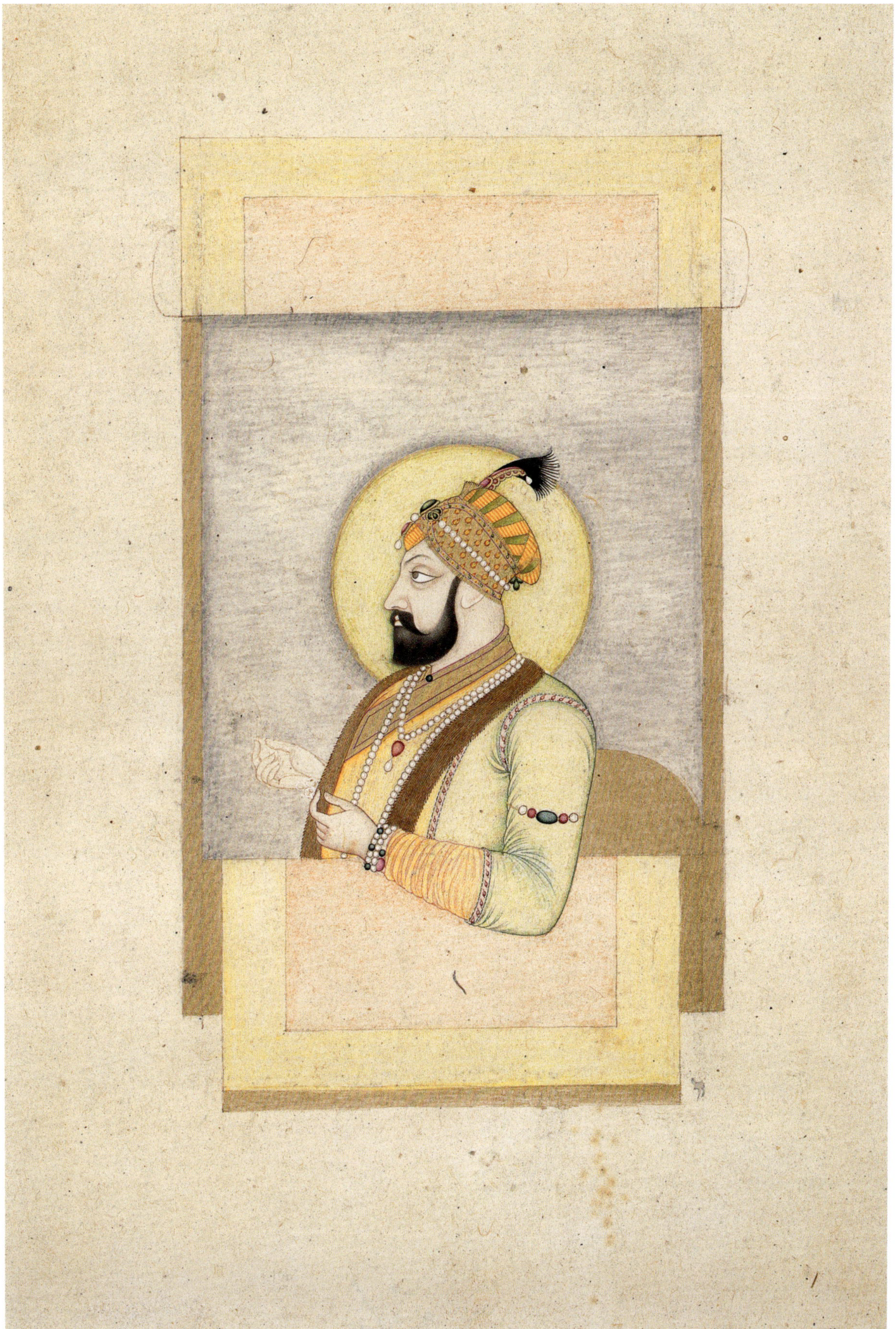

12 A royal lady visits an ashram

Attributed to Mihr Chand
Mughal style at Faizabad, c. 1770
48.1 × 33.3 cm (folio), 18.3 × 10.9 cm (painting)
Inscribed above in an oblong cartouche framed in gold:
taswir-i darwish sannyasi ("Picture of a *sannyasi* dervish")
Museum Rietberg, Collection Danielle Porret, 2011.390

In India, where extremes beget many a paradox, those who enjoy untold wealth have often sought the blessings of those who have turned their backs on even the meanest amenities of the material world in their quest to know God. The theme of the indulgently rich beseeching the deliberately destitute for spiritual alms is represented frequently in Mughal painting, as male and female members of the royal household appear in the guise of humble supplicants before holy men, both Muslim and Hindu. In this case, it is a single royal woman, head and neck visibly bedecked in jewels, who has forsworn the safety and comfort of her customary entourage and has wrapped herself in a modest white traveling cloak to make the journey to the ashram. Having come into the presence of two venerable Hindu yogis and a female disciple, she is distracted momentarily by a small child, towards whom she turns and dotingly offers a piece of fruit. Circumstances suggest that he is the son of the yogini rather than her own, for the toddler is garbed in simple white clothing with a belled chain around his waist, the normally indispensable nursemaid is nowhere to be seen, and the lady, like countless barren women before her, must be driven to avail herself of any intervention that might bring much-desired offspring.

The *sannyasis* ply the usual accessories of ascetic life. The yogini, dung-matted hair bound up in an elaborate topknot and skin rubbed gray with ash, wears a grimy salmon-colored robe as well as beads and an ascetic's whistle about her neck. She raises one hand in address and with the other holds a peacock-feather *morchhal* in a way more suited to display than to any practical whisking purpose. The two yogis are coiffed and dressed in a similar manner. The white-bearded elder, crowned with a dense, looped mass of dung-encrusted hair and covered with a voluminous salmon-colored cloak, holds a rosary in both hands, and sits on a tiger pelt on which a conch and a cloth with two open books are arrayed. His younger companion sits nearby with an open book in one hand and his knees held upright with the aid of a meditation strap. Beneath the five figures is a reed mat with a muted diamond-shaped design along the perimeter, and behind them is a rather fastidiously constructed reed hut, its roof overgrown with vines. Two intertwined trees at the back edge of the compound ease the transition to a stretch of ground receding into the distance, traversed by a river and punctuated by a cluster of tall, white buildings.

All these elements occur in mid 17th-century Mughal art, but this particular example is decidedly a later revivalist painting that can be attributed to Mihr Chand (active c. 1759–1786), a versatile artist who brought his considerable talents to bear on such work made at the behest of Nawab Shuja' al-Daula and the Swiss adventurer Antoine Polier at Faizabad, the one-time capital of Oudh [Awadh].[1] Many individual features support this conclusion. Foremost among them is the royal lady, whose fully modeled facial type not only appears consistently in 18th-century painting, but also in this case is practically identical to one attributed to Mihr Chand and assigned to Lucknow or Faizabad, c. 1760–1770.[2] Moreover, the three *sannyasis* and especially the reed hut are rendered with a pervasive explicitness – even verging on fussiness – that is a defining characteristic of late 18th-century work. Finally, the twinned trees with an exceedingly schematic fringe of foliage, the formulaic shape of the relentlessly regular tufts, and the bright blue sky are all found in other works in an album compiled for Shuja' al-Daula.[3]

The painting was extended on the left and bottom edges, an addition necessary to match the proportions of other paintings in the album; the difference between the two stages, which seemingly were not many years apart, is particularly evident in the rendering of flowers in the two distinct bands before the ashram's platform. On the reverse of the folio are four lines of verse written in fine Nasta'liq by the calligrapher Muhammad Latif Tabrizi. | JS

1 Leach 1995, vol. 2, pp. 654–656, gives a useful overview of Mihr Chand's career, and suggests that he often turned to Shahjahan-period models.
2 Leach 1998, no. 50.
3 Leach 1995, vol. 2, pp. 654–656.

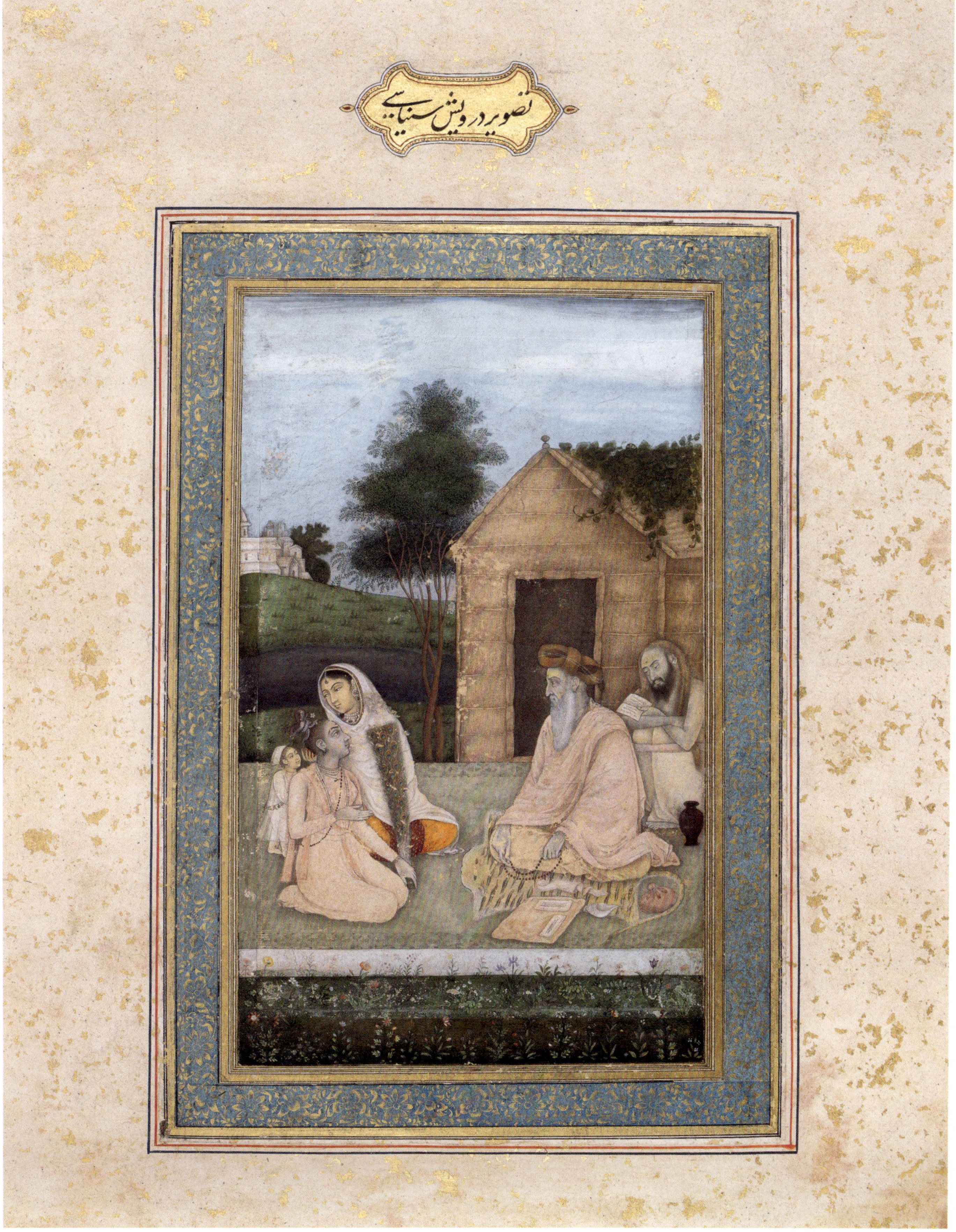
تصویر درویش سنیاسی

13 Sultan Muhammad 'Adil Shah

Bijapur, c. 1650–1655
33.3 × 21.6 cm (folio), 21 × 13.2 cm (painting)

Purportedly representing Muhammad Sa'id Khan, whose name – including the misspelled epithet "Bishapuri" – is written spuriously at the top of the painting, this half-length portrait depicts a figure with smooth, tawny skin, an elegantly coiffed beard, a broad dark sash draped over his shoulder, and a turban tied in the manner of mid 17th-century Bijapur, especially by Sultan Muhammad 'Adil Shah II (r. 1627–1656). The figure holds a morsel of *pan* up to his mouth with one hand and clutches a small cloth with the other. The basic format, dress, and gesture correspond almost exactly to those features in a smaller portrait of Muhammad 'Adil Shah attributed to Muhammad Khan, deviating only slightly in the cut of the beard and the angle of the bridge of the nose.[1] The artist even describes the bulge of the sitter's neck, a feature associated with Muhammad Khan,[2] though in overall quality it more closely resembles another portrait not attributed to him.[3]

Yet there is something amiss here, and it is not merely surface damage, seen primarily in the sash, turban, and background. Rather, the painting is left unfinished in a curiously haphazard way, so that the fingernails of the right hand are refined down to a polished state while the normally prominent eyelashes are still to be supplied, and the dainty web of white lines criss-crossing his diaphanous *jama* is already in place while the ear and left hand remain unarticulated lumps. There is little doubt, too, that a jeweled pendant, pearl necklace, turban ornaments and pom-pom would eventually have been added, and that the contours of every element would have been strengthened with a crisp outline.

The portrait is set crudely within an album page with elaborate late 16th-century Khurasani stenciled borders. The stenciled design on this side consists largely of floral arabesques, but has pairs of demonic and *qilin* heads in a lobed medallion in the center of the outer border. Four oblong cartouches inscribed with poetical couplets are complemented by paintings of a male and female youth in the upper and lower corner medallions. Surrounding the four-line 17th-century calligraphic specimen set into the reverse is a still more flamboyant design that has a youth and cupbearer in the outer corner medallions, four oblong cartouches with couplets written in white Nasta'liq, three star-shaped or lobed medallions, and dozens of fully colored disembodied human and animals heads leering from the intervening spaces. | JS

1 The British Museum 1937 4–10 04, published in Zebrowski 1983, fig. 98.
2 Zebrowski 1983, p. 128 and note 14.
3 British Library, India Office Collections J.A. 1.10, published in Falk and Archer 1981, no. 407.

Published: Sotheby's, New York, 6 October 1990, lot 72

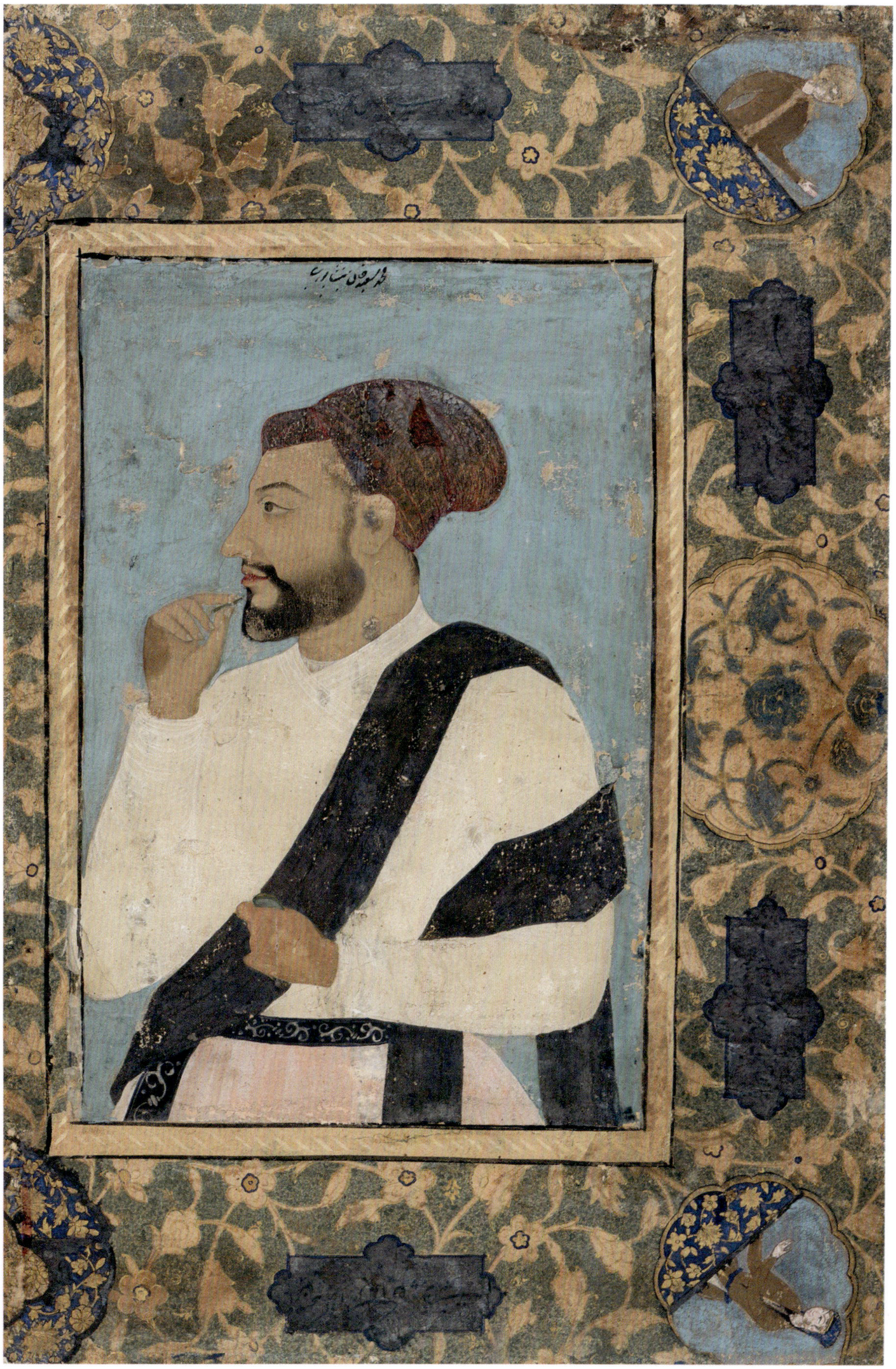

14 Royal women lounging beneath a canopy

Golconda, c. 1680–1685
21.8 × 17.8 cm (folio), 19.9 × 14.5 cm (painting)

Scenes of royal women indulging in sensuous activities were a popular genre in Deccani painting. Like most examples, this scene takes place outdoors, in this case on a terrace shaded by a sizeable canopy and graced by an adjacent garden and fountain. At the center are two princesses, one lounging against a pile of massive cushions and ostentatiously displaying her bared torso as she cradles her head in an upraised and bent arm, and the other – also bare-breasted – leaning forward to gaze into her eyes. Increasing the sexual atmosphere of the situation still further is the second princess, who grazes her forearm against her companion's breast as she plies her with a cup of wine. Both women are of similar status, for they wear identical golden medallions and jasmine bud necklaces as well as triple-pearled earrings. They are attended by a coterie of three servants: one pouring wine from a flask into a cup, another holding a small fan, and a third tendering a small cloth. Two wear only a diaphanous *dupatta* with a thick gold hem across their otherwise naked torsos, while the other is dressed in the customary *choli*, whose teal blue color sets off a gleaming pearl necklace.

Despite these many enticing details, the scene exudes a curious sense of lassitude. Most of it stems from the women's heavy-lidded and drooping eyes, which together with the oddly pursed mouths make for rather joyless, even glum expressions. The bodies, too, have a stiff and contrived quality often found in Golconda painting, a quality most pronounced here in the severe shapes of the torsos and the indistinct rendering of the breasts. And while the strongly delineated radiating leaf patterns and whittled markings of the trees' foliage clusters and trunks contribute to the power of the painting's overall design, the only elements truly imbued with a semblance of organic freedom are the oversized salmon-colored blossoms on the dark blue carpet. The palette is dominated by gold, beige, and teal blue, an unusual combination made more striking by patches of discoloration and paint loss, especially in the whites of several skirts.

The painting relates closely to two other works assigned to Golconda at the end of the 17th century, a resemblance seen in the rendering of the eye and the milky white pleated folds of the skirts and *jamas*. The first is a beautiful if conventional image of a woman standing beneath a tree.[1] The second is a Golconda painting among the cache of works seized by Bikaneri forces during the conquest of the fort at Adoni (Kurnool Dtt.) in 1689.[2] Such a connection probably accounts for the exceptional appearance of the Golconda facial type in the work of Ibrahim, son of Ruknuddin, in at least two *Rasikapriya* illustrations produced in Bikaner in 1692.[3] A painting in the same vein a generation later shows the same compositional structure, facial type, and odd palette, but also polished surfaces.[4] | JS

1 Spink 1982, no. 94.
2 Goetz 1950, fig. 90.
3 Krishna N. 1985, fig. 2, and an unpublished work in an American private collection. From other known works by this artist, it seems clear that he was experimenting with a new facial type even as he maintained a distinctly Bikaneri figure type, which is far more petite.
4 Gahlin 1991, no. 47.

Published: Heeramaneck 1984, pl. 240

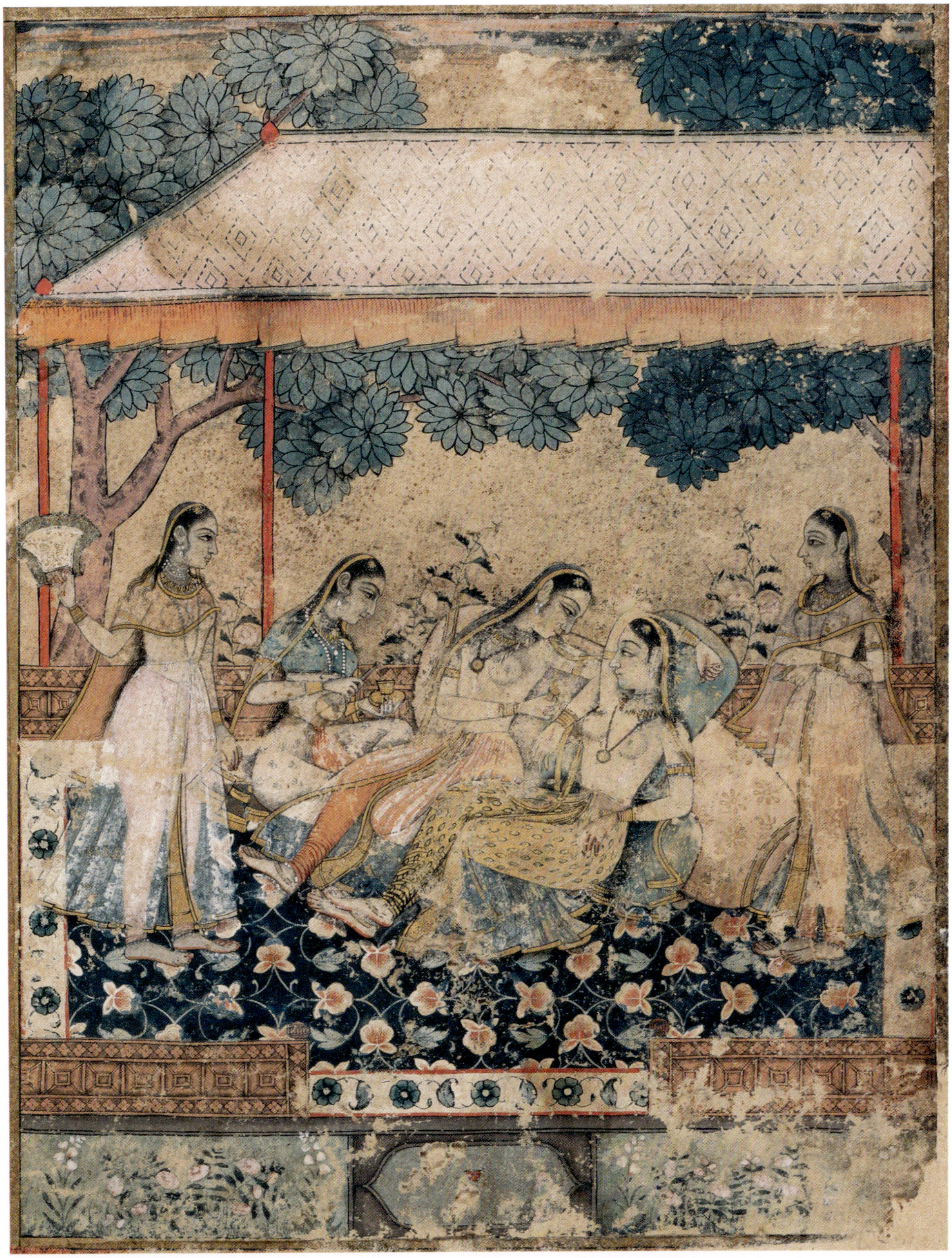

15 Krishna playing the flute

North Deccan, possibly Burhanpur, c. 1670
37.6 × 24.4 cm (folio), 30.2 × 17.3 cm (painting)

Krishna's resplendent and alluring nature is brilliantly conveyed here as he strikes an iconic pose – standing with legs crossed jauntily and playing his flute – before a tree fashioned into a spreading mass of brightly variegated leaves. Two *gopis* wave whip-like, red-tipped flywhisks, and their two cows raise their heads in homage. The compact composition culminates in the sun, which appears directly above Krishna in a streaky blue sky and radiates long, golden rays.

The painting has been tentatively identified as Meghamalar *raga*, which initially seems plausible for a figure of a dark-skinned male dancing and playing the flute. It is numbered 3 in the appropriate places (upper left and lower right) on the border, and has the same rulings as a well-known *ragamala* series generally assigned to the northern Deccan about 1670.[1] However, the three lines of Sanskrit text above the painting do not name the particular *raga* as the other pages do, describing instead *kama* (desire) as well as Krishna's crown and regal power.[2] Matters are further complicated by the existence of a Meghamalar *raga* from that very series. That painting is numbered 76, which would place it at the end rather than the beginning of the *ragamala* series, and has very different imagery – a dark-skinned figure in a lightning-filled monsoon sky hovering above a landscape with peacocks perched in trees – that accords more closely to Mesakarna's textual description.[3] In short, in both format and style this enigmatic painting is akin to the illustrations of at least two of four very similar *ragamala* series produced in a single workshop, but cannot be placed definitively in any of them.

As many scholars have observed, this group of paintings has both Rajasthani or Central Indian elements, notably the grid-like composition, strongly patterned trees, and basketwork-patterned water. These features, however, are blended with at least as many Deccani ones, especially the small-headed and full-cheeked facial types, the wealth of geometric, floral, and arabesque decorative motifs, and a palette featuring pastels, lapis lazuli, a peculiar avocado green, a shrill magenta, and copious amounts of gold. All this points to a regional center in the northern Deccan, most likely Burhanpur or another city in Berar, where these two traditions might have mixed on an *ad hoc* basis, either as the result of a noble from one of those areas of northern India being posted to a Mughal garrison in the Deccan or as the natural hybrid of adjoining regional styles. | JS

1 For a comprehensive list of paintings from this series, see Seyller with Seitz 2010, no. 40, note 2. Seitz erroneously dates this and a related *ragamala* series to c. 1640–1650.

2 One stylistically identical but unidentified painting sold at Christie's, London, 3 July 1980, lot 115, also lacks the customarily explicit identification of the *raga* in the text area. The unsteady writing on this folio also differs clearly from the neatly written text on the other *ragamala* paintings. I am grateful to Ilyse Morgan-stern-Fuerst of the University of Vermont for sharing her thoughts on the substance of this text.

3 Cincinnati Art Museum 1982.250, published in Smart and Walker 1985, no. 23.

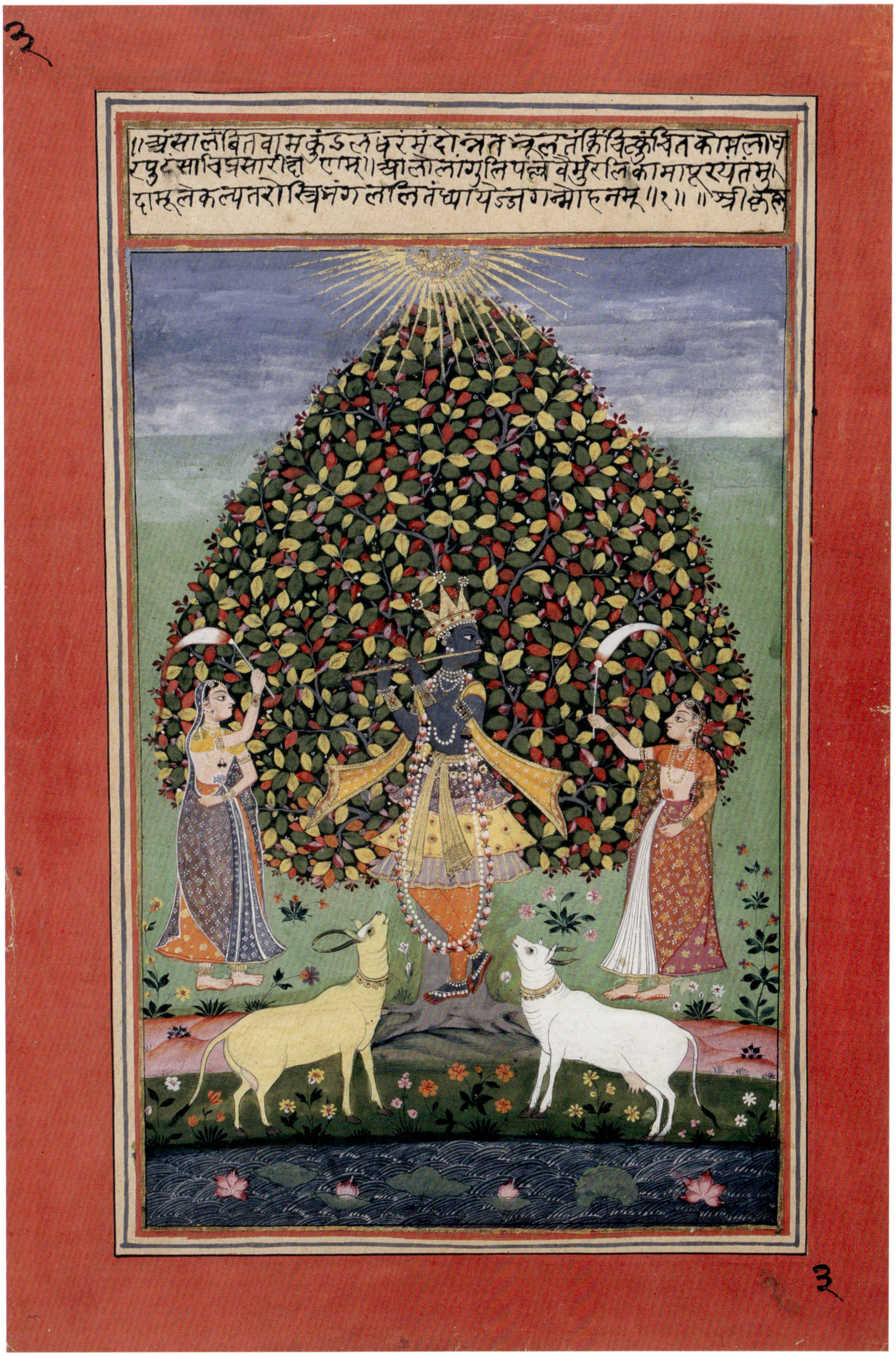
३
॥अंसालंबितवामकुंडलधरं मंदोन्नतभ्रूलतं किंचित्कुंचितकोमलाध
रपुटं साचिप्रसारीक्षणम्॥ आलोलांगुलिपल्लवैर्मुरलिकामापूरयंतं मु
दामूले कल्पतरोस्त्रिभंगललितं ध्यायेज्जगन्मोहनम् ॥२॥ ॥श्रीकेल
३

16 Standing noble

Golconda, c. 1700–1710
17.7 × 12.1 cm (painting)

By the late 17th century, Mughal portraiture had become so conventionalized and abbreviated that artists working at regional courts under Mughal sway were able to approximate both their form and finish. Along with several closely related examples, this portrait demonstrates how effectively a painter from the defeated Deccani kingdom of Golconda was able to apply that formula to the local nobility.[1]

The unidentified subject stands here in a well-established pose, that is, in a strict profile view with the right hand gripping a long, straight-bladed sword with a flaring finial. The relaxed left hand rests against the hilt of a shorter sword slung from a decorated strap, the curving index finger accentuated by the sword's cleverly positioned tassel. A long-handled *katar* (dagger) protrudes from the waist-sash even beyond the abdomen. A black buffalo-hide shield with a flat gilt rim and bosses asserts itself against the ankle-length white *jama*, whose floral design does not allow pleats and folds in the relatively stiff fabric to disrupt the absolute regularity of its pattern. The short *patka* has a basic leaf design, and its fringe is minimally articulated. The turban, tied in typical Deccani fashion, is rendered as three discrete shapes that complement the stylized curves of the closely cut hair and beard. But the coolly formal Deccani character of the portrait is most pronounced in the fluid, abstracted shapes and smooth surfaces of the subject's eye and hands. In these features as well as in the tufted olive-green ground and the muted background topped off by gold-outlined clouds, the last remnants of Mughal naturalism are visibly tempered by the legacy of the Persian tradition in the Deccan. | JS

[1] Comparable examples are *Portrait of 'Azam Shah*, published in Smart and Walker 1985, no. 26; Michell, Lampert and Holland 1982, no. 41, p. 74; Christie's, London, 21 November 1986, lot 137; and Sotheby's, London, 9 October 1975, lot 227.

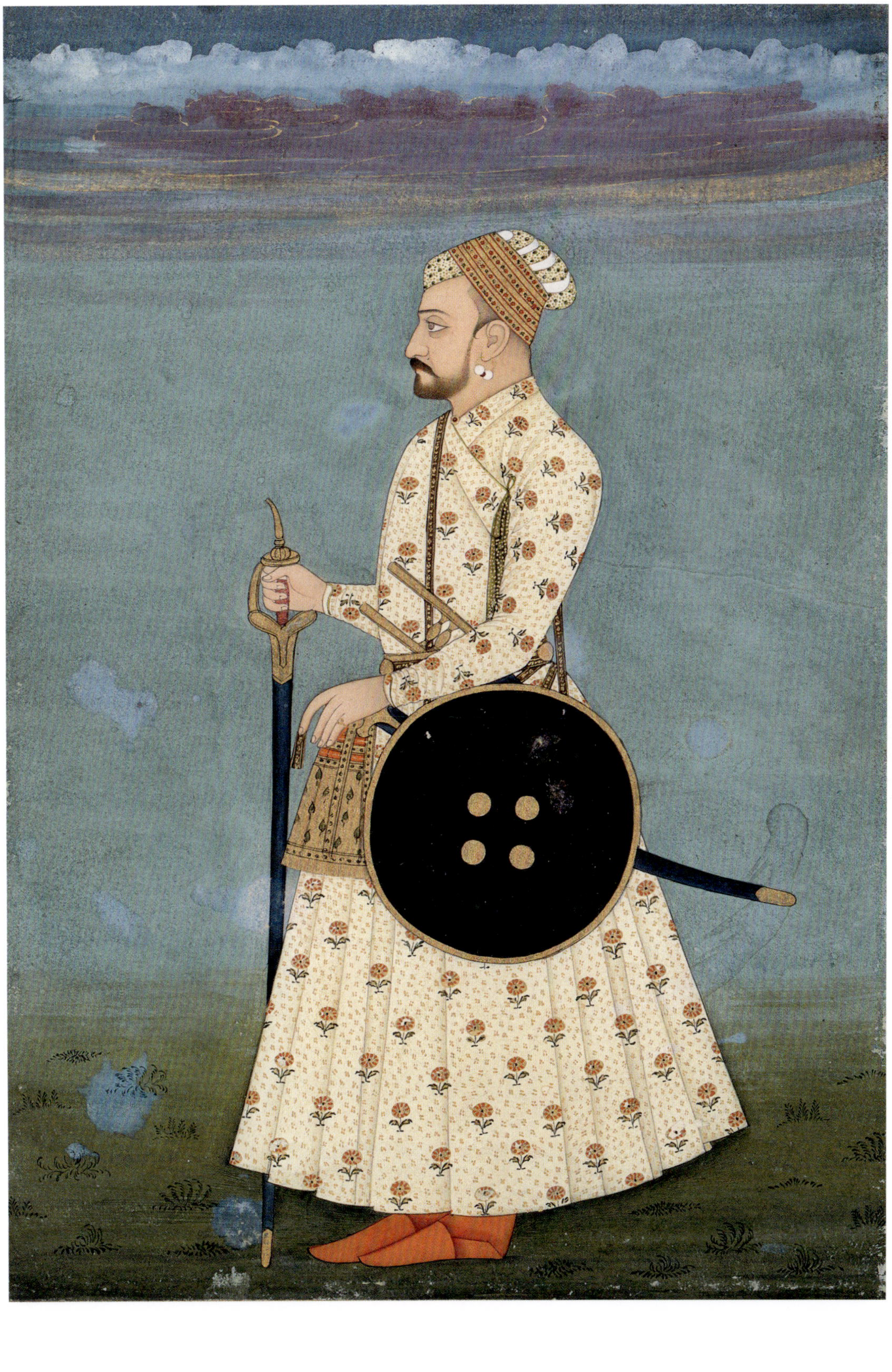

17 Mahout on an unruly elephant

North Deccan, c. 1720
27 × 25.2 cm (folio), 19.7 × 22 cm (painting)

Scaling a small rise to push against a mango tree, this royal elephant exhibits the first signs of unruly behavior that may soon get out of hand. Unperturbed, the bare-chested mahout remains seated well back on the creature and merely tugs on the harnessing ropes. A saluki hound is a chance bystander to this developing situation, and reinforces the lack of drama at the moment by looking away distractedly.

The artist reduces the composition to a few big, solidly colored shapes – the elephant, mahout, hill, tree, and band of sky – and arrays them against and around a starkly plain ground of creamy yellow-white. The juxtaposition of dark and light forms focuses attention on the elephant, and particularly on the undulating lines of his trunk, domed crown, back, harnessing rope, and tail, all of which are features with close counterparts in contemporary elephant paintings from Kota.[1] Other details familiar from Kota examples are the ears fanning forward, a view that accentuates their veining and spotted, crinkly, and rose-colored edge, and the saluki. Still more distinctive is the dense cross-hatching applied systematically to the elephant's skin, but also insistently on the tree trunk and the ground. Such a rich tactile network is exceedingly rare, occurring almost exclusively in early 18th-century Kota paintings, especially in paintings attributed to Niju.[2] The mango leaves have similarly busy veining, and the clouds are a swirl of wetly blended streaks. The mahout's awkwardly articulated stocky body, heavily modeled red shorts, and green waist-sash are also consistent with this artist's work. Conversely, the mahout's face is not, showing greater three-dimensionality than elsewhere, and the style of his turban seems more Deccani than Rajasthani.[3] In short, the intriguing blend of features seen here suggests an ongoing exchange of visual ideas between the northern Deccan and Kota, a process that probably involved the recruitment or migration of an artist trained in the Deccan to that Rajasthan state. | JS

1 Topsfield 2012, nos. 84, 106, and p. 275.
2 Beach 2011a, pp. 476–477 and figs. 10–12. Coincidentally, perhaps, one of these paintings (Beach 2011a, fig. 10; and Leach 1995, vol. 2, no. 10.41) depicts an elephant climbing a hill to shake fruit from a tree.
3 Compare Sotheby's, London, 4 April 1978, lot 252.

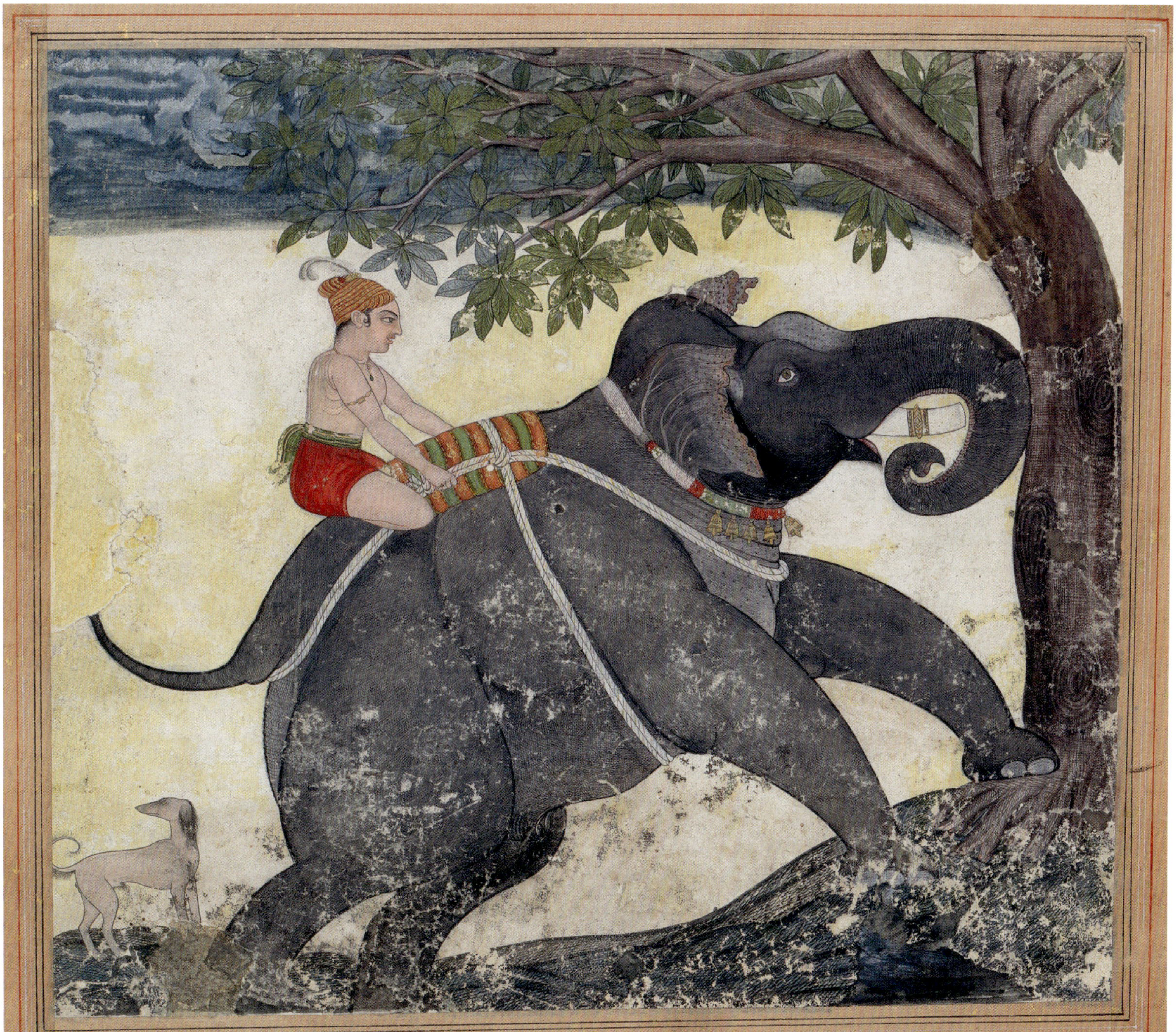

18 Guru Nanak Dev and Mardana

Attributed to the "Jaipur Painter"
Deccan, probably Aurangabad, c. 1750
24.6 × 16.8 cm (folio), 17.7 × 12 cm (painting)

These two venerable figures are Guru Nanak Dev (1469–1539), the founder of Sikhism, and his disciple and companion Mardana (1459–1534). Both hailed from the village of Talwindi (now Nankana), Pakistan. After losing six children in childbirth, Mardana's mother was so pessimistic that she named the newborn Marjana ("he who dies"). But the child survived, and eventually became the companion of Nanak, his junior by ten years. Guru Nanak celebrated his companion's unlikely survival by bestowing on him the name Marda-na ("one who would not die"). Raised in a family of minstrels of the Mirasai clan, Mardana was adept at the *rabab*, and entertained audiences that gathered to listen to Guru Nanak's teachings and hymns. They traveled together for twenty-five years, praising the One God until Bhai Mardana's death in 1534.

The pair is depicted as white-bearded figures standing beneath a flowering tree. In keeping with his non-sectarian beliefs, Guru Nanak wore clothing that adapted the customs of both Hindu and Muslim holy men. Accordingly, Guru Nanak is depicted here in plain traveling garb, with the domed cap of a Muslim *qalandar* (Sufi dervish) on his head, a Hindu-style saffron *tilak* mark on his forehead, and a modest *patka* about his waist. He holds a long staff though not the customary *mala* (rosary), while an enigmatic object hangs from a *gatra* (thick strap) looped over his right shoulder.[1] A hitherto unknown symbolic expression of Guru Nanak's ecumenical outlook lies in his impractically mismatched footwear, which consists of one Hindu-style wooden *khandava* (Punjabi sandal) and one nondescript cloth slipper of a type worn by Muslims. Mardana, for his part, wears a standard Muslim turban and shoes, and actively plays a *rabab* with an elaborate wood-grain pattern on the face of the instrument.

Deccani images of Sikh gurus are far less common than northern Indian ones, but images such as this may have been commissioned by the distinct Dakhni Sikh community that was established in Maharashtra and Andhra Pradesh during the time of Guru Gobind Singh (1666–1708), the Sikhs' tenth spiritual leader.[2] His assassination at Nanded, a site in southeastern Maharashtra located approximately midway between Aurangabad and Hyderabad and absorbed into the territory of the Mughal successor state headed by Asaf Jah (1671–1748, r. 1724–1748), led to the founding of the shrine of Hazoor Sahib, one of Sikhism's five most sacred *takhts* (throne of spiritual and temporal authority).

The painting itself is characterized by fine drawing and a keen sense of design dominated by sharp-edged shapes, the latter quality most pronounced in the figures' juxtaposition against a solid olive-green background, but also present in the ornamental mass of the tree's gold-outlined foliage and the hard strip of ground brightened by a band of varied but stylized flowers. The large figure scale, the rendering of the mask-like facial features and beards, the curling shapes and subtle modeling of the fingers and hands, the general stiffness of the clothing, and the smooth, polished surfaces all relate closely to features seen in works attributed to an artist known as the "Jaipur Painter."[3] An attribution to this anonymous but distinctive artist is strengthened by several minor details, notably the varieties of flowers below, the flat streaks of colored clouds at the upper edge, and the red border with golden floral designs. One of the paintings attributed to the Jaipur Painter has an inscription that indicates that it was "the gift of Purushottamdas, son of Damordardas, in the city of Bhagnagar [Hyderabad]."[4] Yet since the court of Salabat Jang (r. 1751–1762), the fourth Nizam of the Hyderabad State, remained at Aurangabad until 1762, when it moved to Hyderabad, it is likely that this painting was produced at Aurangabad during the 1750s. | JS

1 The same object appears less distinctly in an image of Guru Nanak published in Stronge 1999, p. 32.

2 A Deccani representation of the master and disciple along with other Sikh gurus and some political luminaries is published in Mittal 1963, fig. 10.

3 See Zebrowski 1983, pp. 234–237, figs. 208–210 and pl. XXII; the artist was designated by this misleading name because one painting is in the City Palace Museum, Jaipur. Other works attributed to him are in the Baroda Museum and Picture Gallery no. IA 711, published in Doshi 1995, p. 69; Fondation Custodia 1971-T.45, published in Gahlin 1991, no. 47; Khalili collection MSS 891, published in Leach 1998, no. 74; Falk and Digby 1979, no. 39; Bharat Kala Bhavan, published in Khandalavala, Chandra and Chandra 1960, no. 158; and Jagdish and Kamla Mittal Museum of Indian Art D30, published in Mittal 1963, fig. 3. Many other scholars have dated these works to the early 18th century or even c. 1700.

4 Khandalavala, Chandra and Chandra 1960, p. 62.

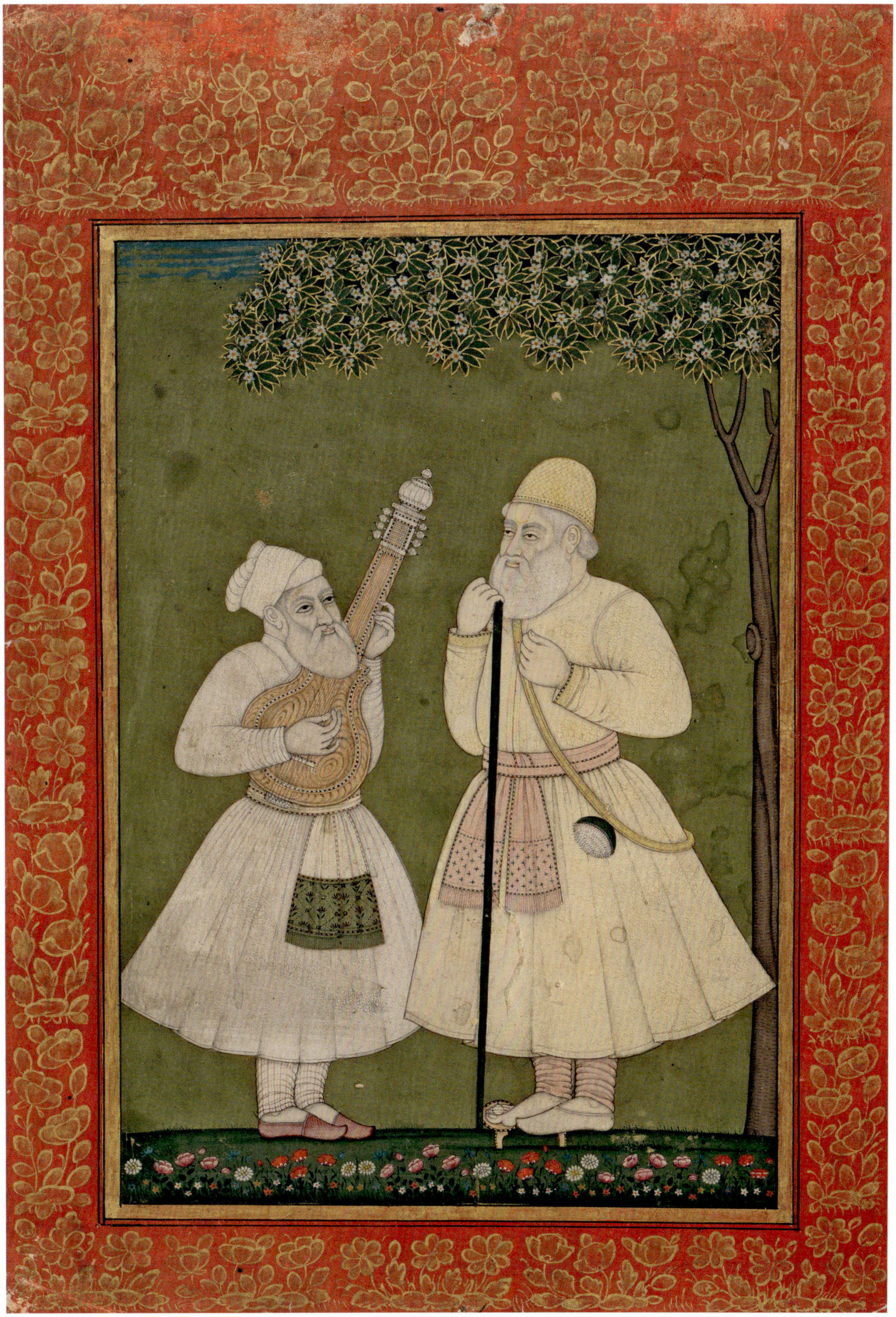

19 A king entertained by female musicians

Deccan, c. 1775–1800
24.6 × 36.8 cm (folio), 23.6 × 35.8 cm (painting)

Old customs, modern times at an Indian court, in this case, one in the central or southern Deccan in the late 18th century. In a secular ritual enacted by many a predecessor, a Hindu ruler pauses to savor a flower's fragrance while he enjoys a traditional pastime, a performance by a small troupe of female musicians and dancers. The setting, too, is familiar: he, within the portico of a canopied, single-chambered pavilion decorated with conspicuously deep ornamental niches, and they, moving about a narrow white terrace surrounded by an ancillary building, a high wall, and gardens with unwavering rows of red poppies. He assumes the classic Indian seated position of royal ease, though his silver-clad throne mimics the high, rectangular, scalloped back and curving armrests of European chairs. Five members of his military guard affect snippets of British fashion, sporting several varieties of mutton-chop sideburns along with different types of South Indian *jamas*, *dhotis* and turbans. Outfitted more pretentiously in military chic is the musket-bearing retainer who wears the upper half of a British redcoat uniform, but forgoes the accompanying trousers and boots in a concession to the heat.

The remainder of the scene is untouched by such foreign novelties. The seven entertainers – a singer with hand raised demonstratively, a dancer, and musicians playing cymbals, flutes, a drum, and a *sruti upanga* (drone bagpipe) – all look and dress in the most traditional of South Indian manners, including heavy jewelry, coiffures, and bare torsos. No less varied in complexion and behavior are the group of men to the left. Several figures dressed in proper *jamas* and turbans watch enthusiastically as they hold bows, dagger, and swords, while other bare-chested tribesmen, farmers, and priests raise up a spear, a plough, a begging bowl, a coin, and solicitous hands.

While no work directly comparable to this painting has come to light, the late Doris Wiener plausibly proposed an association with Shorapur, a minor central Deccani court where painting in a Hyderabad-inspired style is known from about 1750. The naïve figure style, frontal faces, and minor Europeanizing details point to a late 18th-century date. | JS

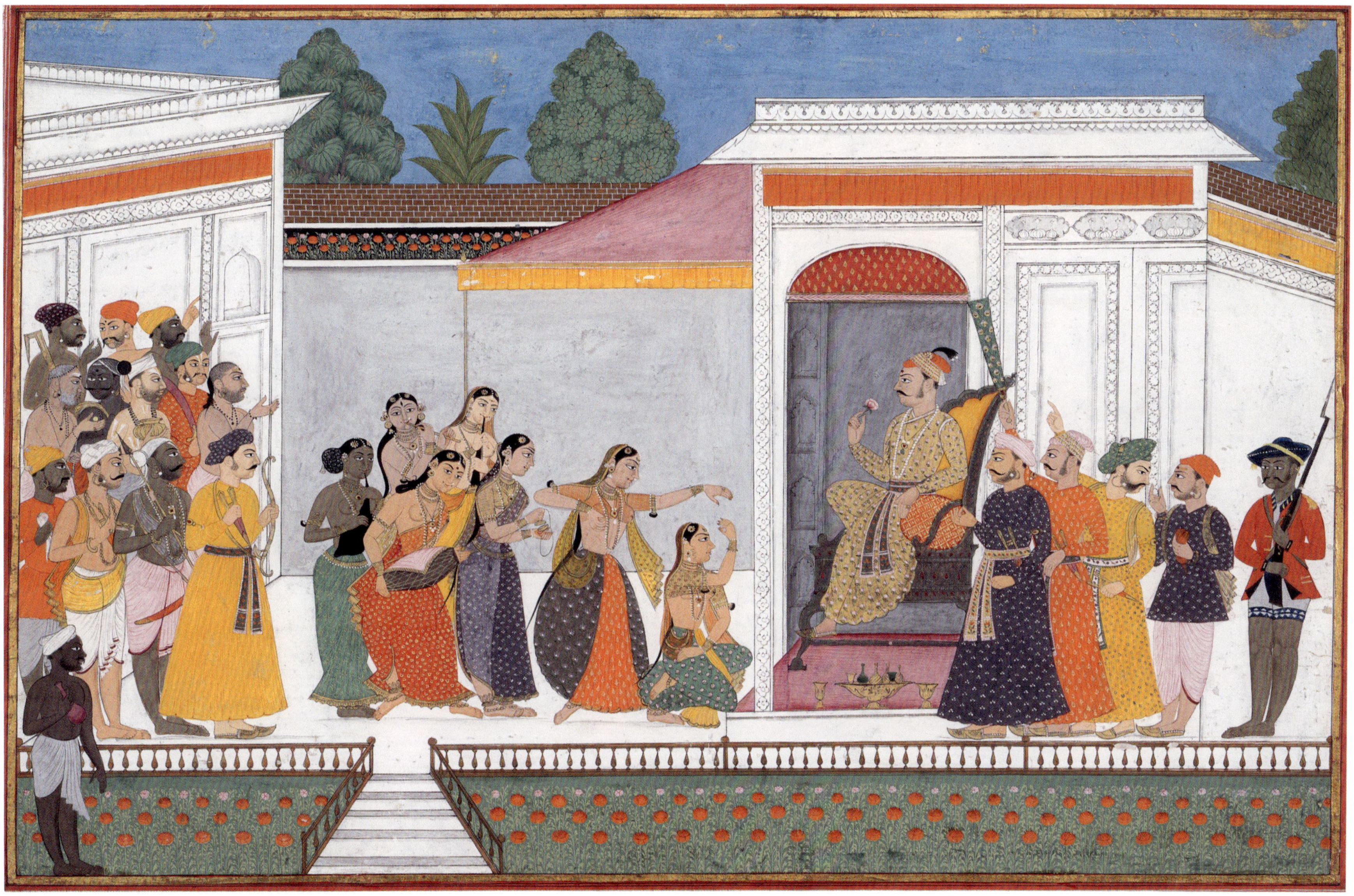

20 Woman on a terrace watching pigeons

Style of Venkatchellam
Hyderabad, c. 1820
20.9 × 15.1 cm (painting)

In a stereotypical scene of idle pleasure, a beauty on a terrace draws on a huqqa pipe while watching pet pigeons feed from a dish. She cuts a wonderfully flamboyant figure. Her scarlet and dark blue pleated skirt fans out in luxurious arcs before and behind her, exuding such irrepressible energy that even the angular base and scalloped back of the woman's blue chair are caught up in the rhythms of its white-beaded segments. Complementing this striking design unit is the dark huqqa hose, which swoops in a great arc in the opposite direction and loops around to join a coiled mass hung from the huqqa proper. These curving forms are played off against the straight lines of a raised white terrace, which is bordered by two different balustrades, a fountain-centered garden subjected to the rules of mathematical perspective, and some low-lying floral clusters.

Most of this composition is based on a model of c. 1800 attributed to Venkatchellam, the Hyderabad court artist of Nizam 'Ali Khan, Asaf Jah II (r. 1762–1803).[1] The woman, chair, huqqa, terrace, and even the pigeons are practically identical in form and position, though this version forgoes the master artist's delicate floral patterns and gold trim in favor of starker shapes and stronger tonal contrasts. Here, too, such details as two low tables holding cups, flasks, and fruit, the woman's removed shoes, three large flower pots overflowing with plants, two trees with voluminous, white-tipped foliage, and the cloud-streaked sky are eliminated, and the elaborate architectural bracket in the foreground is supplanted by a conventional staircase and geometric flower garden. An intermediate version of this composition with fewer deviations is known as well, indicating that Venkatchellam's work remained in favor in the region for decades after its creation.[2] | JS

1 Jagdish and Kamla Mittal Museum of Indian Art D16, c. 1800, published in Mittal 1963, fig. 9.
2 Christie's, London, 11 June 1986, lot 152 (also Zebrowski 1983, fig. 250).

Published: Sotheby's, London, 10 October 1977, lot 44; Archer 1963, pl. 12

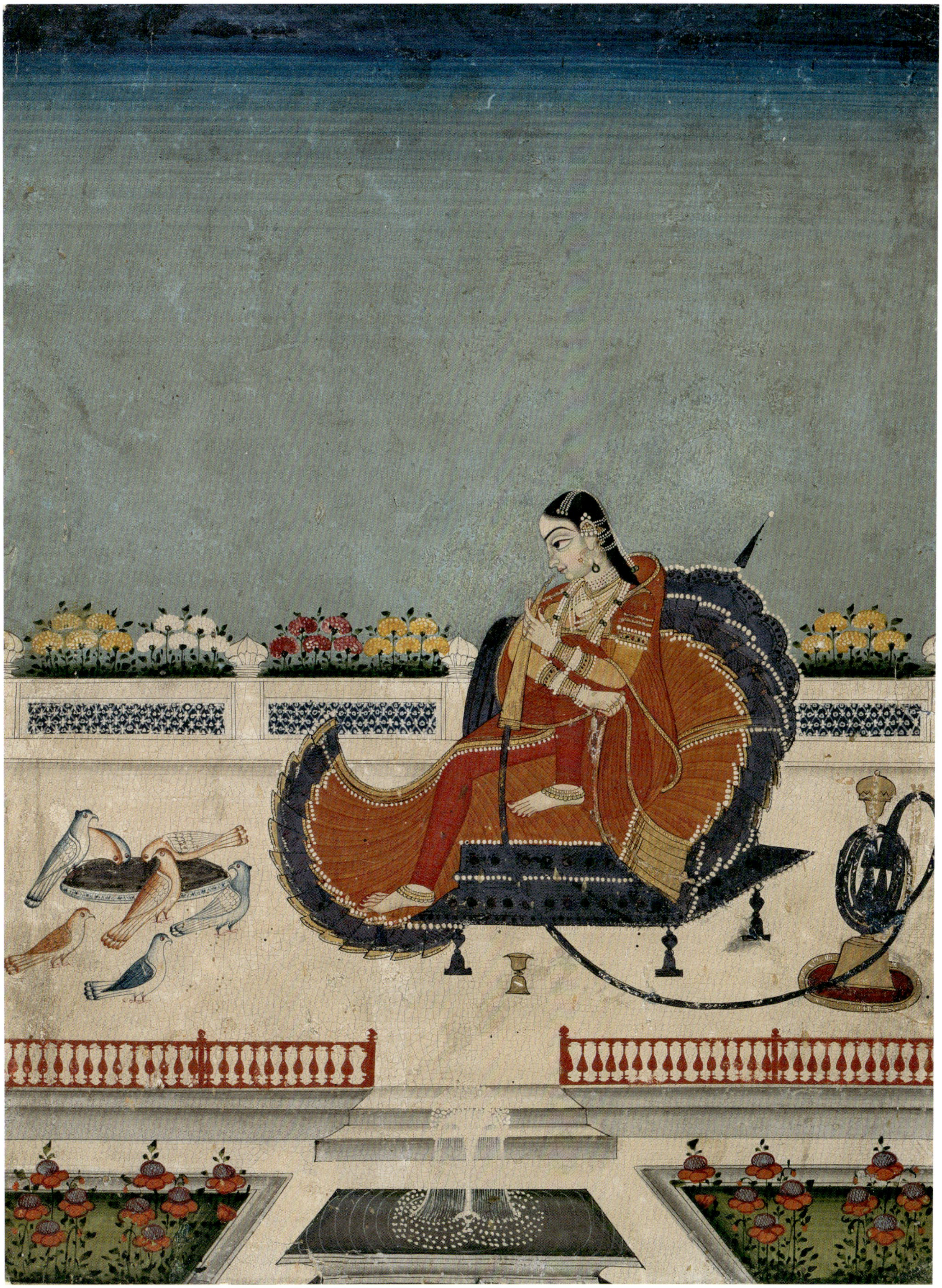

21 Intoxicated yogis

Hyderabad, c. 1830–1840
29.5 × 19.5 cm (folio), 22.8 × 14 cm (painting)

Indian artists revere individual ascetics, and routinely present their remarkable impassivity and weatherworn bodies as outward signs of profundity. By contrast, cynical observers are inclined to look askance at larger groups of ascetics, and frequently hold them up to visual ridicule for their drug-induced antics or stupor.[1] Here, in a late Hyderabadi example of this tradition, an artist caricaturizes the ascetics' dissolute behavior, setting up a distant and impersonal view of seven isolated and evenly spaced yogis. Dressed in the scantiest of loincloths and distinguished from each other primarily by the shape of their matted locks and pointed beards, all the figures have a gleamingly light complexion, a device that in combination with the dark brown ground and a smattering of schematic vegetation produces a composition dominated by a caustic inventory of poses and actions. Two yogis lean against a shrub or on a meditation crutch as they actively smoke opium from a huqqa, and two reach a hand into a bowl to knead or scoop *bhang* (cannabis). Several yogis with shuttered eyes have lapsed into a state of stupefaction, and one looks apprehensive and clutches his wrist.

The artist pays little attention to the figures' emaciation, preferring to emphasize their awkward cross-legged or slumped poses and distended bellies. Their faces and bodies are quite loosely drawn and painted, and even the fire pits, gourds, and rocks strewn about the ground are distinguished chiefly in terms of color. A smattering of flowers that are little more than splashes of green and orange, and red huqqa pipes and brown sticks used to stir the drug add a bit of surface liveliness to the central portion of the composition. This minor decorative interest continues in the silvery river, jagged shoreline, and minuscule waterfowl in the foreground, and in the charmingly naïve moon and stars overhead.[2] | JS

1 Representative examples are published in Ehnbom 1985, no. 39; Leach 1986, no. 42; Leach 1995, vol. 1, no. 4.40; Pal 2004, no. 78; and Habighorst, Reichart and Sharma 2007, fig. 72.

2 An illegible inscription in Devanagari script is written across the band of water.

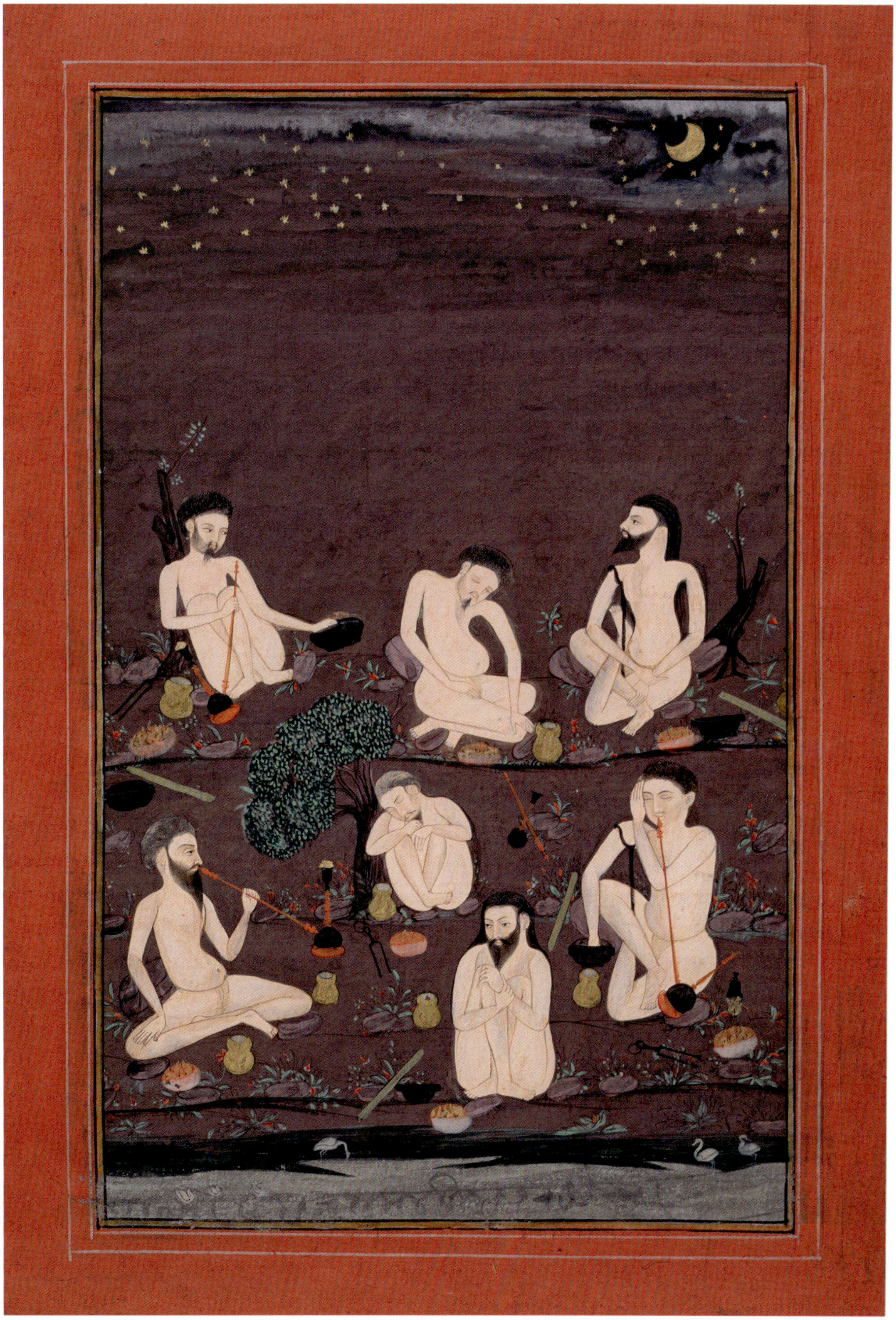

22 Imam Husayn, the Martyr of Kerbala

Hyderabad, c. 1830–1840
59.1 × 35.3 cm (folio), 46.7 × 25.4 cm (painting)

Given the seemingly incongruous attributes of a richly adorned turban, European-style curly hair, and a radiant halo, it is something of a surprise that this grand figure represents Imam Husayn, an identification established definitively in an inscription written above a smaller and earlier version of the same image type.[1] Husayn (626–680), son of 'Ali and grandson of the Prophet Muhammad, is, along with his brother Hasan, revered as one of the principal figures in Shi'a Islam. He is celebrated for his martyrdom at the hands of the overwhelming forces of the Umayyad ruler Yazid I, whom the Shi'a regarded as apostate. Husayn's death on the battlefield of Karbala on 10 Muharram AH 61/10 October 680, and the ignominious mutilation of his body are commemorated annually throughout the holy month of Muharram, and are the focus of special celebrations on the date of Ashura, which sometimes take the form of ritual flagellation. Husayn's shrine at Karbala in Iraq has been a major pilgrimage site for the Shi'a practically since his death.

Many popular images on scrolls depict a mounted Husayn riding across the battlefield of Karbala with his infant son 'Ali Asghar in his arms. Here, by contrast, he is neither embattled nor bloodied, but a standing, stately figure dressed in a plumed turban, a long red cloak, and boots. His piety is expressed in the meditation staff and rosary that he holds.

There are reportedly numerous examples of this subject, many produced in Hyderabad, where Shi'a Islam is strong. This is a late work, obvious from the hard rendering of the face and hands, and the very schematic treatment of the ground and flowers. | JS

[1] The painting is published in Pal 1983, D14.

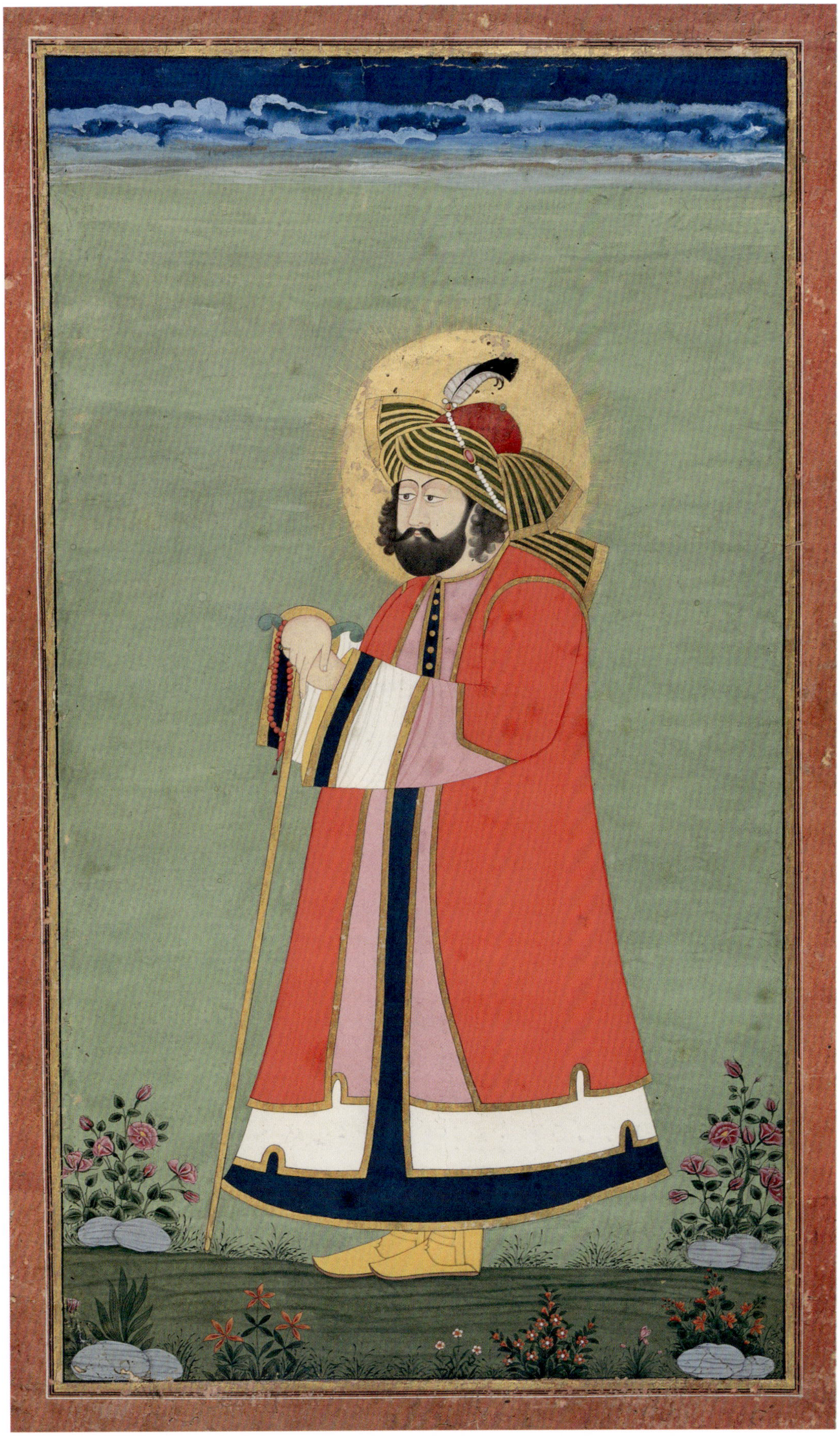

23 Krishna and Radha on a terrace

Hyderabad, c. 1840
22.5 × 16.3 cm (folio), 15 × 9.5 cm (painting)

Krishna and Radha, archetypal lovers in whose guise members of Indian royalty often fancifully saw themselves, huddle together on a terrace amidst a pile of luxuriant cushions. Krishna is endowed with his iconic blue complexion and a crown topped by a central plume of peacock feathers, but he also uncharacteristically sports a pencil-thin mustache, a nod to secular custom. He reaches out to cradle Radha's bare head, and she reciprocates by tenderly laying one hand on his arm to prolong his caress. So close are they that their radiant haloes conjoin and their lips are separated by only the span of her large nose-ring. Their intertwined bodies remain visually indistinct, deprived of normal outlining and concealed beneath a busy surface of lace-like patterns, long scarves, and thick necklaces. The gold of the crown, earrings, bracelets, and necklaces is tooled in a characteristically late technique to increase its glimmer, while that of bolsters, balustrades, hems, and vessels is merely applied with a thin layer of paint.

The faces have more pronounced modeling than earlier 19th-century examples, and the flowers on either side of the steps leading up to the terrace are rendered in a cursory painterly manner adapted from European art. These features build on elements seen routinely in slightly earlier works.[1] | JS

[1] See, for example, Binney 1973, no. 171.

Published: Christie's, London, 9 November 1977, lot 39

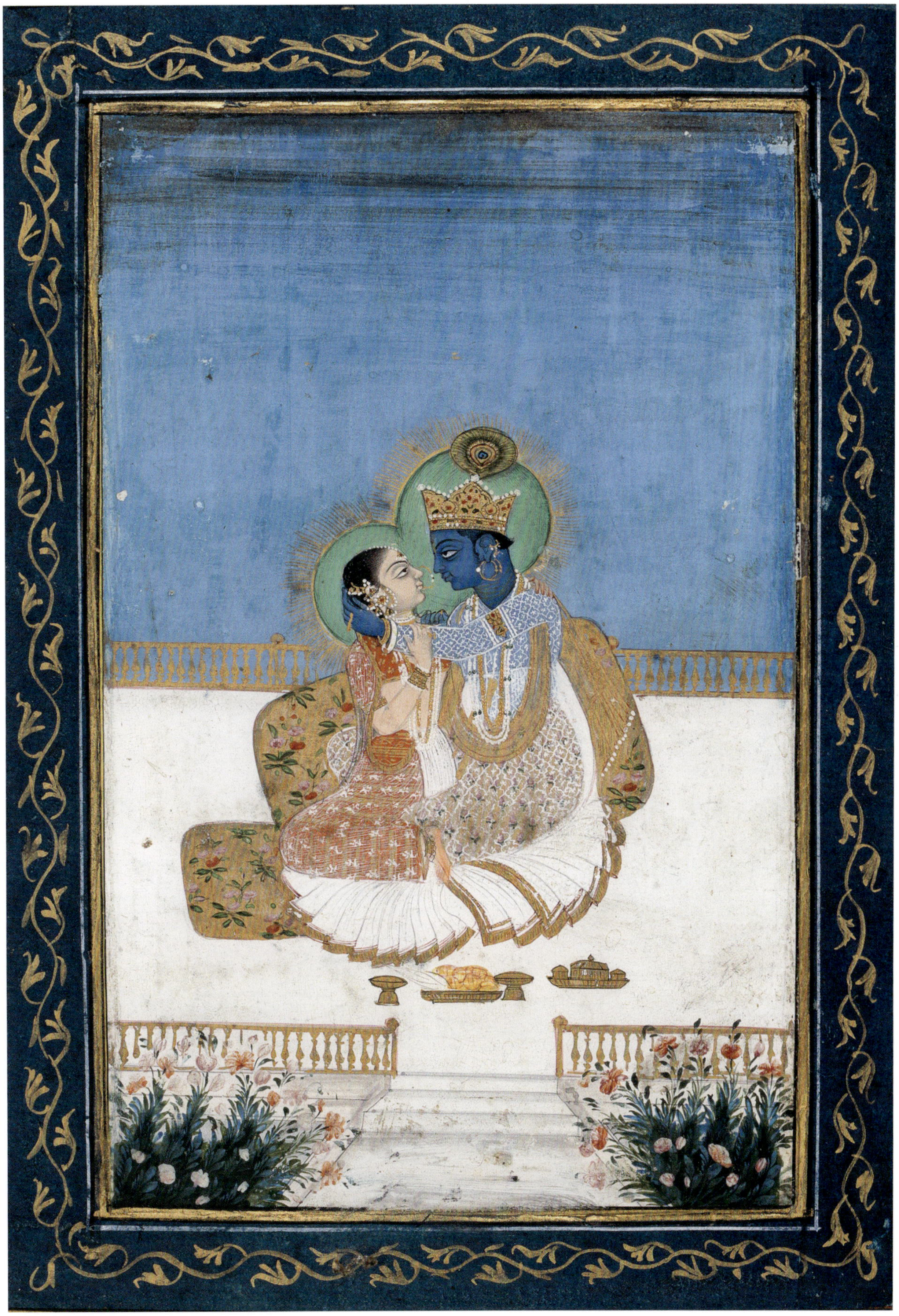

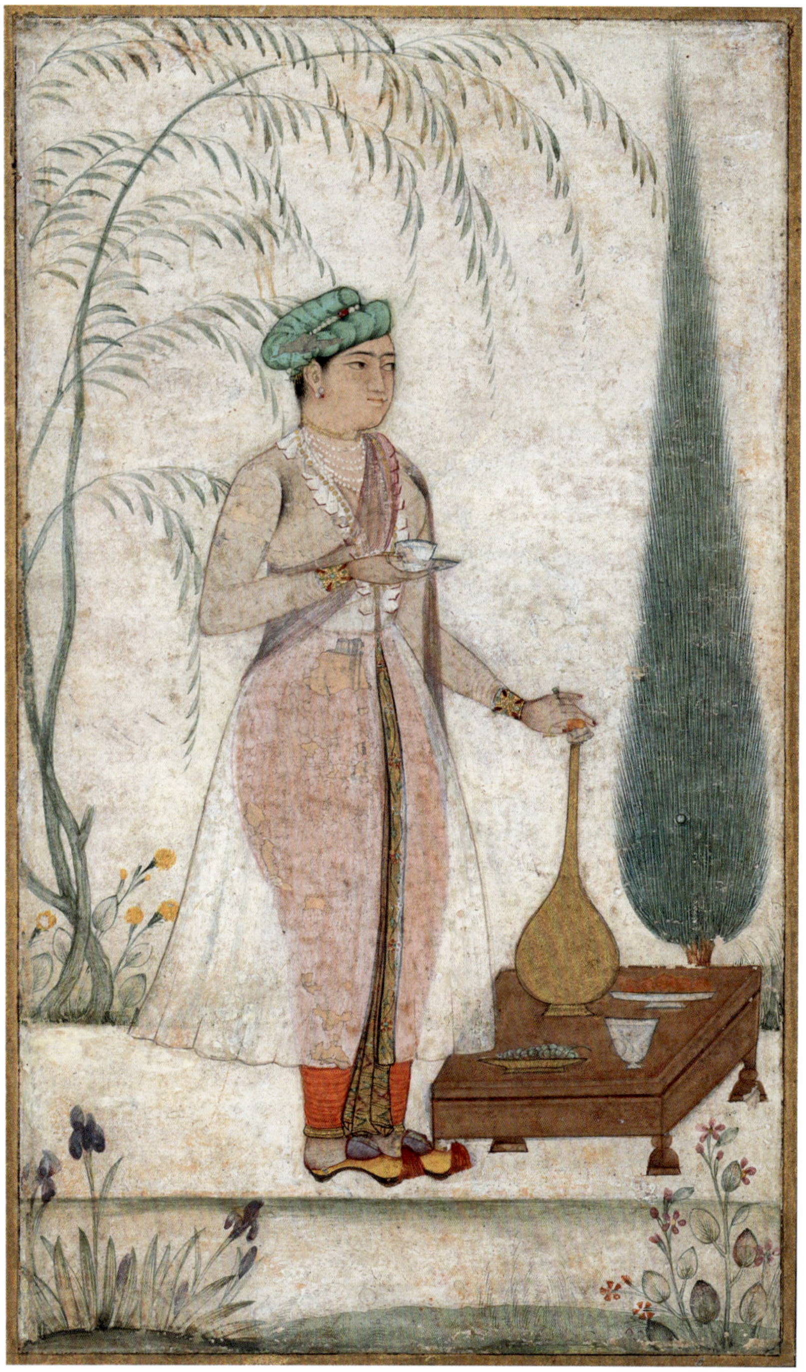

24 A royal lady with a wine bottle

Mughal style at Bikaner, c. 1625–1630
15 × 9 cm (folio), 14.2 × 8.1 cm (painting)

Although royal women normally remained beyond the covetous eyes of male artists, they were served up as regular if fanciful fare in Mughal painting. This painting of a solitary princess or lady-in-waiting with wine flask and cup in hand exemplifies a particularly common image type, a woman whose natural allure is enhanced by the presence of the fruits of the vine. Here, she is dressed more modestly than usual. In keeping with her handsome, unconventionally squarish face, her most distinctive article of clothing is actually an item of male attire: a turban festooned with a strand of pearls and a single ruby and complemented by matching pearl-and-ruby earrings. Her main outfit, however, is traditionally feminine: a white *peshwaj* with traces of musk stains at the armpits, a broad sash slung over the left shoulder and draped down her side, a reddish-orange *paijama*, a thin, ankle-length golden *patka* decorated with an arabesque design, and brightly colored shoes. While the material of the white *peshwaj* itself is more gauzy than diaphanous, the customary ruffles around its neckline are made unexpectedly opaque, their lower edges thrown into relief by red lines. Most of the rest of the painting – including the later extension of the painting added just below the figure's feet – has a similarly thinly painted chalky surface.

Together with the distorted shape of the woman's Jahangir-period turban, the simplified rendering of her handsome face and of many other elements suggest that the painting was made outside the imperial atelier at the end of the 1620s, probably at Bikaner, a court with strong Mughal connections. The low table beside the figure is noticeably ungainly in shape, and the implausibly outsized golden flask has no sense of modeling. Likewise, the cup, two dishes of grapes and pomegranates, and even the cypress tree lack the full and precise articulation of imperial painting.

A romantic scene with a turbaned woman in an essentially similar style but by a different artist has erroneously been associated with Prince Salim's atelier in Allahabad.[1] A related scene of lovers rendered in a more fluid version of this style and thus dated slightly later is also known.[2] | JS

1 Leach 1998, no. 23. She also provides references to several other works attributed to that artist.

2 Leach 1986, no. 36. Two *ragamala* paintings in that same variant of the Mughal–Bikaner style are published in Bautze 1991, nos. 25–26.

25 Lion attacking a dragon

Ascribed to Ghulam Hamid Umrani
Bikaner, late 18th century
19.2 × 26.6 cm (painting)

In theory, at least, this animal combat pits raw power against viperous wiles. Planting his rear leg against a rock, the lion launches his massive body at the dragon, whose nightmarish form combines a serpentine body, a lupine snout and teeth, a single horn, clawed feline feet, and slender wings. The great beast has already closed in too much to be held off by any of these attributes, and he clamps his jaws onto the dragon's back even as he tears at it with his claws. The sinuous dragon counterattacks, twisting about his upper body and head to bite the lion's neck. Each creature draws blood from its opponent, but there is no doubt that it is the rangier one that is doomed.

While images of such fabulous bestial battles traveled widely, passing from China to Iran and thence to Golconda and Rajasthan, this artist prefers pattern to gore, making the lion's head proper surprisingly small, fixing the eyes in a blank stare, and concealing the teeth. All these features are eclipsed by his focus on the lion's magnificent mane, whose whorls of hair are arranged in six concentric arcs overspreading almost half his body. The dragon, too, is envisioned less as a full-bodied creature than as a looping ribbon-like form with mottled green coloring and golden spots. Such a highly ornamental rendering represents a late stage in the process of transmission of this compelling motif, and is the work of Ghulam Hamid Umrani, a Bikaneri artist whose name is ascribed on the reverse below a freely drawn design of a floral scroll.[1] Ghulam Hamid is not included in any of the published lists and genealogies of Bikaner artists, but the simplified shapes of the rocks and clouds, the delicate plants in the foreground, the fine line, and the thinly applied colors establish a Bikaneri provenance. By coincidence, another Bikaneri artist with a similar name, Hamid Umrani, is known from a far more substantial version of the confrontation of lion and dragon in a rocky landscape that is dated to c. 1700.[2] | JS

1 The inscription reads *li kam* Ghulam Hamid Umrani ("written work of Ghulam Hamid Umrani" [*li* is apparently an abbreviation for *likhatam* – written]). Umrani is the family name of a prominent artist family working in Bikaner.
2 Gahlin 1991, no. 57.

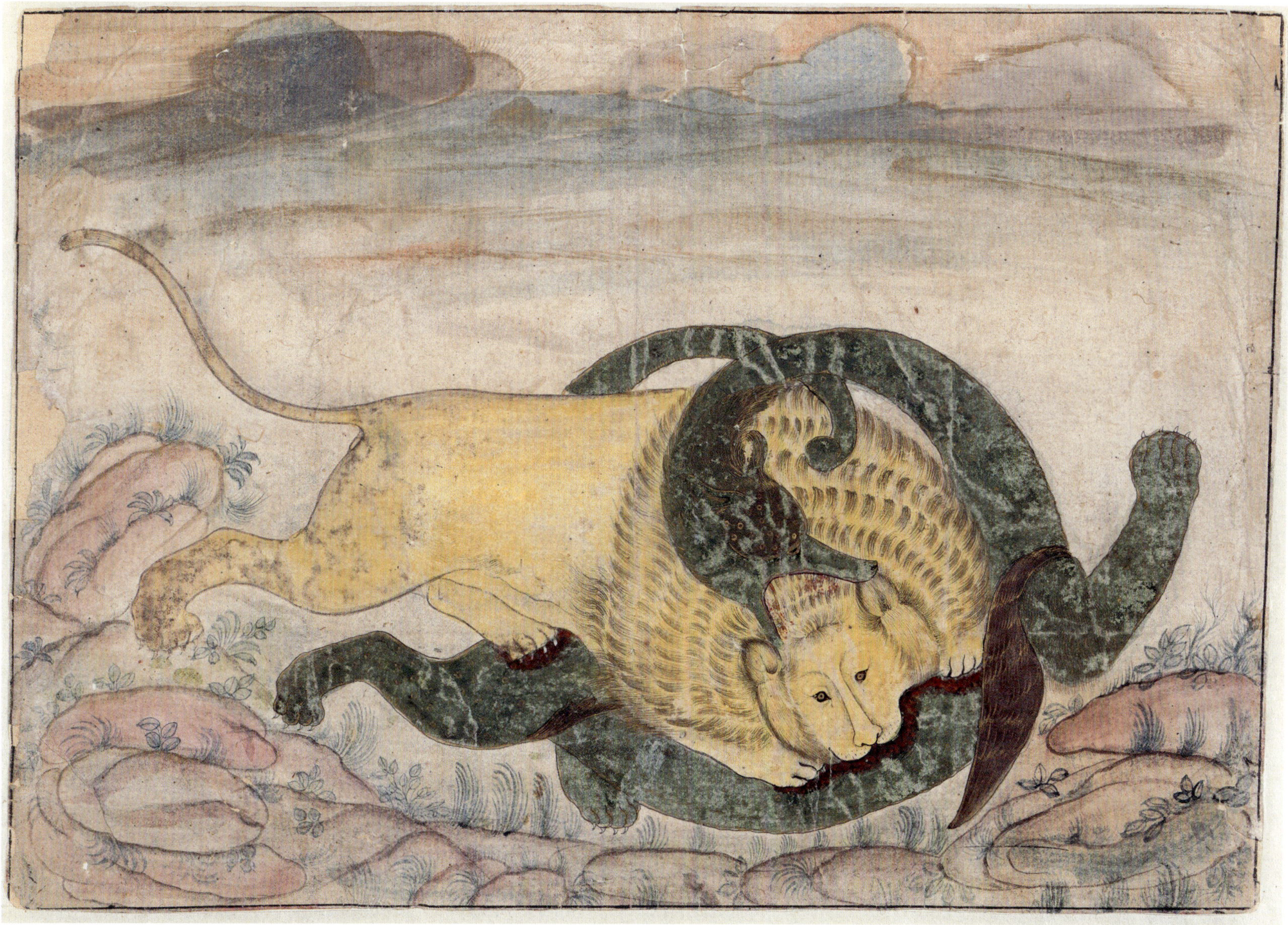

26 Krishna standing on a lotus

Bikaner, c. 1800
22.6 × 14.8 cm (folio), 14.4 × 9.2 cm (painting)

Standing on a large and brilliantly colored lotus, a solitary Krishna holds a flute in his outstretched hennaed hand. His pose – feet splayed and head turned away from the flute – is a variation of an exceedingly common devotional image type that customarily depicts the deity full-face with flute raised to his lips. Obviously the simple pastime of a cowherd, Krishna's flute playing is a much-celebrated metaphor for his irresistible summons to devotees, who flock to him to slake their yearning for union with the divine.

This painting, which was formerly in the collection of the Maharaja of Bikaner, was produced at that court around 1800. It shares with contemporary Bikaner paintings the disproportionately large head set on a lithe body, the lotus-shaped eye, the curling sidelock, and the pearl-outlined crown with tall prongs, conical cap, and peacock-feather plume.[1] Particularly noteworthy is the dark aura that surrounds the figure, a penumbral effect created by a series of discrete, even scratchy brush marks paralleling the contours of Krishna's body and clothing. Together with more basic accents placed just inside those same contours, this device counteracts the flatness found in most schools of Rajasthani painting, and adds atmospheric depth to the unusual gray-green background, which is plain but for some rhythmic ridges and tufts of grass below and loose streaks of white overhead. Krishna's muted yellow *dhoti* takes on a similarly unearthly sense of volume. It is modeled with dense, scratchy lines emanating from the waist and both sides of the *dhoti*'s central fold; this network of hairy marks is intersected by a peculiar frond-like set of lines behind each thigh and knee. Displaying many of these same qualities is a painting of a seated Krishna dated 1801, a work that anchors the chronology of this group.[2] | JS

1 Isacco and Dallapiccola 1982, figs. 50 and 112; and Khandalavala, Chandra and Chandra 1960, fig. 80. A version sold at Sotheby's, New York, 6 October 1990, lot 21, shows Krishna with his legs crossed and the flute at his mouth; one offered at Sotheby's, New York, 21 March 1990, lot 146, depicts him with three women and two cows.
2 Asian Art Museum, San Francisco F1996.6, published in Aitken 2010, fig. 5.58.

Published: Sotheby's, New York, 21 March 1990, lot 145

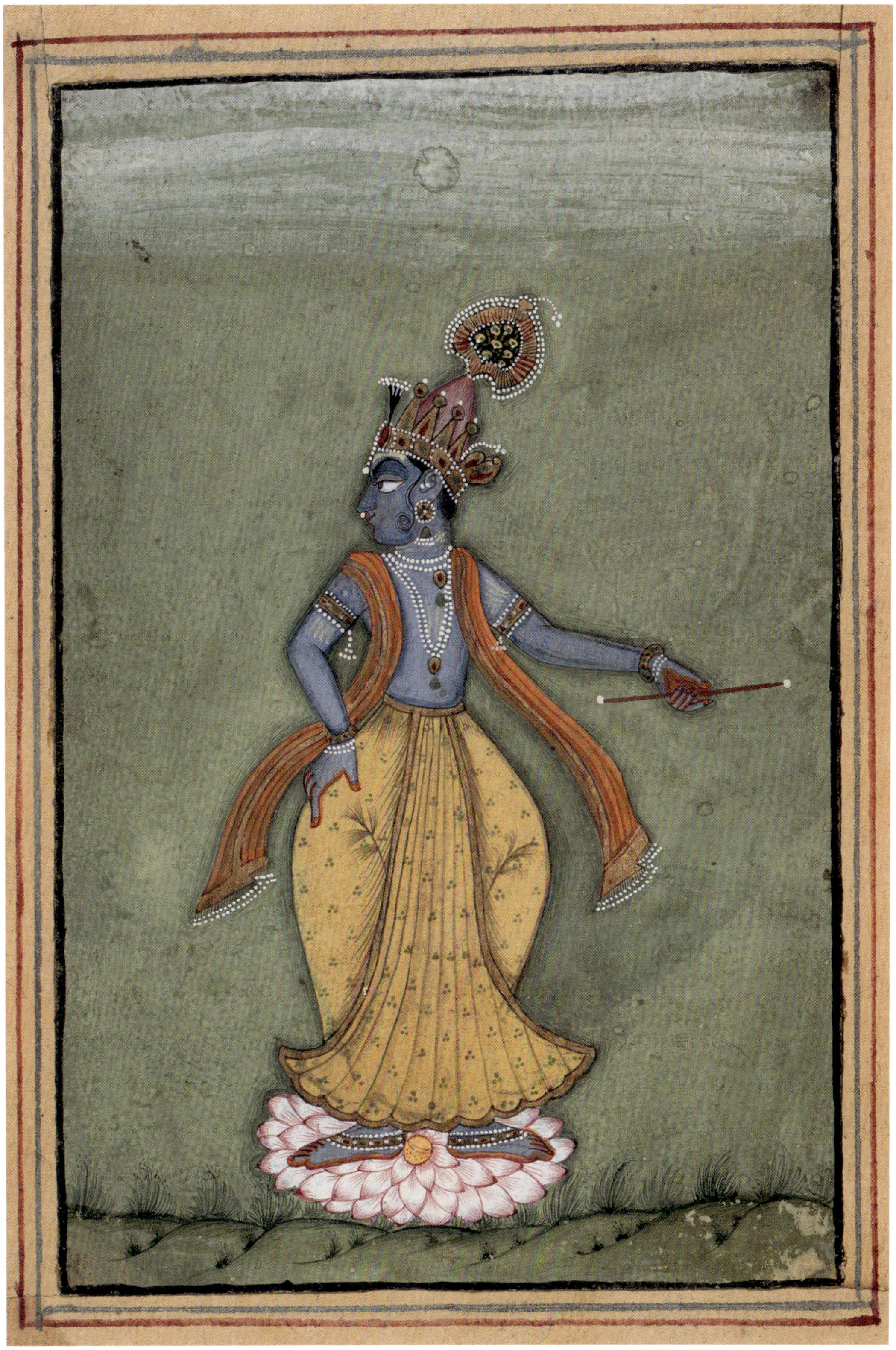

27 The Bower of Quiet Passion

Attributed to Nihal Chand
Kishangarh, c. 1750
23.5 × 32.5/33 cm (folio)

The fully colored, finished version of this preparatory, tinted drawing, now in the Binney collection in the San Diego Museum of Art, has a long text in Hindi verse inscribed on its back.[1] "Thus the night passed, lying in pleasure and comfort," it reads, "When dawn came, knowing it was Hari's time, the *sakhis* came together/ The sweet and skillful Lalita took the *vina* and played on it/The wondrous raga *vibhasa*, its sounds spreading all around the grove/ The birds were chirping in this blissful moment/The cool breeze, blowing over the pollen of lotuses and over water, came to them." It is all part of what is often called the *kunj lila*: Krishna's sports in the grove of love.

Remarkably little is stated directly and yet everyone understands: the lovers decided to escape to their favorite grove in the forest, away from others' eyes, and there they spent the night, cooled by breeze and surrounded by fragrance. But the *sakhis* caught up with them as the day dawned and there they stood all around them, playing upon instruments, breaking into song. But the royal poet, Sawant Singh who wrote under the *nom de plume* Nagaridas and for whom Nihal Chand must have painted this work,[2] also suggests in this verse, subtly: how can anyone be certain that it is not they who, playfully, will tell everyone in the village where they found them?

The completed painting is filled with lush foliage, greenery covering almost every inch of the surface of the painting. Under this emerald green cover, the lovers are seen still asleep as it were, bodies fully stretched out on a bed of lotus leaves and flowers. Their arms are still a bit entangled – the fingers of his dark hand on her golden stomach looking, as a poet said in the context of another painting, as if these were lines of gold scratched on a black touchstone – and an expression of utter peace reigns on the faces of the two who are lost to the world. Even when one *sakhi* peeps through the branches of a close-by tree to look at them, or when music pervades the surrounding air, it seems not to matter.

The interest of this freely drawn work lies in the fact that it lets us see the process, almost hear the initial thoughts of the painter. Here, there is no bevy of *sakhis* playing music, only Lalita who sets herself up close by, *vina* in lap. No one is bending down here to pluck lotus flowers; no one is crowding close to the lovers' lotus couch. The artist, however, is clear that the figure of the lover must be recognizable as Krishna, and as no ordinary lover; carefully therefore he has clad him – almost the only color one sees in this drawing – in his yellow garment, the *pitavastra* that almost identifies Krishna. The bare outline of the trees, or of how lotuses in the river are suggested, tells us as much of the manner in which the mind of the painter worked as of the process of painting: the correcting patches in white stand out boldly wherever the painter had paused to re-think or re-plan. | BG

1 See Goswamy and Smith 2005, no. 32.
2 For a recent summary of Nihal Chand's œuvre see Haidar 2011.

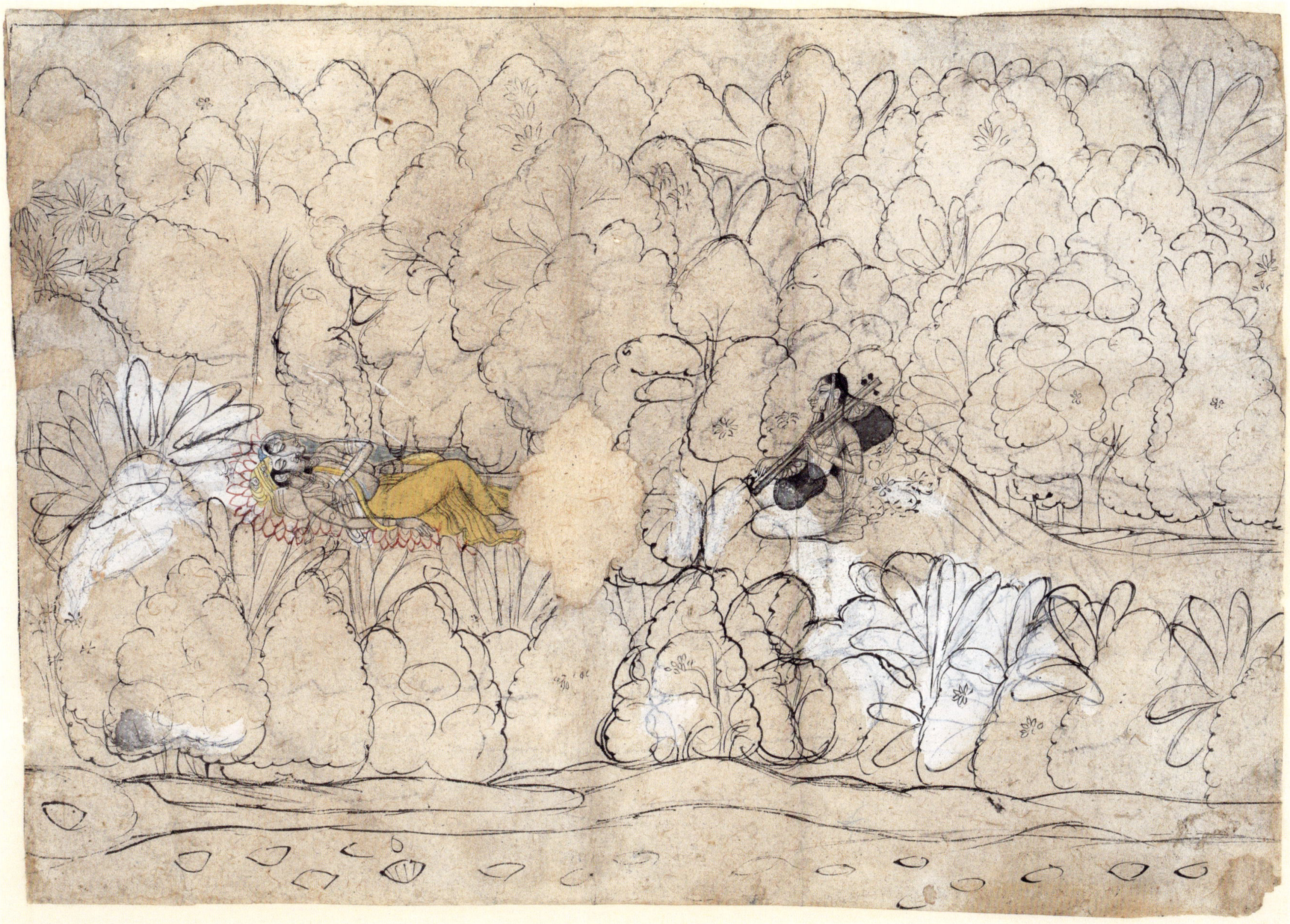

28 Portrait of a Vaishnava priest

Ascribed to Nihal Chand
Kishangarh or Rupnagar, c. 1750–1764
28 × 18.9 cm (folio), 10.4 × 8.4 cm (painting)
Museum Rietberg, Collection Danielle Porret, 2010.5

The subject of this modest figure study is identified on the reverse by two inscriptions. The first, written at the top in Persian, reads: "Portrait of Misr Mohan, resident of Brindavan. Work of the painter Nihal Chand. Price one rupee." The second, written in Hindi in Devanagari script in the center of the folio, reads: "Mohan Mishr. He recites text at Pulani. Work of Nihal Chand."[1]

Together, they establish that the seated figure is a brahman who lived at Brindavan, a site about 10 km from Mathura that is venerated for its association with Krishna. Misr Mohan's duties presumably included the recitation of sacred texts in that vicinity. When the artist Nihal Chand recorded the priest's likeness at Brindavan is a matter of speculation, but his great patron Savant Singh (1699–1764, r. 1748–1757) spent time in that holy city, some 300 km from Kishangarh and very near his maternal home, during the struggles of succession in the aftermath of the death of his father, Raj Singh, in 1747, and retired there permanently upon abdicating the throne in 1757.[2] It is likely that the artist had occasion to visit Brindavan during one of his patron's sojourns there in the 1750s.

The portrait depicts a seated young religious figure with a vertical *tilak* on his forehead, a necklace of tulsi beads, an unadorned chalky-white *jama*, a plain *angavastram* over his shoulder, and a simple rose-colored turban. The priest looks up and away as if contemplating lofty matters, a pose that accentuates his thin mustache and prominent Adam's apple. While his sketchy right hand rests passively on his thigh, his fully articulated left hand is shown with its index finger suspended in mid motion, a discreet gesture that adds a sensitive touch of humanity to the portrait.

The painter, Nihal Chand, (c. 1710–c. 1782), who belonged to a family of brahmans of the Surdhaj sect, was the dominant artist at Kishangarh and nearby Rupnagar for much of the 18th century, and under the auspices of the poet-king Maharaja Savant Singh produced a series of hauntingly lyrical images of Krishna and Radha in panoramic landscapes.[3] Many of his works are ascribed in Persian, albeit in a different hand than the one used here. This sketch portrait represents a type known from at least three other works. Two ascribed sketches depict older priests, one unnamed and the other identified in Devanagari as Nar Hair Dasji.[4] The third, which is unascribed, portrays another Vaishnava priest, one Gosain Radhavallabhi Chand Lalji, in a very similar format and style.[5]

One instructive element of the inscription is the valuation of one rupee, modest but typical remuneration for an artist whose monthly stipend of twenty-five rupees was augmented by sums given periodically in acknowledgment of the formal presentation of individual works.[6] | JS

1 Both readings have been adapted from translations provided by B.N. Goswamy.
2 Dickinson and Khandalavala 1959, p. 11.
3 Haidar 2011, p. 596.
4 These works, respectively, are in the collections of J.P. Goenka and the late Kumar Sangram Singh.
5 Goswamy and Bhatia 1999, no. 139.
6 Haidar 2011, p. 597.

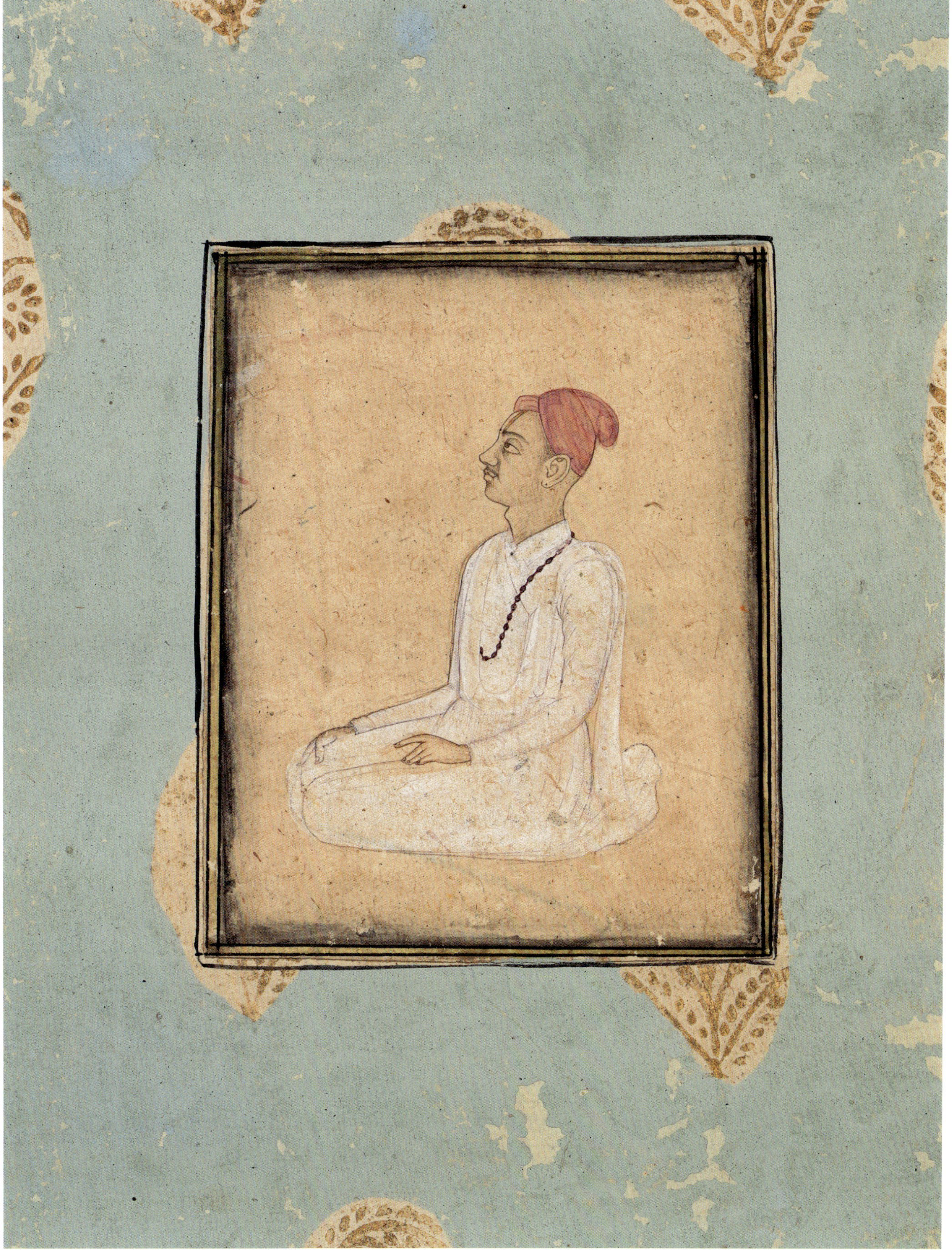

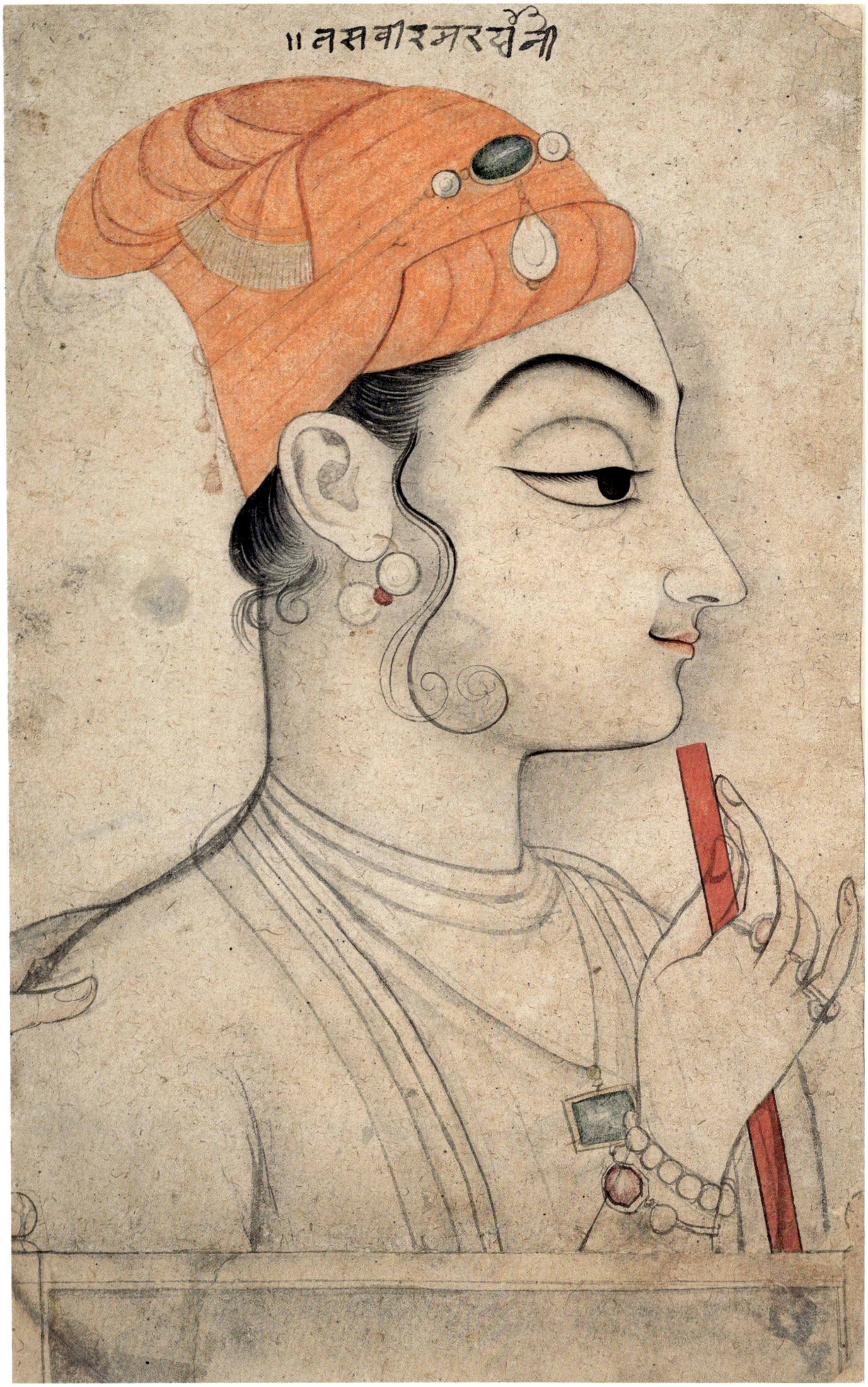

29 Krishna holding a flute

Attributed to Budh Lal
Kishangarh, c. 1795–1800
33 × 20.4 cm (painting)

To judge from a peripheral detail – the remnants of a left hand resting on the shoulder of this handsome youth wearing a bejeweled turban – this drawing was once part of a larger composition, probably a scene of Radha and Krishna, whose identity is invoked not only by the red flute that passes through his hand and decidedly over his thumb but also by the sheer elegance of his idealized features.[1] Yet the rendering of these features is telling in another way as well, for they help identify the painter as the artist Budh Lal, son of Suratram; the pair presented works to the Kishangarh court but were employed by Bagh Singh, the third son of Bahadur Singh (r. 1755–1781) at the *thikana* of Fatehgarh, some fifty-two km south of Kishangarh.[2] The key detail is the ear, which has both a well-defined dark oval depression (triangular fossa) near the top and a dark groove (scaphoid fossa) inside the outer rim (helix). This distinctive feature appears in Budh Lal's ascribed portrait of Maharaja Bhim Singh of Jodhpur (r. 1793–1803), though not in Jodhpur images of that ruler.[3] It recurs along with several other diagnostic features in four lightly colored and similarly sized paintings of a woman holding an infant, a vase of flowers, a wine cup, or her *odhni*, and thereby establishes a small corpus of works associated with Budh Lal.[4]

One of these features is the delineation of the highly geometricized arch of the eye socket, which echoes the springing arc of the meticulously plucked eyebrow and answers the upswept curve of the elongated eye. This element, widely regarded as the defining characteristic of Kishangarh painting, must ultimately be derived from Bijapuri painting, specifically from portraits of Sultan 'Ali 'Adil Shah II (r. 1656–1672).[5] Common to these four paintings, too, are the delicate articulation of the upper and lower eyelashes, the hint of modeling around the thin lips and along the jaw, the sinuous earlock and curling nape hair, and the fluid contour lines. In each case the hands assume the same graceful proportions and position, the attenuated fingers curving in virtually the same arrangement and bedecked with almost the same sequence of rings. Although in every example the colors are thinly applied and the skin remains altogether uncolored, this painting is more selectively colored than the others, the result of its incomplete state. Were it finished, the turban, jewels, clothing, and fingertips would certainly have been enhanced with stronger color accents. | JS

1 The inscription above, written in informal Devanagari script, is merely descriptive: *Taswir-i mardhani* ("picture of a youth"). Navina Haidar reports that this same inscription appears above a bust-length portrait ascribed to Bhavanidas in the royal collection at Kishangarh. Accordingly, in 1995, she published this painting (fig. 164) as a c. 1760 copy after an original by Bhavanidas.
2 Khan 1979–80, p. 67.
3 Crill and Jariwala 2010, no. 39.
4 Sotheby's, New York, 22 March 2002, lots 21–22; Pal et al. 1989, no. 8; and San Diego Museum of Art 1990:769.
5 Compare, for example, Zebrowski 1983, figs. 107–110; and Crill and Jariwala 2010, no. 33.

Published: Tooth & Sons 1974, no. 57; Tooth & Sons 1977, no. 35

30 Krishna with Radha and a princely figure

Attributed to Surdhaj Nanagram
Kishangarh, c. 1825
19.7 × 15.5 cm (painting)

Having plucked two petals from the once-full lotus blossom in his left hand, Krishna bestows them upon his beloved Radha, who reaches out to accept them with one hand. Gracefully arching the forefinger of her right hand, Radha plies a wooden needle strung with a thin black cord and adds the petals to a floral garland in the making. This tender, mundane act has a devotional aspect as well. While Radha will undoubtedly offer the finished garland to the nimbate Krishna as any devotee would do to a temple idol, the repetitive but focused process of preparing it becomes a meditative exercise in its own right, freeing her mind to fixate on her divine lover, a trance-like condition conveyed here by her smoldering gaze. Radha enters into this state of union as the intercessor for all others, including the princely figure that sits immediately behind her. His supplication of Krishna is indicated by both the lotus stalks resting before him and the inscribed sheet of paper laid out on the low table located at the edge of the white floor cloth on which Krishna sits.[1]

The figure style that dominated Kishangarh painting for much of the 18th century continues here in the figures' slender physiques, arched backs, and bow-like legs. Their faces have the sloping profile, elongated nose, and pointed, highlighted chin of late 18th-century examples, though the upward sweep of the eyes is less exaggerated than in most works from that period. Radha's coiling sidelock is an elegant touch, as is Krishna's loosely tied and trailing turban. The substitution of a dark brown complexion for Krishna's typically light blue one is a rare feature.

The element that dates this painting well into the 19th century is the hard, discrete striations in the barren and receding background – dark green and dense at first, lighter and disintegrating into rows of dots in the distance. The landscape culminates in a broad crest articulated with three symmetrical ridges dabbed with unusually schematic trees. Streaks akin to those in the landscape traverse the entire sky, a treatment of the ground and sky associated with the artist Surdhaj Nanagram (active c. 1813–1873), son of Surajmal and grandson of Nihal Chand, in his early work of the 1820s.[2] The feather-like foliage of the large tree on the right is quite naturalistic for the period, and helps mitigate the geometric division of the composition. | JS

1 The fragmentary three-line dedicatory inscription, which is oriented to Krishna, has not been deciphered, but ends in the number 83.
2 Haidar 1995, p. 202. This same feature appears in a painting ascribed to Surdhaj Nanagram and published in Sotheby's, New York, 21 September 1985, lot 410.

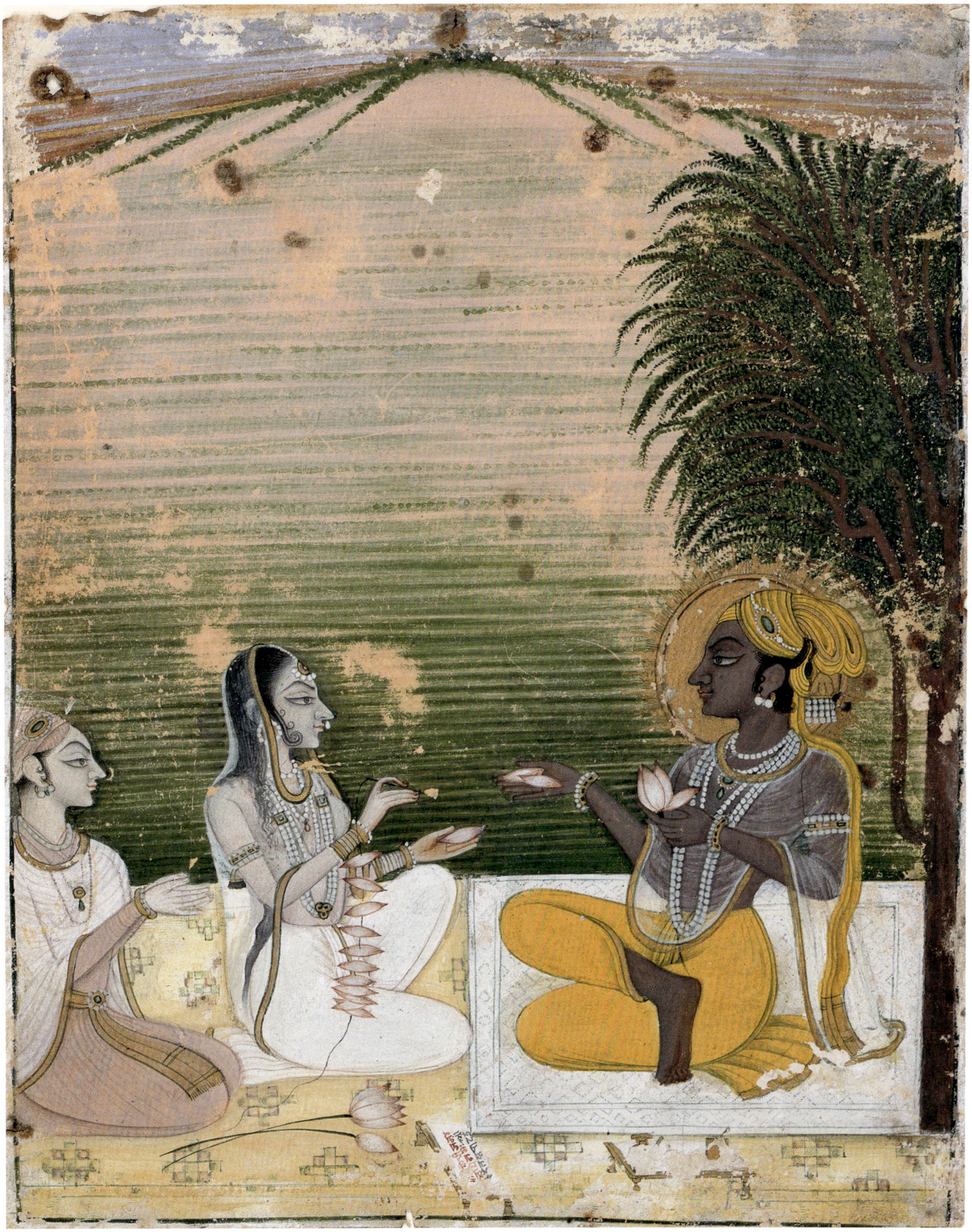

31 Guru and disciple

Attributed to Surdhaj Nanagram
Kishangarh, c. 1835–1840
10 × 15.2 cm (folio), 9.5 × 14.3 cm (painting)

If the guru and disciple in this small painting seem abnormally aggrandized for a Kishangarh scene of figures of their nature, it is because this fragment of a painting must be about one-third of a far more spacious, vertically oriented composition.[1] Fortuitously, however, the intimate confines of this cut-down composition lead us to focus on the two figures, and to grasp the change they represent from Nanagram's earlier phase (see cat. no. 30).

The *dhoti*-clad figure, whose radiant blue nimbus and red *gomukhi* (prayer sleeve) imply a high degree of sanctity and piety, is too old to be identified as the sage Shukadeva, whose image was established in a number of earlier Kishangarh paintings, including two ascribed or attributed to Nanagram.[2] It is likely that he is a venerable priest in the area, for another aged figure with the same distinctive curving helmet of white is shown seated immediately behind the throne from which Shukadeva preaches.[3] The disciple, his hair gathered in a tight bun behind the head, displays a manuscript page inscribed with four lines of text. Between teacher and acolyte are two oblong books wrapped in red cloth, a sign that the discourse entails religious matters. Returning to the formula employed in cat. no. 30, the artist reinforces the scene's visual hierarchy by depicting the guru seated on a strongly colored carpet placed atop a bright yellow reed mat with a checkered motif. Each element – carpet, mat, and checkered motif – becomes more assertive, initiating a series of high-key contrasts and a new penchant for broader forms.

Nanagram's bodies exhibit newfound heft, and his faces become less mannered, finally breaking with the longstanding Kishangarh tendency towards more exaggerated eyes. This particular painting is most closely related to an ascribed portrait of Raja Mohkam Singh (b. 1817, r. 1839–1841) with courtiers on a terrace.[4] Since Mohkam Singh acted as regent from 1832 until his own accession in 1839, this work can safely be dated to the latter half of the 1830s. | JS

1 The lack of ruling and irregular edge at the top are two telltale signs that this painting has been cut down significantly.
2 Sotheby's, New York, 6 October 1990, lot 107; Sotheby's, London, 21 September 1985, lot 410.
3 Sotheby's, New York, 6 October 1990, lot 107, behind the back left corner of the throne.
4 Harvard Art Museums, published in Welch and Beach 1965, no. 79. The ascription is erroneously recorded as Nanak Ram.

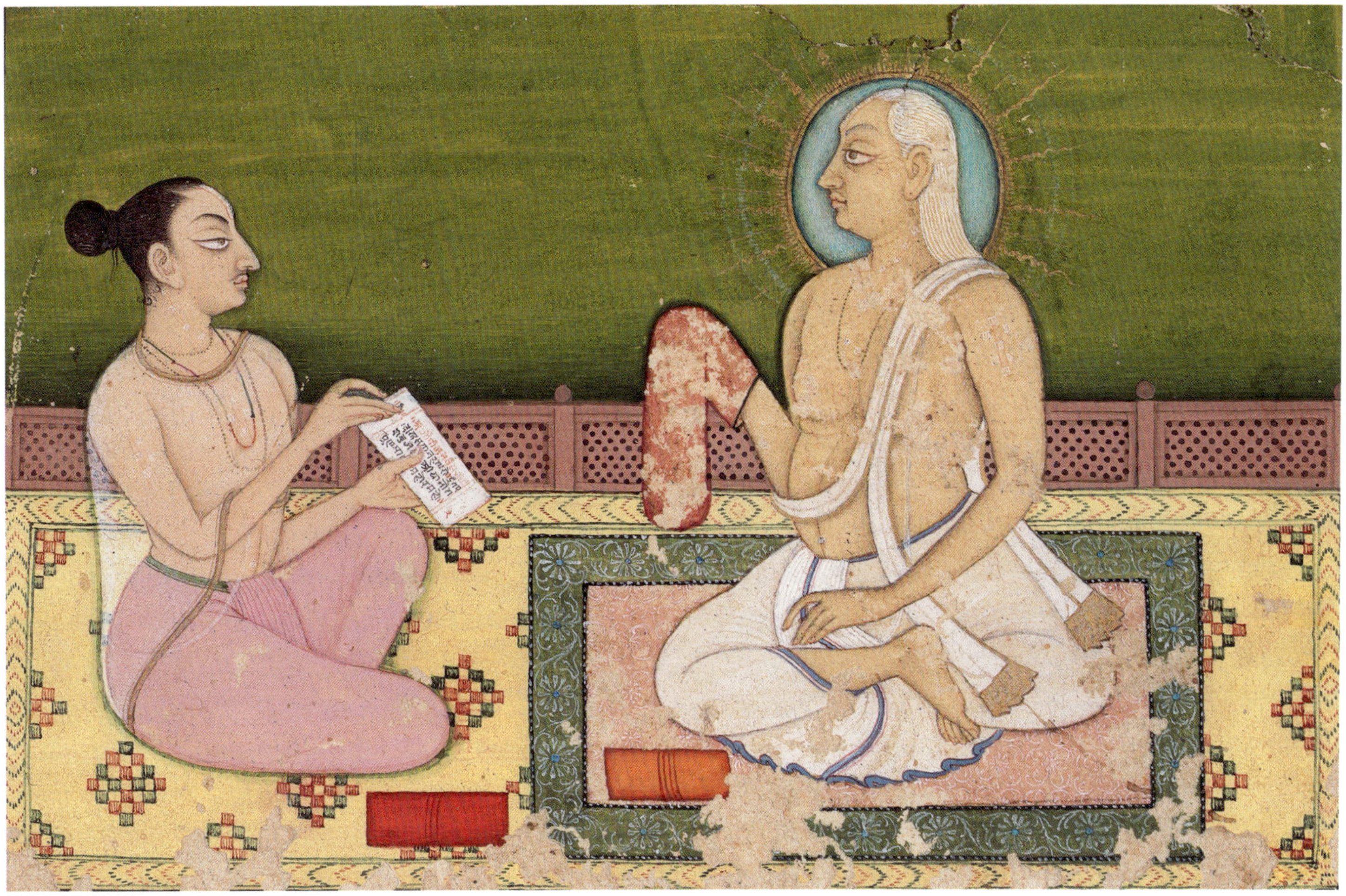

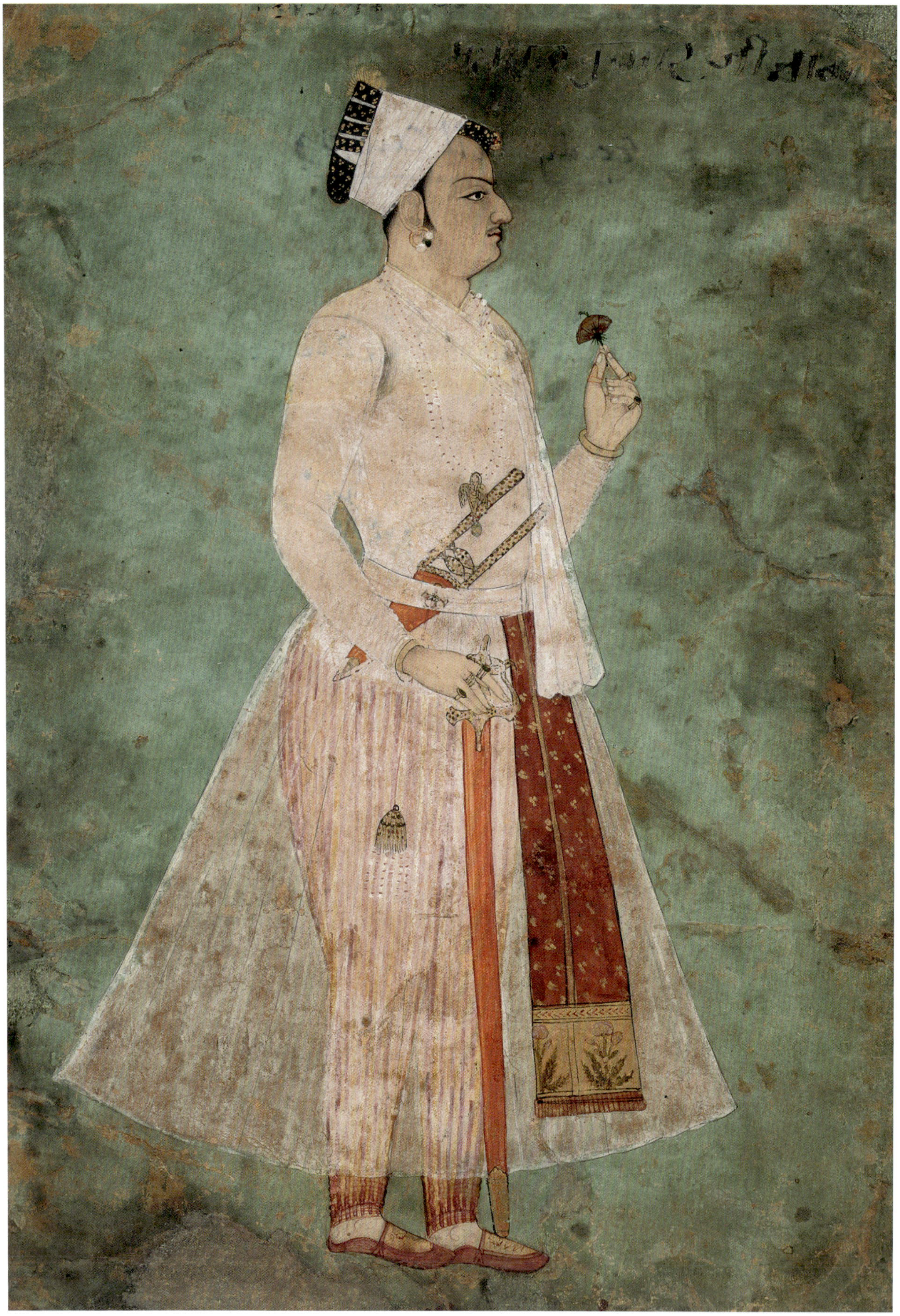

32 Maharaja Ajit Singh of Jodhpur

Jodhpur, c. 1720
23.2 × 15.5 cm (painting)
Inscribed above in Devanagari: *Ajit Syanghji maharaj kumar ji …* ("Ajit Singh as a prince …")

Maharaja Ajit Singh of Jodhpur (r. 1707–1724) stands facing right holding a poppy in his left hand, while his right hand is on the hilt of his long straight sword. A large *katar* is stuck in his *patka* (cummerbund). The artist seems to have intended to portray a jeweled pendant in the shape of a bird attached to his double pearl necklace, but its position is wrong and it is painted over one of the hilts of the *katar*. He wears a simple long transparent white muslin *jama*, *paijama* striped in purple and gold, and a dark brown *patka*, with poppies decorating the end pieces. On his head is a dark blue brocaded turban with a large white band, of comparatively simple design for Jodhpur, where turbans by the mid century became much more elaborate (e.g. cat. nos. 34 and 35). The painting is severely abraded; most of the white blobs of pigment that made up the Maharaja's pearl necklace are lost as well as the details of the cummerbund that encircles his waist. The inscription seems to mean that the subject is portrayed as he was as a prince.

Ajit Singh was the posthumous son of Raja Jasvant Singh (r. 1638–1678), born in 1679, but never recognized by the Emperor Aurangzeb. The infant heir was smuggled out of Delhi and hidden by loyal Rathor chiefs and clansmen, while Aurangzeb put various claimants on the Jodhpur throne and then instituted direct rule. He was vigorously opposed by the Rathors of Jodhpur in defense of their chief and their autonomy. Only after the Emperor's death in 1707 was Ajit Singh able to fully claim his inheritance. This period was inevitably not conducive to the production of paintings.

Isolated standing portraits were a Mughal convention, whereas Rajput rulers preferred to be portrayed seated and surrounded by their nobles. This portrait resembles another highly finished one in the Ashmolean Museum, Oxford, also from about 1720, but portraying him as he was some years earlier.[1] Early portraits of Ajit Singh such as the Oxford one and this one adhere to the Mughal standing convention, suggesting that the Mughal artist Dalchand, who painted highly Mughalized portraits of Ajit Singh's successor Abhai Singh (r. 1724–1749) in the 1720s, might already have reached Jodhpur. This might have been in the train of Ajit Singh's daughter Indra Kunvar, who had been married to the Emperor Farrukhsiyyar (r. 1713–1719) but who returned to Jodhpur after her husband's dethronement and death. As in the case of the Oxford portrait, our artist has a delicate touch in his modeling of the subject's features and hands; other portraits of Ajit Singh are much flatter in the traditional Jodhpur manner.

This portrait does not show a singular trait displayed by the Oxford one and other portraits of Ajit Singh, i.e. his eyes turned up towards the sky. It does however have Ajit Singh's very noticeable large curved nose (a feature not inherited by any of his sons)[2] as well as the same facial hair. His small mustache was later curved round toward his ears while his sideburns, here still vertical, were encouraged to grow across his cheeks. Ajit Singh was murdered by his second son Bakhat Singh at the instigation of his first, Abhai Singh (r. 1724–1759), who succeeded him and gave his co-conspirator the principality of Nagaur. Both were ardent patrons of painting. | JL

1 Crill 2000, fig. 29.
2 For all five of them with their father, see Crill 2000, fig. 34.

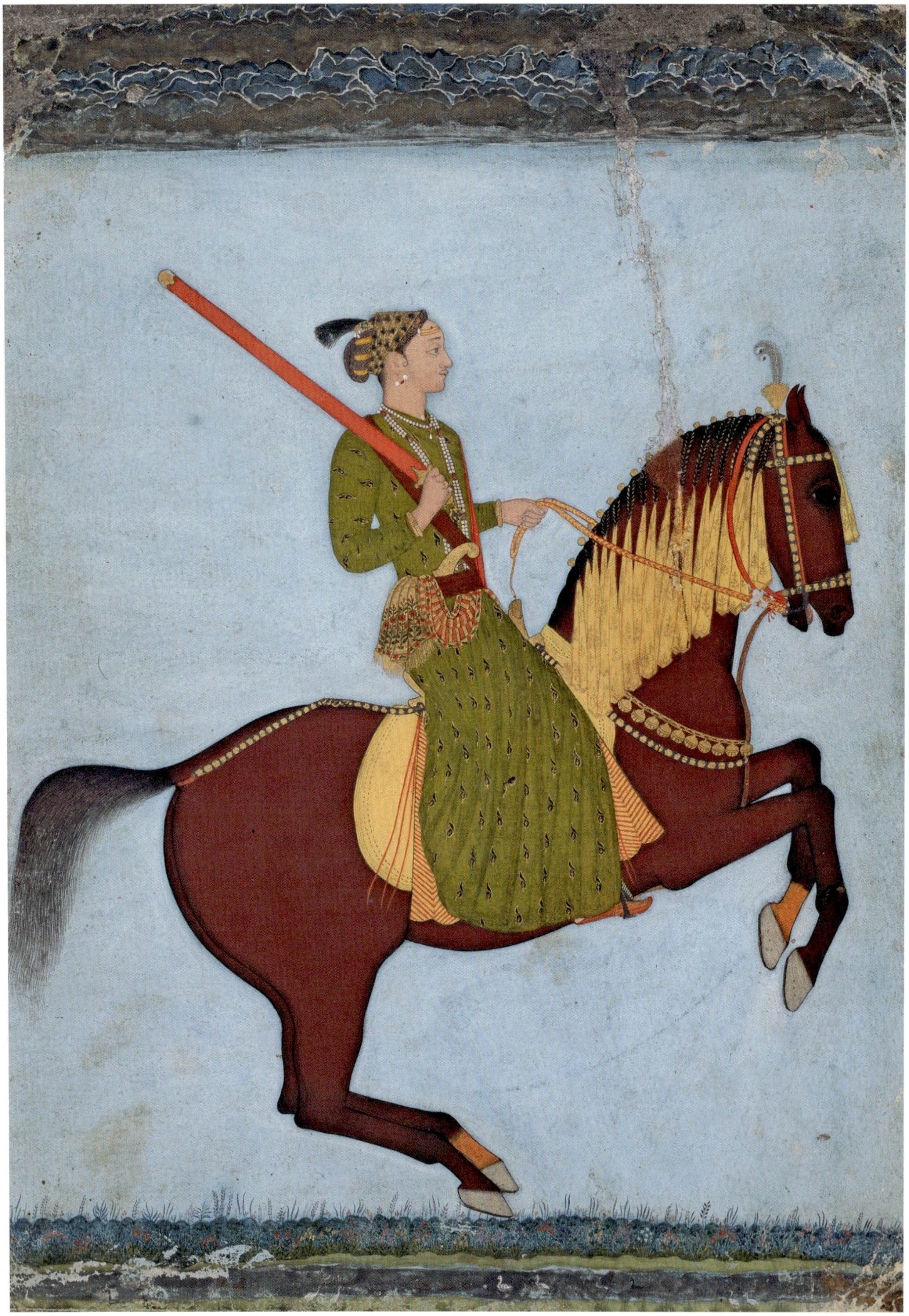

33 Equestrian portrait of a Rathor prince

Attributed to Dalchand
Jodhpur, c. 1724–1727
27.1 × 18.4 cm (painting)

Most Indian artists, named and anonymous alike, work in a style readily associated with one court or another. A few painters, however, transcend such nominal categories and by virtue of their exceptional talent and innovativeness actually transform them, acquiring and disseminating visual traits as they move from place to place. One such figure is the artist Dalchand, who, according to a recent comprehensive study, trained at a princely Mughal atelier in Lahore, joined the imperial workshop at Delhi about 1707, when the long antipathy toward the arts at the capital abated upon 'Alamgir's death, moved to the court of Jodhpur in Rajasthan about 1724, and shifted to the nearby court of Kishangarh in 1728.[1] The fruits of Dalchand's artistic journey can be sampled in this stylistically complicated equestrian portrait of a young prince.

Impressive initially is the sheer elegance of the painting's design, a quality evident in everything from the fluid contours and long gold mane ribbons of the springing mount to the complementary lines of the lithe figure, reins, and great sword. One's appreciation of this artist's mastery deepens with every detail: the subtle black modeling of the chestnut brown horse; the rhythm and delicate floral designs of the mane braids, which also flare out from the other side of the forehead; the pliancy of the prince's *jama*, whose soft, twisting folds are picked up in the directional changes of the ornamental leaf motif on the garment's surface; the jaunty loop of the *patka* over the brown waist-sash allowing the display of both the lively horizontal stripes and the meticulous floral motifs; the vibrant zigzag pattern of the saddlecloth; and even the orange dye selectively applied to the pastern of the horse's left foreleg and hind leg.

Yet what connects this magnificent painting to Dalchand are four easily overlooked elements. The most telling one appears at the painting's lower edge, where a band of undergrowth and water is articulated with astonishingly dainty flowers and grasses and at least eight even more miniaturized waterfowl. Such an elaborate element – especially including the minuscule waterfowl – occurs in a comparable ascribed equestrian portrait of c. 1715 of Emperor Farrukhsiyar,[2] in another of c. 1725 of Maharaja Abhai Singh of Jodhpur, and occasionally in Deccani or even Deccan-inspired works made at Kishangarh or Bikaner.[3] The second is the broad swath of a uniformly light blue sky, a distinctive color found in another contemporary portrait ascribed to Dalchand.[4] The third is situated in the uppermost register, where a dark band comprises dark blue and brown clouds, a compressed version of a Mughal-inspired motif used in the aforementioned portrait but here with the crinkly cloud edges outlined in white.[5]

Finally, there is the rendering of the subject's turban and face. The turban does not rise as high as the typical Jodhpur turban of the period, but it does have nearly the same shape, rich fabrics, and jeweled ornaments – including a drop pearl at the brow but not the large medallion above it – as other portraits of Abhai Singh. The prince is young enough to have only a wisp of a mustache, which would suggest that he is no more than eighteen years old. The rendering of the eye socket, eyebrow, and lips is sensitive but conventional, a feature again in keeping with Dalchand's style. There is no reason to believe that this figure lacking the customary royal halo is Abhai Singh himself, whose likeness is known from one painting by a different artist dated 1721[6] and another by Dalchand of the newly accessioned maharaja at a dance performance,[7] but it could well be one of his younger brothers, particularly Anand Singh or Raj Singh, both of whom would seem to be the appropriate age in the mid 1720s.[8] Another possibility is suggested by a work from Nagaur, a *thikana* of Jodhpur, in which a local artist seems to take Dalchand's work as his model for an equestrian portrait of the same Nagaur prince at a slightly older age on a dark steed with similar mane braids.[9] A two-line inscription on the reverse might provide a definitive answer to the subject's identity, but it is too abraded and torn to be deciphered. | JS

1 McInerney 2011.
2 Victoria and Albert Museum, Large Clive Album (I.S. 133–1964), f. 104a.
3 McInerney 2011, fig. 4, and Crill 2000, fig. 38. For a Deccani painting with versions of these elements, see Zebrowski 1983, fig. 207.
4 McInerney 2011, fig. 7, and Crill 2000, fig. 40.
5 Compare these elements to those in a contemporary equestrian portrait of Muhammad Shah published in Topsfield 1994, no. 23.
6 Crill 2000, fig. 34.
7 Crill 2000, fig. 37.
8 Crill 2000, fig. 34, the third and the fifth figure from the top on the right.
9 Khandalavala 1987, fig. 5.11, p. 93.

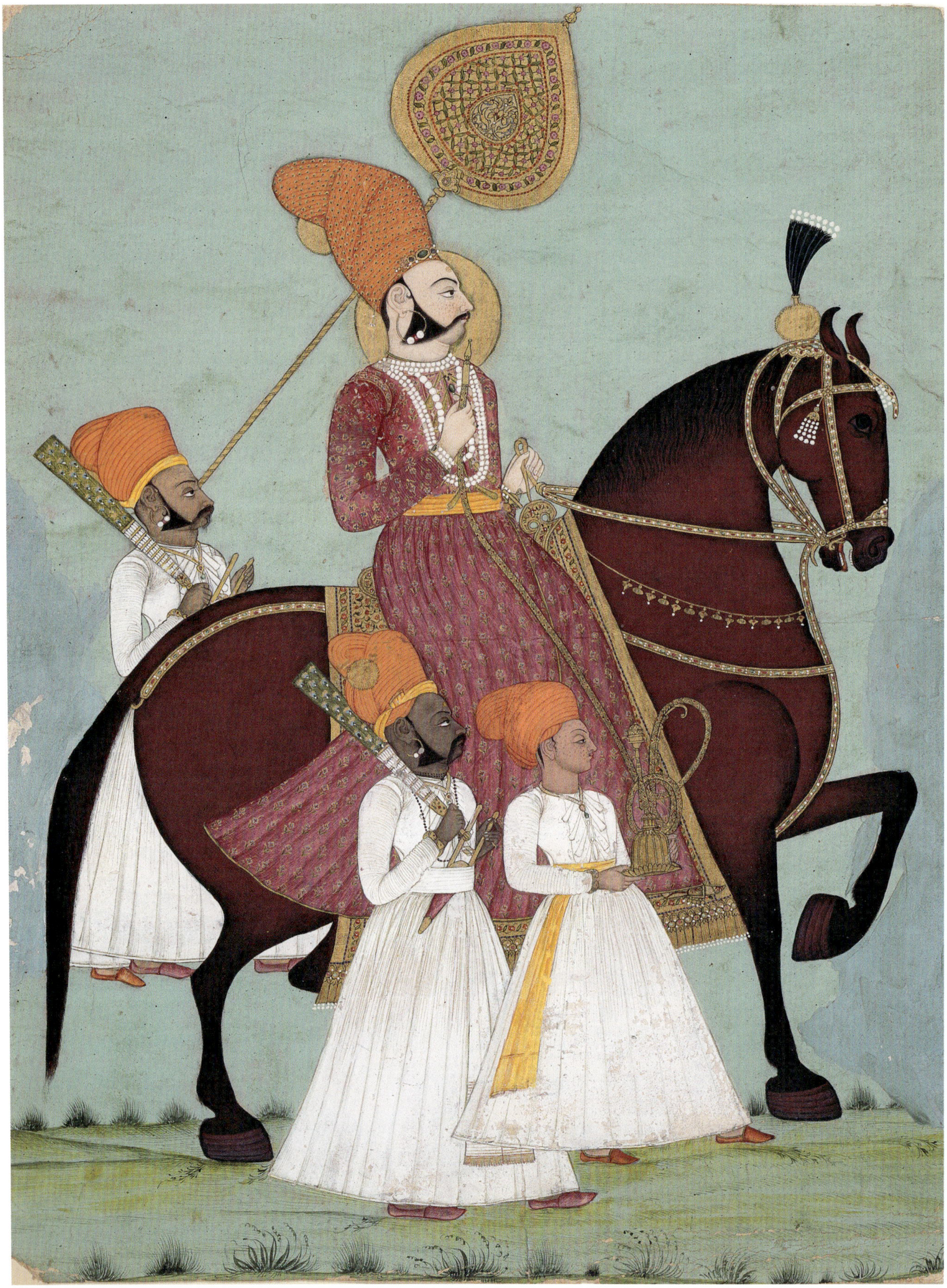

34 Maharaja Ram Singh of Jodhpur

Jodhpur, c. 1750
30.1 × 22.4 cm (painting)
Inscribed on the verso in Devanagari: *Maharaja Sri Ram Singh ji Jodhpur ko raja*

Abhai Singh was succeeded on the *gaddi* of Jodhpur by his nineteen-year-old son Ram Singh (r. 1749–1751). In Ram Singh's brief reign he managed to antagonize many of the leading Rathor chiefs who sided with the rival power source of his uncle Bakhat Singh based in Nagaur. A brief civil war ended with Bakhat Singh's victory at Merta in 1751 and Ram Singh fled to the Marathas. He never regained his throne and died in Jaipur territory in 1773.[1] Bakhat Singh also had a short reign and died in 1752, the year after he had gained the throne, murdered in his turn according to James Tod.

Ram Singh's weak and capricious character can perhaps be gauged from this splendid portrait of him in which his luxurious whiskers uniting sideburns and mustache fail to hide his weak mouth and chin. He also seems to be suffering from smallpox scarring. He wears a sumptuous purple *jama* and a magnificently tall turban formed of an orange tie-dyed textile. A nimbus surrounds his head, a Mughal device introduced by Dalchand into Jodhpur painting with his portraits of Maharaja Abhai Singh. Our artist's sensitive modeling of the Maharaja's features is also extended to the attendants, especially to the bearer of the *morchhal* behind him who gazes devotedly up at his master. The attendant behind him holding the staff of the royal *chattri* has unfortunately been lost; a boy is represented in this position in a very similar portrait of Ram Singh in the Victoria and Albert Museum.[2] An attendant on this side of the horse holds another *morchhal* and a third holds the royal huqqa, the snake of which is held close to his mouth by Ram Singh. These portraits are again most sensitively painted – the latter attendant is also scarred by smallpox. The ground is lightly painted beneath the horse's hooves but has not been extended for the far attendant to stand on, so that he seems to be floating in the air.

Several equestrian portraits of Ram Singh are known, as well as of his contemporary *thakurs*, many in a very similar style with figures floating in the air,[3] albeit somewhat flatter. Our artist may have inherited his naturalistic traits and the nimbus from Abhai Singh's artist Dalchand, although it is also possible that he has been influenced by the Bikaner artist who seems to have been in Jodhpur in Ram Singh's reign and who painted two terrace portraits of the Maharaja that are still in the Jodhpur collections.[4] | JL

1 Crill 2000, pp. 86–91.
2 Crill 2000, fig. 60.
3 Crill 2000, figs. 60–61.
4 Crill 2000, figs. 62–63.

Formerly in the personal collection of the Maharaja of Bikaner
Published: Cran 1980, no. 71

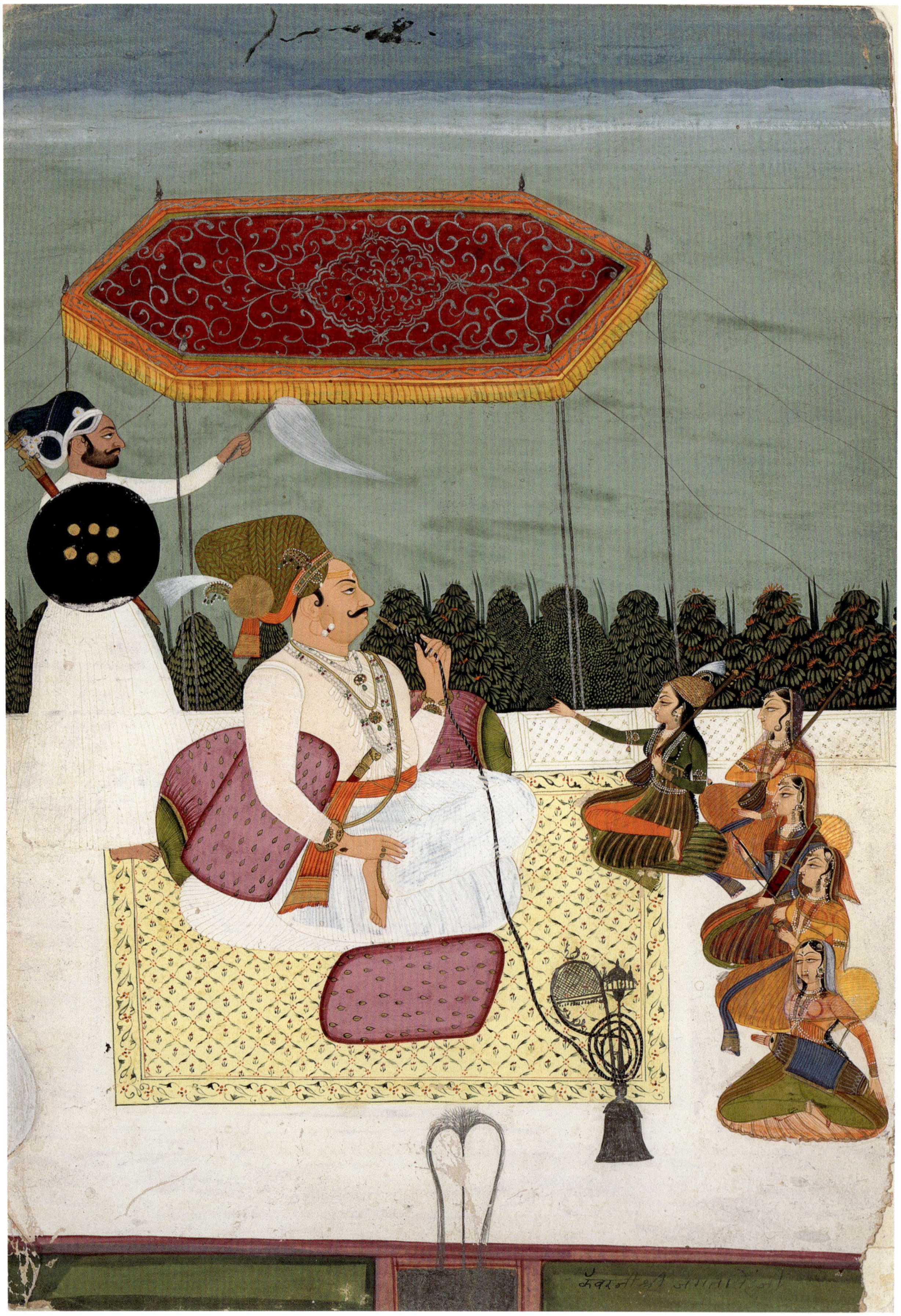

35 A Rathor nobleman listening to music

Marwar *thikana*, 1760–1775
37 × 25 cm (painting)
Inscribed in a modern hand at the bottom: *kunvarji Jagat Singh ji* [1]

A Rathor nobleman is seated on a summer spread on a terrace under a rich canopy while smoking from a huqqa. He is being entertained by five female musicians. The lead musician is singing to the accompaniment of her *tambura*, while the four behind her play respectively another *tambura*, a *sarangi*, cymbals and a double-ended drum. An attendant behind the nobleman fans him with a chowrie while holding his sword and shield. In the foreground is a small fountain and beyond the terrace is a line of trees separated by pairs of cypresses.

The inscription unfortunately is modern and of little help. The style of the painting, however, is unmistakeably Jodhpur and from the later part of the 18th century. Parallels to the setting with the trees in the back are found in a double portrait of Rathor noblemen or *thakurs* now in the National Museum, New Delhi.[2] The *thakur* in our portrait has a very distinctive hairstyle with a curl in front of his ears and no sideburns, but this youthful style is denied by his vigorously curling mustache; he also wears Shaiva sectarian marks on his forehead and the distinctive tall turban of his Rathor clan. Some of these characteristics are found in other Jodhpur paintings of this period in what Rosemary Crill names the *thikana* style[3] but not all united in the same person; Kunvar Jagat Singh's identity and place in Rathor history remain for the moment unknown. | JL

1 A stamp and signature of Sangram Singh of Nawalgarh are also found on the verso.
2 Crill 2000, fig. 77.
3 Crill 2000, figs. 79–81.

36 Maharaja Bhim Singh of Jodhpur

Jodhpur, c. 1793
22.5 × 17.8 cm (folio)

Bakhat Singh was succeeded in 1752 by his son Bijay Singh (r. 1752–1793), whose forty-year reign was preoccupied with the Maratha incursions. Still, he was a vigorous patron of artists and in his time Jodhpur court conventions spread to the minor courts of the *thikanas* (e.g. cat. no. 35). At his death in 1793, his grandson Bhim Singh by one of his younger sons rushed to occupy the throne of Jodhpur and ruthlessly made away with his uncles and cousins with a better claim to the throne than his. The only survivor was his young cousin Man Singh who eventually succeeded him.

This ruthless streak in Bhim Singh (r. 1793–1803) is surely caught in this splendid unfinished standing portrait done probably about the time of his coup, since he has yet to acquire the nimbus he liked to have in his later portraits.[1] The artist has admirably caught his strong features and the determined expression on his face as well as his formidable head set on a bull neck. This seems a true-to-life portrait sketch that served as the basis of other more finished but less intense portraits such as one in the British Museum that seems based on it.[2] The artist has also given a darker tinge to his skin which Bhim Singh clearly disliked, since he is portrayed with a lighter skin in his other portraits. | JL

1 See, for example, Crill 2000, figs. 86–87.
2 Ahluwalia 2008, fig. 54.

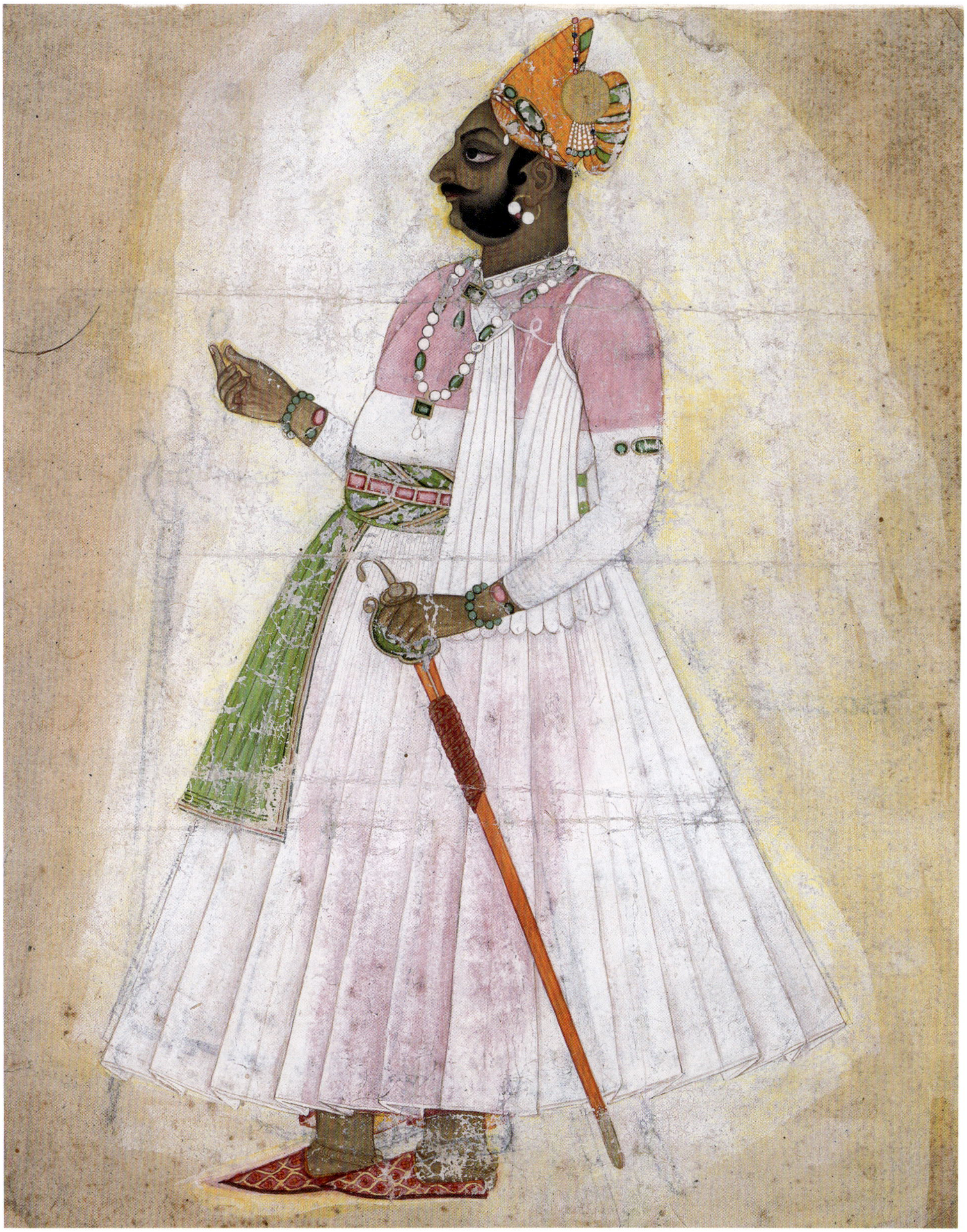

37 Thakur Saheb Bakhtawar Singh and a lady

Ascribed to Bhati Shiv Das
Jodhpur, dated 1815
33 × 25.4 cm (folio); 27.5 × 19.9 cm (painting)
Inscribed on the reverse in Devanagari: *//Thakur Sayab Raja Sri Bakhtavar Singh ji//Botala ri ji sri Cundavat ji.* And below: *kalam citara Bhati Siv Das Udai Ram ra ri//samvat 1872 ra Bhadrava su dha 15//budh* ("Thakur Saheb Raja Bakhtawar Singh. Botala Cundavat. Work of the artist Bhati Shiv Das son of Udai Ram, dated the 15th day of the bright half of Bhadrapada in the year 1872 [1815] on a Tuesday.")

In this striking painting the young Bakhtawar Singh stands facing his lady friend, who seems to be named Botala, gently holding her under the chin while she casts her eyes down. The composition is dominated by the swirling patterns made by the couple's brocaded clothes – his *dupatta* (scarf) and *patka* (cummerbund), her *odhani* (veil) and both of the hems of their gowns, which are curled upwards in a manner typical of the 19th-century Jodhpur style. Also notable in this style is the way the eyes curve upwards at their extremities, a mannerism borrowed from Kishangarh painting. The rich clothes stand out against the plain white muslin of the Raja's gown and the eau-de-Nil plain background, which is relieved only by a geometrically arranged pool in the foreground.

The identity of Bakhtawar Singh is not immediately apparent from the inscription, which despite being on the back of an obviously Jodhpur painting, refers to Bakhtawar Singh's lady friend as a Chundawat, one of the septs of the Sisodiya Rajputs of Mewar. It is unlikely that a Rathor would be consorting with a Chundawat, but that seems to be the import of the inscription. Her name is mysterious.

Bhati Shiv Das is an artist who worked for Maharaja Man Singh (r. 1803–1843) and Takhat Singh (r. 1843–1873) of Jodhpur.[1] In Man Singh's reign, according to Rosemary Crill,[2] the artists produced hundreds of equestrian portraits of the local *thakurs* and notables, the best using "bold colours and strong lines that fill the whole frame of the painting."[3] Shiv Das is one of these artists and his best examples are so vigorous that they flow out into the margins.[4] Our painting done in 1815 is somewhat earlier than any of these. Shiv Das is still a young artist perhaps innovating here, since his curvaceous skirts and upcurved eyes are among the earliest dated examples of these stylistic traits. Shiv Das contributed as did all the court artists to the lavishly illustrated manuscripts of the sacred texts of the Nath sect with which Man Singh was so intimately associated, as well as other large-scale series.[5] More personal to Shiv Das perhaps is one of the most striking of Man Singh's devotional images of himself and the Nath guru Jallandharnath painted c. 1820–1825, showing the Maharaja receiving a shawl from the enthroned guru at Diwali (Mehrangarh Museum, Jodhpur).[6] In Takhat Singh's reign he produced highly decorative but well-composed portraits of the Maharaja and his ladies around 1855 also now in the Mehrangarh Museum, Jodhpur.[7] | JL

1 For paintings by his father Udai Ram, see Crill 2000, figs. 74, 126.
2 Crill 2000, p. 140.
3 Crill 2000, fig. 115.
4 See Losty 2013, no. 40 for an example from 1824.
5 Crill 2000, pp. 150, 156.
6 Diamond, Glynn and Jasol 2008, no. 32.
7 Crill 2000, figs. 143–144.

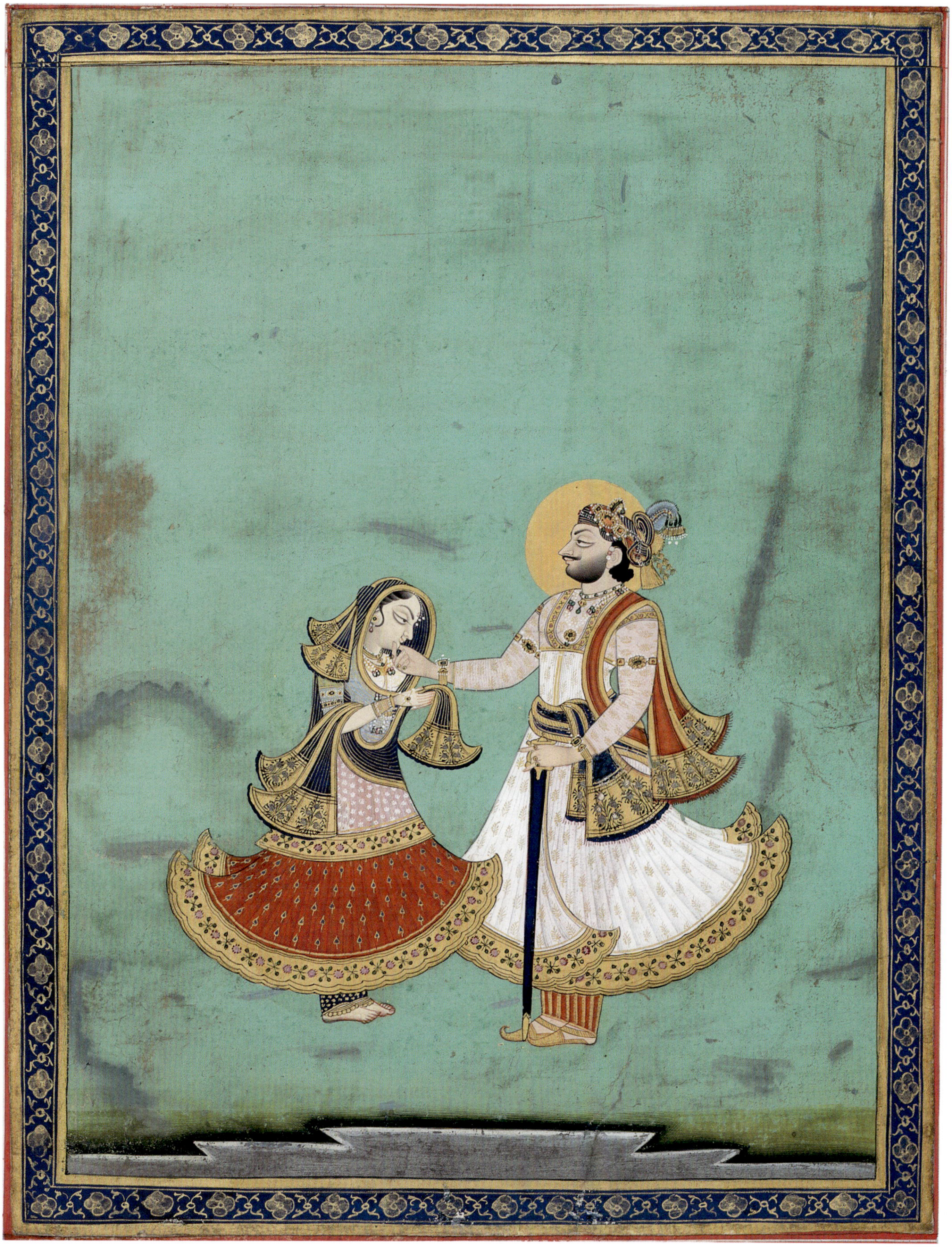

38 Krishna playing his flute

Jodhpur, c. 1820
31.1 × 22.8 cm (painting)
Inscribed in Devanagari above the figures: *gopi* and *krsna vamsi vajavai* ("cowgirl" and "Krishna the flute player")

Krishna is playing his flute standing on a *chauki* beneath a mango tree, while a *gopi* brings him an offering in a silver box (perhaps a *pandan* containing the necessities for *pan* or betel chews), while a cow and its calf and two peacocks listen to the music at his feet. The artist has painted Krishna in the traditional stance of *tribhanga*, with the three breaks of the body facing different ways, yet managed to convey a posture of great elegance. He is the center of the devotion expressed by the cow and its calf and the peacocks. Indeed the cow is licking his extended foot. The image is an ancient one in Hindu iconography, that of *Venugopala*, the flute-playing cowherd. Here the *gopi*, although devoted to Krishna, seems to have other things on her mind as she approaches him, a sentiment Krishna is very much aware of as he fixes her with his gaze. The painting is a symphony of hot oranges, yellows and ochres, expressive of the emotion latent in the composition.

A similar but much flatter version without the cows and peacocks is in the British Museum.[1] | JL

[1] Unpublished, 1956,0714,0.33.

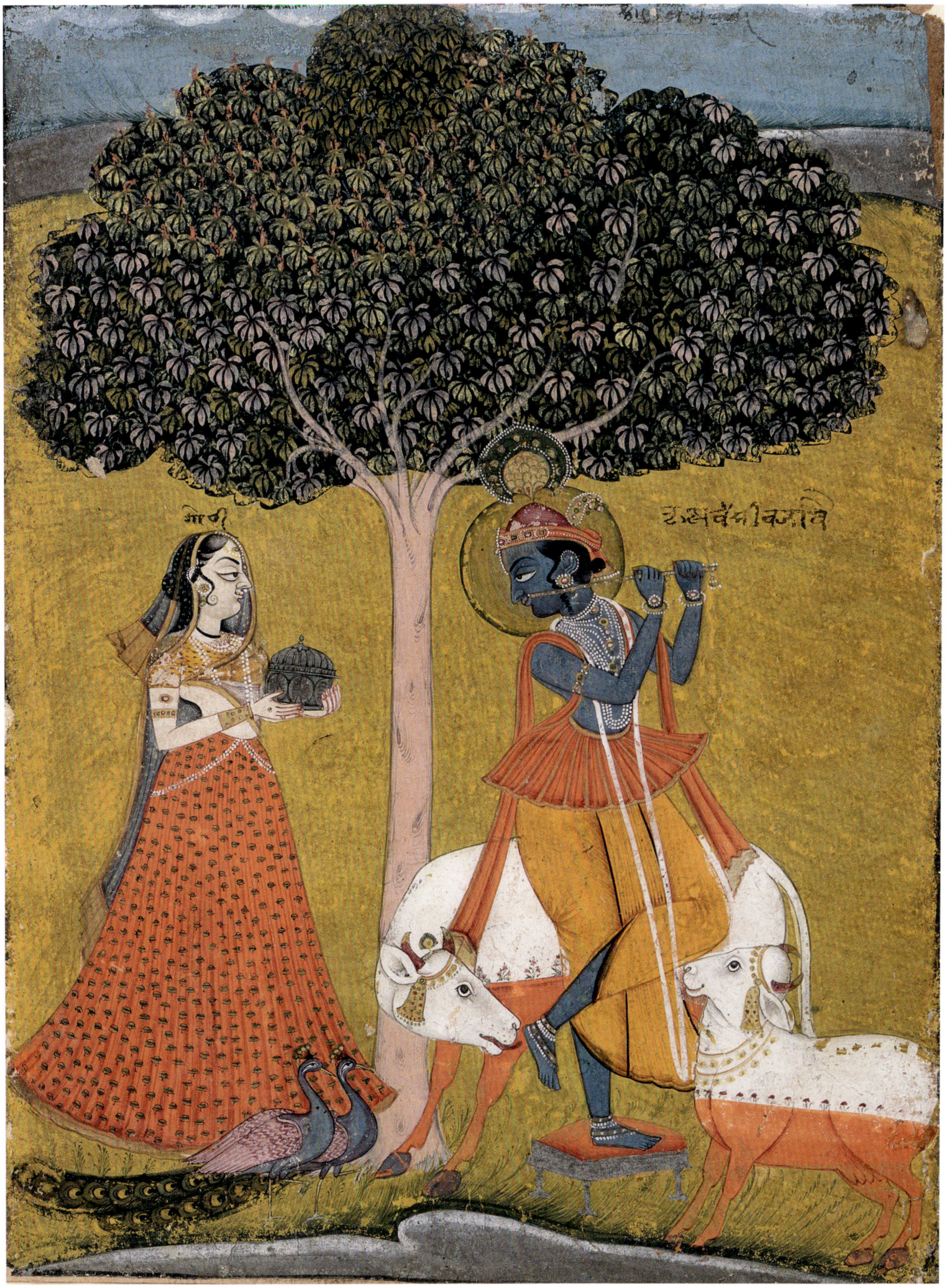

39 The sakhi approaches Krishna while Radha waits in a grove

Folio from a *Gita Govinda* series
Mewar, c. 1665
19.1 × 23.9 cm (folio), 16.8 × 21.7 cm (painting)

The page is from a series of the *Gita Govinda*, Jayadeva's 12th-century *Krishna-lila* poem on the love between Krishna and Radha. Radha waits in anticipation in a grove with a jasmine creeper around her neck, as her companion or *sakhi* approaches Krishna who sits calmly waiting beneath a tree. There is no text to this series and this subject is treated several times in the poem. The artist has cleverly called on the ancient painterly practice of dividing up the picture plane into different sections to indicate happenings at different places, but instead of compartments, makes use of the central tree to divide the space. Krishna and the *sakhi* are silhouetted against a yellowish ground while the ground behind Radha is dark reddish brown as she waits in the shadows. Nonetheless, their eventual union is signaled by the stream that unites them across the bottom of the page, while the creepers coiled round the trunks of trees are an early example of Rajput artists making use of the expressive qualities inherent in the depiction of nature.

The Mewar style in the 17th century is one of the most consistent and recognizable of all the Rajasthani schools. It was forged and consolidated by its greatest master Sahib Din (act. 1628–1655), while other known artists such as Manohar follow the same basic idiom. The only exception is this particular Mewar sub-style that shows an obvious Deccani influence in its coloring and composition, but in fact has very close links to the fourth and fifth books of the great *Ramayana* of 1649–1653 done for Rana Jagat Singh of Mewar (r. 1628–1652), which were painted in Udaipur in a mixed Mewar–Deccani style.[1] Deccani artists were brought to Mewar to assist in this great project consisting of over four hundred large-scale paintings illustrating the Hindu epic. Krishna's grown-up appearance in our page also links him to the Mewar artist of the school of Manohar who painted a similar Rama in the *Uttarakanda* of the *Ramayana* done for Jagat Singh in 1653, also dressed in contemporary costume apart from the crown.[2] In other paintings from this *Gita Govinda* series, Krishna wears a crown with a *dhoti*.[3]

Other series in this group in the Mewar–Deccani style comprise a manuscript dated 1650 and done in Aurangabad for a minor Mewar nobleman, containing among other texts an illustrated *Rasamanjari* of Darya Khan, and two illustrated *Gita Govinda* manuscripts.[4] All these series were found in Mewar or in nearby Ghanerao, and there is controversy as to whether this group was painted in the Deccan for Rajput patrons who brought them to Mewar,[5] or whether it was painted in Mewar by Deccani painters, who had accompanied their returning patrons and were recruited to the Mewar studio as argued here and elsewhere.[6] Aurangabad served as one of the military headquarters for the Mughal assault on the kingdoms of the Deccan and was a melting-pot of Mughal, Rajput and Deccani influences. Although, unlike the other Rajput chiefs, the Ranas of Mewar themselves were exempt from Mughal military service, they did send various Mewar nobles to the Mughal army to fight their expansionist wars in the Deccan. It was perhaps in the train of such noblemen that Deccani artists found their way to Mewar or even in that of Rana Jagat Singh himself when he went on pilgrimage to the shrine at Omkareshwar on the river Narmada (the boundary between Malwa and the Deccan) in 1647.

The present *Gita Govinda* series, of which several pages were in the collection of Kumar Sangram Singh of Nawalgarh, is now widely dispersed.[7] | JL

1 Losty 2008, pp. 14–16, pls. 47–74.
2 Losty 2008, pls. 125–128.
3 For example in Topsfield 2002, fig. 54.
4 Goswamy and Bhatia 1999, nos. 95–96.
5 Argued among others by Doshi 1972, Zebrowski 1983, pp. 46–50, and Seitz in Seyller with Seitz 2010, pp. 124–127.
6 Losty 1995 and 2008, and Topsfield 2002, p. 77.
7 For others in the series see Poster et al. 1994, no. 157; Chandra M. 1957, pl. 6 (also 1971, pl. IV) as well as references cited above.

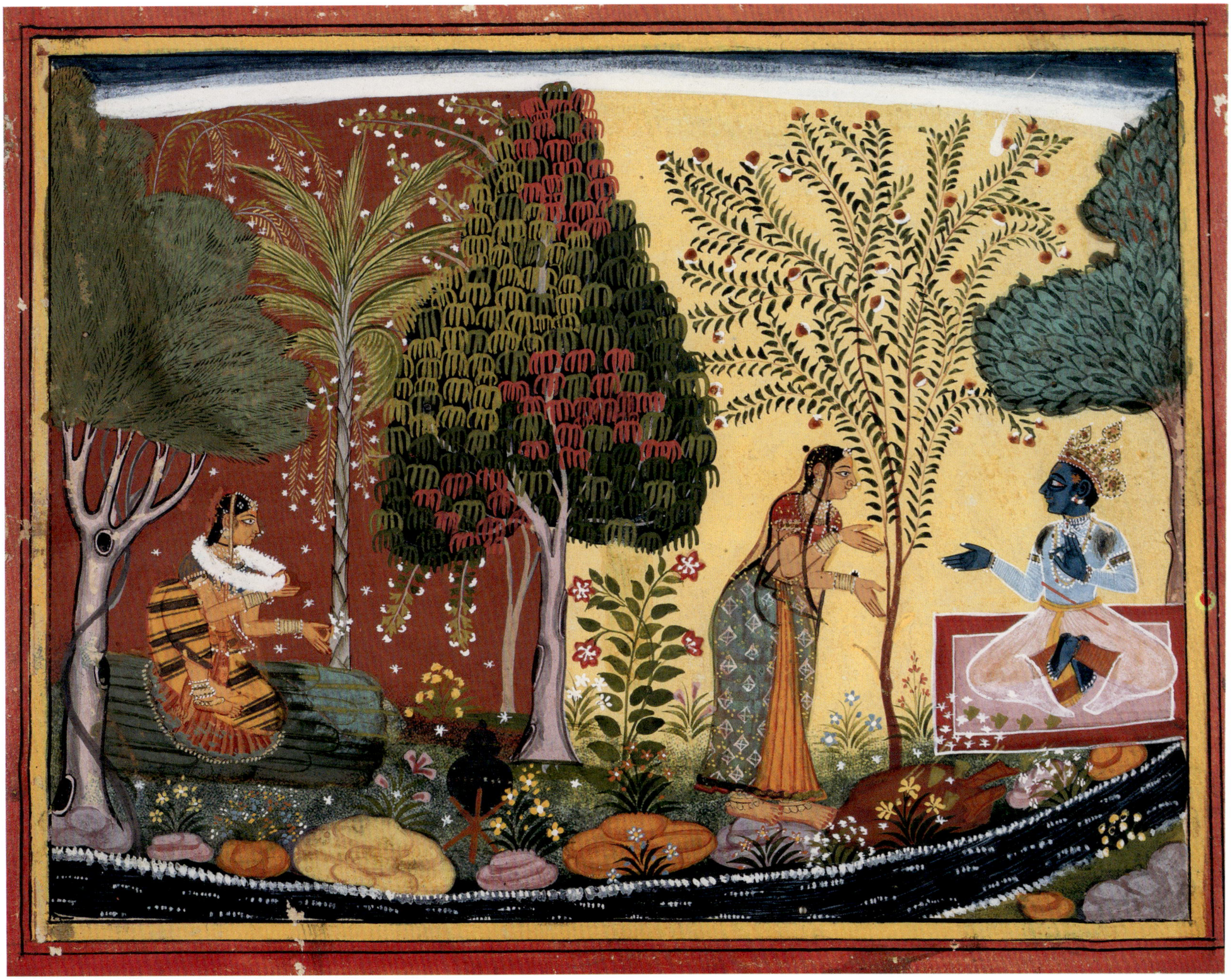

40 Krishna stealing butter

Folio from a series of the *Sursagar* of Surdas
Mewar, c. 1680
36.4 × 25.3 cm (folio), 32.2 × 21.2 cm (painting)
Inscribed above with a verse numbered 37 of the Braj-bhasha Hindi text of the *Sursagar*, set to the *raga* Dhanasri: "Yashoda, you are so mean, my dear: Though Fate/Brahma granted you milk and curd a-plenty, you keep it hidden from your son. I don't see so *many* children, you've just the one – Kunvar Kanhai [Krishna]. He it is who roams from house to house, eating butter on the sly. Your abundant old-age pieties have brought you much wealth. So why this scheming, [asks] Sur, about his food and drink?"[1]

The artist depicts a scene from daily life at Braj, as imagined by the blind poet Surdas (c. 1483–c. 1563) in his *Sursagar* (Sur's Ocean). The poet sits at the bottom right corner singing his poem and clapping time. The context of the verse is the complaint by a woman of Braj to Yashoda about how the child Krishna is stealing her butter. Each element of the verse has its counterpart in the artist's vision. The cows have been brought in from their pastures and are being milked by the cowherds, who bring the pots of milk to the women to make curds or to be churned to make butter. The benevolent Nanda, Krishna's foster father, sits giving out alms to a passing Brahmin. Krishna's foster mother Yashoda at the top left is directing the making of curd and butter when she is made aware by a woman of what Krishna is up to. At the top right the child Krishna asks one of the maids for a drink, and then when she is distracted elsewhere climbs up to steal the butter from the pot that is hanging from the ceiling. In the sky an image of Brahma, in his role of Fate, presides over the proceedings, holding his usual water pot and lotus as well as two manuscript pages inscribed with *Sri Ramji*.

Surdas is renowned as one of the *Astachap* or eight principal followers of Vallabhacharya. The sage Vallabhacharya founded the Vallabha sect of Krishna worship based around the image of Srinathji found by him at Govardhan in Braj and now enshrined at Nathdwara in Mewar (see cat. no. 53). Surdas's *Sursagar* is a very large collection of verses based on the stories of the childhood of Krishna contained in Book X of the *Bhagavata Purana*. The poems are particularly rich in the details of daily life in Braj, something that our artist has faithfully illustrated. For instance, apart from the obvious village activities, we notice that the child Krishna has the front of his hair shaved leaving three long loose tufts, indicating that he has undergone the ritual (*samskara*) of *mundana* (hair-shaving) or *cuda-karana* (arranging the hair in tufts). Nowadays one tuft is normally left, but it used to be common to leave the number of tufts corresponding to the number of *pravaras* or ancient sages associated with that family's genealogy, in this instance three.

The first known Mewar attempt at illustrating this text is attributable to Manohar and his studio in c. 1655–1660.[2] Manohar was the ascribed artist of the *Balakanda* of Jagat Singh's *Ramayana* of 1649–1653 and was the head of one of the three main Mewar studios toward the end of the reign of Jagat Singh. Our painting comes from a dispersed series done later in the 17th century and is more dependent on the style of the principal artist of the *Ramayana*, Sahib Din, with slightly more elongated female figures and faces.[3] Various small series of the *Sursagar* were made in the later 17th century.[4] Another page from our series showing Yashoda playing with the baby Krishna is in the Goenka collection, Mumbai.[5] Another set in the Government Museum, Udaipur is of smaller size than our set but also has the blind poet sitting in the bottom corner beating time with his clappers to the music of the verse.[6] | JL

1 The verse has been kindly translated here by Rupert Snell. The verse is no. 325/943 in the Nagari Pracharini Sabha edition of the *Sursagar*, ed. Nandadulare Vajpeyi, Varanasi, 2029/1962, pp. 368–369 with slightly different readings.
2 Topsfield 2002, pp. 88–89.
3 For a discussion of the artists of the *Ramayana*, see Losty 2008, pp. 11–18.
4 Topsfield 2002, p. 97 and n. 74.
5 Goswamy and Bhatia 1999, no. 101.
6 Andhare 1987, fig. 80; Cimino 1987, fig. 16.

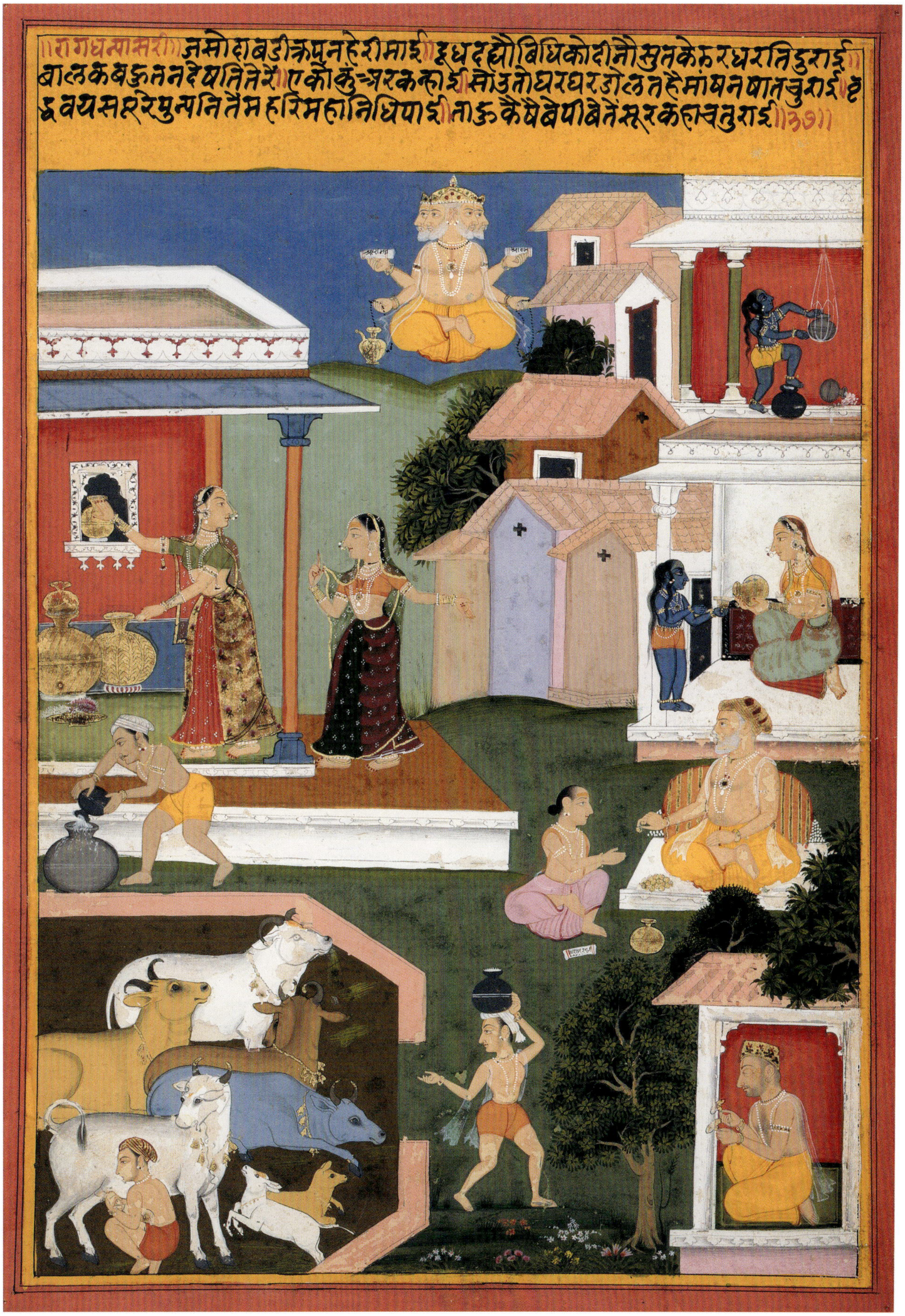
॥राग धनासरी॥ जसोदा बडी कृपुन हेरी माई ॥ दूध दह्यौ बिधि को दीनौ सुत केऊ रघर रति दुराई ॥
बालक बकुतन न देषति तेरैं ॥ एकौ कुंअर कन्हाई ॥ सोउ तो घर घर डोलत है मांषन षात चुराई ॥ २
वय सहरे मुनमति तैंम हरि महा निधि पाई ॥ ताकुं कैषे बे पावे तें सूर कहा चतुराई ॥३७॥

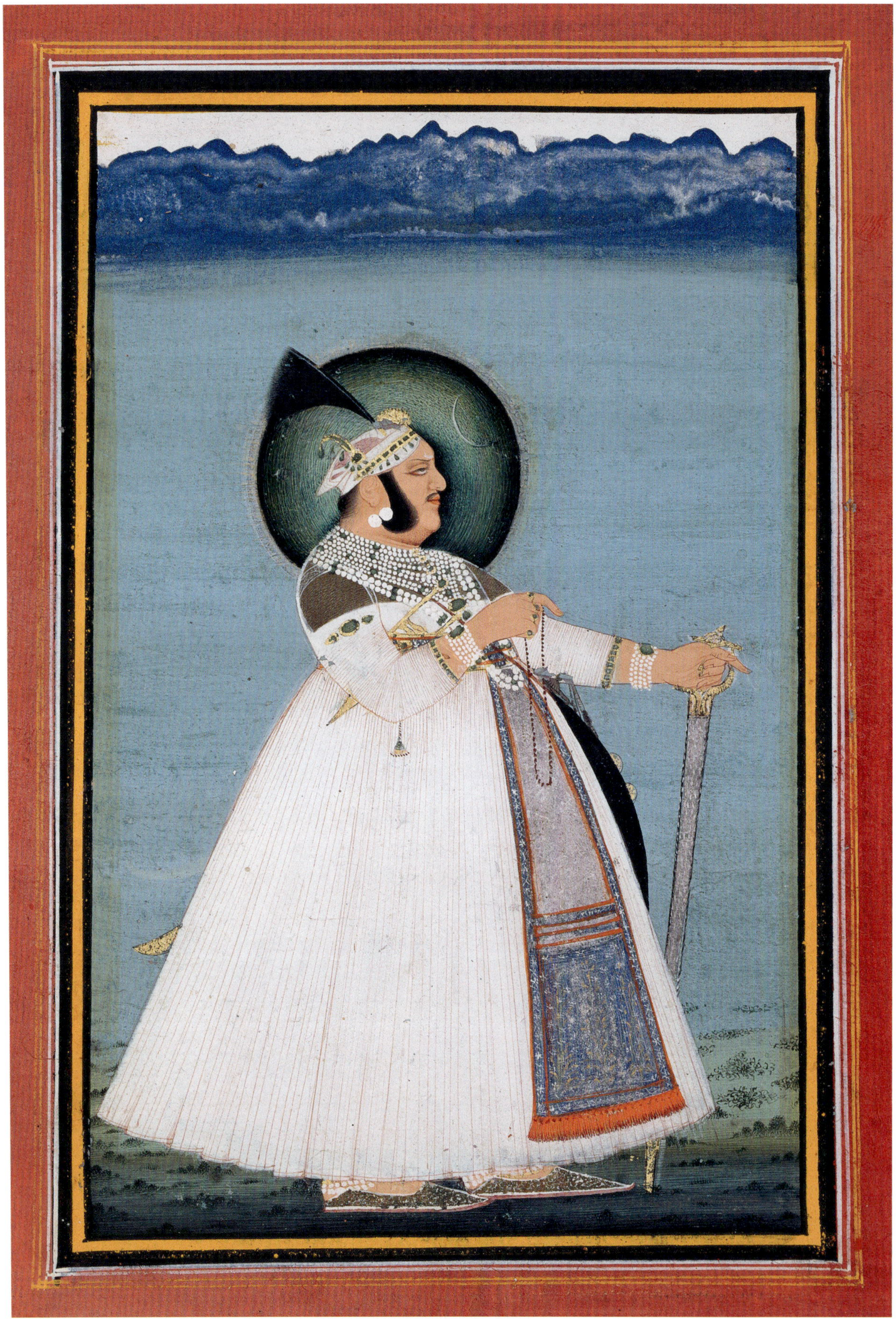

41 Maharana Raj Singh of Mewar

Attributed to Bagta at Devgarh
30 × 22.4 cm (folio), 20.9 × 13 cm (painting)
Devgarh, c. 1780
Inscribed on the reverse in Devanagari: *Maharana Raj Sighji Pratapsighot* ("Maharana Raj Singh son of Pratap Singh")

Series of portraits of the Ranas and Maharanas of Mewar are a feature of painting in Udaipur in the 18th century and the life-size ones were meant to be displayed in the palace, either painted onto walls or on cloth. An almost life-size portrait on cloth of Rana Karan Singh for instance is in the British Museum,[1] while a similar life-size portrait of Amar Singh II in the Victoria and Albert Museum may be contemporary to that ruler in the early 18th century.[2]

Small-sized series of these rulers were also produced. Such a series was presented to Maharana Ari Singh shortly after his accession by the painter Sahaji, of which two of the portraits are now in Melbourne,[3] while another series was produced in the Mewar *thikana* of Devgarh c. 1780[4] including apparently Devgarh rulers as well as those of Mewar. The present painting seems to be from this set, which is generally attributed to Bagta. Early in the reign of Maharana Ari Singh of Mewar (r. 1761–1773), the exactions of the Marathas caused him to run out of money to support an artistic studio and by 1769 (or possibly earlier) the artist Bagta had moved to the small Mewar *thikana* of Devgarh north of Udaipur.

Although intended as a portrait of Maharana Raj Singh II of Mewar (r. 1754–1761) according to the inscription on the reverse, it in fact bears no resemblance to him. Maharana Pratap Singh died in 1754 and was succeeded by his ten-year-old son Raj Singh "who had a cruel and unattractive nature and his death at the age of seventeen was probably caused by poison."[5] His few portraits show him to be a rather plump and beardless young man.[6] The subject here has a dark green nimbus, the rays of which imitate the sun in splendor of the Mewar rulers as well as the crescent moon of Shiva, the tutelary deity of Mewar enshrined at Eklingji, leaving no doubt that a ruler of Mewar is intended. Many of these portraits of rulers show them as rotund hence prosperous, but our subject here has attained the dimensions of the obese Madho Singh of Jaipur (r. 1751–1768). His posture, body, clothes, jewels and accoutrements seem to be closely modeled on a portrait of Madho Singh done by a Mewar artist, possibly Bagta, about 1760–1765,[7] but his features seem instead to be modeled on those of Bagta's patron Rawat Ragho Das of Devgarh (r. 1776–1786) with his very distinctive long sideburns curving backwards and his hooked nose.[8] Madho Singh was closely connected to Devgarh through his Rani, Kundan Kumari, who was the daughter of Rawat Jaswant Singh. Both the Rawat and Bagta would seem to have visited Jaipur around 1768.[9]

An apparently later set of such portraits has been attributed to the artist Kavala, son of Bagta, at Devgarh, c. 1810.[10] While our series normally shows the rulers standing against a green ground with indications of landscape at the foot and sky at the top, the one attributed to Kavala shows a background suffused with a vivid blue as here. Kavala's career is known from paintings done at Udaipur, Devgarh and Badnore between 1780 and 1815,[11] although Ainsley Cameron suggests that this so-called later series is actually the same as our series and attributable to Bagta.[12] | JL

1 First published as c. 1670–1680, Topsfield 2002, fig. 2, redated as a 19th-century replacement, Crill and Jariwala 2010, no. 41.
2 Jackson and Jaffer 2009, pl. 1.
3 Topsfield 1980, nos. 181–182.
4 Christie's, New York, 19 March 2013, lot 301.
5 Topsfield 2002, p. 193.
6 For instance Topsfield 1980, nos. 150–152.
7 Topsfield 1980, no. 183.
8 Beach and Singh 2005, fig. 50.
9 Beach and Singh 2005, p. 33.
10 Tuli 1999, lots 37a–c.
11 Beach and Singh 2005, pp. 39–47.
12 Private communication.

42 Krishna making music with the sages

Mewar, c. 1820
38 × 29 cm (folio), 26.5 × 19.5 cm (painting)

Krishna, very dark in color and dressed as the cowherd god with a tall oval peacock-feather finial to his crown, is seated playing his flute among a company of sages and ascetics, one of whom accompanies him on the *tambura* while the rest have little hand cymbals. One sage waves a scarf over Krishna while another is engaged in mixing *chapattis* or perhaps in the production of narcotics. All the sages are in ecstasy at hearing Krishna's flute. The scene is set in the sparsest of landscapes with a dark green ground shading upwards towards a lighter sky ending in a brilliant royal blue at the top. The subject may be from chapter 84 of the *Bhagavata Purana*, where Krishna is visited in Kurukshetra by all the great sages who listen eagerly to his words about life and how to live it. This is supposed to be the heroic Krishna of the *Mahabharata*, the expounder of the *Bhagavad Gita* to Arjuna, but he has here been substituted by the amorous flute-playing cowherd of popular Krishnaite devotion.

This type of Krishna's headdress is seen in Mewar paintings of Krishna in the first half of the 19th century, e.g. *Krishna and Radha exchange clothes* c. 1835 in Melbourne,[1] although our artist is much more sophisticated. The monochrome ground shading into the sky is seen in various portraits, also in Melbourne, attributed to Bagta's son Chokha,[2] while the overall tonality is favored by him elsewhere.[3] On the other hand, a painting of a comparable subject, also attributed to Chokha and now in Paris, depicts Shukadeva reciting the *Bhagavata Purana* to sages and children,[4] and is rather more varied in style. It shows the fairly squat figures with large heads and wide eyes that are typical of Chokha's work. By contrast, the figures here are taller and more elegant. What most impresses about this picture is the marvellous spiritual and aesthetic ecstasy achieved by the simplest of means – the closing of the eyes or their being raised slightly towards heaven. While this is undoubtedly a Mewar painting, it is difficult to assign an artist to it or to find comparable work from this period. | JL

1 Topsfield 1980, no. 253.
2 Topsfield 1980, nos. 211–213.
3 See, for example, Beach and Singh 2005, figs. 98, 99, 107.
4 Gahlin 2002, no. 33.

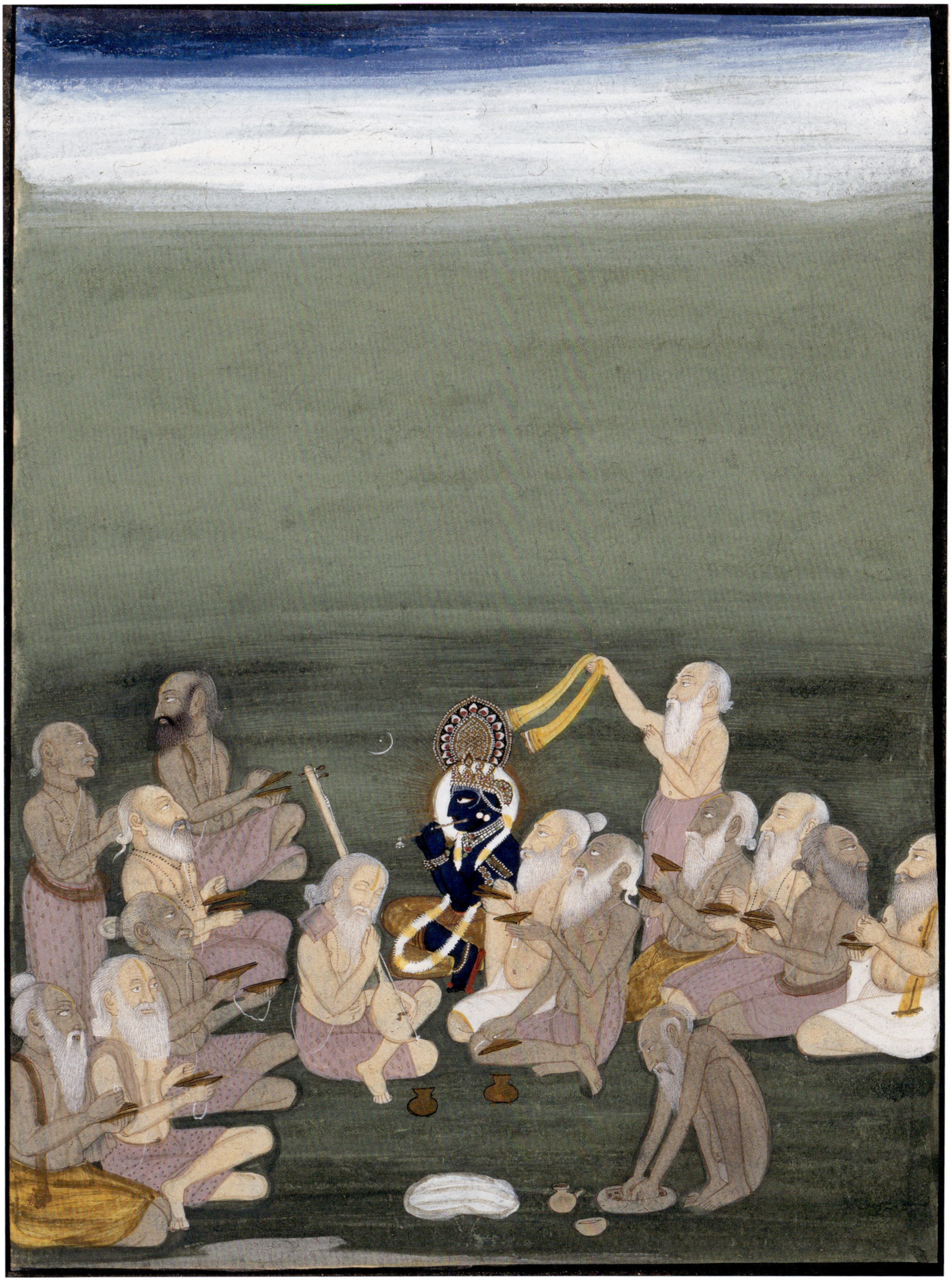

43 Maharana Jawan Singh of Mewar hunting tiger

Mewar, c. 1830
25.7 × 36 cm (folio), 23.8 × 33.5 cm (painting)
Inscribed on verso (erroneously) in modern Devanagari: *Maharana Bhim Singhji Udaypur* and the old number 32

Portraits of Maharana Jawan Singh of Mewar (r. 1829–1838) may be distinguished from very similar ones of his father Bhim Singh by the considerable upward curl at the end of his mustache. Here he is depicted galloping forward to skewer with his lance the tiger that has leapt onto one of his huntsmen, who tries in vain to fend off its teeth and claws. One of the Maharana's companions is also galloping forward to assist and manages to fire his rifle into the beast's flank. The scene is set on the banks of the stream that crosses the bottom of the page. Another tiger, half submerged in the water, eagerly watches the events as they unfold. Small undulating hillocks and two large dark trees on the left complete the scene. There is otherwise no landscape, just a greenish-gold background color.

In a painting showing Rawat Ragho Das hunting boar of c. 1780,[1] the Mewar and Devgarh artist Bagta has eschewed all notions of depicting deep space in favor of the furiously energetic activity happening just behind the picture plane and parallel to it. Here, the same compositional mode as Ragho Das hunting is used, but it lacks its energy. Bagta's son Chokha left Devgarh for Udaipur in 1799 where he worked for Maharana Bhim Singh (r. 1778–1828); his early work in Udaipur shows him still under his father's compositional influence. Our equestrian portrait of Jawan Singh riding a short-backed and unduly plump horse with massive chowries hanging at the saddle may be compared with other very similar ones showing his father Bhim Singh returning from a hunt, now in San Diego, or hunting boar, now in Paris.[2] Chokha's landscape innovations, his small hillocks impressionistically painted with pads rather than the brush for instance, lingered on in Udaipur even after he had returned to Devgarh around 1811, as can be seen in this painting, even though they became progressively more stylized. The foreground hillocks have their paint applied with pads and their ridges outlined with bold brush strokes and covered in rows of little trees. Such innovations soon diminished into a more routine approach to the foreground landscape as in another portrait of Maharana Jawan Singh hunting in the Victoria and Albert Museum (c. 1830–1835), but this time the prey is boar.[3] | JL

1 Beach and Singh 2005, fig. 50; Losty 2010, no. 11.
2 Topsfield 2002, fig. 197 and Gahlin 1991, no. 75, pl. 76.
3 Cimino 1987, fig. 94; Topsfield 2002, fig. 223.

Formerly in the Jeffrey Paley collection
Published: Lerner 1974, no. 31

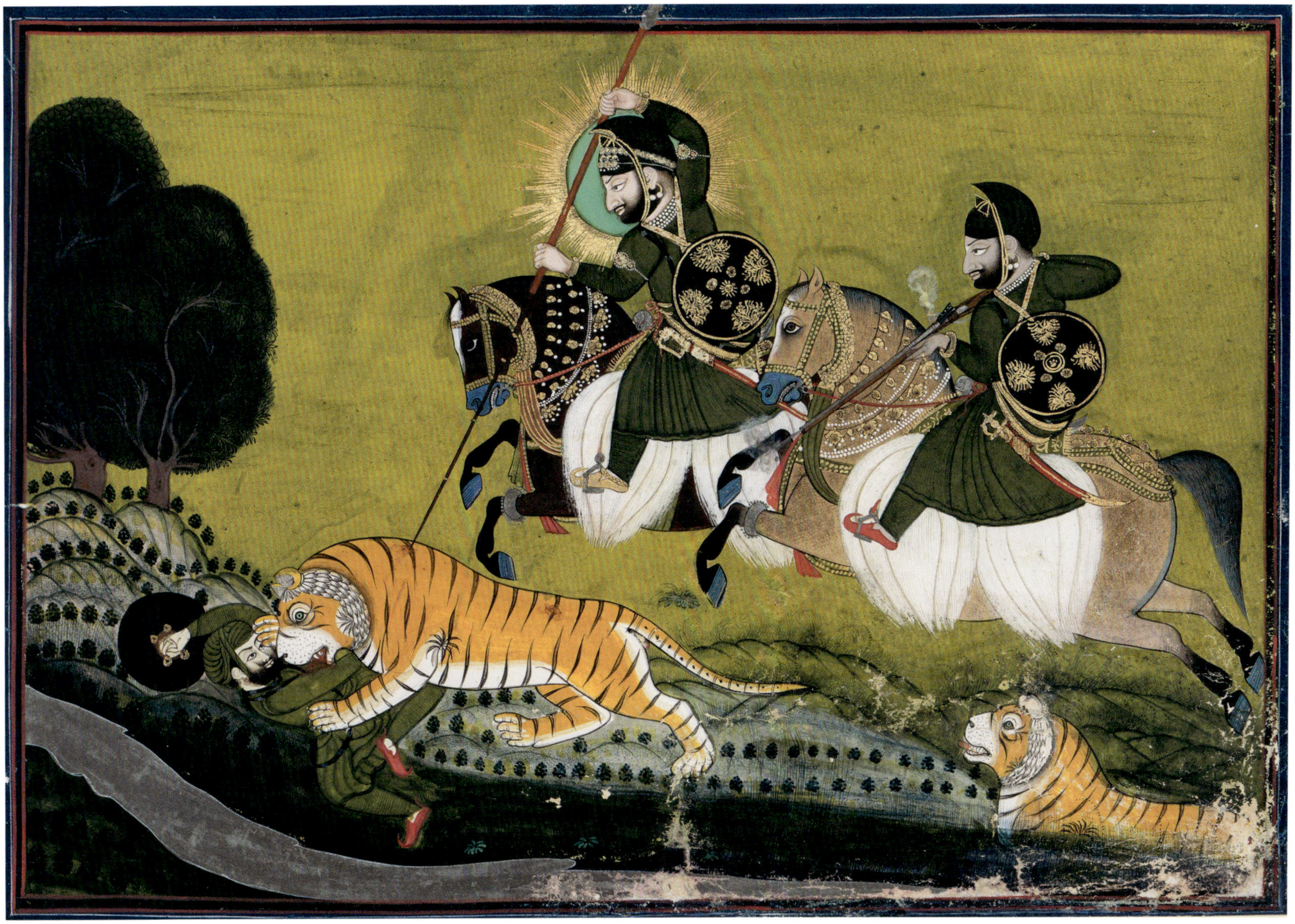

44 Maharana Sarup Singh of Mewar in procession at the Gangaur festival

Ascribed to Tara
Mewar, dated 1844
47 × 64.5 cm (folio), 42.5 × 59.9 cm (painting)
Inscribed on verso in Rajasthani: "Maharana Sarup Singh riding the elephant Gajnayak at the Gangor Festival on Caitra sudi 4 samvat 1901 [23 March in the year 1844]. The picture was presented as a *nazar* to the Maharana by Tara on *Bhadrapada sudi 14 samvat 1901* [15 September 1845]."[1]

Maharana Sarup Singh of Mewar (r. 1842–1861) is riding in procession on the elephant Gajnayak (Hero among Elephants) along the banks of the Pichola Lake at Udaipur on his way to celebrate the Gangaur festival. This was one of the major festivals in Udaipur. The image of the goddess Gauri was borne in a procession of women round the city, while the Maharana and his nobles were rowed round the lake in barges. The artist Tara also painted this stage of the festival in c. 1845.[2] At night there were illuminations and firework displays. The Maharana is accompanied in the present painting by attendants bearing all the insignia of royalty associated with the Mewar rulers: chowries waved by attendants on top of the elephant, the fan-bearer before, and the solar standard and umbrella holder behind. An elderly man walks alongside the elephant holding the Maharana's huqqa, whose long snake stretches up to the Maharana's hand. Besides attendant foot soldiers and cavalry, we notice the gold and silver stick bearers and lion-headed mace-bearers in front (*sontar-bardars* and *chobdars*) without whom no important man could set foot out of doors in India. Other men prudently bear long lances and *charkis* (mini Catherine-wheels on long sticks) used to control elephants that got out of hand.

Tara was the principal artist of the court studio in this reign and the next. This painting comes from his early period before he was too much influenced by European conventions. As in his contemporary paintings of 1844–1845, the Maharana in the royal barge at Gangaur noted above and also the Maharana hurling a spear through a papaya tree,[3] Tara liked to stack his attendant figures up in rows and made formal designs of great elegance. The restricted color scheme of orange and brown set against the blue of Lake Pichola reflects the bare, parched landscape of Mewar in March waiting for the rains to reinvigorate the land.

Tara's early starkly impressive equestrian portraits of Sarup Singh, silhouetted against a plain ground with low rolling hills in the background, are now in Melbourne.[4] There was increasing European influence in Tara's work from about 1850 occasioned by the visit of the itinerant artist William Carpenter in 1851, whose portrait of Sarup Singh now in the Victoria and Albert Museum was frequently copied by other Mewar artists. | JL

1 The long inscription gives the names of all the *sirdars* and officials participating.
2 Topsfield 2002, fig. 230.
3 Topsfield 2002, fig. 228.
4 Topsfield 1980 figs. 267–269.

Published: Maggs (London), *Oriental Miniatures & Illumination*, Bulletin No. 39 (December 1985), no. 31

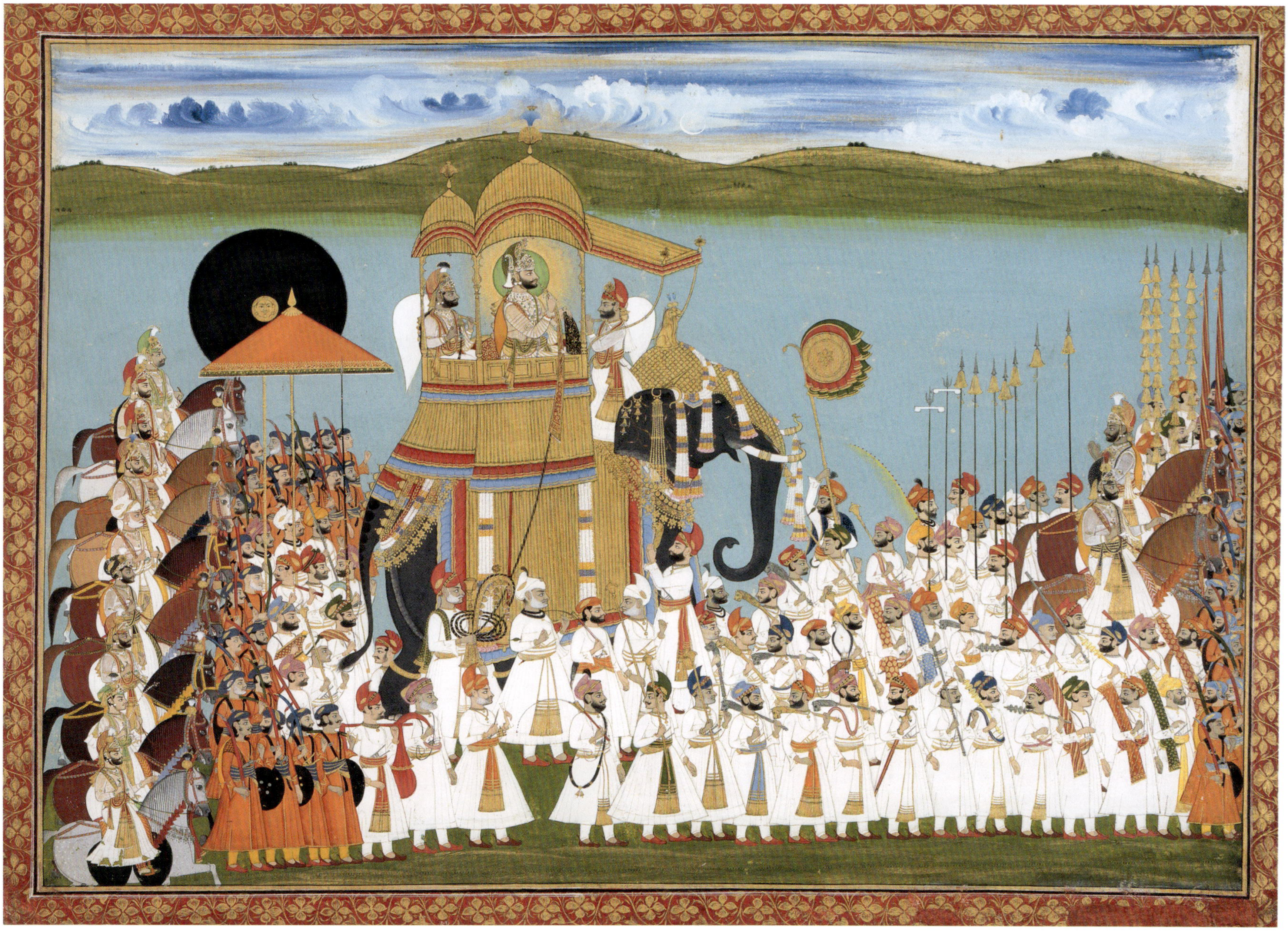

45 Gauri ragini

Folio from a *ragamala* series
South Rajasthan, perhaps Bundi, c. 1610
21.4 × 12.4 cm (folio), 19 × 10 cm (painting)
Inscribed above: *Godi*

The *nayika*, holding sprays of flowers in her hands, walks through a verdant field that stretches to a distant hill, all covered with meadow flowers. She is framed by four peacocks that wait expectantly at her feet and by four stylized trees on the hillside behind her. The dark sky is streaked with white as is the water in the stream below, which is rendered in a kind of straight basket pattern. Both are unsophisticatedly stylized, hovering between the conceptualizations of the Early Rajput style and the more naturalistic conventions of the Popular Mughal style. Gauri *ragini* usually but not invariably involves a lady walking through the forest holding sprays of flowers or, somewhat later, more stylized flower wands.

The appearance of the *nayika* clearly shows her direct descent from Popular Mughal and early Bundi painting. The well-known dispersed set of the *ragamala* from Chunar of 1591,[1] painted by Mughal artists displaced from the imperial atelier, forms the foundation stone on which all later Bundi and Kota *ragamalas* are based. For two centuries the Bundi artists of *ragamala* sets followed the iconography and composition of the 1591 set for their own work. A particular concern in these Bundi *ragamalas* is an interest in three-dimensional representation of architecture inherited from the earliest set of 1591, although of course not visible here. The *nayika*'s appearance, with her square head and pompoms attached to her wrists and elsewhere as well as her skirt (*ghaghra*), bodice (*choli*) and enveloping transparent veil (*odhani*) gathered at the front into folds, is little different from the women in the 1591 *ragamala*. Milo Beach discusses in the context of the similar Kamod *ragini* (a seated lady in the forest plucking flowers from a tree) the means by which the compositions of the earlier set were traced and reused in later Bundi *ragamala* sets.[2] The original Gauri *ragini* from the 1591 set has yet to come to light but Joachim Bautze, when discussing a c. 1800 version[3] lists the various Gauri *raginis* from Bundi. The earliest then known to him was a drawing apparently of the 1620s sold at auction that has already changed somewhat from this version in that the girl is looking to the right not the left, although her body is in the same posture, while one of the peacocks has turned its head to go after a water snake.[4] In the present version although one of the peacocks has turned its head, the snake does not appear. This same iconography together with the water being confined to the lower left corner of the painting rather than running across the bottom is continued in the "Kanoria" Bundi *ragamala* of c. 1680.[5] These slight differences in iconography, not of any consequence in another school, should perhaps prevent a too ready attribution of this painting to Bundi until the 1591 version comes to light.

Another painting from this series inscribed Kakubha *ragini*, marked by identical handling of the panel above and with the same borders, was formerly in the Heeramaneck collection.[6] There the *nayika* holds out garlands to the four peacocks around her and she is likewise in a dark green forest glade between trees. The water running across the base of the painting there is depicted as white with thin dark lines in the same pattern as here. Sets of *ragamala* drawings from Bundi c. 1625 in the National Museum, New Delhi, have scarcely yet been published.[7] A fragmentary Bundi *ragamala* set from the Khajanchi collection and now in the National Museum also dates from the same time but is obviously somewhat later than our painting.[8] | JL

1 Skelton 1981.
2 Beach 1992, pp. 160–162.
3 Bautze 1987b, no. 43.
4 Sotheby's, London, 20 June 1983, lot 97.
5 Archer 1959, fig. 8.
6 Heeramaneck 1984, pl. 227.
7 Mentioned in Ebeling 1973, p. 166; Welch 1976, no. 41 publishes Kamod *ragini*, Beach 1974, fig. 10 publishes Nat *ragini*.
8 Khandalavala, Chandra and Chandra 1960, no. 33a–f; Sodhi 1999, pls. 16, 39, 66.

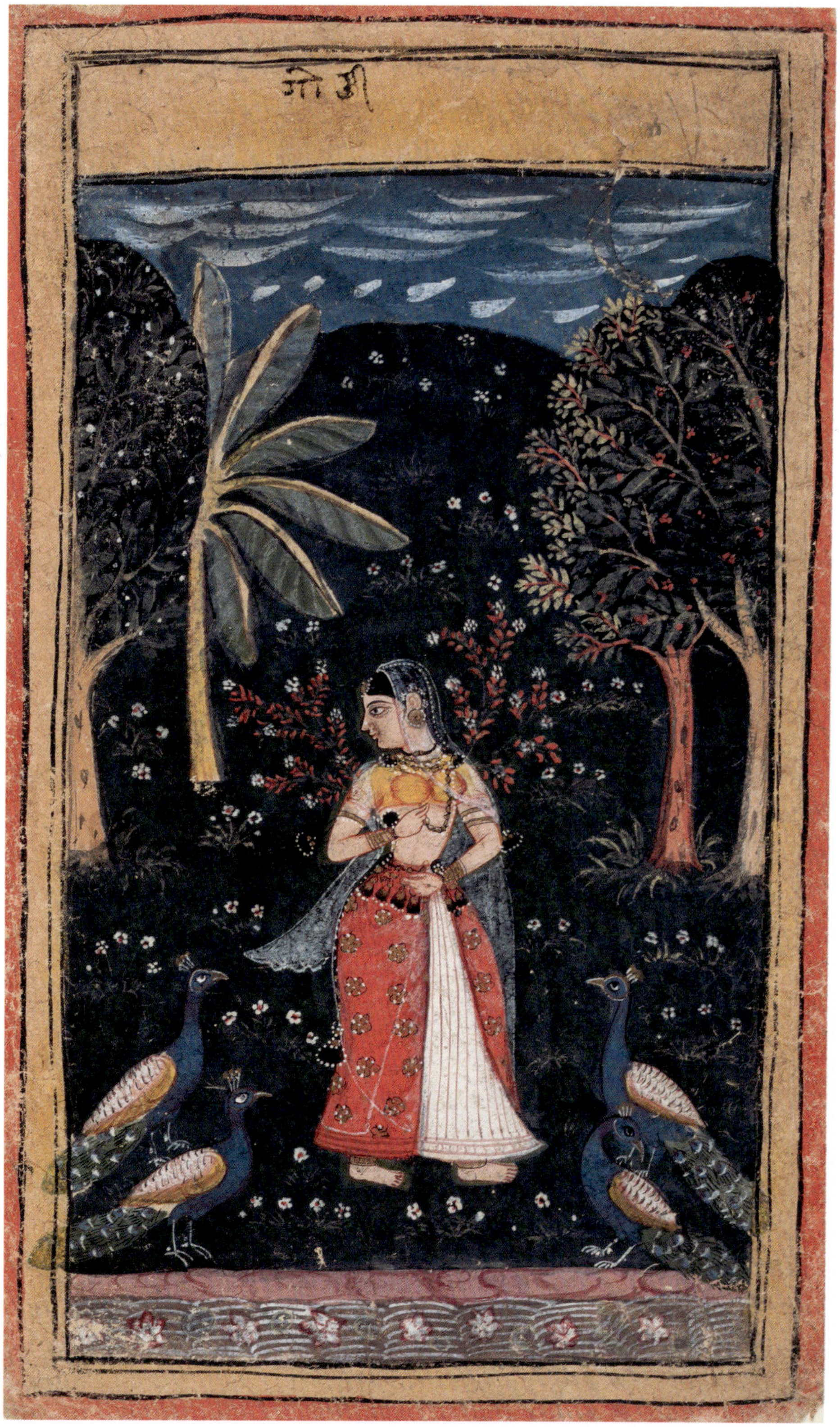
गोडी

46 A seated armed nobleman, perhaps Raja Bir Singh

Bundi, c. 1750
28 × 21.5 cm (folio), 22.5 × 15.6 cm (painting)

A Hindu raja is seated on a terrace, wearing a white *jama* over his mauve *paijama*. His right hand rests on his upright shield with its straps slung loosely around his extended arm; his left hand holds a spear aloft, while his curved sword is still in its scabbard attached by its hanger to his *patka*. Ground and background are simply divided into rectangles of white and blue. The raja's head is tilted slightly up as he stares at something unseen. He has a proud aquiline profile and a drooping mustache. His neatly trimmed sideburn with two distinctive curls in front of his ear extends forwards across his cheek into a sharp point. A jeweled ornament is attached to his red and yellow turban and a spray of roses is stuck into the turban band. A half nimbus centers on his profile rather than his head.

The portrait is of an unknown raja but stylistically must come from Haraoti. His finely modeled features strike a note more in accordance with Bundi taste than with the flatter idioms associated with Kota portraiture. His facial hair conforms to the fashions of the 17th and early 18th centuries, although the two curls before his ear are fairly rare at any period. A portrait of a standing Rao in the Brooklyn Museum inscribed as Rao Bir Singh son of Raghubir, bears a considerable resemblance to our Raja in his aquiline nose and hairstyle, especially the fairly rare two curls in his sideburn, although his mustache is not yet as luxuriant.[1] He too sports a half halo. The Brooklyn portrait is apparently from a series of portraits done in Uniara in c. 1780–1790, mostly copies of earlier Bundi portraits. | JL

1 Poster et al. 1994, no. 132.

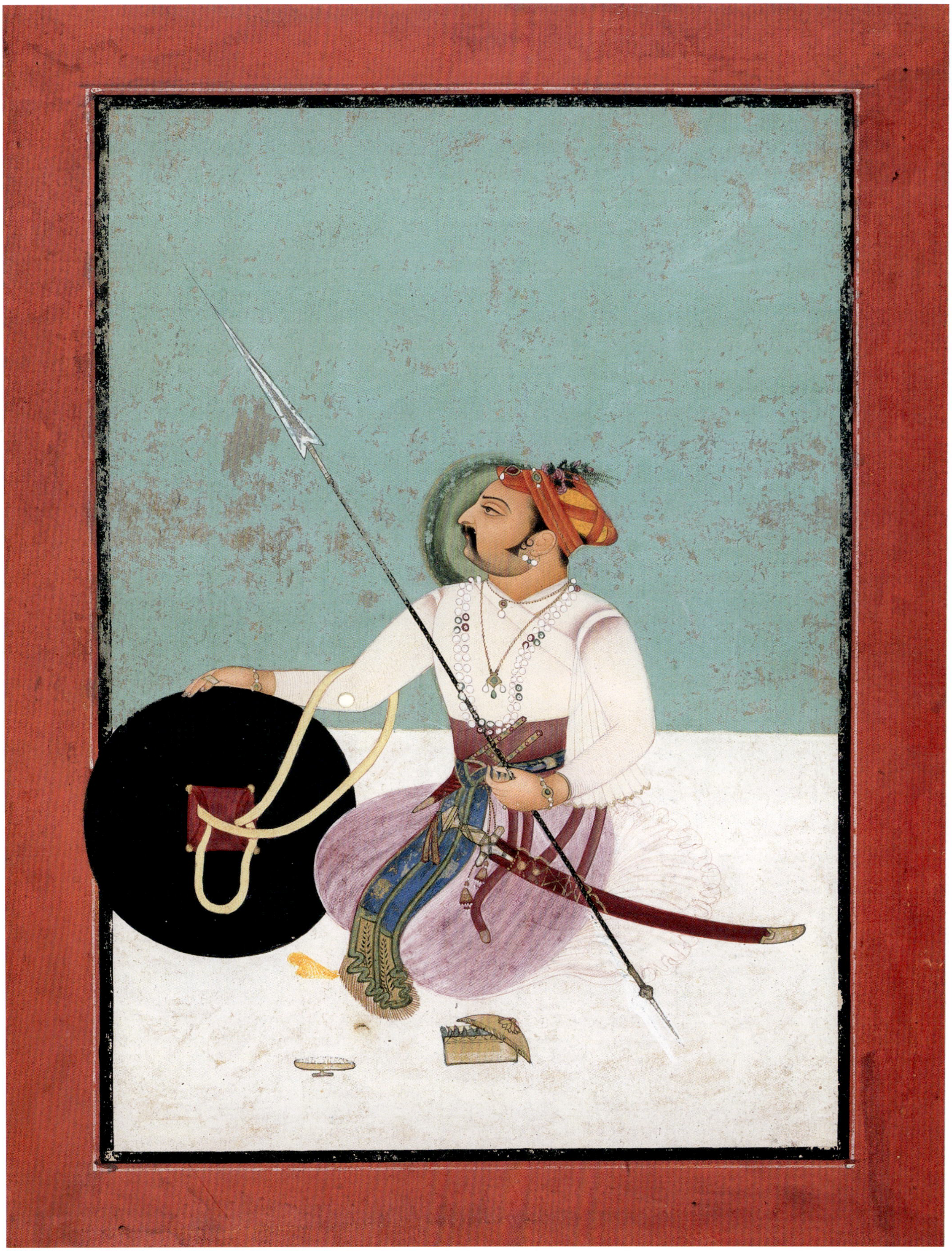

47 Three ladies with a firework

Bundi, c. 1760–1770
25.7 × 17.5 cm (folio), 21.5 × 14.5 cm (painting)

Three ladies are standing on a terrace at night; one holds a single sparkler type of firework. Two are holding hands and the third has her hand on her companion's shoulder. The sparks from the firework are falling into the little tank at their feet, mingling with the drops of water from the fountain, much to the consternation of the ducks. The dark night sky above is sprinkled with stars. Fireworks by night in a Hindu context normally signify the festival of Diwali with its rituals of illuminations and worship of the goddess Lakshmi, but the solitary firework and the three women by themselves perhaps additionally signals their loneliness in the absence of the husband.

Amidst the somewhat chaotic compositions of later 18th-century Bundi paintings (see cat. no. 48 for example), this one impresses with its calmness and the almost geometrical order in which the solid blocks of color are arranged. The shadows around two of the women's faces are indicative of Bundi painting around 1760 when it became something of an affectation in the so-called "white" period.[1] | JL

[1] Compare to Archer 1959, figs. 17–19 and Binney and Archer 1968, no. 16.

Published: Colnaghi 1978, no. 66

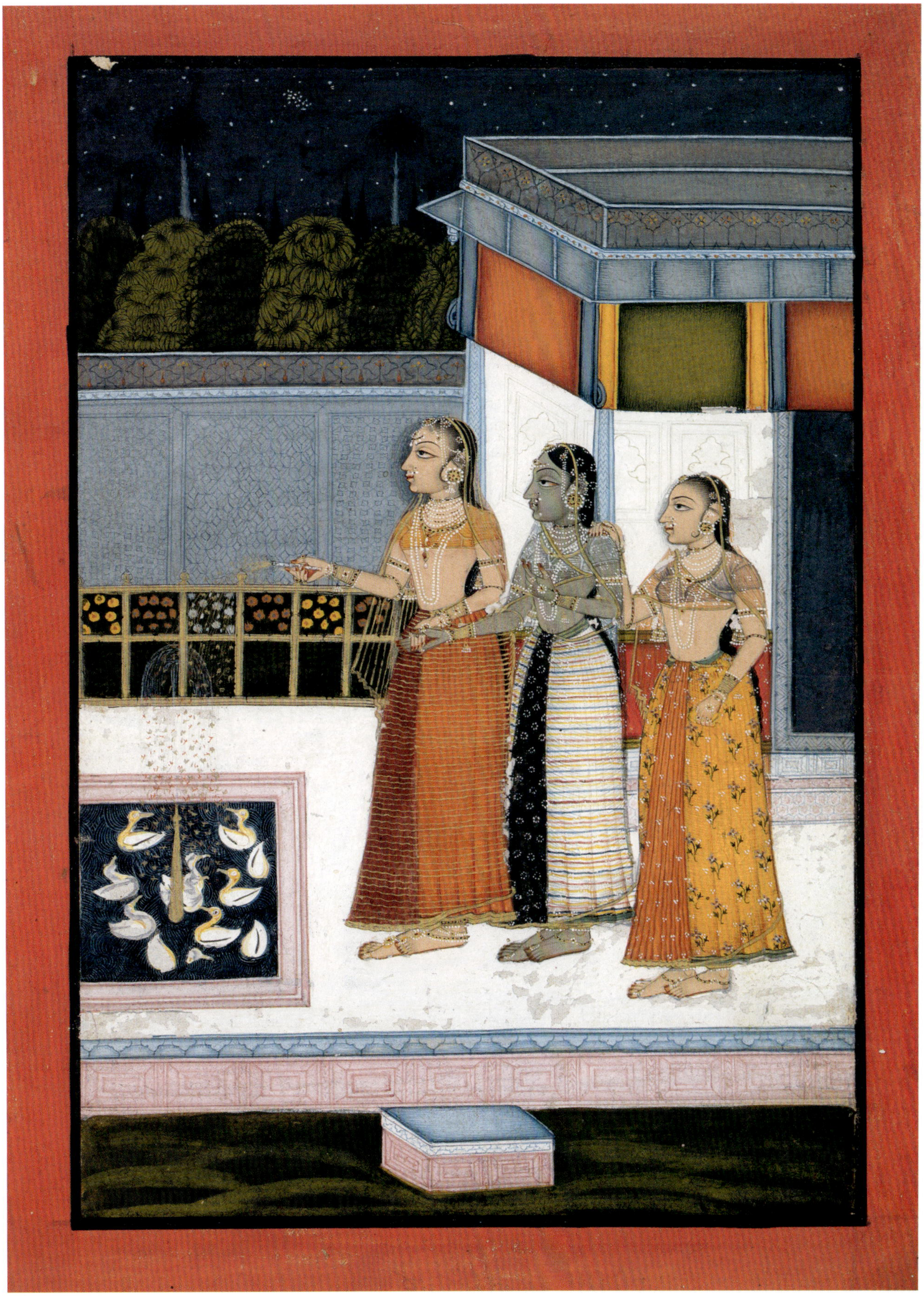

48 A lady being prepared for bed

Bundi sub-style, perhaps Uniara, c. 1770
33.8 × 25 cm (folio), 25.5 × 17 cm (painting)

A lady is seated on a terrace having her hair combed by an attendant while she drinks from a cup and is entertained by two female musicians playing the *vina* and the double-ended drum. They are seated under an awning attached to the lady's house – her prepared bed is visible behind her in front of the door to her house, while another is waiting on an elevated terrace above. Beyond the wall, we see the trees in her garden silhouetted against a fiery red evening sky. The house is richly decorated with colored dadoes and painted vessels in niches on the walls.

The increasingly precarious positions of the Rajput kingdoms under the Maratha dominance of Rajasthan in the second half of the 18th century resulted in various changes in their painting styles. In Bundi joyous genre scenes, erotic encounters and ladies at play as subjects for painting largely replaced the *ragamalas* and *Rasikapriyas* of earlier decades.[1] The present painting seems to embody just a gentle mood of relaxation of an evening, but the anticipated arrival of a lover is suggested by the prepared couches and beds and the unusually (for Bundi) violent sky. A very similar composition of a maiden being led reluctantly to the *nayaka*'s bed with the ladies' veils and skirts raised by the wind is in the National Museum, New Delhi, while the painted architecture is also echoed in another Bundi painting of Varari *ragini* in the same collection.[2] Bundi painting, however, rarely has tumultuous skies such as these, although there are exceptions, such as a painting of Maharao Dip Singh hunting (c. 1750, now in the Israel Museum).[3] On the other hand tumultuous skies are a feature of the Bundi-influenced school of Uniara – there is a possibility that this painting might come from that little state, where Bundi artists such as Mira Bagas and Dhano worked in the middle of the 18th century.[4]

The clouds in scroll formation and the structure of the terrace balustrade in particular are features of the Bundi style of this period which influenced that of Jodhpur in the time of Maharaja Man Singh (r. 1803–1843), to which Rosemary Crill has drawn attention.[5] Bundi paintings of the late 18th century have the same type of balustrade delimiting the terrace.[6] The interest that the artist of this painting takes in three-dimensional architecture harks back to the earliest Bundi *ragamala* series of 1591 (see cat. no. 45), although here the perspective difficulties of the *Bangla* canopy over the upper terrace defeat him. | JL

1 Archer 1959, figs. 17–28.
2 Sodhi 1999, pl. 89 and Sharma 1974, no. 44, pl. 43.
3 Losty 2000, fig. 5.
4 For Mira Bagas see Beach 1974, pp. 23–27 and for Dhano see Losty 2000, *passim*.
5 Crill 2000, p. 118.
6 See, for example, Archer 1959, nos. 24, 26–27; Bautze 1987b, no. 39 and Sodhi 1999, pl. 73.

Published: Cran 1980, no. 56

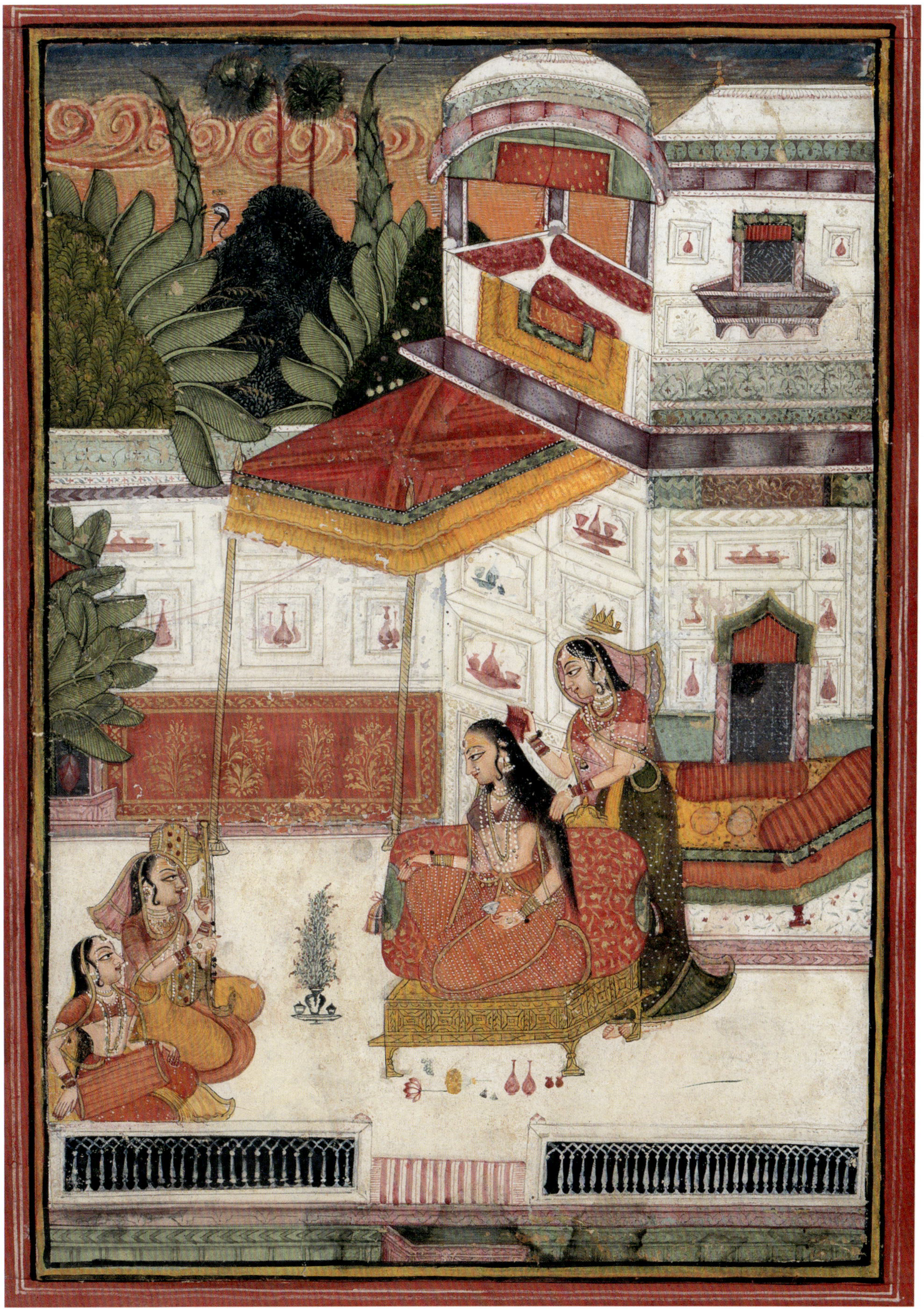

49 Kamod ragini

Bundi, c. 1770
28 × 21.6 cm (folio), 18.6 × 12.6 cm (painting)
Inscribed above: *ragani devagari sri? ki 5*

The *nayika* is seated on a lotus seat on the ground and reaches up her right hand to pluck a blossom from a nearby tree. She is in a glade and all around her are blossoming trees laden with huge flowers or entwined by flowering creepers. Large white birds stand on the water's edge at the front, while other white birds populate the trees in the glade. The trees recede on either side, their dark green or blue foliage relieved by the lighter gray-green of the plantains. The overall dark tonality is set off by the brilliant whites of the birds and lotus petals.

The iconography of a lady seated on a bed of lotus petals in a forest glade and reaching up her hand is found in other Bundi *ragamalas* where it is labeled Kamod.[1] Kamod in fact is difficult to pin down to a single iconography, since it can also involve ascetics or worshippers at a *lingam* shrine.[2] Devagari or Devakari *ragini* as inscribed over the painting is equally difficult to place and normally seems to occur only in Deccani and Pahari *ragamalas*.

This painting comes from a set labeled by Joachim Bautze in his study of Bundi *ragamalas* as Series V,[3] which seems to have been compiled by several different hands. An Asavari *ragini* in the Virginia Museum of Fine Arts from the former Heeramaneck collection is from the same set; it corresponds exactly as to size and border decoration as well as to its figural style and landscape format.[4] A slightly smaller Todi *ragini* in the same collection is possibly also from this set since its landscape elements are the same even though the *nayika* is by a different hand.[5] Both these paintings also have incorrect inscriptions written apparently by the same hand as in the present painting. | JL

1 Ebeling 1973, fig. 212.
2 See, for example, Waldschmidt and Waldschmidt 1975, figs. 131–132.
3 Bautze 1987a, pp. 95–97, where known examples from the series are listed.
4 Dye 2001, no. 108.
5 Dye 2001, no. 107.

Published: Cran 1980, no. 55

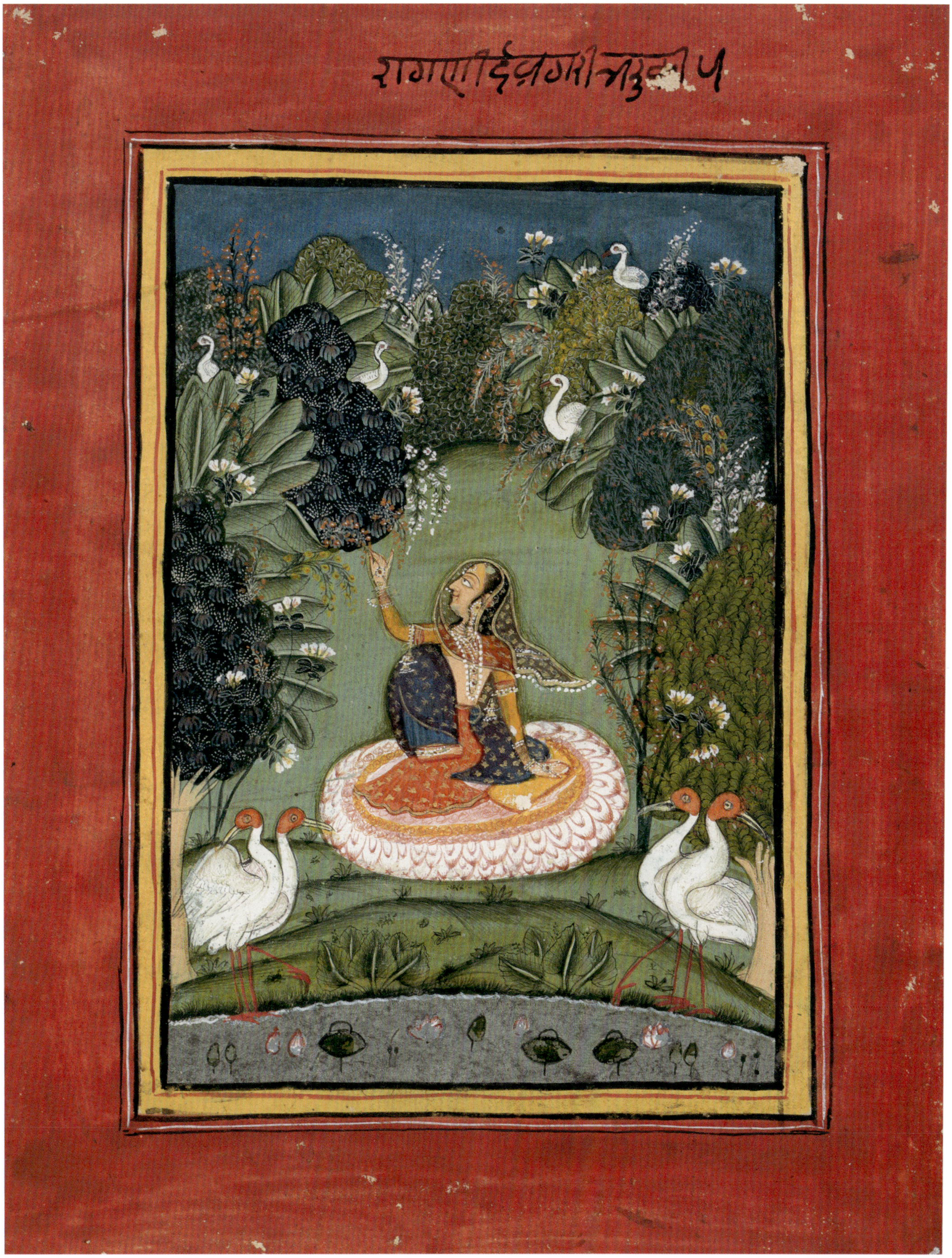

50 Two women at a window

Bundi, c. 1790
25.7 × 17.5 cm (folio), 21.5 × 14.5 cm (painting)
Inscribed on verso in Hindi in Devanagari: *29 Maharaja a[ur?] Patsah ki baita donu chaili?* ("Daughters of the Maharaja and Emperor, both of them dandies?").[1]

Two women stand in the embrasure of a window, indicated by the thick black frame around the painting, with a rich textile carpet over the parapet. This is in imitation of the *jharokha* portraits of the Mughals.[2] The motif was at first the prerogative of the Emperors alone. When Aurangzeb discontinued the daily *darshan* at the *jharokha* and forbade artists to paint representations of it, the motif was seized upon by artists in their increasing eagerness to depict women. Such a motif in this new context perhaps suggests, despite the frequent but inaccurate inscriptions identifying the ladies as particular princesses, that they were "public women." Here the accompanying inscription also suggests that the two girls are princesses, in fact the daughters of a Maharaja and of the Emperor.

The woman in front wears a typical Bundi male turban of the Umed Singh and Budh Singh period, while the other wears the Chagtai type of headdress worn by high-born Mughal women. That they are play-acting these roles is indicated by the Shaiva sectarian marks on their foreheads. The "Mughal" woman has her right hand feeling the "Rajput" woman's right breast and her left arm round her shoulders, while the latter grasps the other woman's arms. The "Rajput" woman in addition to her male turban is wearing a gown that is more typical of masculine dress. This would seem to be a male artist's erotic fantasy of goings-on behind the closed doors of the royal zenana.

This is another example of the *fin-de-siècle* atmosphere that envelops Bundi painting at the end of the 18th century (see cat. no. 48). A strange shadow round the face, as seen here, became the norm at this time in Bundi painting. With their smoothly modeled, almost identical features and their dark hair streaming down their back, curling locks before their ear and immensely long eyelashes shadowing their eyes, these two ladies strike a sensuously erotic note. The repetition of the facial features and especially the identical eyes with their jutting block of eyelashes combined with the interlacing of the arms show the artist's interest in conceptual pattern-making.

One of the finest paintings in this *fin-de-siècle* genre shows an intoxicated courtesan at a window c. 1775, now in the Brooklyn Museum.[3] A picture very similar to the present one showing two women with their arms around each other at a window was in the collection of J.K. Galbraith (there called Bundi style at Kota, c. 1740, but dated surely too early).[4] Double portraits of women are a feature of Bundi and Kota painting in the 18th century as seen in a full-length study in the Kota Fort Museum of two women preening themselves.[5] Paintings in this genre again influenced that of Jodhpur in the next century, as in a window portrait from Jodhpur of two ladies embracing and staring lovingly at each other, now in the National Museum, New Delhi.[6] As with our two ladies, one is dressed in male costume and the other in female, the latter wearing a Mughal headdress. | JL

1 A cut-off inscription on a repair paper with an inspection or presentation date of samvat 1856 [1799–1800] is also found on the verso of this painting.
2 See Losty [forthcoming] for the origin of the format.
3 Poster et al. 1994, no. 129.
4 Welch and Beach 1965, no. 32.
5 Welch et al. 1997, no. 33.
6 Crill 2000, fig. 119.

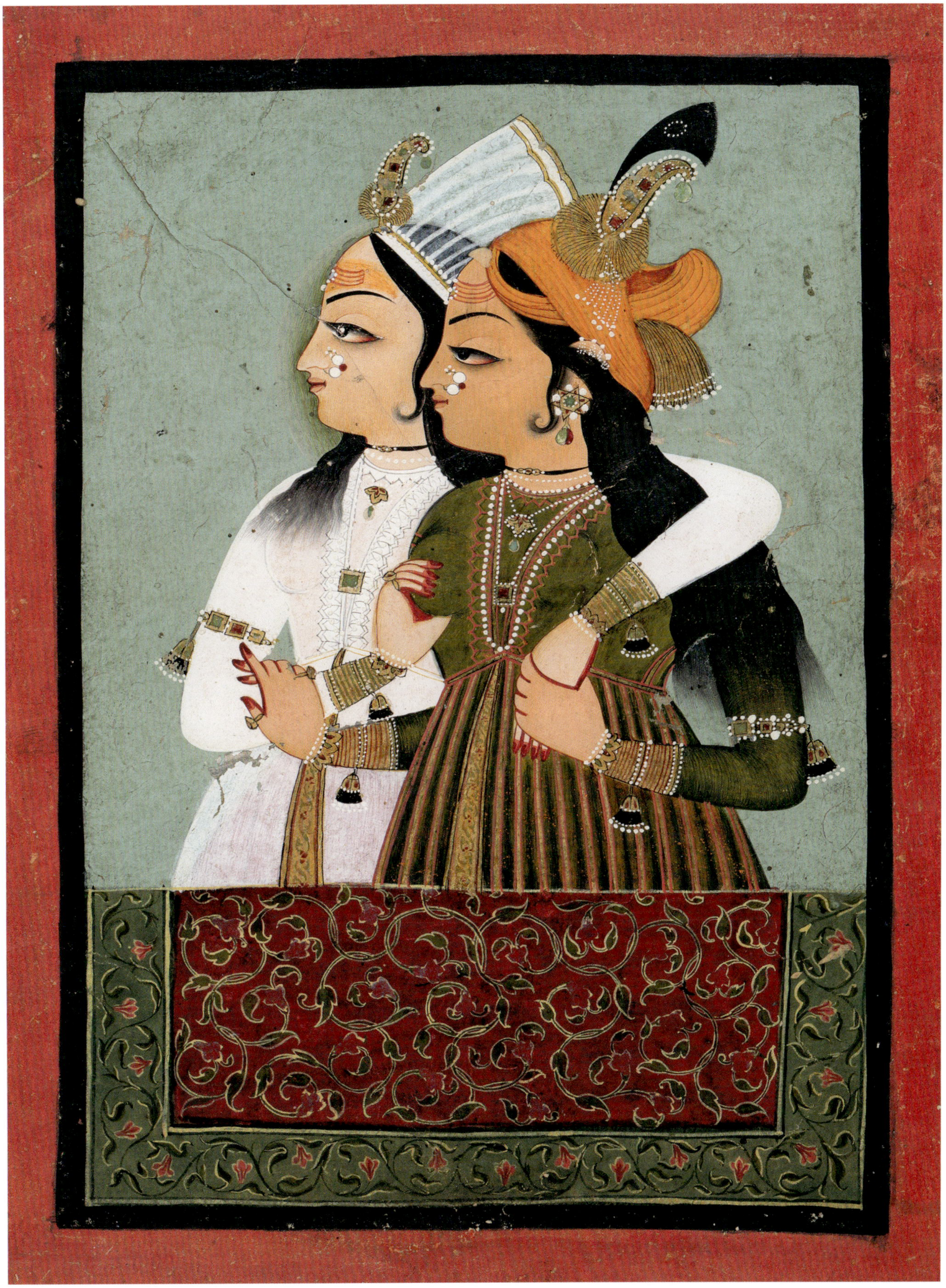

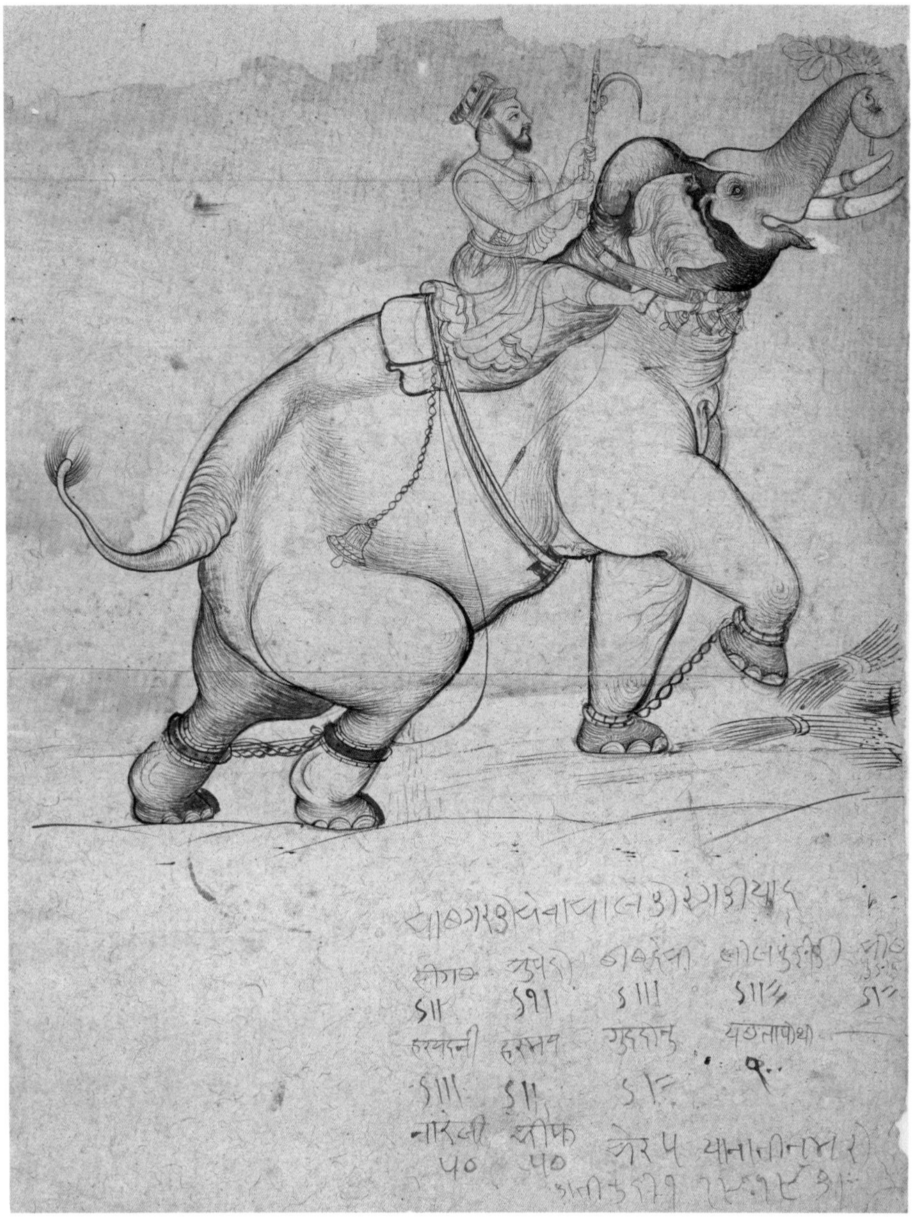

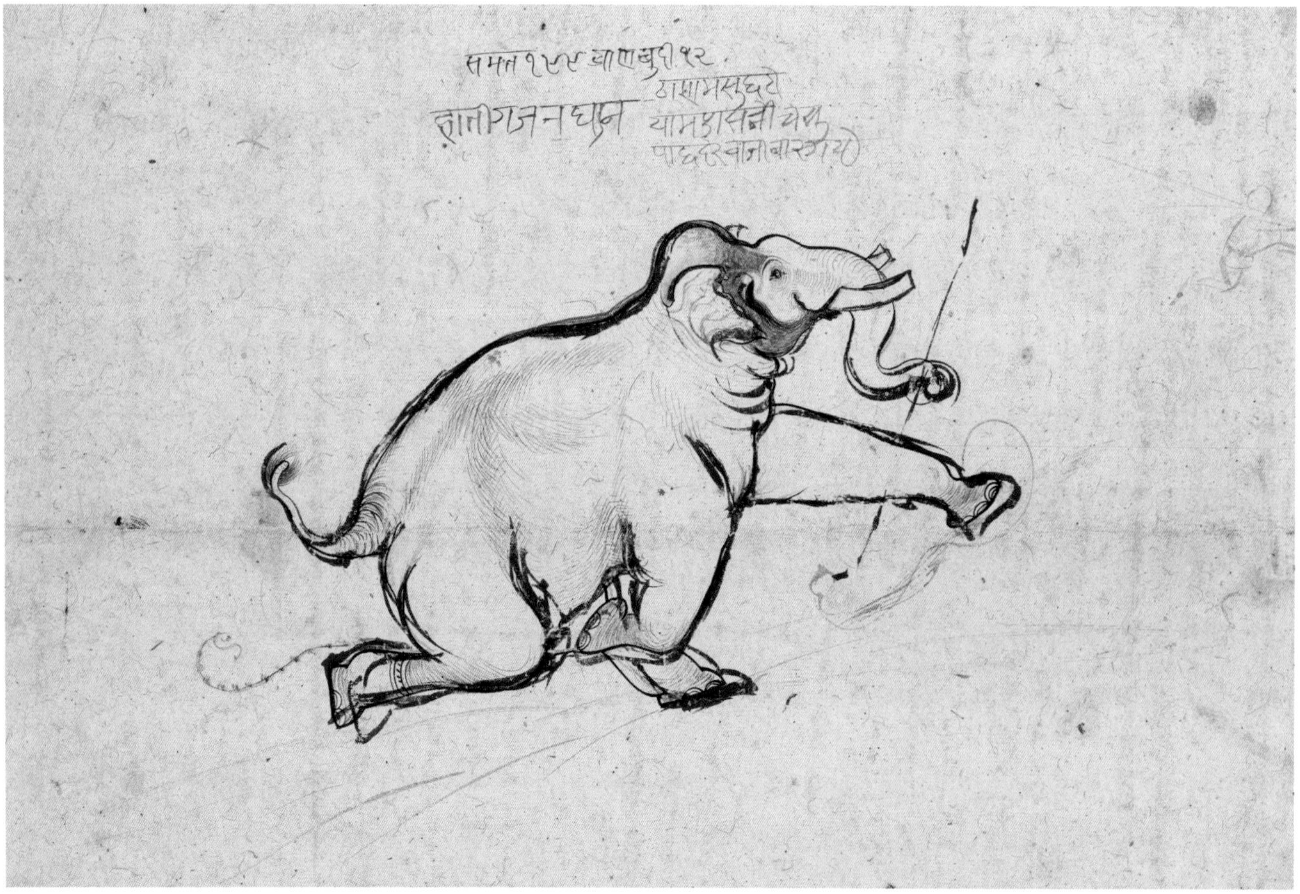

51 A chained elephant breaking a branch
52 A running elephant

Kota, c. 1761–1762
32.5 × 24 cm (folio)
Inscribed beneath in Hindi with measurements of the various parts of the animal and the date of samvat 1818 [1761–1762]
Museum Rietberg, Collection Danielle Porret, 2010.11

Kota, c. 1823
25 × 33.8 cm (folio)
Inscribed above with the date *samvat 1880 Sra[va]n budi 12* [1823], the name of the elephant: *hati gajan dhyan* ("the elephant 'Elephant-wealth'") and a brief description in Hindi
Museum Rietberg, Collection Danielle Porret, 2010.10

Under the Emperor Shah Jahan (r. 1627–1658), Bundi was divided in two and half of it given as his *jagir* to Madho Singh, a younger son of Rao Ratan of Bundi (r. 1608–1631). Both had rendered distinguished military service to the Mughals and Madho Singh (r. 1631–1648) was rewarded with his own principality when Rao Ratan's young grandson inherited Bundi. The earliest definite paintings from Kota share the same characteristics and preoccupations as those of Bundi and were presumably painted by artists from there. Kota *ragamalas* retain the same conventions and iconography as those of Bundi, descended from the 1591 Chunar *ragamala*. Later in the 17th century Kota began to develop its own conventions. Its patrons and artists were fascinated by *shikar*, the royal hunt of lions and tigers, and hence this subject became a major theme over two centuries of development. Drawings of elephants frequently repeated the same compositions over this long period, so that without dates only stylistic considerations serve to distinguish them.

In the first vigorous drawing (cat. no. 51) the elephant is rearing his head up to break the branch that it is holding in its trunk from a tree. Its rider nonchalantly tucks his bare feet into the neckband, from which three bells are merrily swinging. Another larger bell swings from the saddle as the animal prepares to rear. Its feet are chained together to prevent too vigorous a movement. The bearded mahout dressed in *jama* and turban holds up his *ankusa* (goad) as if about to strike the animal's head. Judiciously applied painted lines convert a linear drawing into a modeled one. The mahout wears the loosely tied turban of the Shah Jahan period in the mid 17th century indicating that our artist is relying on an earlier model. The mahout's vigorous upright stance, his raised *ankusa*, his pose with his feet tucked into the band round the elephant's neck are found in many earlier drawings,[1] but a certain stiffness in his carriage here suggests a slightly later date. Nonetheless the artist's draughtsmanship is still vigorous as can be seen in the reworking and refining of his ideas on the drawing.[2]

The second drawing (cat. no. 52) shows an elephant having broken its chains and running off with a smile on its face. In its trunk it holds the pole of a *charki* (a pole with a wheel at the top with burning brands used for controling elephants). The drawing is rough but done with great spirit. The same elephant (his name similarly inscribed) taken apparently from the same *charba* appears in another drawing chasing a mounted spearman.[3] | JL

1 Welch et al. 1997, no. 24 for example, which he attributes to Shaikh Taju and dates to c. 1730.
2 For a drawing from a century later based on a *charba* allied to this one, see Christie's, London, 19 April 1979, lot 108.
For other Kota drawings of elephants see in particular Beach 1974, figs. 71–75; Welch et al. 1997, nos. 12–13, 24–25, 27, 29–31; Beach 2011a, pp. 463–469; and Topsfield 2012, pp. 194–203.
3 Christie's, London, 10 April 1979, lot 109.

53 Srinathji dressed for the Rakhi Bandhan festival

Kota, c. 1830–1840
27.1 × 20.5 cm (folio); 23.4 × 16.9 cm (painting)
Inscribed above: *rakhi ko ucchav hai* ("this is [a picture of Srinathji] at the Rakhi festival")

The idol of Srinathji had been miraculously found buried underground at Govardhan near Mathura by the sage Vallabhacharya (1479–1531). When uncovered, it turned out to be an image of the divine child Krishna in the act of holding up that very mountain. Vallabhacharya enshrined it at Govardhan and built a sect and a philosophy around it. The idol takes the form of the divine boy Krishna holding his left hand up, as he did in the *Bhagavata Purana* to lift the mountain Govardhan in order to shelter the villagers and their cattle. The god Indra, displeased with the villagers, had sent a fearsome thunderstorm down on them. In 1669 in order to escape imminent possible destruction by Aurangzeb at its temple in Govardhan, the image was moved into Rajasthan on a *ratha* or chariot. The chariot kept on moving ahead confronting all the hurdles, until two years later it finally stopped at Sinhada in Mewar territory, and no amount of effort could get it to move again. Believing that this was a sign of the will of the deity, Maharana Raj Singh of Mewar granted it land for the building of a shrine. This became the great shrine at Nathdwara, where the deity occupies not so much a temple as a *haveli* or mansion that also became the seat of the *Tilakayats*, the hereditary succession of the supreme pontiffs of the sect descended from Vallabha's successor, Vitthalnathji. They all took the title *Dauji* (elder brother), a name peculiarly associated with Balarama, the elder brother of Krishna.

In the daily rituals at Nathdwara the image is woken up, washed, dressed, its clothes changed and fed several times a day before being finally put to bed. The Vallabhacharis also celebrate a large number of festivals in the course of the year, for many of which the image has to be dressed accordingly with the correct hangings around it. The clothes, ornaments, hangings, etc., for each separate occasion for worship are known as *sringars*. This painting illustrates one of the *sringars* of Srinathji for the festival of *Rakhi Bandhan* or "tying the thread." Robert Skelton writes that the festival "celebrates the occasion when the goddess Lakshmi descended to the lower regions in order to release her husband from an agreement to reside with the king. As it would have been immodest for her to speak to Bali, she first made him her brother by tying a silk thread around his wrist. This precedent is still followed by Indian girls, who tie the *rakhi* to the wrists of male friends on the full moon of Sravan."[1] For this festival, the god is dressed in a long red skirt and a jaunty turban with a broad peacock feather headdress known as a *chandrika* and he carries his flute. He wears innumerable ropes of pearls attached to gold plaques while the rest of his body is adorned with multiple jewels. His *chutilla* or decorated artificial braid is fanning out to the side. A saffron-colored hanging covers the stele to which the image is attached and behind that hangs a plain red *picchavai*. Srinathji's main garment is worn in the female manner to suggest that he is Lakshmi for the day. At Srinathji's feet are his *banta* (box for sweets, for he is still a child), his *pan* or betel chews and his *jhari* (covered water pot).

The chief priest of the Vallabha cult at Nathdwara, Tilakayat Dauji II or Damodaraji (1797–1825)[2] is present on the left holding the *rakhi* which he will tie onto Srinathji/Lakshmi's wrist. He became *Tilakayat* at the age of ten in 1807. Beside him is another priest holding a tray of sweets while two priestly musicians on the right ring the bell and bang the gong. Another man who does not seem to be a priest and who wears a turban blows into the conch. All are dressed appropriately for worship in loose garments of a *dhoti* and a wrap although the *Tilakayat*, as befits his status, wears richer garments and a panoply of jewels. All wear the appropriate U-shaped *tilak* of the Vallabha sect on their forehead.

Tilakayat Dauji II is remembered particularly for the festival in which he brought together seven of the *svarups* or key images of the sect in 1822 and for vigorously defending his "extensive diocese," as James Tod calls it, by assuming arms himself "at the head of 400 horse, two standards of foot and two field pieces." A depiction of Dauji armed with a spear and on horseback[3] closely resembles this second Dauji and obviously shows him towards the end of his comparatively short life, which serves to date the original portrait to the 1820s. He appears in several paintings from Nathdwara and Kota showing him engaged in worship.[4] Tod met him at Nathdwara when he was "about thirty years of age. He is of a benign aspect with much dignity of demeanour, courteous, yet exacting the homage due to his high calling; meek as becomes the priest of Govinda, but with the finished manners of one accustomed to the highest society."[5] He was also responsible for commissioning many mural paintings, *picchavais* and other works of art.[6]

Although Vallabha came from the south, his sect became particularly important in Rajasthan and Gujarat and some of the ruling dynasties of Rajasthan such as that of Kota were devout followers of the cult. While at Vrindavan in 1719, Maharao Bhim Singh of Kota became a devotee of the Vallabhacharya cult and was given an image of Brijnathji, a small golden image of Krishna in a similar pose to Srinathji. Brijnathji has been the tutelary

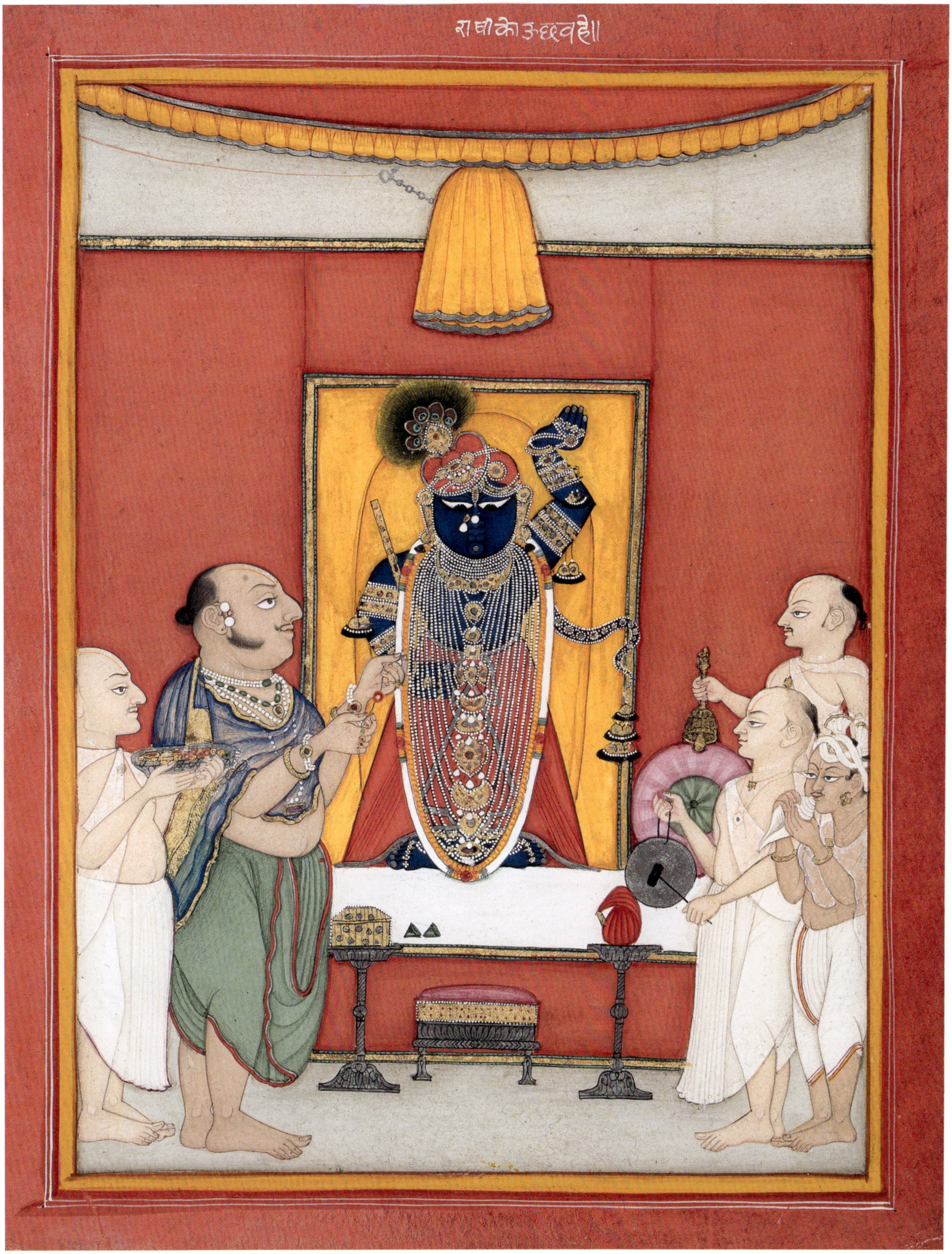
राधीकोउछवहै॥

deity of the Kota state and the Maharaos of Kota have followed the Vallabha *sampradaya* ever since. Maharao Kishor Singh of Kota (r. 1819–1827) fled to Nathdwara in 1821 after the Battle of Mangrol[7] and was entertained there by the Vallabha pontiff Dauji for three months, where he was given an image of Brijrajji, identical to Brijnathji, as his personal deity. After his reinstallation he seems to have brought back artists from Nathdwara to Kota, whose paintings done in Kota are almost indistinguishable from Nathdwara work.[8] Several sets seem to have been produced that show him both in worship of Brijrajji and of the various *sringars* of Srinathji during the reign of his successor Maharao Ram Singh (r. 1827–1866), sometimes with priests in attendance as here.[9] Almost all these paintings have the same kind of inner saffron border and an outer wider red one with two thin white lines and inscriptions in white above. Tilakayat Dauji was dead by 1825 but is often depicted in later paintings as if still alive, e.g. with Maharao Kishor Singh worshipping Brijnathji from c. 1831,[10] and in many of the later *pichhavais* or painted hangings associated with the Nathdwara cult.[11] Another Kota painting of Srinathji dressed for the *Rakhi Bandhan* festival and a contemporary portrait of Tilakayat Dauji II in a non-religious context were published in 2007.[12] | JL

---

1 Skelton 1973, p. 89.
2 Ambalal 1987, pp. 60, 112.
3 Ambalal 1987, p. 65.
4 Ambalal 1987, pp. 66, 112–113; Goswamy and Smith 2005, pp. 74–75.
5 Tod 1920, II, p. 642.
6 For further reference to Dauji II and other portraits, see Ambalal 1987, pp. 64–68.
7 Welch et al. 1997, p. 54.
8 See for example Welch et al. 1997, figs. 56–62, showing Maharao Kishor Singh worshipping Brijrajji.
9 See Bautze 1987c.
10 Welch et al. 1997, p. 77, fig. 2.
11 Skelton 1973, *passim*.
12 Losty and Galloway 2007, nos. 24 and 23.

54 Kakubha ragini
55 Patamanjari ragini
56 Kamoda ragini

Three folios from a *ragamala* series
Amber, c. 1710–1720
42.5 × 32 cm (average folio size); 31 × 20.3 cm (average painting size)
Each inscribed at the top with the relevant verses from Paida's *ragamala* text in Braj-bhasha Hindi

54 Kakubha *ragini*
Inscribed: "With her lover, she had sexual pleasure. The woman's limbs were pressed and crushed. Her hair was loosened and her bodice was torn. She became erotic and her necklace was loosened. Her eyes look beautiful, having remained awake all the night. The modest lotus[es] are enchanted by the lady." [1]

55 Patamanjari *ragini*
Inscribed: "A garland of dried up flowers is round her neck. The lonely one is extremely stricken. One moment she is revived, the next moment her life fades. She does not relish food [or her] living quarters. She does not sleep and (sits) alone on the couch. She is bent into two [due to pangs of separation]."[2]

56 Kamoda *ragini*
Inscribed: "She is yellow complexioned and wears a white bodice. Her charm radiates, she looks beautiful. Her sari is red and she is stricken by Kama [i.e. Cupid]. The cooing of cuckoo is poison to her. She is looking all round to find out the path of her lover. [This is how] the lady, sitting in the wood, adorns it."[3]

The set has been prepared as an album with matching inner and outer borders of a fern-like creeper and flowering plants which echo those found in the paintings themselves. The fern or vine-like border is also found on other Amber paintings.[4] The artist has a very distinctive palette of slate blues, cold greens and grays. The style is located in Amber, the old capital of the Kacchwaha Rajput state of Jaipur, through a *ragamala* dated 1709 done at Amber and now in the royal Kankroli collection.[5] This serves to locate to Amber an even earlier *ragamala* of c. 1680 now mostly in the Victoria and Albert Museum, as well as some pages from a smaller dispersed early set.[6] Other *ragamalas* in the same artistic tradition include several in the City Palace Museum, Jaipur.[7] They would to have been commissioned by Maharaja Sawai Jai Singh II of Amber (r. 1699–1743) near the beginning of his reign. Jai Singh was one of the most original and innovative of Rajput rulers, being interested in painting and architecture as well as literature and astronomy. Under him the new capital of Jaipur was built in the plain below the old fort. He is also one of the most elusive of the great Rajput patrons, since little has been published that comes definitely from Amber/Jaipur during his long reign, of which these *ragamalas* are the most well known.[8]

The set when intact in a private collection was discussed by Ebeling.[9] The iconographies of these Amber *ragamala* sets follow two traditions, what Ebeling calls the Rajasthani and the distinctly separate Amber tradition. The latter are all closely linked by style and iconography. The present set obviously depends on an earlier set such as the Kankroli 1709 *ragamala* and is presumably slightly later. All share the same slender elegant women with doll-like features, the tall stylized flowering trees, and the architecture of a single-storeyed pavilion with heavy *chajja*. The pavilions all have painted cornices, dadoes with flowers and walls decorated with painted bottles in niches.

Paida's Braj-bhasha text is inspired by the relevant Sanskrit verses of Damodara's *Sangitadarpana*. Each inscription above the painting has a verse in *Modaka* metre describing the *raga* or *ragini* followed by a *Doha* with specifications of musical data.[10]

Kakubha *ragini* (cat. no. 54) shows a woman lying on her bed with her lover at night on a terrace in the open. He is wrapped up in a sheet and wears a night turban (his day turban is on a stand nearby). He seems to have fallen asleep as his eyes are closed and he rests his head on his forearm lying on the pillow. Despite this he reaches forward to cup the woman's breast in his hand. She is fully awake and still dressed for the day as she gazes at him, obviously expecting more. The pavilion walls are painted with flowering plants and vases of flowers and the fern motif of the inner border is imitated in the painted decoration of the cornices above the heavy *chajja* and along the top of the adjacent walls.

The Kakubha *ragini* in the Kankroli *ragamala* of 1709 is very similar, with the difference that the lovers occupy a canopied bed on the terrace and the *nayaka* wrapped in his sheet lies face up.[11]

The deserted heroine is one of the tropes of Indian poetry, here utilized as part of *ragamala* iconography in Patamanjari *ragini* (cat. no. 55). A woman sits in a pavilion in mourning, waiting for her lover to come to her. She has equipped the pavilion with wine and other necessities. It is night since a tall lamp is burning despite the blue sky above. The pavilion behind her is decorated similarly to that in Kakubha *ragini*. It looks out onto a delightful *char bagh* garden with a central fountain and water channels. The four parterres contain miniature cypresses interspersed with irises and poppies as well as the fern-like plant seen in the border and on the cornices.

Again the iconography is derived from the 1709 Kankroli Amber *ragamala*.[12] There the whole effect is more three-dimensional and viewed from on high, with the *nayika* occupying a canopied bed in the middle of an octagonal court in front of the pavilion which has angled *jalis* on either side. Only part of the *char bagh* garden is visible below.

Kamoda *ragini* (cat. no. 56) shows a woman sitting alone on the flowery bank of a river with tall trees on either side. Behind her a hill rises to a rocky summit. The sun is shining and the artist has depicted it with a face. She is waiting for her lover and has brought flasks of wine for a picnic.

The trees are beautifully and individually depicted bursting into flower in spring. Between the trees are stylized plants matching the fern-creeper on the inner border. When compared with the Kamoda *ragini* in the 1709 set,[13] it can be seen that some of the irregularities of that painting have been smoothed out: the trees have become more evenly sized and regularly spaced, the stream has been straightened out and so on. The tall plants between the tree trunks in our painting are based on much smaller and more irregular plants in the earlier one. | JL

---

1 Verses 16 and 27. Translation based on Rai Krishnadasa's, Ebeling 1973, p. 138.
2 Unnumbered verses. Translation based on Rai Krishnadasa's, Ebeling 1973, p. 140.
3 Verses 44 and 45. Translation based on Rai Krishnadasa's, Ebeling 1973, p. 140.
4 See, e.g. Pal 2004, no. 3.
5 Andhare 1972; Ebeling 1973, p. 187.
6 For the first set see Ebeling 1973, no. 50, col. pl. 12; for the latter Spink 1987, nos. 23–25.
7 Das 1986, pl. 1.
8 For other paintings commissioned by Jai Singh II, see Findly 1981, pp. 55–56; Das 1986 and 2000; and Spink 1987, nos. 26–29.
9 Ebeling 1973, no. 47. Two pages from this set are in the collection of the Brooklyn Museum (Poster et al. 1994, nos. 101–102), while others were sold at Christie's, New York, 21 September 2007, lot 9.
10 The translation of the whole text by Rai Krishnadasa is published in Ebeling 1973, pp. 136–144. This set has its verses normally numbered consecutively throughout, in contrast to the Kankroli set where the numbering begins again for each page.
11 Ebeling 1973, fig. 205.
12 Ebeling 1973, fig. 217.
13 Andhare 1972, fig. 3; Ebeling 1973, fig. 213.

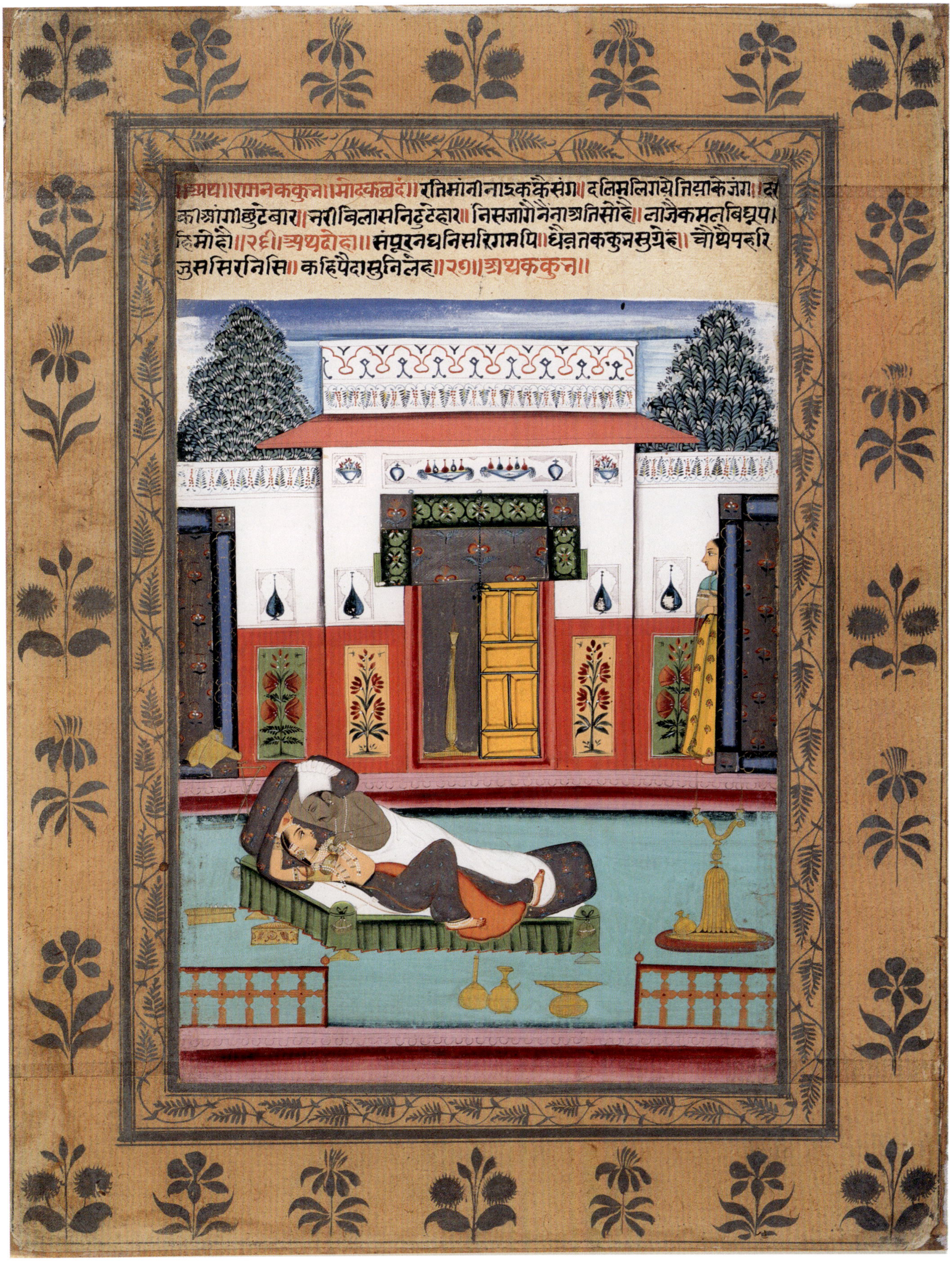
॥अथ॥रागनककुन॥मोदकछंद॥ रतिमांनी नाइककै संग॥ दलिमलि गाये तियाके अंग॥ द
का आंग छुटे बार॥ नरी बिलास निठुटे हार॥ निसजागे नैना अति सोहे॥ लाजे कमल बिध्रुप॥
हि मोहे॥२६॥ अथदोहा॥ संपूरन धनि सरिगमपि॥ धैवत ककुन सुग्रेह॥ चौथे पहरि
जुस सिर निसि॥ कहि पैदा सुनि लेह॥२७॥ अथककुन॥

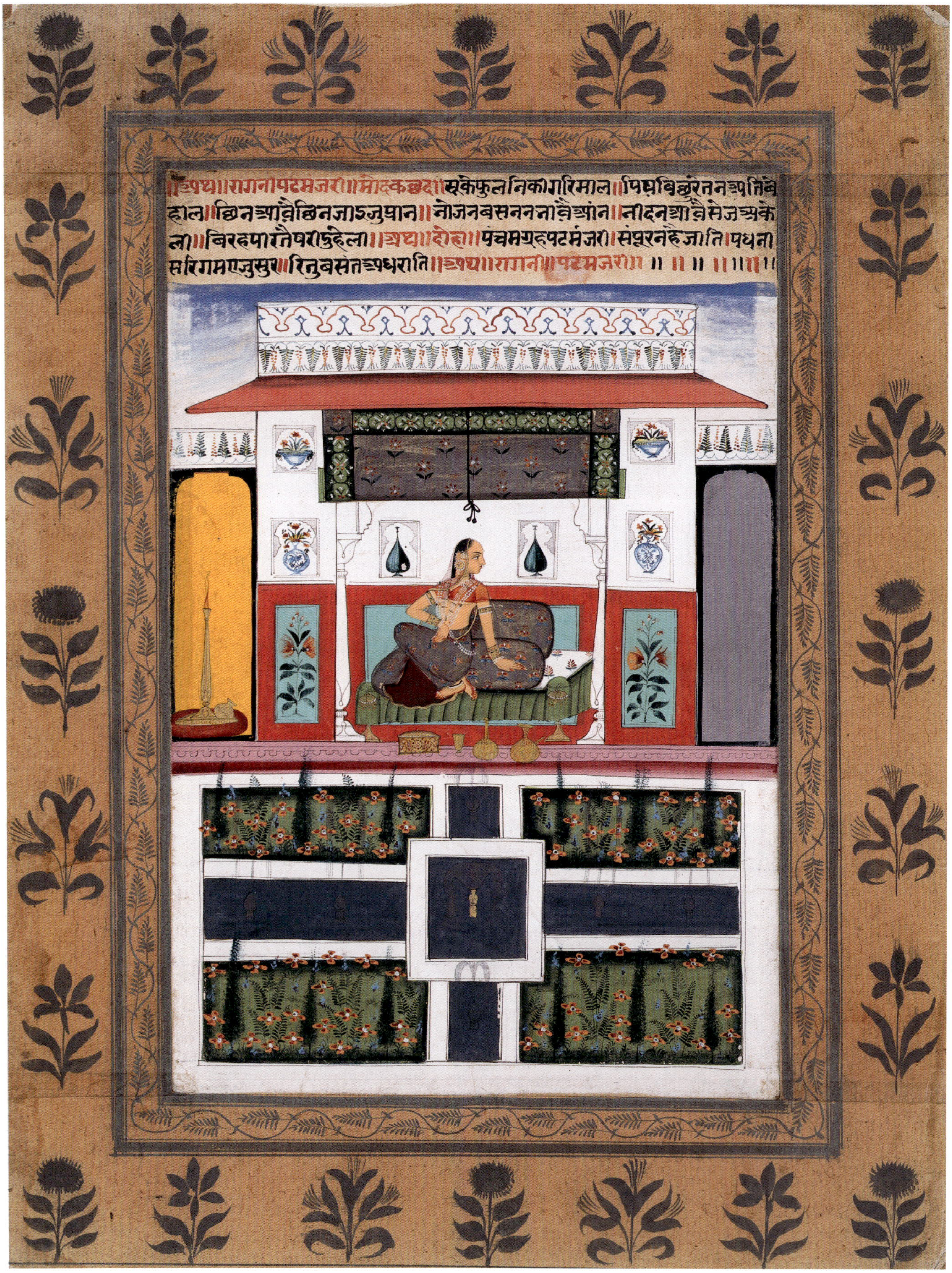

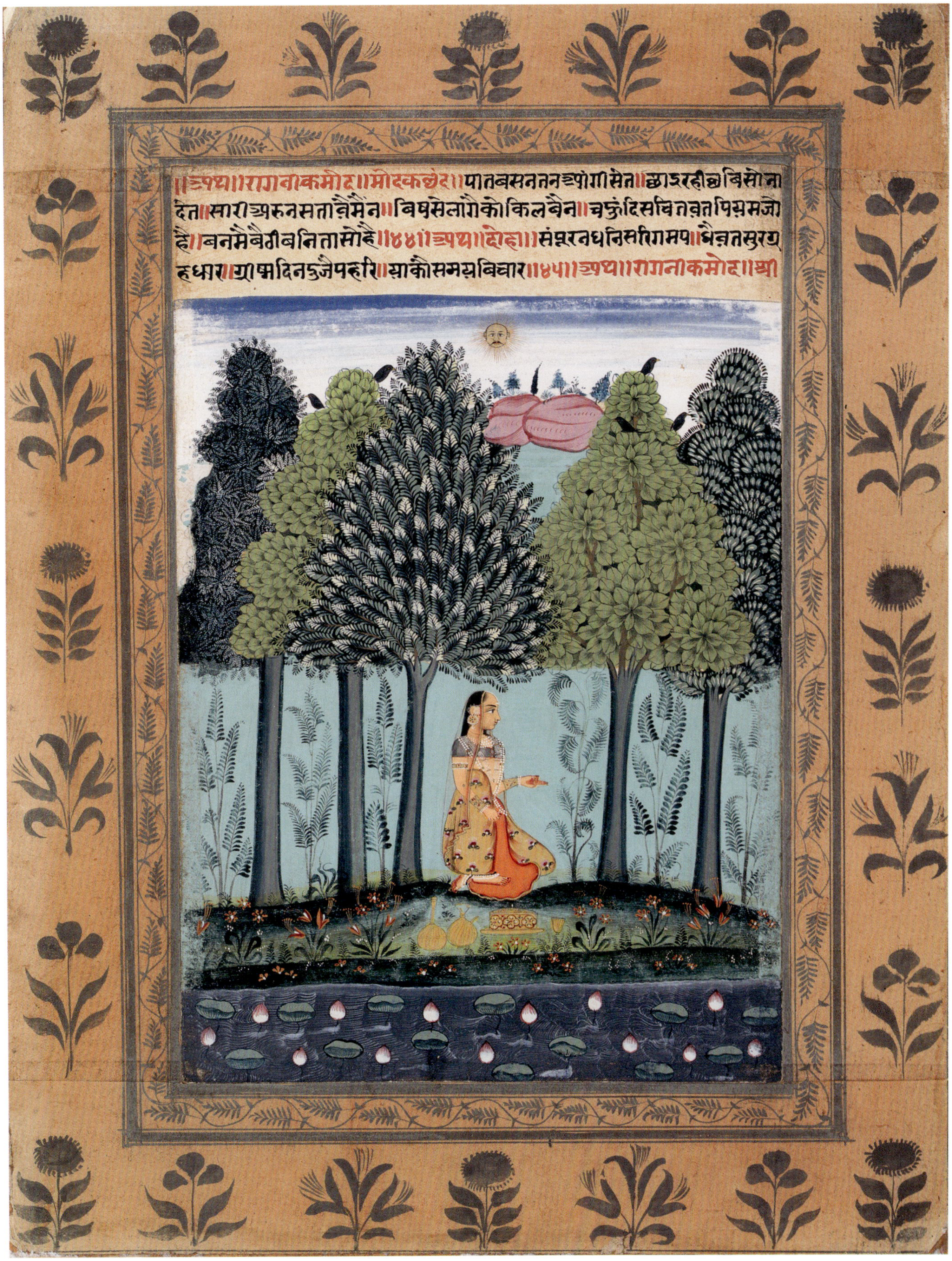

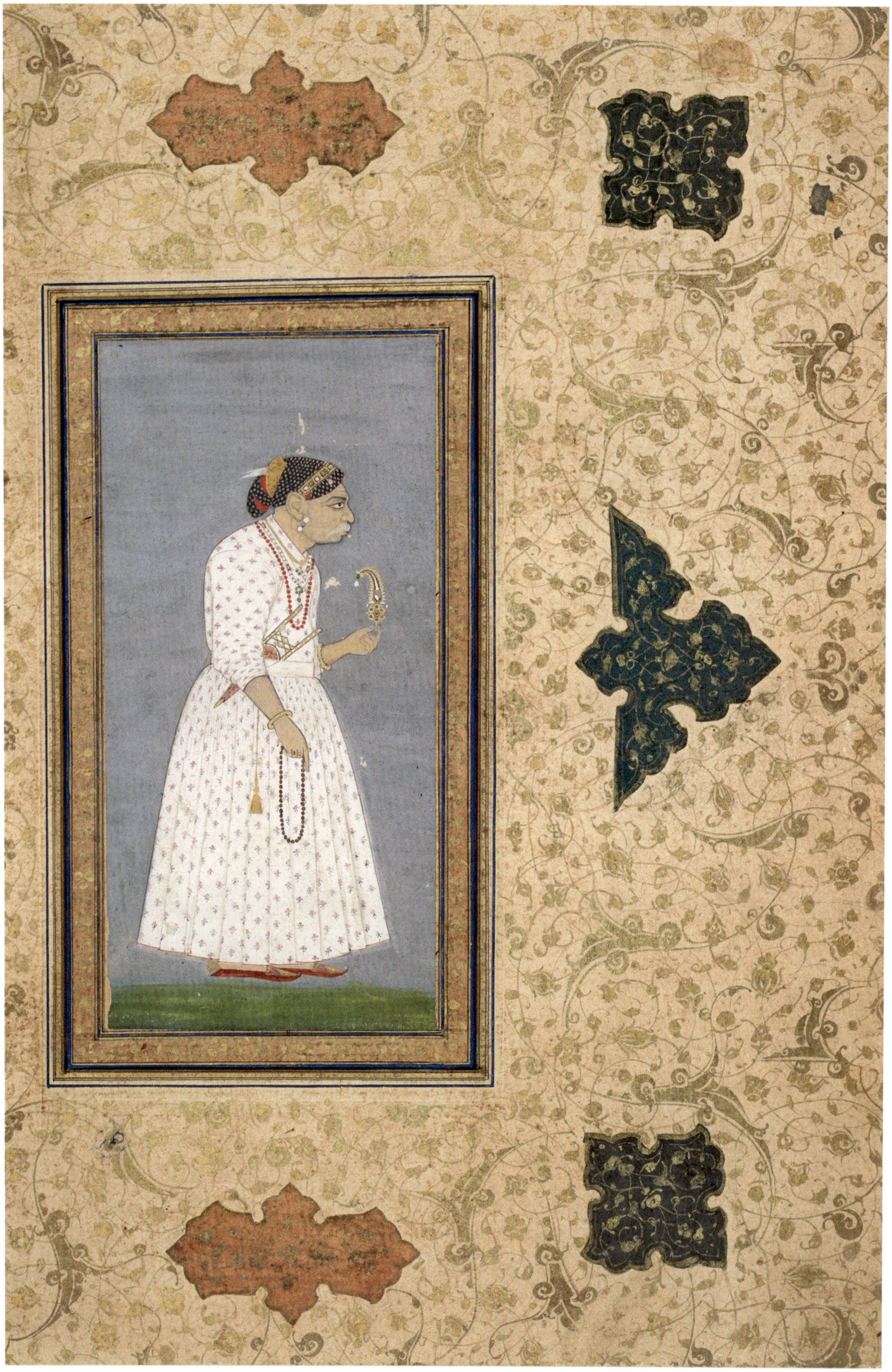

57 Rao Kushal Singh of Jhilai

Jaipur, c. 1740–1750
28.5 × 19.8 cm (folio), 14.4 × 7 cm (painting)

This portrait of a white-haired ruler, his brow furrowed and shoulders stooped with age, depicts Rao Kushal Singh of Jhilai, a *thikana* (feudatory state) of Jaipur in the Tonk district. A member of the important Rajawat sub-clan in line of succession to the Jaipur throne if the ruler were without issue, Kushal Singh is first known for his surrender of the fort of Jhilai to imperial Mughal forces in November 1704. With Jhilai granted as a *jagir* to Sawai Jai Singh of Jaipur in 1717, Kushal Singh soon joined Sawai Jai Singh in a confederated effort of Rajasthani kingdoms against the Mughals. From 1729 to 1734, he sided with Sawai Jai Singh in the conflict between Jaipur and Bundi, and is named as one of five *thakur* signatories to a political agreement dated 1742.[1] He is identified here by comparison to an equally old figure presiding over a *darbar* scene inscribed on the border with the inflated title of Maharaja Kushal Singh.[2] A second and slightly later portrait of this same figure is in the collection of the late Kumar Sangram Singh of Nawalgarh.

Kushal Singh is depicted here holding a jeweled *sarpech* (turban ornament) and prayer beads, symbols of political authority and piety that complement the bejeweled dagger tucked into the waistband of his long white *jama*. The artist dwells on the rao's face, on which he sculpts the eye socket, adds a hint of red to the corner of the eye, and applies a strong black outline around the nose and chin, a device that throws part of the face into relief against the flat blue background. Elsewhere, the painter notes the rao's slouching abdomen, the hairy forearm exposed by his bunched-up sleeve, and the well-articulated left hand. He is little concerned with the lower half of the *jama*, whose hem is delineated simply in red, and with the ground, which is no more than a basic strip of green set just below the rao's feet and a flat, bright blue sky.

The painting has been inserted into a folio with buff borders decorated with gilt arabesques and five cartouches of applied blue and salmon-colored paper. Folios ornamented in this manner were produced in mid 16th-century Bukhara or Tabriz. | JS

[1] The last of these is published in G.N. Bahura and Chandramani Singh, *Catalogue of Historical Documents in Kapad Dwara Jaipur*, Jaigarh Charitable Trust, 1988, no. 1023, p. 136. I am indebted to Shailka Mishra for this and other information about Kushal Singh.
[2] Christie's, New York, 25 May 1978, lot 54.

Published: Maggs, London, *Oriental Miniatures & Illuminations*, Bulletin No. 12 (September 1967), no. 26; Cran 1980, no. 73 (not illustrated)

58 A sleeping ascetic is visited by a prince

Perhaps Jaipur, c. 1780–1800
21.1 × 31.2 cm (folio); 20.7 × 29.2 cm (painting)

An oversized naked ascetic sprawls against the wall of his hut, asleep. He is being visited by a raja who kneels before him dressed all in white apart from his shawl and his turban. An attendant stands behind him dressed in a natty blue short tunic and *paijama* holding a cloth of honor for his master. Another attendant dressed in white waits below with his master's horse. The ascetic's pink hut with floral decoration in its interior is set on a high pink plinth in the midst of a green landscape with a distant view of a city and round hills.

The style is difficult to place with accuracy. Kishangarh artists took a close interest in ascetics in the 18th century, often for purposes of caricature[1] and a study in the National Museum, New Delhi, shows naked ascetics on a terrace either making or preparing to receive their doses of *bhang* while a fat grocer weighs out the ingredients.[2] This type of open landscape with distant towns is also typical of Kishangarh.[3] The raja's turban, however, recalls those of Jaipur in the Pratap Singh II period (r. 1779–1803), while none of these visitors can be placed in Kishangarh and seem more at home in the crisper idiom of Jaipur. The modeling of the ascetic's shaved head suggests the artist has been influenced by Western ideas, in particular caricature prints of the sort that influenced Mewar artists in the 18th century.[4] Jaipur, moreover, had a rich vein of artistic satire that bore fruit in versions of so-called Callot figures.[5] | JL

1 Haidar 2000.
2 Sharma 1974, pl. 64.
3 See, for example, Cimino 1985, no. 44.
4 Mason 2001, no. 63 is a particularly mean example.
5 Losty 2010, no. 99.

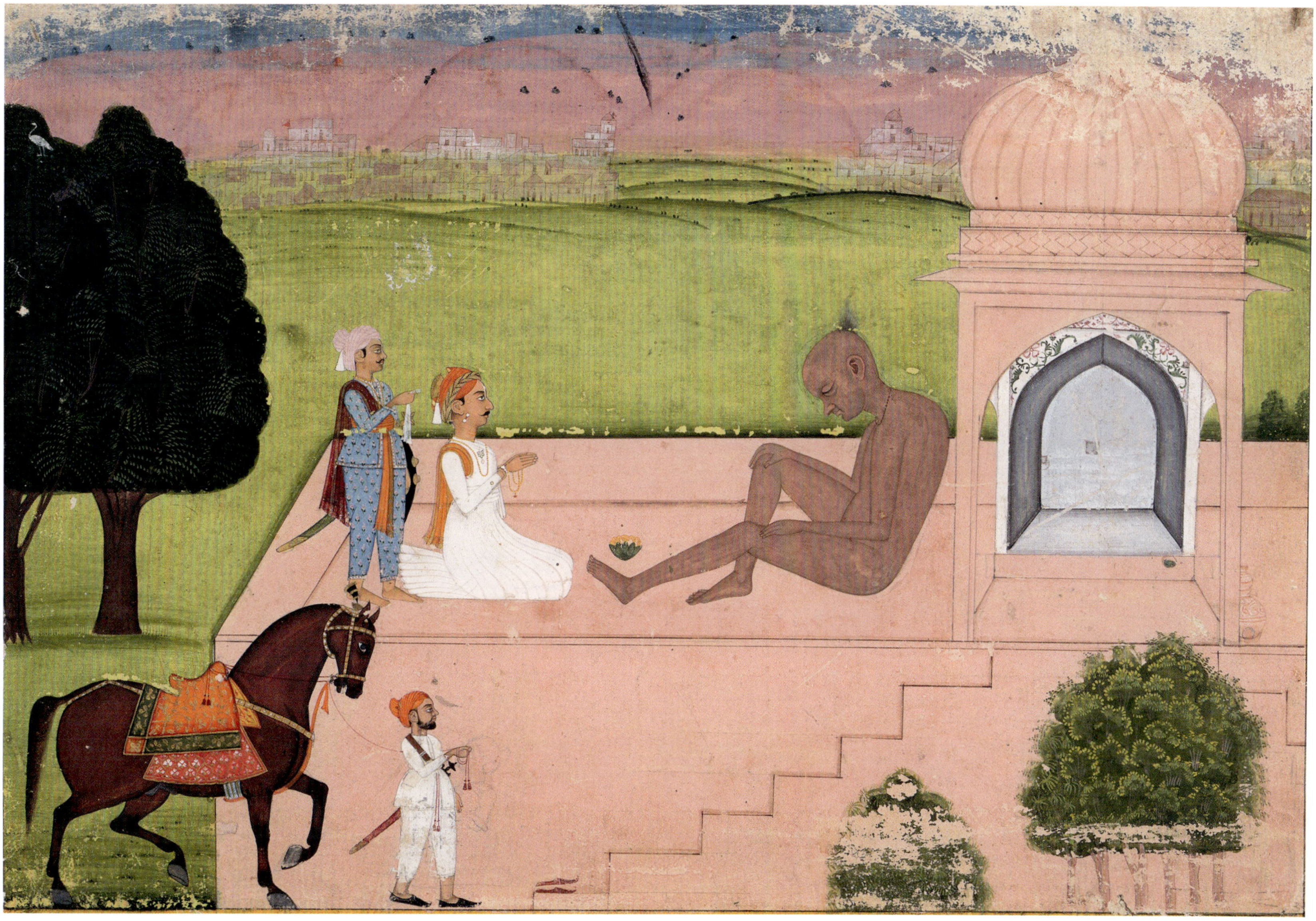

59 A nayika attending to her hair

Ascribed to the artist Mana
Jaipur, c. 1820–1840
16.9 × 12.5 cm (folio); 14 × 9.9 cm (painting)
Inscribed above in Devanagari: *kalam Mana cetara ki* ("work of the painter Mana")[1]

The *nayika* or heroine of poetical literature is depicted at a window with her head thrown back while she runs her fingers through her loose hair. She is naked above the waist with just a loose blue scarf thrown across her shoulder, while below she wears a dull orange skirt with a blue *patka*. She wears lavish jewels: earrings, nose rings, armbands, bracelets, and necklaces. The window embrasure consists of an engrailed arch with a parapet covered by a red textile across the bottom and a rolled-up red blind across the top.

The subject was treated earlier by Sahib Ram, the principal artist of the reign of Maharaja Pratap Singh (r. 1779–1803), to whom are attributed two large paintings (in the Victoria and Albert Museum and a private collection in New York) of *nayikas* attending to their hair at a window.[2] These two figures practically fill the window space and display both a tightness of line and a delicacy of decorative treatment, the latter especially in the treatment of the textiles. Our lady is less monumental and the textiles plainer, but the delicate treatment of the edges of her scarf and *patka* echoes that in Sahib Ram's paintings.

Window portraits had entered the repertoire of Mughal artists in the early 17th century since they were ideally suited for representations of the emperor at the *jharokha*.[3] However, such portraits mostly remained in rectangular format until the middle of the 18th century, when the arched embrasure, engrailed as here, first entered into their vocabulary.[4] The use of the window portrait was restricted to emperors alone until the reign of Aurangzeb, but afterwards it became a favorite format for female portraiture. This convention spread to Rajput studios as in window portraits of Bakhat Singh at Nagaur.[5] A different convention is found in Jaipur in the later 18th century where the arch is semi-circular with a carved leaf voussoir, as in *A Prince and his mistress at a window* in the Polier/ Hamilton albums in the Museum für Islamische Kunst, Berlin.[6] Sahib Ram returned to the Mughal convention of an engrailed arch in which he is followed by our artist. Such window portraits of *nayikas* remained a favorite motif of Jaipur painters well into the 19th century.[7] | JL

1 It is unclear whether the artist's name is to be transcribed as Mana, Amana or Mamana. None of these names appear in Pratap's survey of Jaipur painting (1996).
2 Aitken 2011, figs. 5–6.
3 See Losty [forthcoming].
4 See, for example, Losty 2013, no. 17.
5 Heeramaneck 1984, pls. 81–82.
6 Hickmann and Enderlein 1979, pl. 51.
7 See, for example, Losty and Galloway 2007, nos. 44–45.

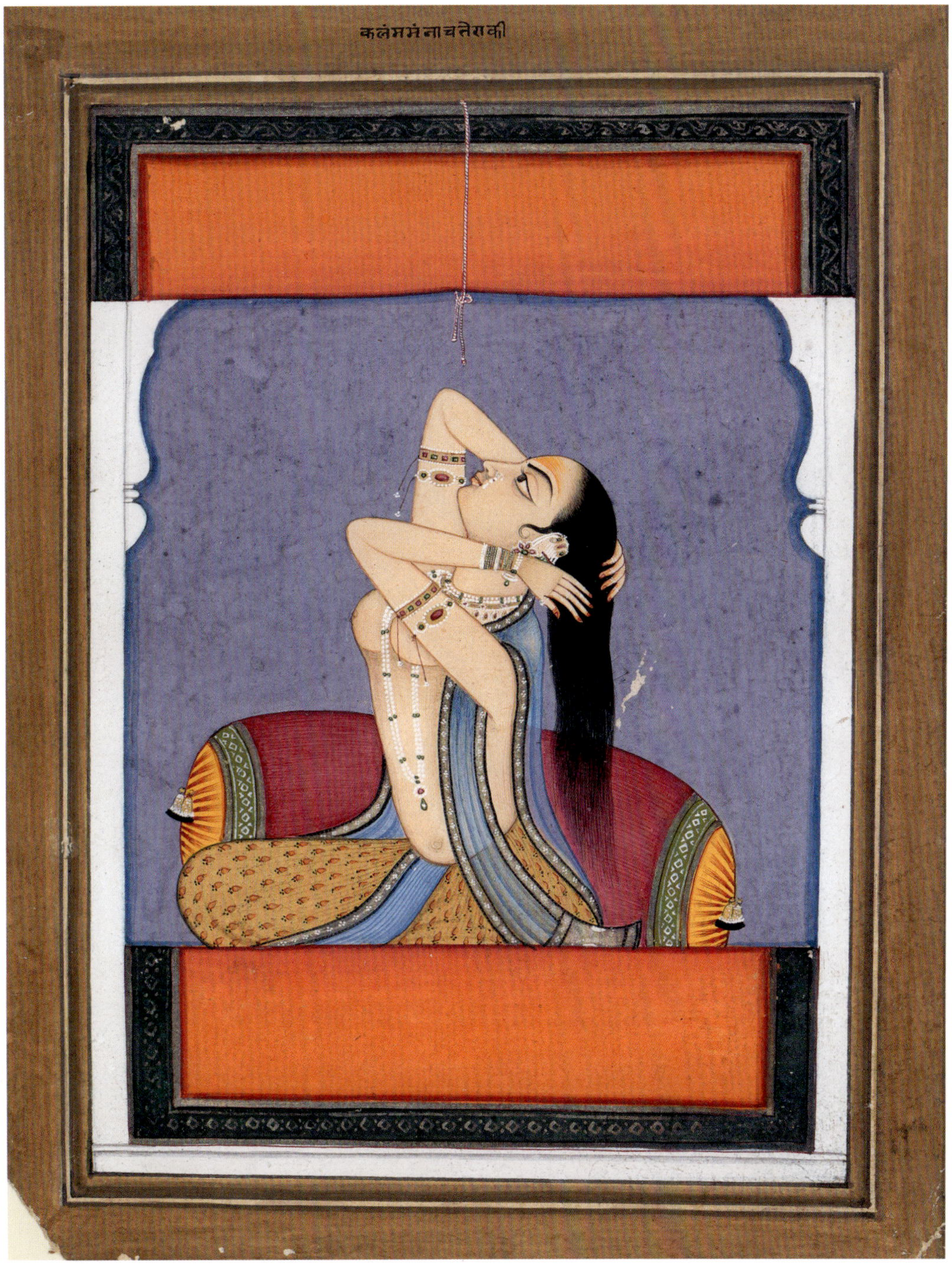
कलंमसंनाचतेराकी

60 A woman smoking a huqqa

Jaipur, c. 1850
32.2 × 23.5 cm (painting)

A woman is seated comfortably on the ground holding the stem of a huqqa to her lips. She wears a red lower garment, probably *shalwar* or loose trousers, a bodice and an all-enveloping dark blue shawl edged with pink that is draped loosely over her upper body and her head. She wears ear ornaments, necklaces, and bracelets. Behind is a pink wall with a blue dado panel. Her white skin contrasts with the generally dark hue of her clothes. The artist has painted her crouched within the frame so that she fills almost the whole of it in a way rarely seen in Indian painting, although Sahib Ram's portraits of courtesans almost filling their window frames seem to be the model for this particular feature here.[1]

Unlike Sahib Ram's similar public ladies (see cat. no. 59), this one gazes out at us and the artist has perhaps meant to have her staring boldly and provocatively at the viewer. But his intention has been thwarted by his not being able to impart life to her eyes by giving her pupils; the woman now looks rather introspective. The way such women were depicted had altered from the standard profile portraits at the window earlier in the 19th century through the work done for William and James Baillie Fraser in Delhi 1815–1819.[2] James Fraser was intrigued by the dancing women of Delhi and had portraits painted of several of them by Delhi artists.[3] Sometimes they were wearing their "off-duty" or "indoor" costume (*khanagi*) of loose-fitting *shalwar* (trousers) and bodice with shawls draped around their upper bodies, as in our portrait. These are obviously portraits of real women, extremely rare in Indian portraiture, and are also depicted individually staring out at us with a frankly appraising gaze. Here our Jaipur artist, untrained in the naturalism of Delhi paintings at this time, has not been able to match their spirit and instead, despite his subject facing out at us, depicts her eyes still turning inward, inhabiting the self-absorbed interior world of Mughal portraiture. He has almost produced a study in abstraction, in which the curves of the woman's clothes, her arms and her huqqa snake stand out against the rectilinear grid of the architecture behind her.[4] | JL

1 Aitken 2011, fig. 5.
2 Archer and Falk 1989.
3 Archer and Falk 1989, pls. 15, 125–128.
4 For a contemporary, more naturalistic portrait of a Jaipur courtesan, see Welch 1978, no. 65, pp. 146–147.

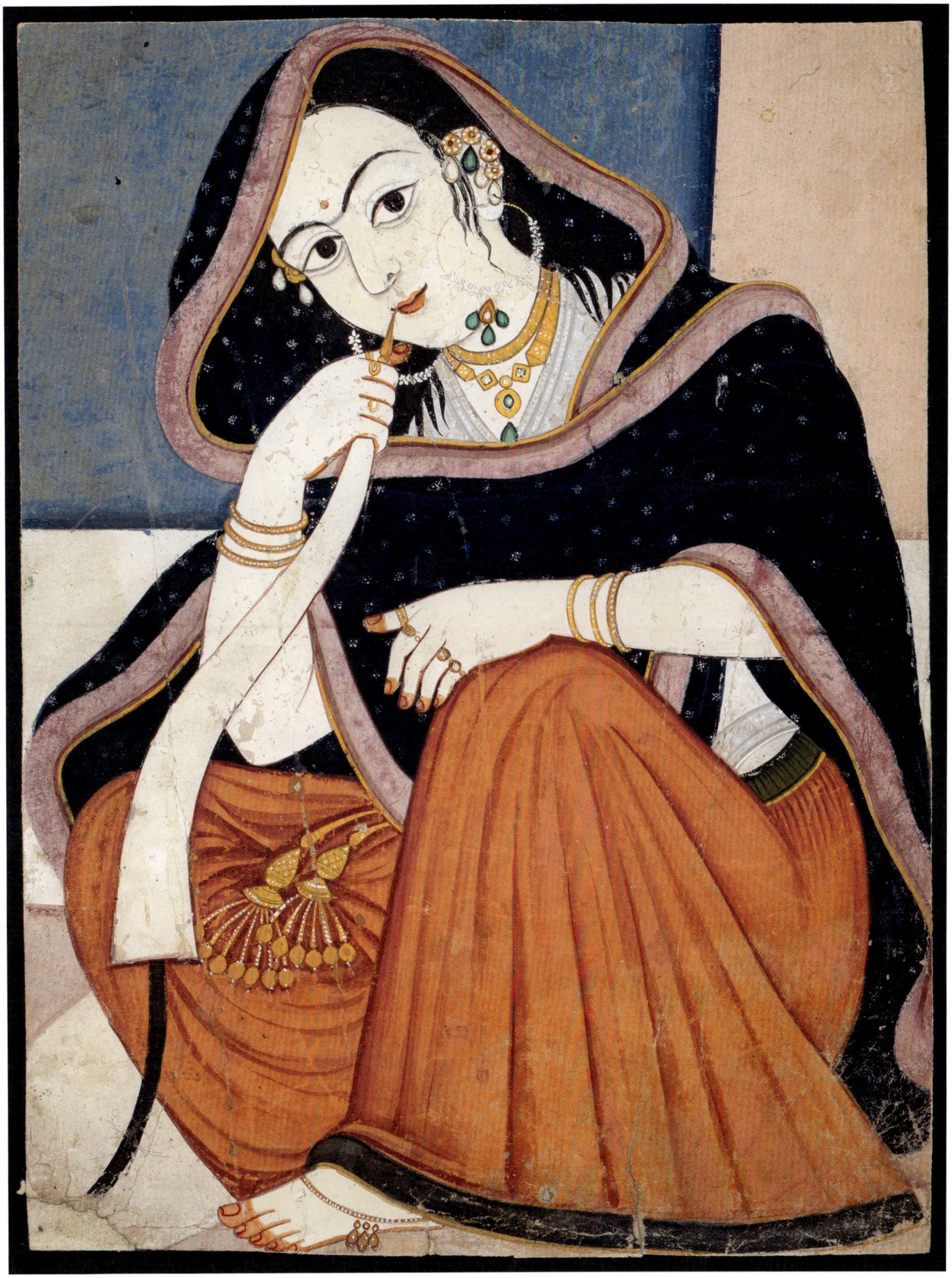

61 Malasri ragini

Folio from a *ragamala* series
Attributed to "The Sirohi Master"
Sirohi, c. 1680
22 × 14.9 cm (folio); 19 × 12.8 cm (painting)
Inscribed above in Devanagari: *Malasri ragani 4*

The iconography of Malasri *ragini* is relatively simple and should consist of two ladies conversing and holding lotuses. Here the artist has seated his two ladies on a terrace holding their lotuses and indicating by their hand gestures or *mudras* that they are conversing. A third girl brings out a tray with a bottle, more flowers and *pan* (betel chews).

Sirohi, a small state in southern Rajasthan between Mewar and Gujarat, seems to have produced various *ragamala* sets in the late 17th century. They are all in a brilliant style of their own, replete with hot reds, yellows and oranges, while they also make use of some highly individual iconographies.[1] None has any of the *ragamala* texts inscribed, merely the names of the *raga* and the numbering in the standard sequence of 36 that all these sets follow. The evidence linking these distinctive *ragamalas* to Sirohi is small.[2] Nonetheless the style seems to be related to contemporary material from Gujarat. Sirohi is just north of the sacred Jain site of Mount Abu and some Jain material in a related style is known.[3] Wall paintings have been found within the palace at Sirohi in an apparently related style.[4]

Milo Beach distinguishes three of the major sets of *ragamalas* from Sirohi as being the work of an artist he names "The Sirohi Master". This artist seems to have been influenced by Sahib Din's *ragamala* of 1628 done for Rana Jagat Singh of Mewar with its tripartite division of the picture space dominated by a terrace with a prominent architectural feature in front of which the action takes place; beneath this is a "below the terrace" area and above are the domes or *chattris* of the building projecting into the divided sky.[5] The present Malasri *ragini* comes from Beach's Set B (figs. 2–4) of similar size and with the same slight damage to the borders. The handling of the architectural details in this set is more refined than in Beach's Set A which he considers a decade earlier. The artist retains the heavy corbels with their pendant bosses found in Sahib Din's *ragamala* and has added Shah Jahani cusped arches linking the pillars or walls together. The lower parts of the compositions with their small niches with cusped arches, steps and pots are also derived from the school of Sahib Din, as are the niches set in the main walls containing pots and flasks. The Sirohi Master makes the architecture an even more dominant part of his composition and also enlarges his heavily modeled figures so that they all seem to burst through the confines of the picture frame into the vivid red borders. Also notable is his addition of tall trees on the side. Often as here they are composed of fan-shaped arrangements of the leaves enclosed within an overall fringe of white blossoms.[6] Other folios of this *ragamala* are in various collections.[7] | JL

1 See Ebeling 1973 pp. 92–94 for an analysis of the iconography of Sirohi *ragamalas* and Beach 2011b for an overview of their style.
2 Beach 2011b, p. 481.
3 Beach 2011b, figs. 11–13.
4 Glynn, Skelton and Dallapiccola 2011, p. 60.
5 Compare Topsfield 2002, fig. 31.
6 Compare Beach 2011b, fig. 4.
7 Williams College Museum of Art (Beach 2011b, fig. 2), Art Institute of Chicago (two folios: Beach 2011b, fig. 3, and Leach 1986, fig. 95A/Ebeling 1973, fig. 220), Cleveland Museum (Beach 2011b, fig. 4, and Leach 1986, fig. 95), Harvard Art Museums (Ebeling 1973, fig. 219) and various private collections (see Beach 2011b, p. 481).

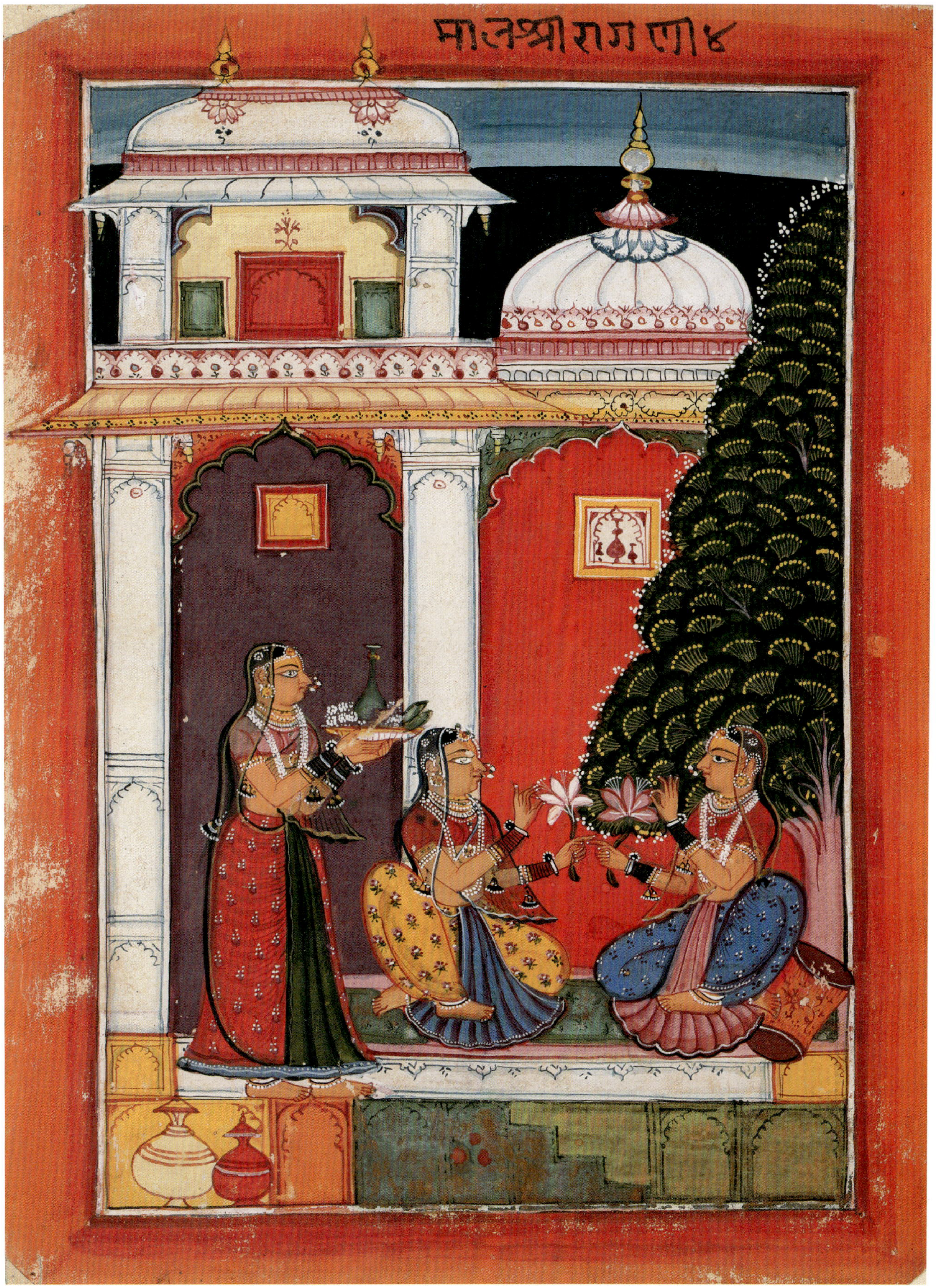
मालश्रीरागणी४

62 Dipak raga
63 Vilaval ragini

Folio from a *ragamala* series
Sirohi, c. 1690–1700
20.9 × 16 cm (folio); 18.6 × 14.4 cm (painting)
Inscribed: *Raga Dipak 19.* On verso: *Dipak raga ni ragani alakh* ("Dipak *raga* not a *ragini*")

Folio from a *ragamala* series
Sirohi, c. 1690–1700
20.7 × 14.9 cm (folio); 18.3 × 13 cm (painting)
Inscribed: *Raga Vilaval 13.* On verso: *Vilaval ragani Hindola raga ni* ("Vilaval *ragini* of Hindola *raga*")

These two paintings come from a slightly later *ragamala* from Sirohi and serve to show how quickly the initial inspiration of a master artist could become jaded in the hands of his imitators. Compared with the elegance and brilliance of Malasri *ragini* (cat. no. 61, see below), this later artist overcrowds his compositions. It is also notable how the fineness of detail seen in Malasri *ragini* has been abandoned. In Dipak *raga* (cat. no. 62) the arches are no longer even an approximation of Shah Jahani cusped arches but instead the artist plays with patterns.

The Gujarati inscriptions on the back (written in the Devanagari script rather than that used later for Gujarati) tend to

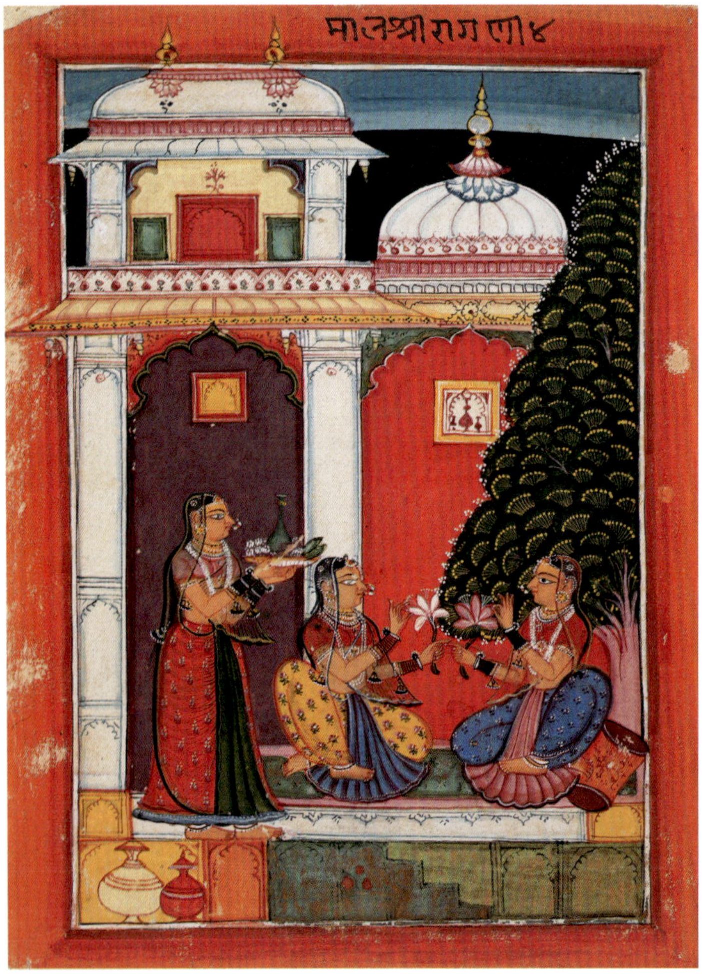

| 61

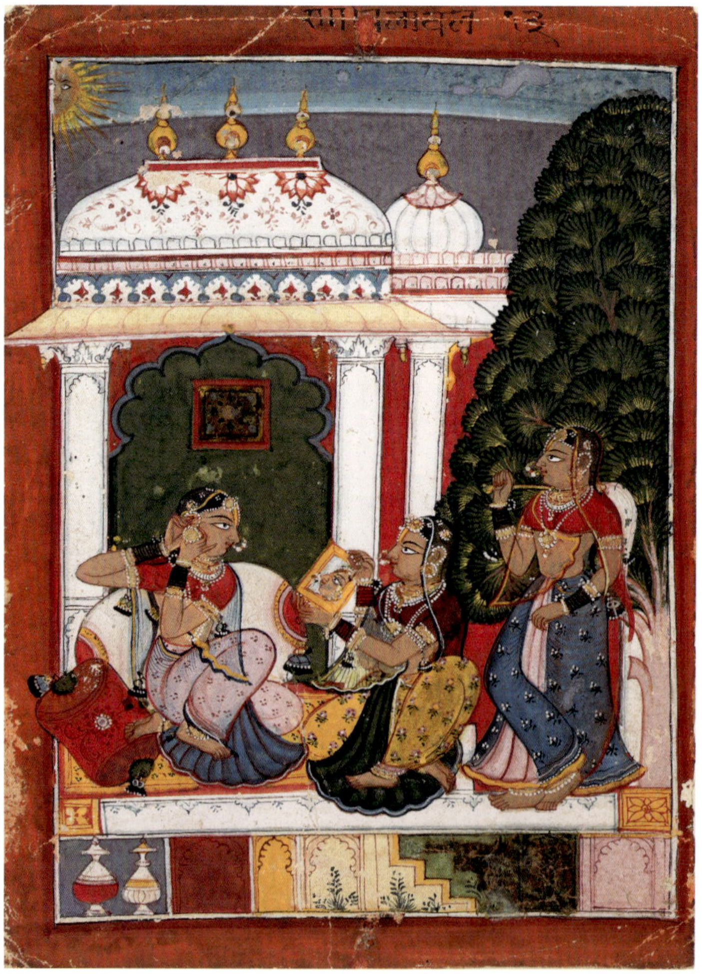

| 63

confirm the south Rajasthani provenance assigned to this school and its closeness to the Gujarati-speaking area south of Rajasthan. Another folio possibly from this set is in the Claudio Moscatelli collection, showing similar traits of overcrowding on the platform that supports the action.[1]

A *ragamala* of thirty-six verses is normally arranged in six sets, each consisting of one *raga*, thought of as male, and his five *raginis*. All the Sirohi *ragamalas* conform to the same system, normally with the same numberings. Thus Dipak is the fourth *raga*, hence numbered 19 (after three sets of six each) and Vilaval the first *ragini* of the second *raga* Hindola should be numbered 14, since Hindola is 13.[2]

The iconography of Dipak *raga* (cat. no. 62) consists of a prince with his beloved normally listening to music as here. The point of the name (*dipak* means "lamp") is that this should be happening by lamplight and here such a light is attached to the wall. The prince has his arm wrapped around his companion and both are beating time to the music played by the lady musician singing and playing her *tambura*. The latter's companion is clapping in time (her little cymbals seem to be absent). The artist made his figures so large that he ran out of space and had to push the female attendant into the left margin and the musicians off the terrace and into the right margin as well.

The iconography of Vilaval *ragini* (cat. no. 63) consists of a lady looking at herself in a mirror, here held by an attendant while the lady adjusts her earring. Another attendant stands to the right with a chowrie in her hand. It appears to be early morning as the sun has just risen and the lady is completing her toilette. Here again there is not enough room for the artist to place all his figures on the terrace. | JL

---

1 Glynn, Skelton and Dallapiccola 2011, no. 11.
2 Compare the table of Sirohi *ragamala* subjects in Ebeling 1973, p. 94.

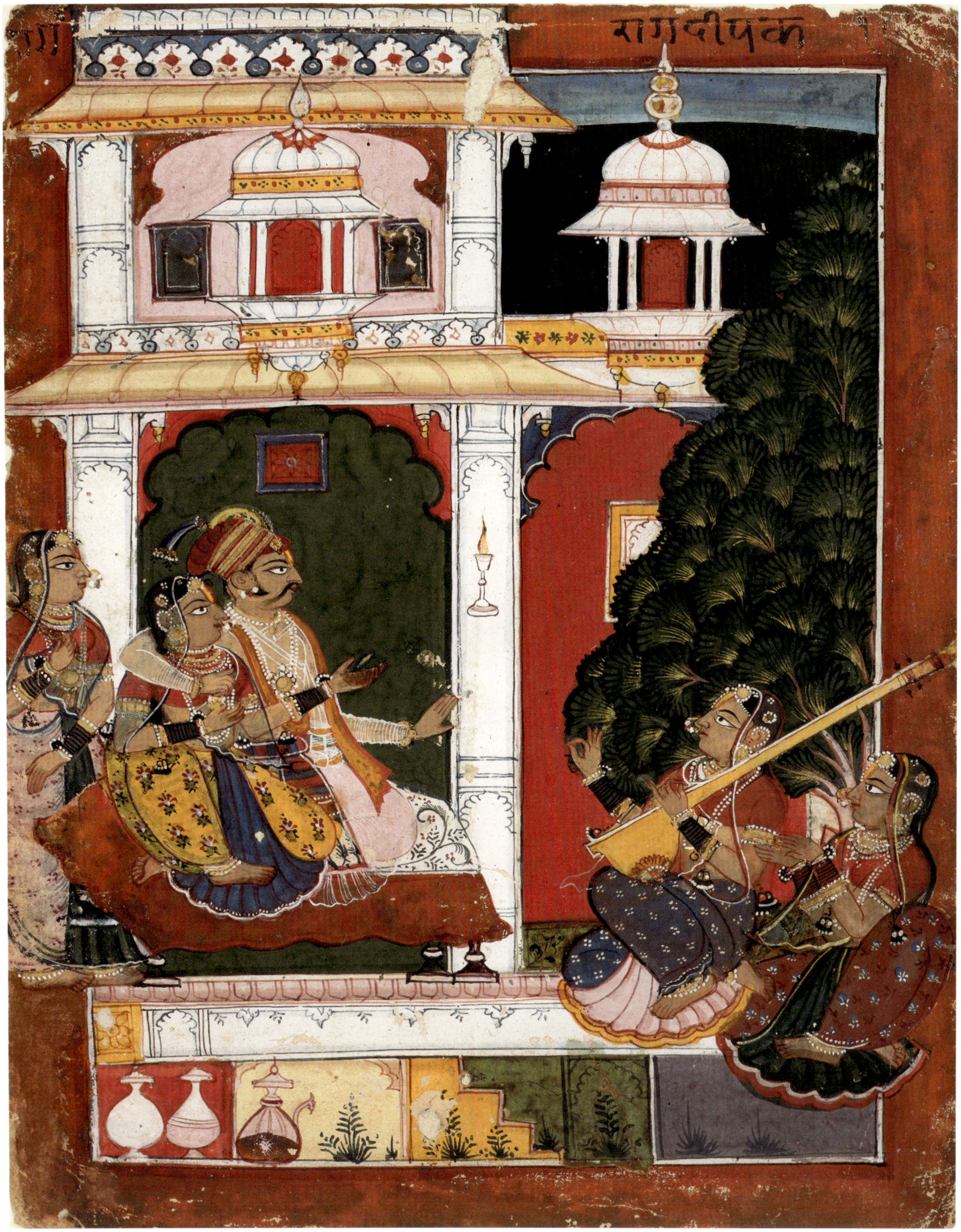
रागदीपक

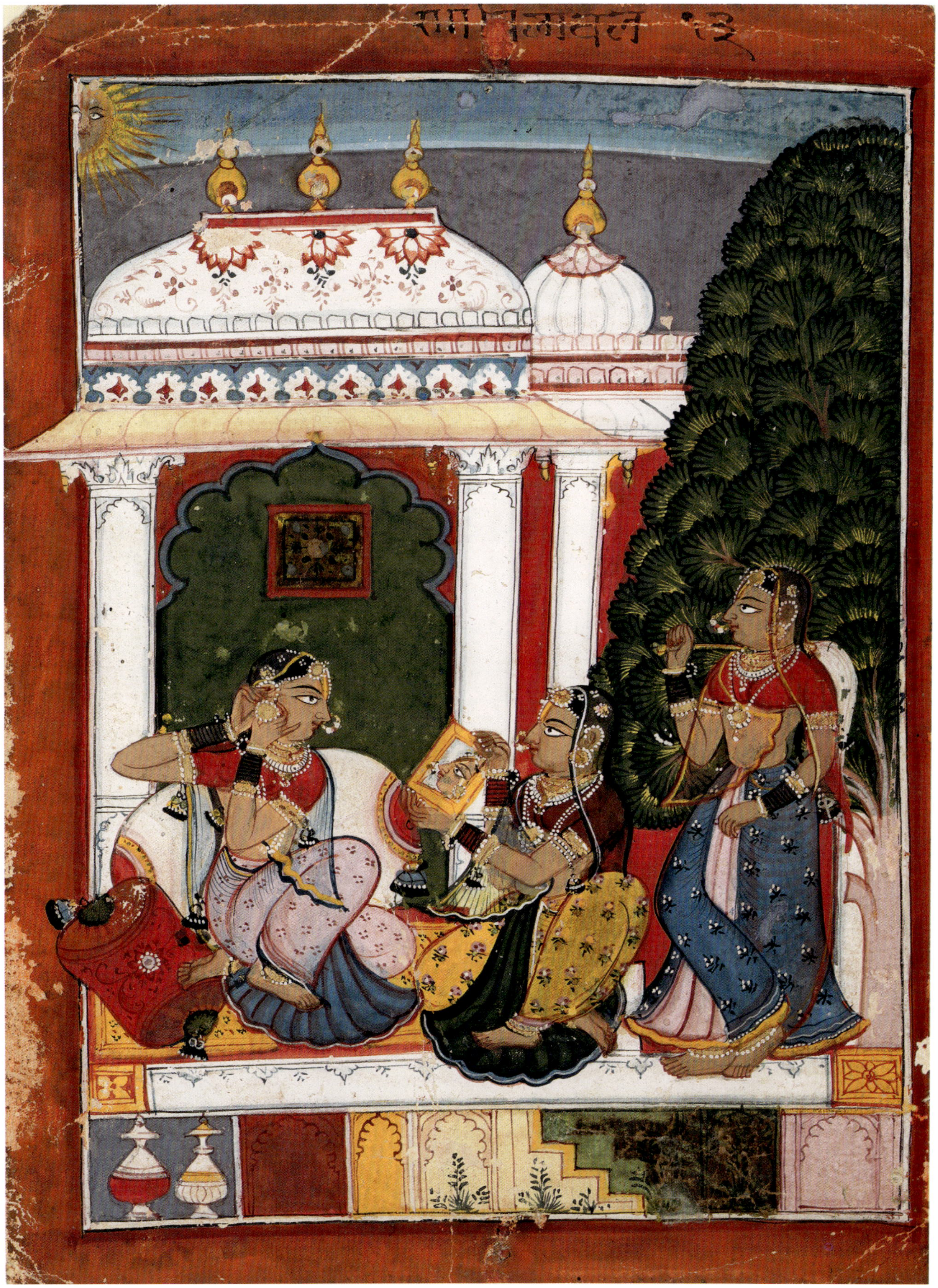

64 Kanada ragini

Folio from a *ragamala* series
Sirohi, c. 1700
27.7 × 20 cm (folio); 24.5 × 15.2 cm (painting)
Inscribed above in Devanagari: *Kanaro ghari 2 ragani 22*

Krishna stands on a terrace outside his palace holding an elephant tusk in one hand and a lotus in the other. He is attended by a chowrie-bearing lady. A well-dressed mahout (elephant-driver) with an *ankusa* (goad) over his shoulder rushes up to him raising his arm above his head in a salute. Below the elephant from which he has dismounted runs angrily at a tree while an attendant seems to be fleeing with his turban knocked askew. While Krishna is often portrayed in *ragamala* iconography, it is normally as a prince surrounded by ladies and not as part of a narrative sequence as here. Something similar occurs in a Kanada *ragini* now at Harvard[1] from the so-called "Boston *ragamala*" from Mewar, c. 1680, where the elephant required by the iconography is also running amok and Krishna has rushed up to the palace to kill the demon king who may be his demon uncle Kamsa. The basic iconography of the *ragini* seems to be a prince with an elephant tusk receiving homage, which artists had to make some sense of in pictorial terms. Sometimes the elephant appears to have his tusk just ripped out, which may be the case here as only one tusk is visible, a reference to Krishna's slaying of the elephant demon Kuvalayapida in the *Bhagavata Purana*.

While still brilliantly colored and animated, Sirohi paintings became progressively more distant from their brilliant beginnings, displaying an increasing lack of finesse. The cusped arches here have yielded to artistic fantasy. | JL

[1] Ebeling 1973, fig. 67.

Published: Cran 1980, no. 46 (not illustrated)

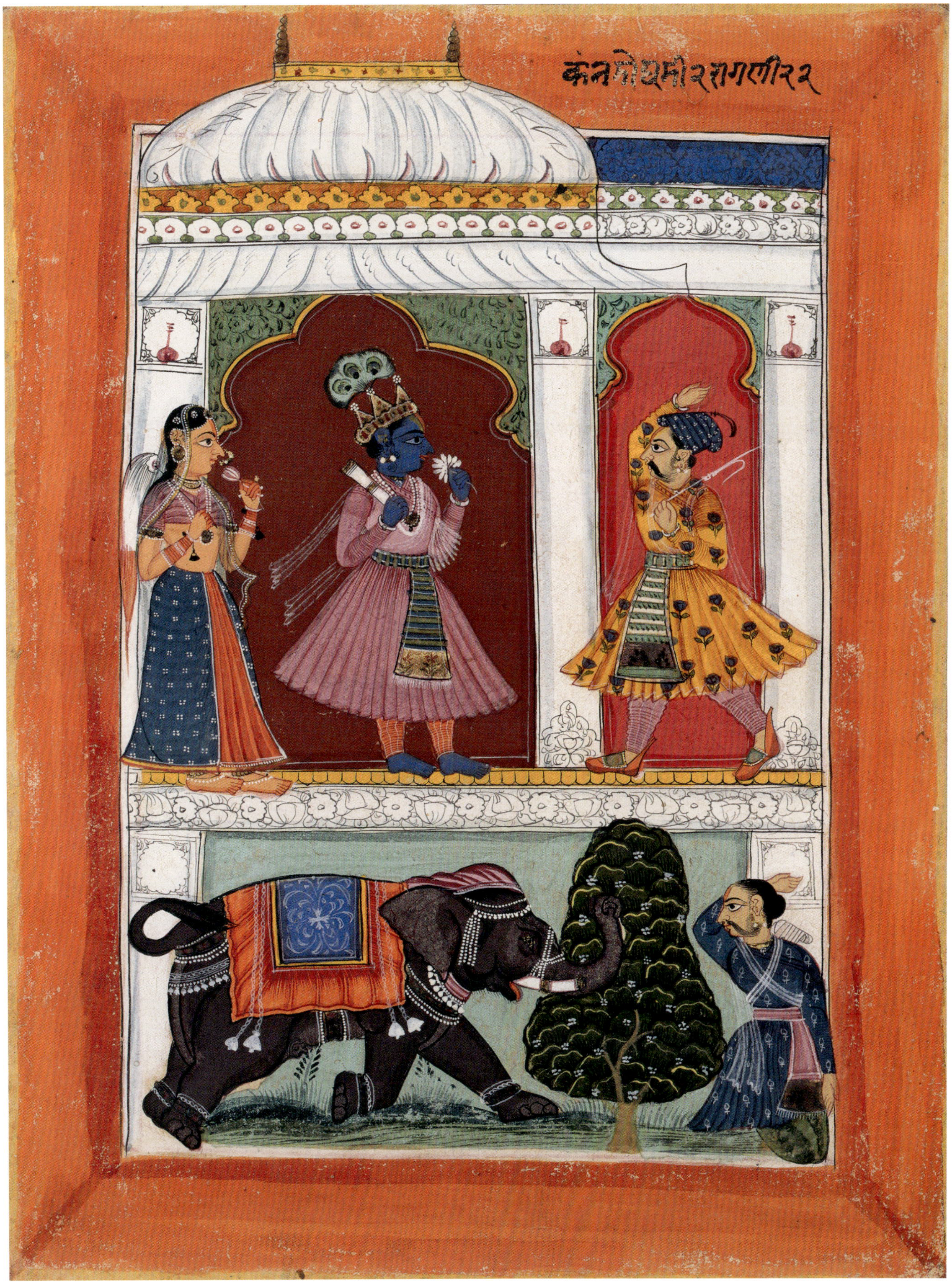

65 Rama shows his prowess
66 Rama's army of monkeys and bears build a bridge

Folio from a *Ramayana* series
Central India, Malwa, c. 1640
18.1 × 16.4 cm (average size)

Folio from a *Ramayana* series
Central India, Malwa, c. 1640
17 × 15 cm (folio)

There may be no sheen on the surfaces, the pigments might be flaking and the borders might be unfinished, but there is in these folios of the *Ramayana*[1] an intensity of feeling, and an almost instinctive understanding of *bhava* that makes them stand out. The simplicity borders on naïveté at times, but the thinking, the imagery, is startlingly abstract. Consider the painting in which Rama proves, in fact is asked to prove, his prowess (cat. no. 65). The episode occurs in the *Kishkindhakanda* of the *Ramayana*: Rama in his search for Sita lands, along with Lakshmana, in the kingdom of the *vanara* kings, Vali and Sugriva. The two brothers have fallen out; Vali, much the stronger of the two, has ousted Sugriva from his kingdom but Sugriva is far from reconciled to the situation. When, through his trusted general Hanuman – whose devotion to Rama is intense – Sugriva meets Rama, the two become friends, with Rama promising to help Sugriva regain his kingdom. But, touched as he is by this promise, Sugriva is not certain of Rama's ability to overpower Vali, not yet at least. He therefore first asks Rama, with no insolence but real concern, to prove his prowess. To give him some idea of his estranged brother Vali's incalculable strength, he narrates to him two feats of his: one, that once he was able to pierce with an arrow the trunk of a full-grown Sala tree; and second, that in a contest with the invincible bull-headed demon Dundubhi, he had killed and beheaded the demon, but so heavy was the head that nobody could lift it, and it still lay there. Hearing this, Rama is impressed, but not unduly concerned. With the calm that almost defines him, he placed an arrow on his bow, took aim, and shot it in the direction in which seven Sala trees were growing in a row. His arrow went like lightning through the trunks of all the seven trees, and then returned, magically, to his quiver. Then, locating the spot where Dundubhi's head still lay, Rama gave it a gentle nudge with his toe and the head was flung *yojanas* away. Surgriva now knew that Rama was the one who would be his savior.

The essence of this long narrative is understood by the painter in completeness. He gets everything right: the number of the trees here is exactly seven; the mountainous setting is established by piles of rocks, one atop another; Vali and Sugriva, looking identical, are seen facing each other inside the cave where the beginnings of their enmity lay, and which is neatly placed, completely open-fronted, in the very heart of the rocky mountain. The colors in the background are changed to suggest different spaces. The devices of abstraction come almost naturally to the folk artist – leaving out as much as possible, and concentrating on the core of the narrative. The painter tells the story with conviction, and in the clear belief that the viewer already knows the story: the image is only a reminder.

One encounters much the same approach in the painting where the bridge across the ocean is being built for Rama's army of *vanaras* and bears as they prepare to march towards Lanka (cat. no. 66). The preceding episode where the ocean had declined to give way to allow the armies to cross, and Rama had threatened to dry it up with the sheer heat produced by his arrow is nowhere in sight here, but the bridge is. The text of the Valmiki *Ramayana* is filled with animated passages about the energy with which the project was executed under the expert supervision of the engineer, Nala. The monkeys "filled the ocean with all types of trees like Sala and Asvakarna, Dhava and bamboo, Kutaja, Arujuns, palmyra, Tilaka, Tinisa, Bilva, Saptaparna, Karnika;" they, "the huge bodied monkeys with mighty strength uprooted elephant-sized rocks and mountains and transported them" to the spot; some others "drew up strings a hundred *yojanas* long in order to keep the rocks in a straight line," and so on. Rama and Lakshmana watched this great engineering feat with satisfaction while the monkeys and bears shouted with delight, "taking long leaps and short leaps" in the air, even as "all others saw the construction of that bridge across the ocean as unimaginable, impossible and wonderful, causing their hair to stand on end in amazement."[2]

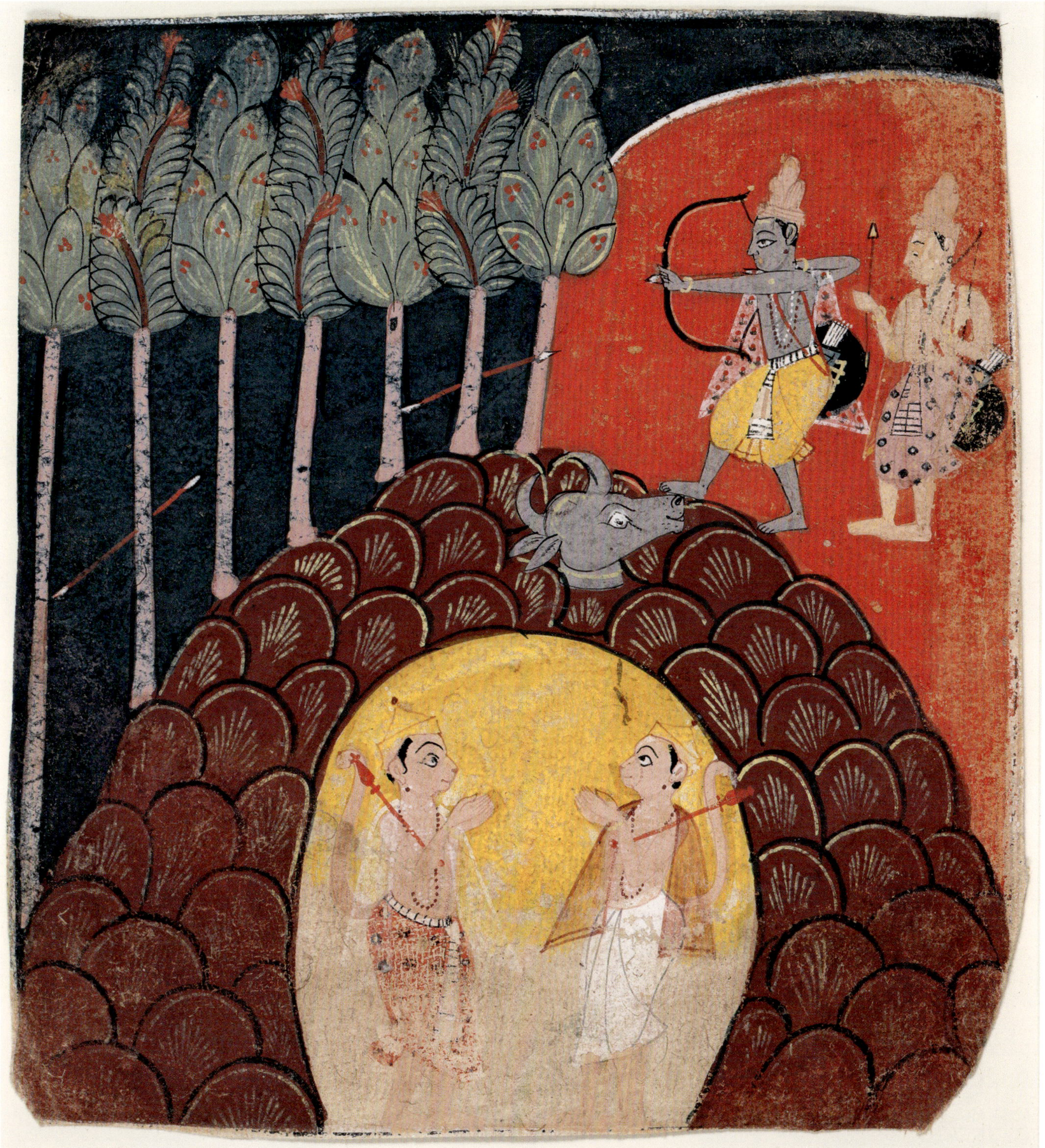

As the painter renders it, one sees the ocean split up, one stream of water – a broad stripe of white and blue, diagonally placed – pushed to nearly one end of the page, and the other – a similar broad stripe – pushed towards the bottom. The text speaks of "a colossal bridge, which was broad, well-constructed, glorious, well postured and held together firmly," which "looked beautiful like a separating straight line in the ocean." Between these two, in any case, where the dry strip of land – the bridge – is now clearly visible, all figures are seen: not hundreds and thousands of monkeys and bears as the text says, but a few, representing all those not to be seen here. Rama is there, and so is Lakshmana, the former crouching at the foot of a small rocky mound. One does not even see it at first but Rama is performing a ceremony: bowing before a *linga* of Shiva, which he has anointed with three ashen horizontal lines, he is seeking the Lord's blessings before embarking upon his assault on Lanka. This ceremony, one notices, is not mentioned in Valmiki's text, but it must have been so much a part of folk belief – Rama's worship of a Shiva-*linga* – that the painter brought it in, almost as a matter of course. Meanwhile, on either shore of the ocean, some trees stand, perhaps those that the army of monkeys and bears had not yet uprooted.

Once again, it is all very simply, but truly effectively, stated. One might find the line wanting and the colors a bit fragile, but there is sophistication of thought here and so much boldness. | BG

---

1 Most of the folios from this series are kept at the Bharat Kala Bhavan in Varanasi, see Poster 1994, p. 188.
2 The relevant episodes are found in Sarga 22 of the *Yuddhakanda*.

Published: Britschgi and Fischer 2008, nos. 42 and 70

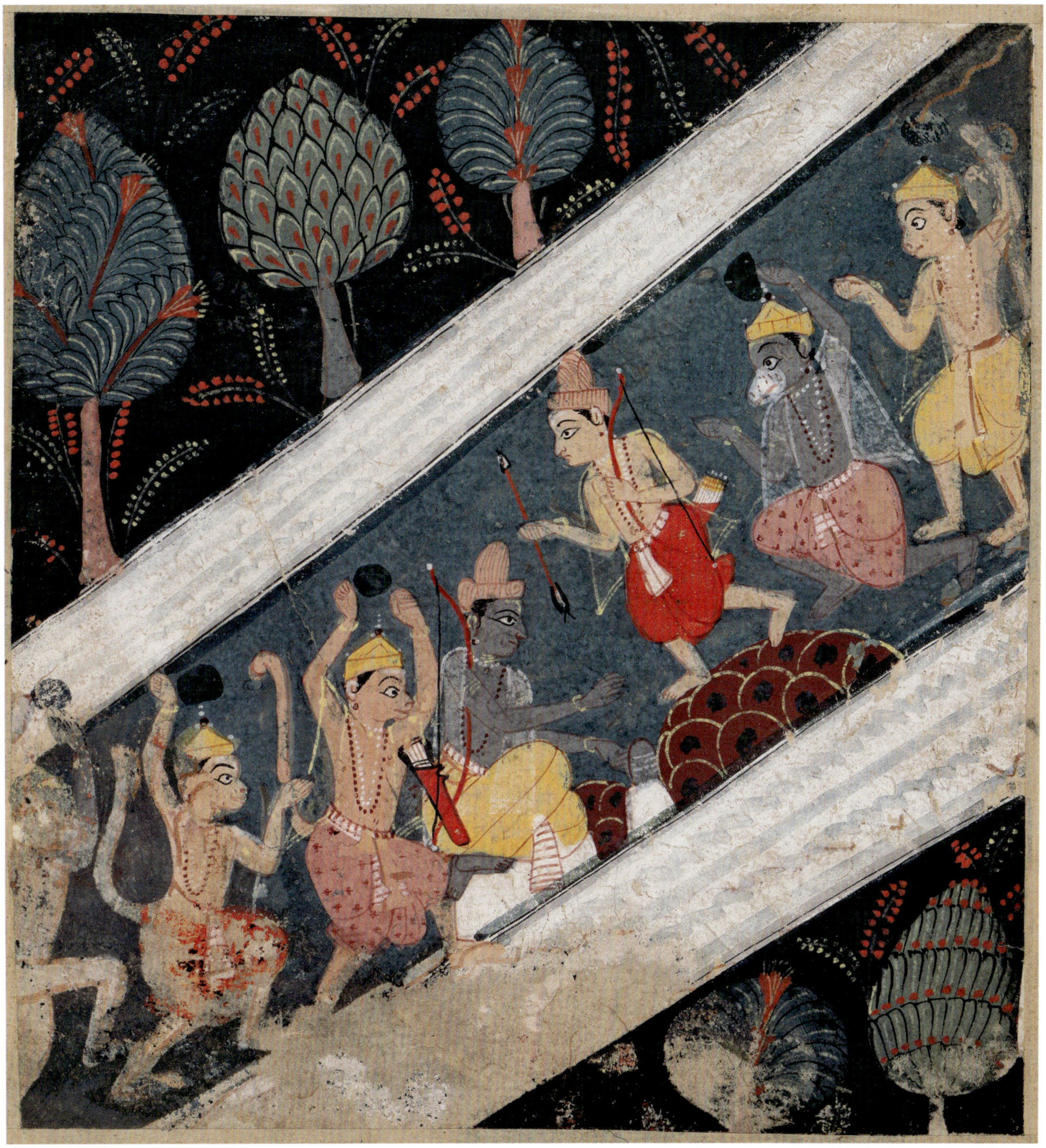

67 The sakhi seeks out Krishna

Folio from a *Rasikapriya* series
Central India, perhaps Malwa, c. 1640
20.4 × 17.6 cm (folio); 18 × 15 cm (painting)
Numbered 18 above and inscribed on the back in Hindi in Devanagari script with verses numbered 18 from the *Rasikapriya* of Kesavadasa[1]

Kesavadasa's *Rasikapriya* was composed in the late 16th century at the court of Orchha in Bundelkhand. It is the most complete of the Hindi texts on the classifications of heroes and heroines and was one of the staple texts of the various Rajput schools for illustration. The hero or *nayaka* and the heroine or *nayika* are often identified in the text and in the paintings based on them as Krishna and Radha. The *sakhi* or confidante acts as a go-between conveying the emotions and wishes of the two lovers to each other.

In this painting the *sakhi* confronts Krishna with her mistress Radha's words that they must part since her love makes her suffer excessively, and Krishna looks suitably downcast. He is dressed in contemporary costume with a jaunty feather in his turban and is seated on a plinth erected between the two flowering trees. A deer prances on either side while two monkeys gambol in the trees above the scene, in contrast to the seriousness of interview going on below them. A very similar image from the same series numbered 255 on the front is in the Cynthia Polsky collection.[2]

Malwa, the upland plateau south-east of Mewar and Kota, is actually a term that defines a style rather than denotes a place of origin. The style is instantly recognizable and definitely from Central India but its few known geographical links are to courts that are outside of Malwa such as Bundelkhand (e.g. cat. nos. 70–73) or in the case of a dated *ragamala* of 1680 to Narsinghgarh, north-east of Malwa proper.[3] Malwa is one of the Rajput schools that had little or no truck with Mughal naturalism and retained direct connections both to the Early Rajput style and to earlier Sultanate painting at Mandu (the former capital of the Muslim Sultanate of Malwa) and elsewhere. In the earliest style there is a total lack of depth and the vividly colored and completely flat figures interact with one another through gestures and eye-glances. Architecture and trees are likewise completely flat and conceptual. Only later in the 17th century do the artists try to come to terms with spatial depth and volume in their paintings.

There are few dated documents in the style. The *Rasikapriya* of 1634 (the bulk of which is in the National Museum, New Delhi)[4] is the earliest, where the text is inscribed on yellow bands above and below the paintings. The present painting is from a slightly later version of the same text, now widely dispersed, with the text written on the back.[5] Narrow yellow bands at top and bottom frame the scene. Figures and architecture are silhouetted against a yellow or deep blue ground with the suggestion of a cloudy sky along the top. | JL

1 This verse illustrates a *prachanna-viyoga* or "open parting". In the *Kesava-granthavali*, ed. V.P. Misra, vol. 1, p. 4, this is verse number 25 of chapter 1: "O fan me not with breezes cool and keep the moon's soft light away, For these my pleasures have removed and sorrowful have made my days. Scatter the flowers, dust camphor off from me, this sandal me afflicts, A dying fish from water cast can be by water saved – not milk! My suffering do you comprehend? Or knowing not, you tend my pain? Who by this fire is burned, my friend, is by that same fire cooled again!" (translated Bahadur 1972, pp. 6–7).

2 Topsfield 2004, no. 61, Christie's, London, 24 April 1980, lot 155.

3 Khandalavala 1950, fig. 24; Binney and Archer 1968, pp. 52–53.

4 Krishna A. 1963, pls. 10–11.

5 For other pages from this series see Bautze 1991, nos. 56–58 (now Museum Rietberg, Horst Metzger collection); Mason 2001, no. 21, and references cited above.

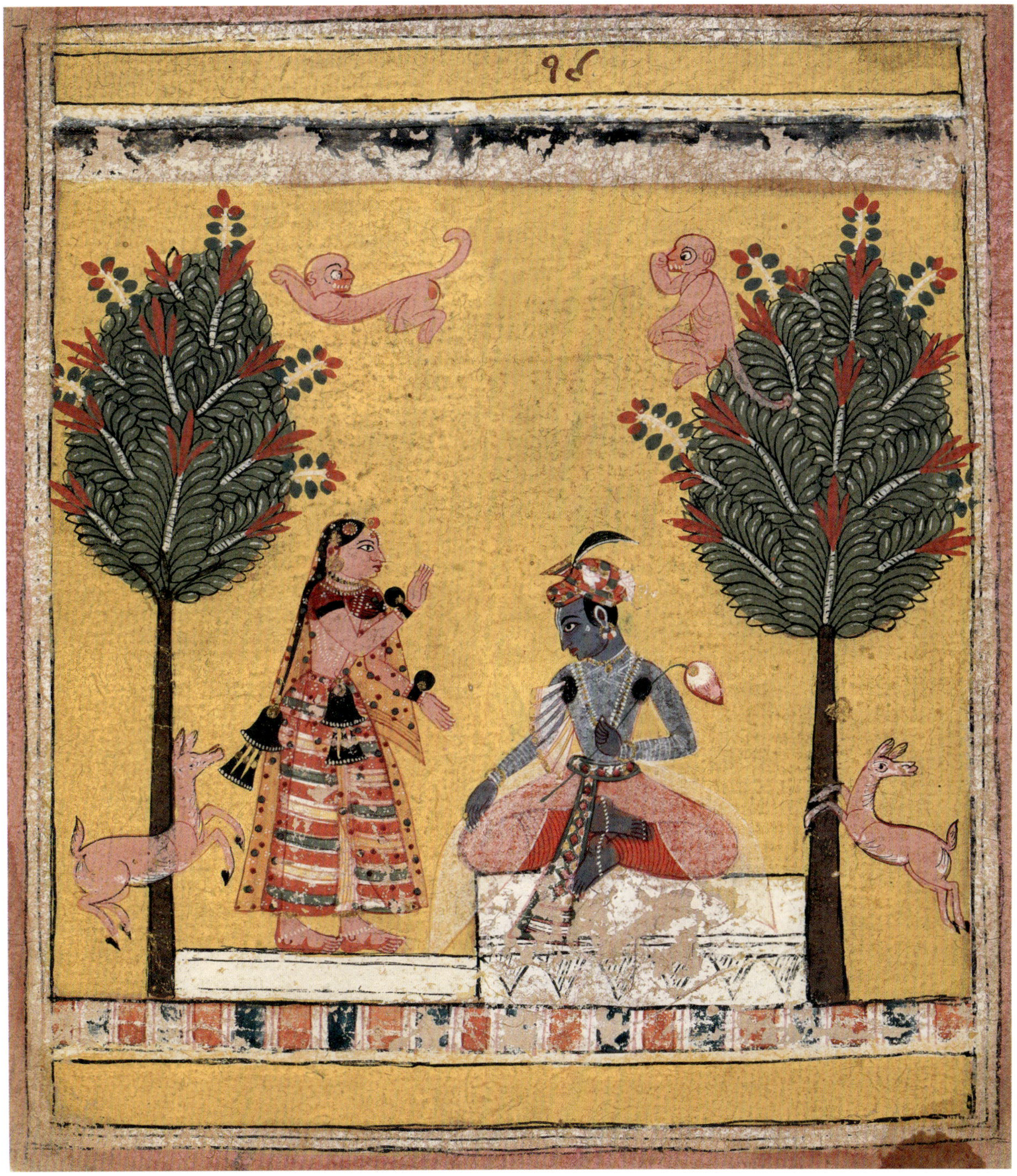

68 The lover attempts to appease his mistress with his tears

Folio from an *Amarushataka* series
Central India, perhaps Malwa, c. 1660
19.5 × 13.6 cm (folio)
Inscribed above in Sanskrit in Devanagari with verse 39 from the *Amarushataka:* "'Slender woman. Drop your silence! Look! At your feet I am bowed. Never was your anger such as this.' Her husband declared, eyes cast down. One huge droplet her eye released, nothing said."[1]

The *nayaka* is attempting to appease his thoroughly annoyed mistress. He leans forward, all ardent eagerness, his hand on her upper arm, but she restrains him with one hand and turns her face away hiding it with her veil. The couple are hunkered down within their pavilion and their posture allows us to see the artist's brilliant control of line with which he is able to express the volume of their bodies. Like others in these series the architecture is a simple elevation and the top and bottom bands of the folio are occupied by the text panel and floral scrolls and palmettes. Within the generally subdued color range of dull reds, ochres and greens, the brilliant blue of the hero's turban strikes an aggressively ardent note. The extended whites of his eyes suggest his tearfulness and sincerity, but she is turning away. The Sanskrit is ambiguous as to whose eyes are cast down and who is crying. The artist seems to have interpreted it to mean that the *nayaka* is the one with the tears forming while the *nayika*'s eyes are cast down, but she has turned away trying to hide the smile that is forming on her lips.

The *Amarushataka* is a collection of Sanskrit lyric verses, traditionally 100 or a *shataka* (century) but more have accumulated, whose subject is erotic love in all its manifestations. The author Amaru is otherwise unknown but is thought to have lived in the 7th or 8th century. As with *ragamalas* and *Rasikapriyas* there are several series of the *Amarushataka* from Central India in this period, which differ only slightly from each other in their marginal rulings, size and scroll bands at the base.[2] One series is tentatively dated to 1652 and from an obscure place named Nasratgarh.[3] Here, the verse and composition are the same as in one of the pages in the collection of the Museum Rietberg, which is in a slightly smaller format, but manages to include a tree to one side and a peacock on the roof of the pavilion.[4] | JL

1 The inscription is somewhat rubbed and illegible in places. Translation by Greg Bailey, in Bailey and Gombrich 2005, p. 233.
2 For other paintings from these series, see Khandalavala 1950, fig. 20; Heeramaneck 1984, pls. 30–31 (now private collection and National Gallery of Canada), Pal 1978, no. 10 (miscalled Mewar), Bautze 1991, nos. 79–80 (now Museum Rietberg, Horst Metzger collection), Dye 2001, no. 127, and Christie's, London, 16 October 1980, lot 216.
3 Mehta 1935, p. 147.
4 See Bautze 1991, no. 79.

Published: Christie's, London, 16 October 1980, lot 217

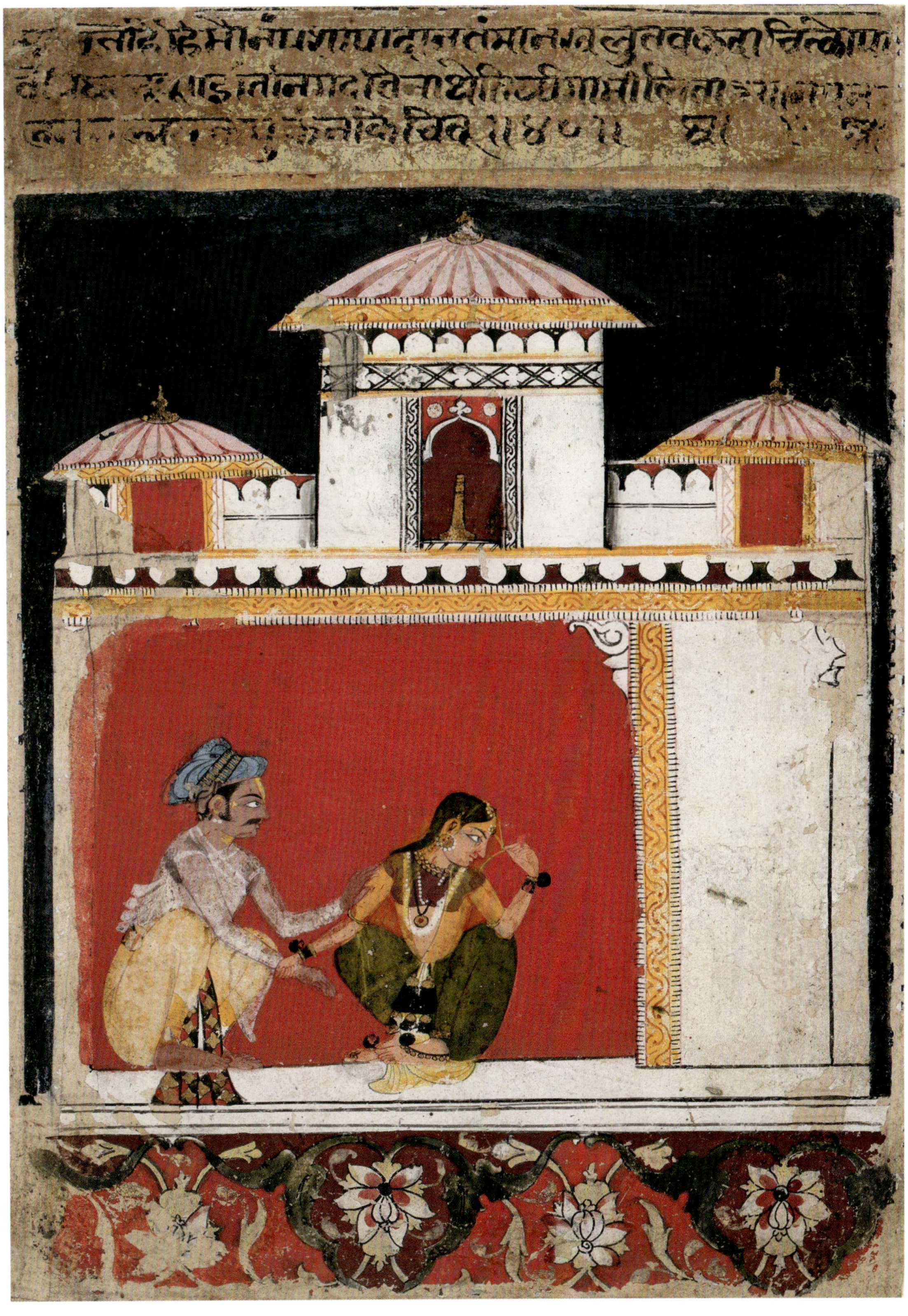

69 The gopis lament their separation from Krishna

Folio from a *Bhagavata Purana* series
Central India, 1650–1660
22.6 × 36 cm (folio); 20 × 33.8 cm (painting)
Inscribed on the verso with four verses in Hindi in *doha* metre from the beginning of chapter 31 of the tenth book of the *Bhagavata Purana*, labeled leaf 54

In the previous chapter of the *Bhagavata Purana*, Krishna, almost overpowered from the attentions of the *gopis* seeking his favor, has vanished from their midst. The girls wander along the banks of the Jumna and through the woods of Vrindavan calling for him and asking the various trees and creepers whether they have seen their vanished love. In this chapter they sing of their love for him and they praise him. Krishna eventually solves his dilemma by dancing with each and every one of them simultaneously, through his divine power making each *gopi* think she is dancing with him alone. Here, this large and beautiful page can illustrate either chapter 30 or 31 if the verses are taken to refer to the painting opposite when the manuscript is open, rather than to what is on the other side of the folio. The *gopis* in four groups are wandering or sitting among the flowering trees of the groves of Vrindavan, asking each other and then the various trees where Krishna has disappeared to. The scene is divided into two registers separated by a white line. The brilliantly clothed girls stand out against the deep blue ground favored in this painting style, apart from a group of three seated girls who are highlighted against a red ground framed by the trees. Though the *Bhagavata Purana* nowhere mentions Radha, to artists of the 17th century she would have been very much in the forefront of their mind when illustrating the Krishna legends and they honored her in this traditional way.[1]

This page comes from neither of the better known series of the *Bhagavata Purana* from Central India, one from the late 17th century or the other around 1700.[2] Both those are highly stylized and conceptual in their approach, with squat, almost folk-like figures, and are often divided into three registers as in the page in the British Museum illustrating the same episode of the *gopis* searching for Krishna.[3] Our tall and elegant *gopis* on the contrary seem related to those in series of the 1650s and 1660s, as do the generally slender trees.[4] Another page from this series, illustrating Krishna slaying the demonic Putana, is in the Norton Simon Museum, Pasadena, likewise divided horizontally by a broad white stripe.[5] | JL

1 Compare with Ehnbom 2011 for the depictions of Krishna similarly silhouetted against red in the dispersed Early Rajput *Bhagavata Purana* series.
2 For the first series see Dye 2001, no. 133, for examples from the second one see Dye 2001, no. 134; Binney and Archer 1968, no. 48; Pal 1978, no. 26.
3 Ahluwalia 2008, no. 72.
4 Dye 2001, no. 129; Heeramaneck 1984, pls. 20–27.
5 Pal 2004, no. 26.

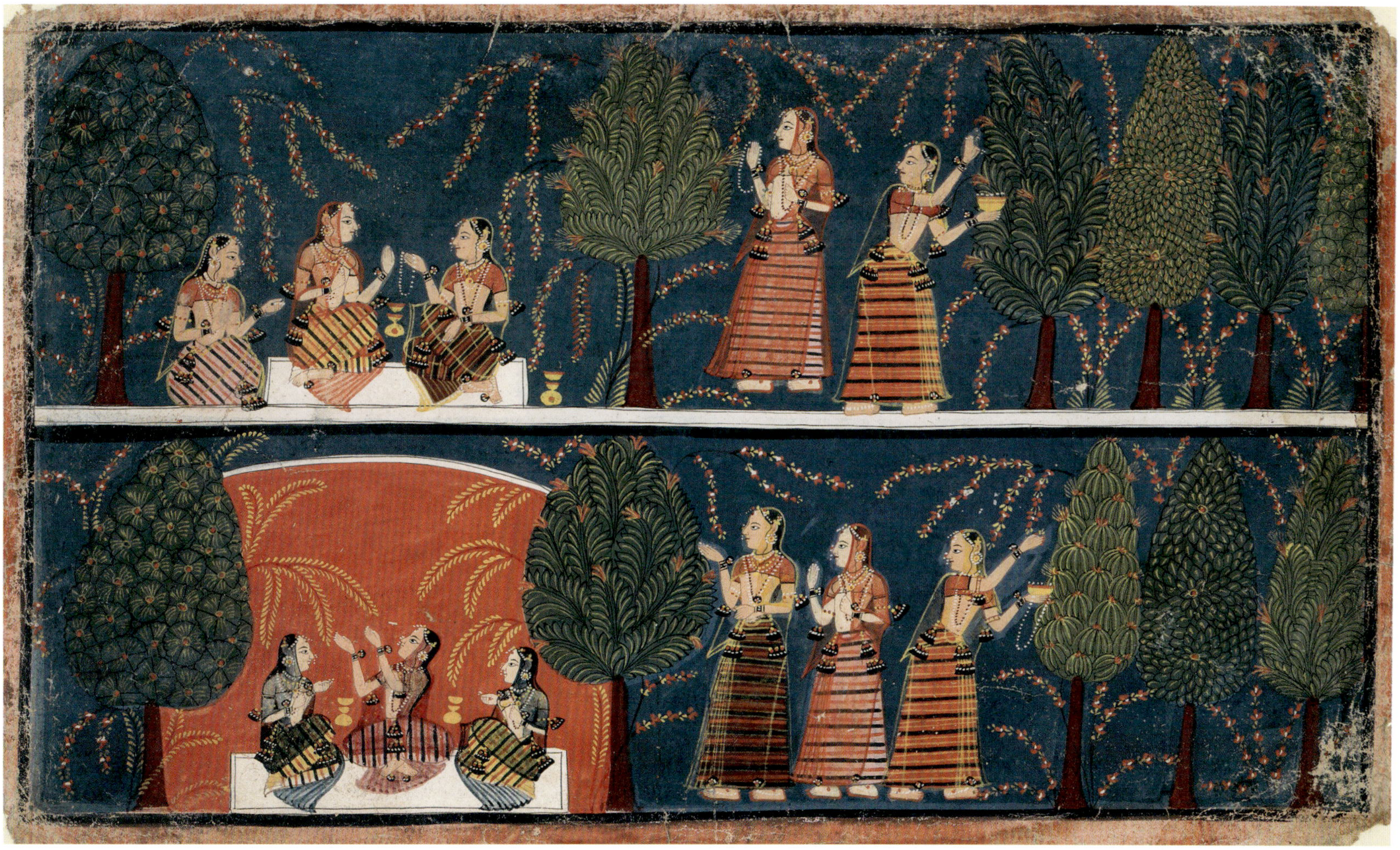

70–73 Lalita, Malava, Gujari and Suddhamalara ragini

Four folios from a *ragamala* series
Bundelkhand, Mahewa or Panna, c. 1680–1700
23.5 × 17 cm (average folio size); 21.5 × 15 cm (average painting size)
Each inscribed on the verso with the relevant verse from Lacchman Das's *ragamala* text in Braj-bhasha Hindi and a brief Persian caption.
Apparently commissioned by Raja Chattar Sal of Mahewa and his son Kunvar Bharti Chand

70 Lalita *ragini*
Inscribed verso: *Lalita ragini Sri raga ki*, followed by the relevant *doha* of Lacchman Das's Hindi *ragamala* text and the number 34.[1]
Below in Persian: *ragini Lalita az Dipak raga*.
Below in a finer and more regular hand: *Sri Maharajadhiraja sri Maharaja sri Raja Chatra Sal ju dev ye te sri Maharaja Kaumara sri Divan Bharathi Canda ju dev kan vancyaum apara sri phukemxx* (the last part is obscure: the writer has added unnecessary *anusvara*s or nasalizations and arbitrarily lengthened vowels but the inscription can be interpreted as meaning "at the command of Maharaja Chattar Sal and his son Divan Bharti Cand, may unlimited fortune be theirs[?]").

71 Malava *ragini*
Inscribed verso: *Malava ragini Dipak ko*, followed by the relevant *doha* of Lacchman Das's Hindi *ragamala* text and the number 21.[2]
Below in Persian: *ragini Malava az Dipak raga*.

72 Gujari *ragini*
Inscribed verso: *Gujari ragini Sri raga ki*, followed by the relevant *doha* of Lacchman Das's Hindi *ragamala* text and the number 33.[3]
Below in Persian: *ragini Gujara az Sri raga*.
Below in a finer and more regular hand: *Sri Maharaja Kaumara Divan Mauhan Singh ju dev*.

73 Suddhamalara *ragini*
Inscribed verso: *Suddhamalar ragini Dipak raga ki*, followed by the relevant *doha* of Lacchman Das's Hindi *ragamala* text and the number 29.[4]
Below in Persian: *Mallar az Dipak raga*.

The important inscription on the reverse of Lalita *ragini* (cat. no. 70, a reproduction of it can be found at the end of this entry) gives us some precious information about the provenance and patronage of Central Indian painting. Normally called simply Malwa painting, this is a misnomer (as Robert Cran pointed out in 1980) that links together separate areas of painting. Malwa (now south-west Madhya Pradesh) is the upland province south-east of Rajasthan, but the inscription links the set to the more northerly province of Bundelkhand (now northern Madhya Pradesh). This was historically the domain of the Rajas of Orchha, who rose to prominence under Rudra Pratap, the first Raja of Orchha (r. 1501–1531) in the wake of Babur's invasion of Hindustan in 1526. His descendant Raja Bir Singh Deo (r. 1605–1627) was an ally of Akbar's son Salim, even going so far as to have Abu'l Fazl, Akbar's friend and historiographer, whom Salim hated, murdered in 1602. When Salim succeeded as Jahangir, Bir Singh Deo rose high in imperial favor, and was able to build the great palace at Orchha.

The apparent patron of this *ragamala* series, Raja Chattar Sal, was descended from Raja Rudra Pratap of Orchha through one of his younger sons, Kunvar Udayajit Singh, who became Raja of Mahewa in eastern Bundelkhand. His descendant as Raja of Mahewa was our Raja Chattar Sal (1649–1731), who led the Bundelas in revolt against the Mughal Emperor Aurangzeb in 1671. With the help of the Marathas under Baji Rao I, the Maratha Peshwa from 1720 to 1740, he eventually established his rule over most of what is now known as Bundelkhand. At some stage he moved his capital from Mahewa to Panna. He had twenty-two legitimate sons and an even larger number of illegitimate ones. After his death his lands were divided between the Maratha Peshwa Baji Rao, who received a third of his dominions, and his sons. Panna went to Hirde Sah (r. 1731–1739). One of his younger sons, Kunvar Dewan Bharti Chand, who is also named in our inscription, became Raja of Jaso (r. 1732–1750), further to the east of Panna. Another son, Kunvar Dewan Mohan Singh, is named on the verso of cat. no. 72. The inscriptions referring to Chattar Sal and his sons are couched in the Bundelkhandi dialect of Hindi. The reference to two of the sons as Dewans or ministers suggests that this inscription cannot have been added much before 1700.

The style of this *ragamala* points to a date near the end of the 17th century. It is less refined than the earlier sets such as the *Amarushataka* (cat. no. 68) and also less vigorous than for instance the dispersed *Rasikapriya* of c. 1640 (cat. no. 67). The figures have lost the elegance of the mid-century styles and become somewhat squat. Less attention is paid to the details of architecture, although they conform for the most part to the traditional rendering of flat elevations topped by *chattris* and domes. The artist has experimented in places so that the architecture has become almost unreadable, for example in the pavilion in Lalita *ragini*, which also has large flowering plants along the bottom tier. These, like the scalloped arch in Suddhamalara *ragini*, show the influence of Shah Jahani painting and architecture. The bottom layer of the painting is no longer occupied by floral scrolls and palmettes. In all these respects it closely resembles an almost complete set in the National Museum, New Delhi, called Malwa c. 1690 by Ebeling.[5] On the other hand, the set differs from the *ragamala* from

Narsinghgarh of 1680[6] in which the figures are still relatively tall and elegant and the bottom floral scroll is sometimes present. The text is common to several *ragamalas* of the Central Indian tradition.[7] The full text of Lacchman Das's *ragamala* comprises a series of lengthy verses mostly in *caupai* metre, followed by a succinct summary of the painting's subject in *doha* metre. In this series only the latter is inscribed.

Lalita *ragini* (cat. no. 70) shows a disconsolate lady lying on her bed in her chamber. Her attendant attempts to console her as her lover is leaving her. He is walking off carrying a garland in each hand and looking back at a black buck which stands before the lady's pavilion amidst flowering plants. The lover leaving his beloved in the morning is the usual iconography for Lalita, but the deer is unusual and seems to have strayed in from Todi, where a deer is the only companion and consolation for an abandoned mistress. The artist has tried something different to the usual background seen in this style of a flat architectural elevation and has attempted to produce an almost three-dimensional building, but the complexities of the perspective seem to have defeated him.

In Malava *ragini* (cat. no. 71), a prince is about to embrace a lady seated in a pavilion while an attendant stands nearby with a *morchhal*. The elongated trees on the left shoot up towards the inky black sky. The iconography of Malava fits, which often shows a prince leading a lady towards a bedchamber. The artist here reverts to the traditional architectural elevation and rendition of trees known in this style.

Gujari *ragini* (cat. no. 72) is visualized as a girl with her hands raised above her head and seated in an elaborate pavilion. A female attendant fans her. Branches of flowering creepers emerging from the tall trees on the left of the pavilion bend their heads in sympathy as the rain falls upon them from the black clouds above. Again the artist uses traditional renderings of the building's elevation and of the trees. Klaus Ebeling writes that in "Malwa" *ragamala* iconography, Gujari is regularly confused with Desvarati *ragini*,[8] which is elsewhere a lady with her arms above her head. But in one of the few complete *ragamalas* from Central India, that in the Bharat Kala Bhavan, Varanasi, the two are quite distinct, Desvarati being number 15, a lady with a man approaching holding a lotus,[9] and Gujari being number 33 with the same iconography as here and inscribed with the longer version of Lachhman Das's verses. The composition of our painting fits the verse perfectly well. A similar iconography to our version from the "Boston" *ragamala* is also inscribed Gujari.[10]

The fourth folio from this series, Suddhamalara *ragini* (cat. no. 73), shows a female ascetic sitting with a *tambura* on a tiger skin by a little tank outside her pavilion. A mango tree towers over her with a peacock in its branches entranced by the rain falling from the heavens. Suddhamalar or Setmalar *ragini* is meant to be sung in the rainy season. The *ragini* has become tired of waiting for her lover and disguised herself as a male ascetic to wait for him. The absent lover is identified in the verse with the *raga* of her group, Megha. Setmalar or Mallar is number 29 in the c. 1650 Malwa *ragamala* in the Bharat Kala Bhavan in Varanasi, linked to Megha and also with Megha in another almost complete Malwa *ragamala* of c. 1680 in the same institution.[11] Our scribe seems to be out on his own when linking Setmalar to Dipak *raga*. | JL

1 Text E and F in Ebeling 1973, pp. 132–136. As translated by Coomaraswamy: "A tiger hero, swaggering and truculent, seeming to be the slave of love. Who can tell when he returns, roaring like an elephant" (cited Ebeling 1973, p. 136).
2 Text E and F in Ebeling 1973, pp. 132–136. The verse describes how the lover approaches his mistress in the evening.
3 Text E and F in Ebeling 1973, pp. 132–136: "She is to some extent self-content while partially anxious as she has left her abode." Lacchman Das says (she is anxious) "whether her hero will come or not" (translation by Rai Krishnadas, cited in Ebeling 1973, p. 134).
4 Text E and F in Ebeling 1973, pp. 132–136: "She is an extremely helpless woman and tender and has fallen prey to separation incarnate. Her peace of mind is drained out, she is eager for the company of Megh Mallar" (translation by Rai Krishnadas, cited in Ebeling 1973, p. 136).
5 Ebeling 1973, no. 33 illustrates Varari *ragini*, a close parallel to cat. no. 70; also Krishna A. 1963, pl. 20.
6 Khandalavala 1950, figs. 24–25.
7 Ebeling 1973, pp. 132–136.
8 Ebeling 1973, p. 173.
9 Ebeling 1973, fig. 198.
10 Ebeling 1973, fig. 46.
11 For the first one see Ebeling 1973, p. 173, and no. 32, for the latter one Ebeling 1973, p. 179.

Published: Cran 1980, no. 42 (Lalita *ragini*, not illustrated); Cran 1980, no. 41 and front cover (Malava *ragini*); Cran 1980, no. 43 (Suddhamalara *ragini*, not illustrated)

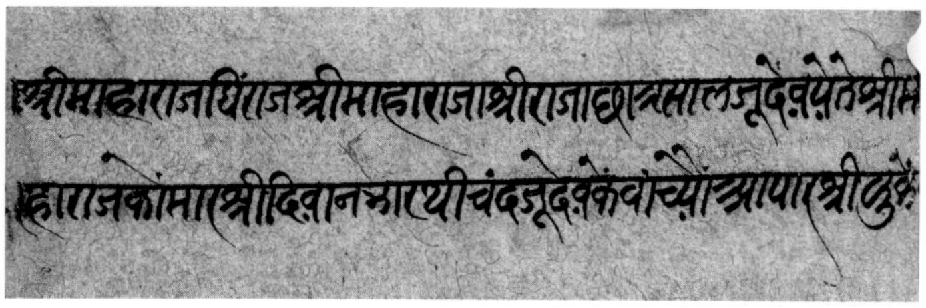

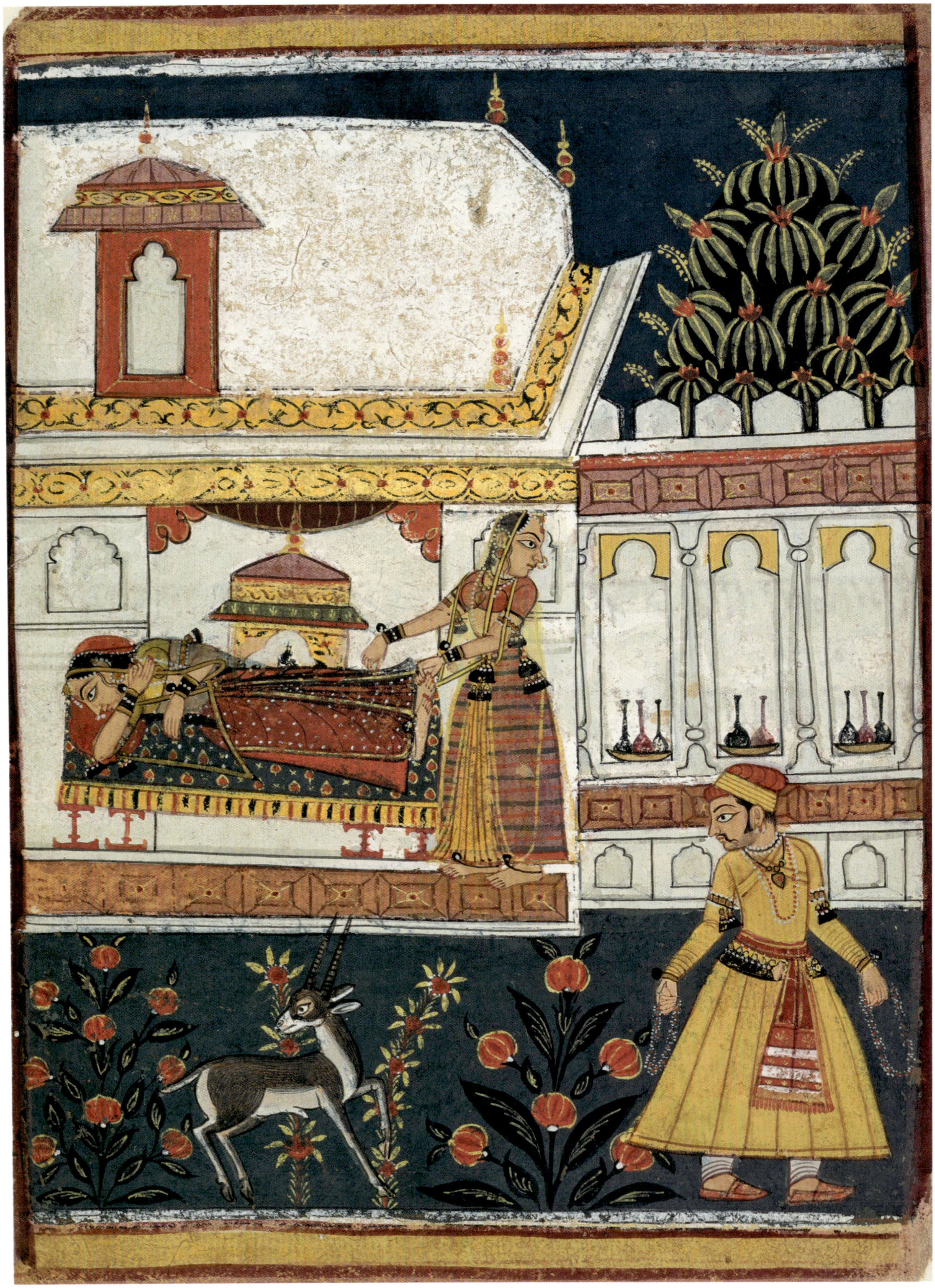

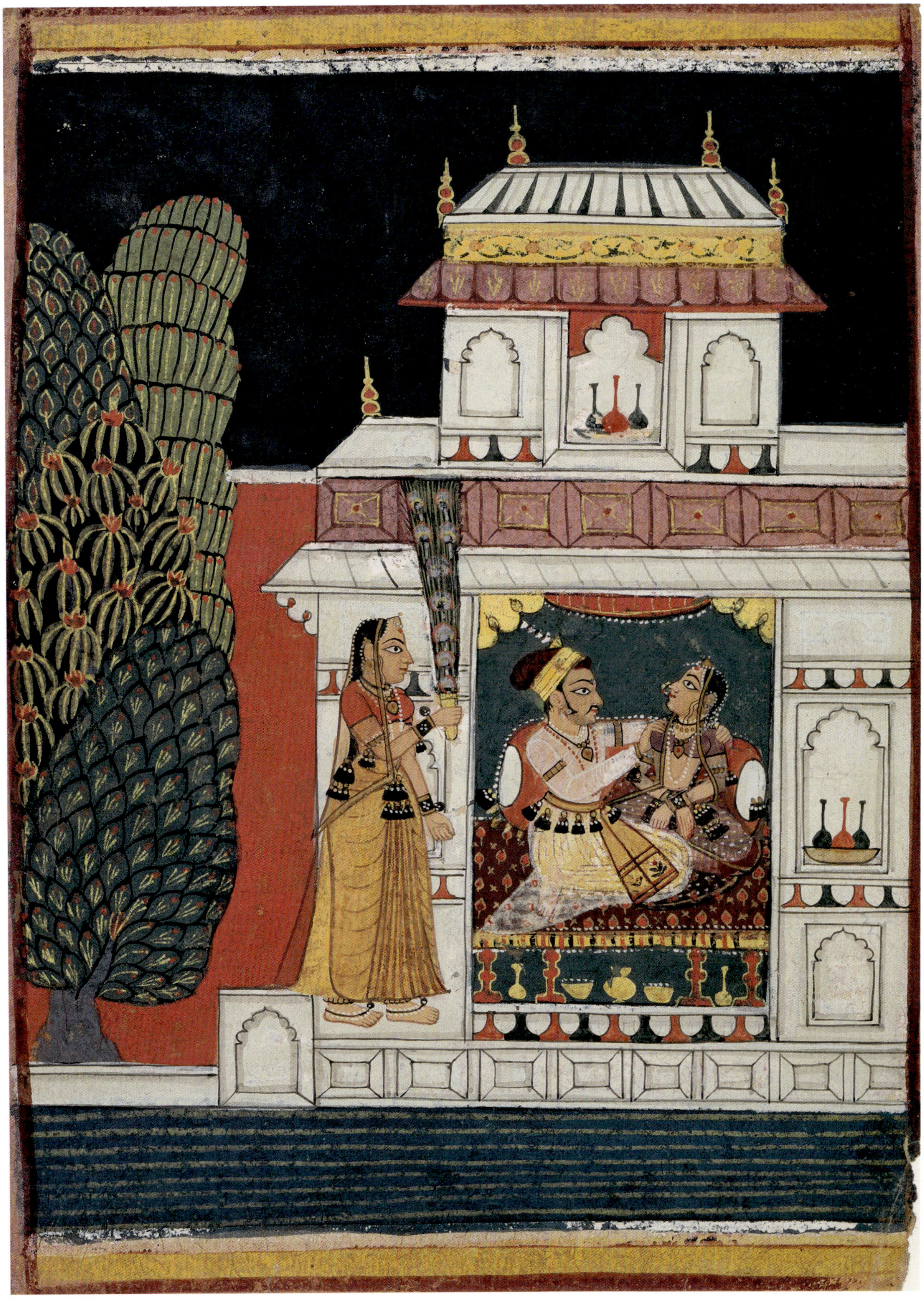

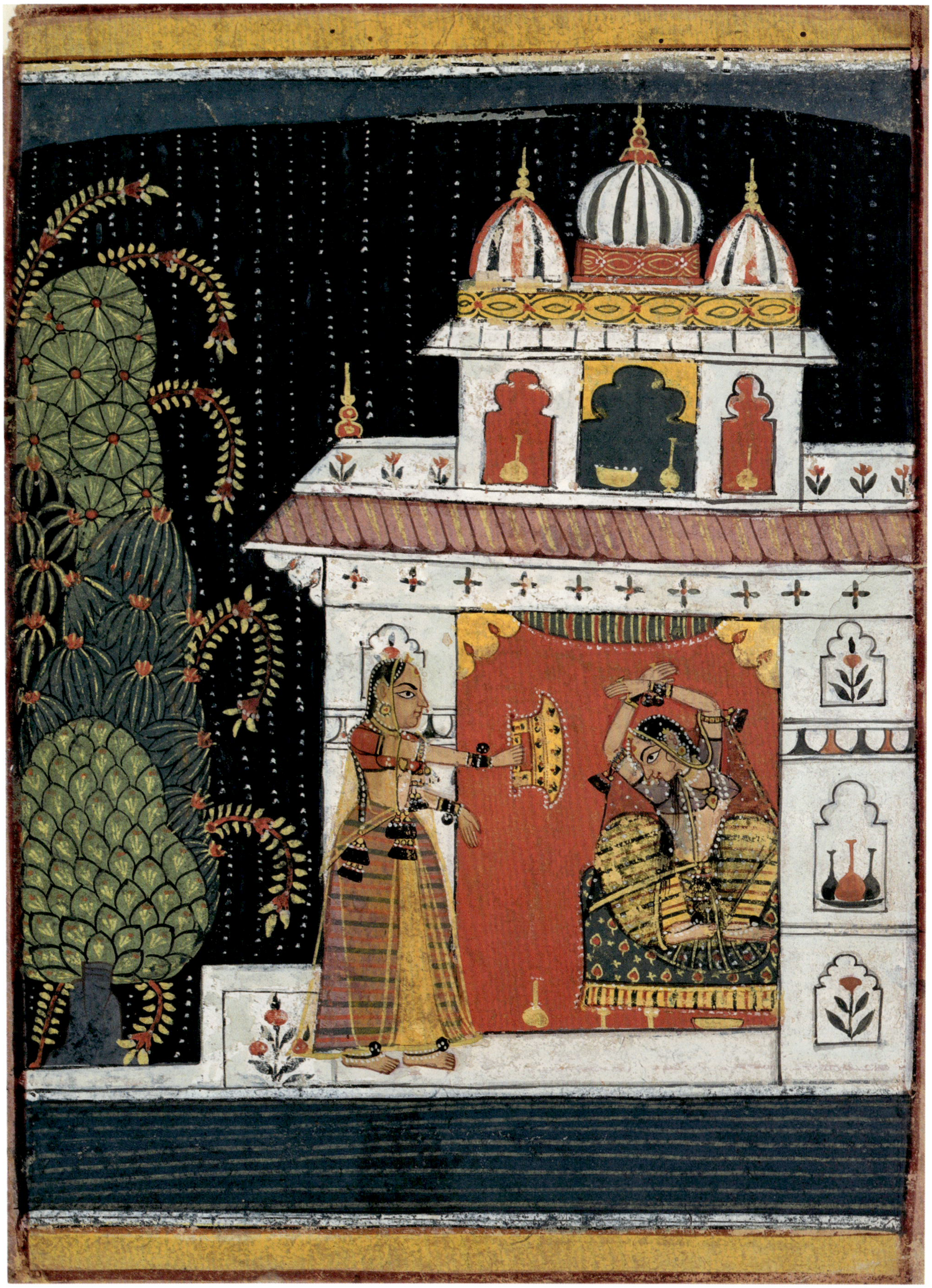

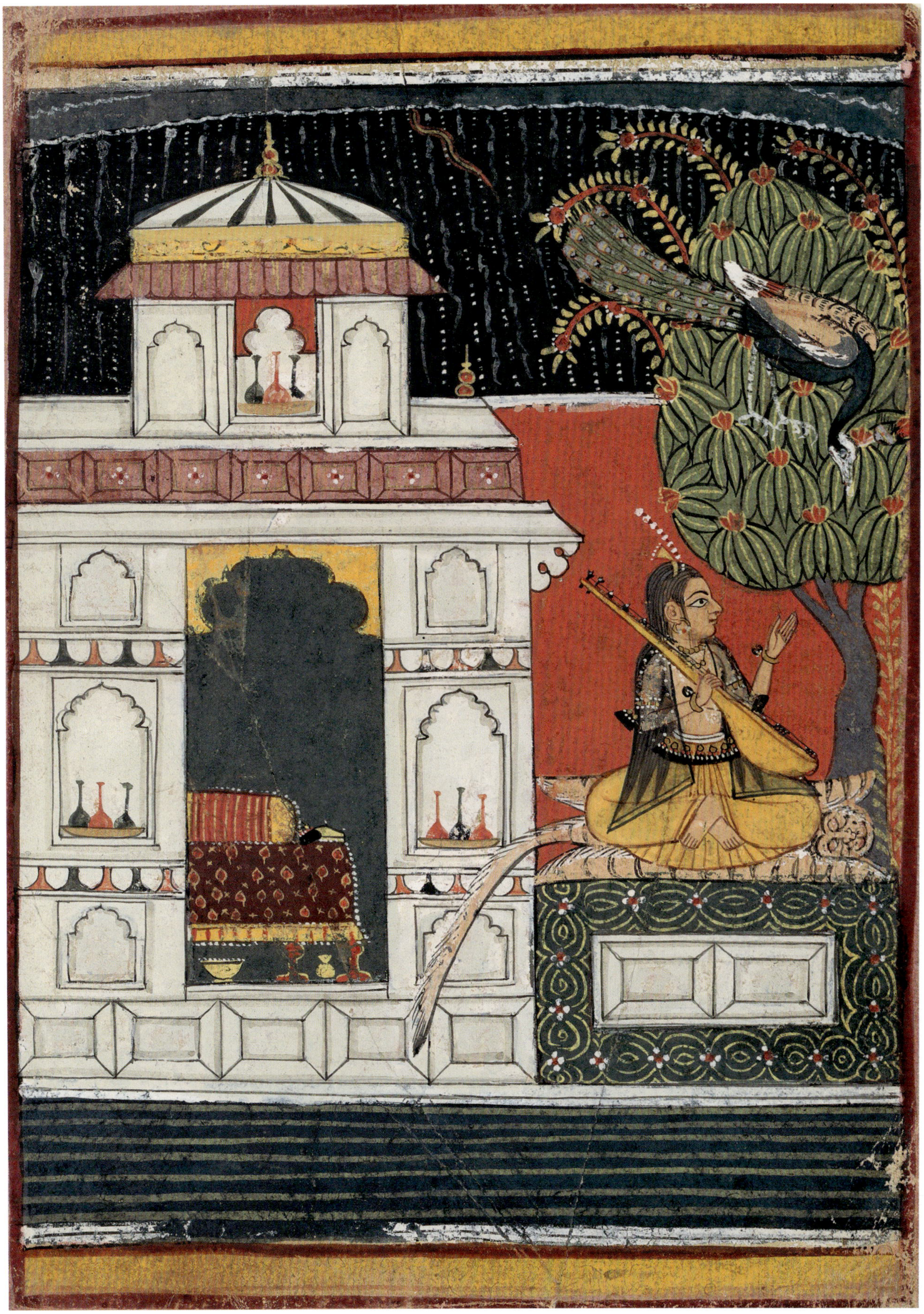

74 Krishna and the gopis, the first meeting of the eyes

Central India, perhaps Bundelkhand, c. 1700
19 × 17.2 cm (folio)

The scene is starkly divided into two parts. Above, Krishna greets two *gopis* who are wandering hand in hand through the groves of Vrindavan, represented by four trees. The first *gopi* stares at Krishna fascinated, although her friend tries to lead her away. They are all three standing on the horizon line above a reddish-brown ground and are silhouetted against a stark blue sky. A dramatically plunging line of a yellowish-brown hillside links the two episodes together. Below, the two *gopis* go on their way and one of them turns her head to look back at Krishna, who has also turned back to look at her. This painting perhaps depicts the first meeting of Radha and Krishna.

The style is hard to place with certainty. Despite the simplicity of construction, the artist draws his figures with sure conviction and individuality. Krishna wears an ochre *dhoti* and a brown cloak as well as his peacock-crested crown. The two *gopis* are distinguished by their dress. The companion wears the normal skirt, bodice and veil, caught at the waist before being pulled over her head, but Radha wears her veil over her head and shoulders and has an elaborate waistband fastened round her middle. She also wears an X-shaped gold ornament across her body. The figures have their faces silhouetted against a darkening of the surrounding color, a characteristic of Bundi painting in its white period around 1760– 1770 but sometimes also found elsewhere. The schematic landscape construction remained a feature of painting in Bundelkhand in the 18th century. A parallel is found in a painting of the same subject similarly arranged in two tiers in the former Khajanchi collection,[1] which the authors were unable to place exactly, but in which the trees seem definitely to be of a Central Indian type. | JL

[1] Khandalavala, Chandra and Chandra 1960, fig. 106.

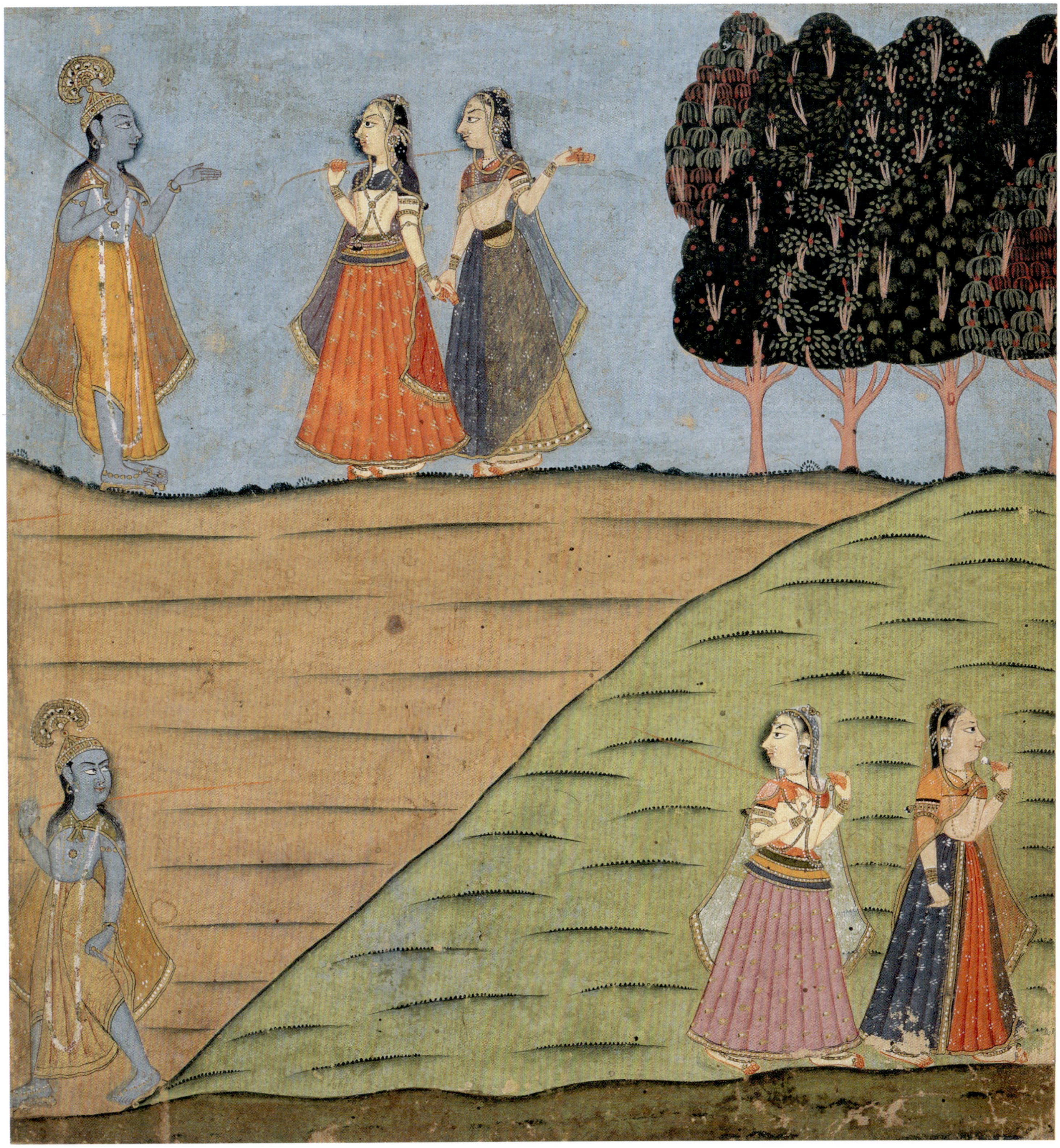

75 Raja Prithvi Singh of Orchha being entertained

Bundelkhand, Datia or Orchha, c. 1770
28×35.8 cm (folio); 25.9×33.7 cm (painting)
Inscribed on the reverse in Devanagari: *sri raj Prithi Sigh* ("Raja Prithvi Singh") and with the stamp of the Datia State

The various early styles attributed to Central India, whether Malwa or Bundelkhand, were transformed around the turn of the century. They still retained their traditional flatness and love of juxtaposing planes of bright color, but adapted to Mughal and Rajasthani architectural conventions with pavilions and terraces viewed from above. The next phase of painting in the region is connected with Datia in north-west Bundelkhand, a state founded in 1626 by Rao Bhagwan Rao, when his father Rao Bir Singh Deo of Orchha divided his realm between his sons. Whether any of the painting styles of the 17th century can be associated with that state we do not know, even though some of the sets have the stamp of the Datia State on the reverse, but the earliest dated works associated with Datia are from the mid 18th century. In a portrait of Rao Indrajit of Datia (r. 1733–1762) dated 1753,[1] the Rao is seated on a terrace with courtiers and musicians and with a garden beyond, showing that the flat earlier style of the 17th century has been decisively influenced by contemporary Mughal painting. Portraits are also known of his successor Rao Satrujit (r. 1762–1801),[2] who was a considerable patron of artists. A somewhat similar portrait from Datia of a Raja on a terrace with musicians is in the National Museum, New Delhi,[3] in which the attendant figure with a *morchhal* is very close to our figure with the fan behind Prithvi Singh and to the young figures in orange *jamas*.

In this portrait the Raja has a considerable presence in his white *jama* and turban, looking quite elderly with a gray mustache. He is presumably to be identified as Raja Prithvi Singh of Orchha (r. 1735–1752). Prithvi Singh was a famous patron of literature and music and was himself a poet known as "Rasnidhi".[4] He is seated on a *takht* on a terrace under a white canopy. He is being entertained by boy dancers accompanied by singers and drummers. Some young attendants hold the customary fan and sword, while another elderly minister sits behind the principal figure. The scene is set at night, lit by torches with the moon and stars above.

The composition recalls that of the terrace scene showing Rao Indrajit, but with the geometrical garden transferred to the foreground of the composition. The sharply observed profiles with heavy details in black, the flat planes of color and the absence of modeling perhaps recall the earlier Central Indian style. Now all figures dress in the contemporary manner, which has been perhaps influenced by that of the Marathas. Raja Chattar Sal of Panna had involved the Marathas in the struggle of the Bundelis against the Mughals and they remained paramount in Bundelkhand until their defeat by the Afghans at the Battle of Panipat in 1761. Vast areas of white show the influence of contemporary Mughal and Awadhi painting. Another portrait shows Prithvi Singh on a terrace watching dancers re-enact the *Rasalila* (the dance of Krishna and the *gopis*).[5] | JL

1 Welch and Beach 1965, no. 38.
2 For examples see Mehta 1926 pp. 40–41, pls. 14–15; Chandra P. 1971, no. 204 and Ahluwalia 2008, fig. 74.
3 Sharma 1974, no. 29, pl. 55.
4 Gupta 1990, p. 157.
5 Asian Art Museum, San Francisco 1991.245.

Formerly in the Datia State collections

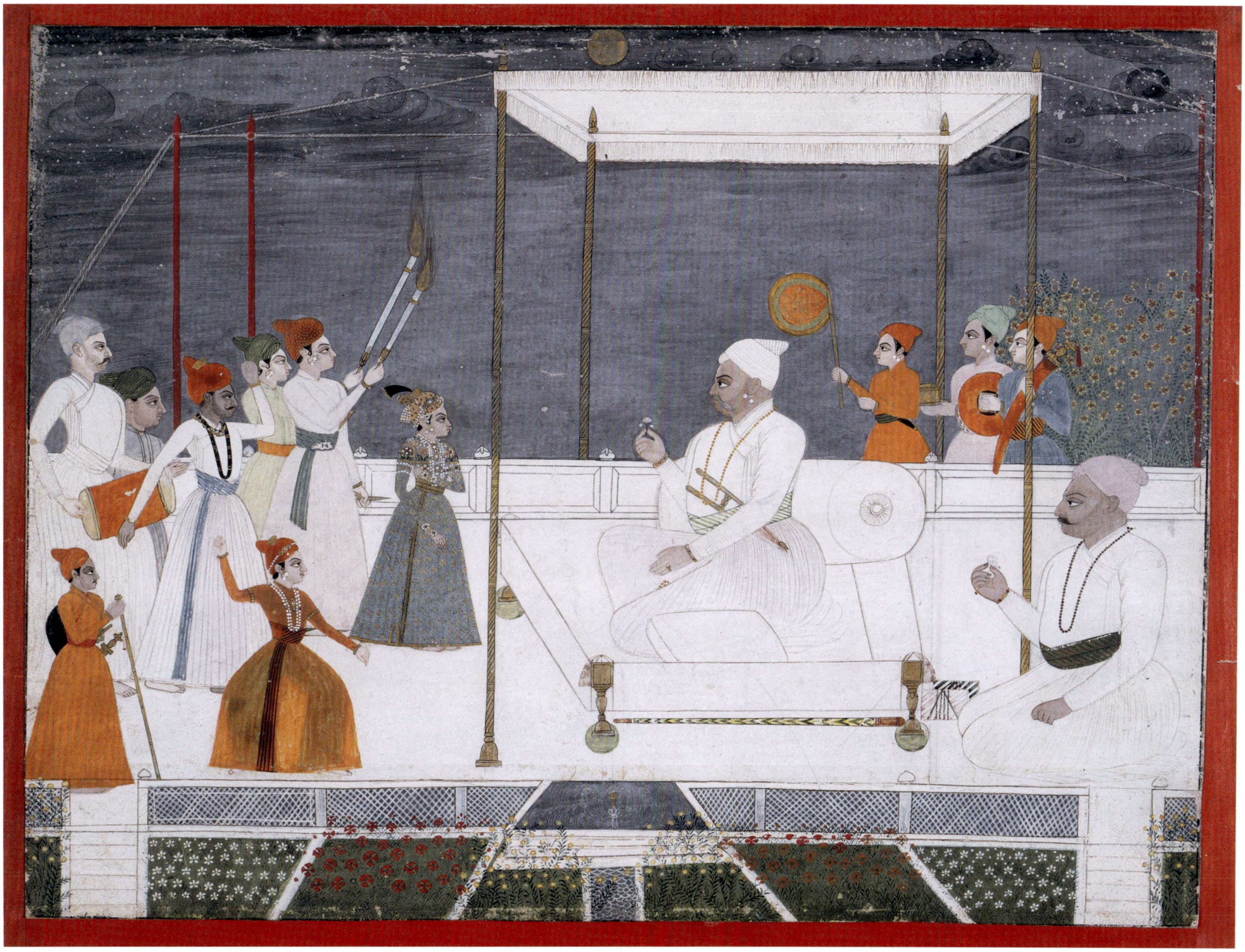

76 Bihari expresses his devotion to Krishna
77 The nayika approaches her beloved

Folio from a *Satsai* series
Bundelhand, Datia, c. 1770
22.5 × 24.5 cm (folio); 17.8 × 19.2 cm (painting)
Number 11 to the side. Inscribed: "Liberate me, Lord, even as you've liberated many sinners. Release me from the bonds of worldly existence: and if it pleases you to keep me bound, bind me with the rope of your devotion."[1]

Folio from a *Satsai* series
Bundelhand, Datia, c. 1770
22.5 × 23.3 cm (folio); 18.2 × 19 cm (painting)
Number 306 erased on the second line and number 580 to the side. Inscribed: "Your co-wives are swaggering about joyfully, their faces bright as blossoming flowers, but the moment they see you go to meet your lover they'll turn pale like stars fading in the morning light."[2]

Bihari (1595–1664) was a poet of the Braj area who was patronized by both the Mughals and by Rajput rulers. His master work is his *Satsai* (literally 700), his collection of over 700 verses addressing every aspect of love. It was finished at the court of Mirza Raja Jai Singh of Amber in 1647 but follows the literary conventions of Keshav Das's *Rasikapriya* of fifty years earlier, so that each verse also illustrates a poetic conceit. Krishna is often treated as the *nayaka* or hero of the poems.

This series of paintings is thought to have been commissioned by Raja Satrujit of Datia (r. 1762–1801) who was a considerable patron of artists and of whom portraits are known.[3] The heroes of the poetic imagery in this series (as in cat. no. 77) bear some resemblance to the Raja with his luxuriant mustache and loosely wound, flat turban. The series is almost of square format with the paintings surrounded by a black border with the verses inscribed at the top.[4]

In the painting *Bihari expresses his devotion to Krishna* (cat. no. 76), which is one of the first folios in this series, the poet is bowing to Krishna with an appropriate devotional verse above. The god and devotee are isolated on a carpeted terrace with the barest of backgrounds and sky, all in planes of strong color. Bihari leans forward in his devotion, his hands joined, while Krishna sits calmly and at ease on his *morha* with the little finger of his right hand raised as if indicating the required devotion to it. It was with his little finger (albeit with his left hand) that Krishna raised the mountain Govardhan to protect the villagers of Braj from the wrath of the god Indra.

In the second painting from the series (cat. no. 77) the poetic imagery has been transferred to a court setting. The verse illustrates the words of the *sakhi* or confidante to her friend who seems to hesitate to approach her husband. Three other women, the co-wives of the verse, stand and watch. The brief comment calls the *nayika* the *abhisarika nayika*, i.e. one who risks the darkness of the woods and their dangers in order to come to her lover. The normal tropes of darkness, lightning flashes, forests and snakes through which the terrified but determined heroine threads her way have been replaced by a civilized court setting at her destination. Her lover sits impassively awaiting her arrival as she is ushered into his presence.

Typical of the style are the tall elegant women, sometimes with their hair caught up in a jutting chignon, and the brilliant colors of clothes and textiles juxtaposed against each other. | JL

1 Translation by Bahadur 1972, no. 674 in his arrangement.
2 Translation by Bahadur 1972, no. 274 in his arrangement.
3 Mehta 1926, pp. 40–41, pls. 14–15; Chandra P. 1971, no. 204; Ahluwalia 2008, fig. 74.
4 The series is widely dispersed, for other examples see Czuma 1975, no. 75; Mason 2001, no. 71, and references; Roy 2008, pp. 118–119.

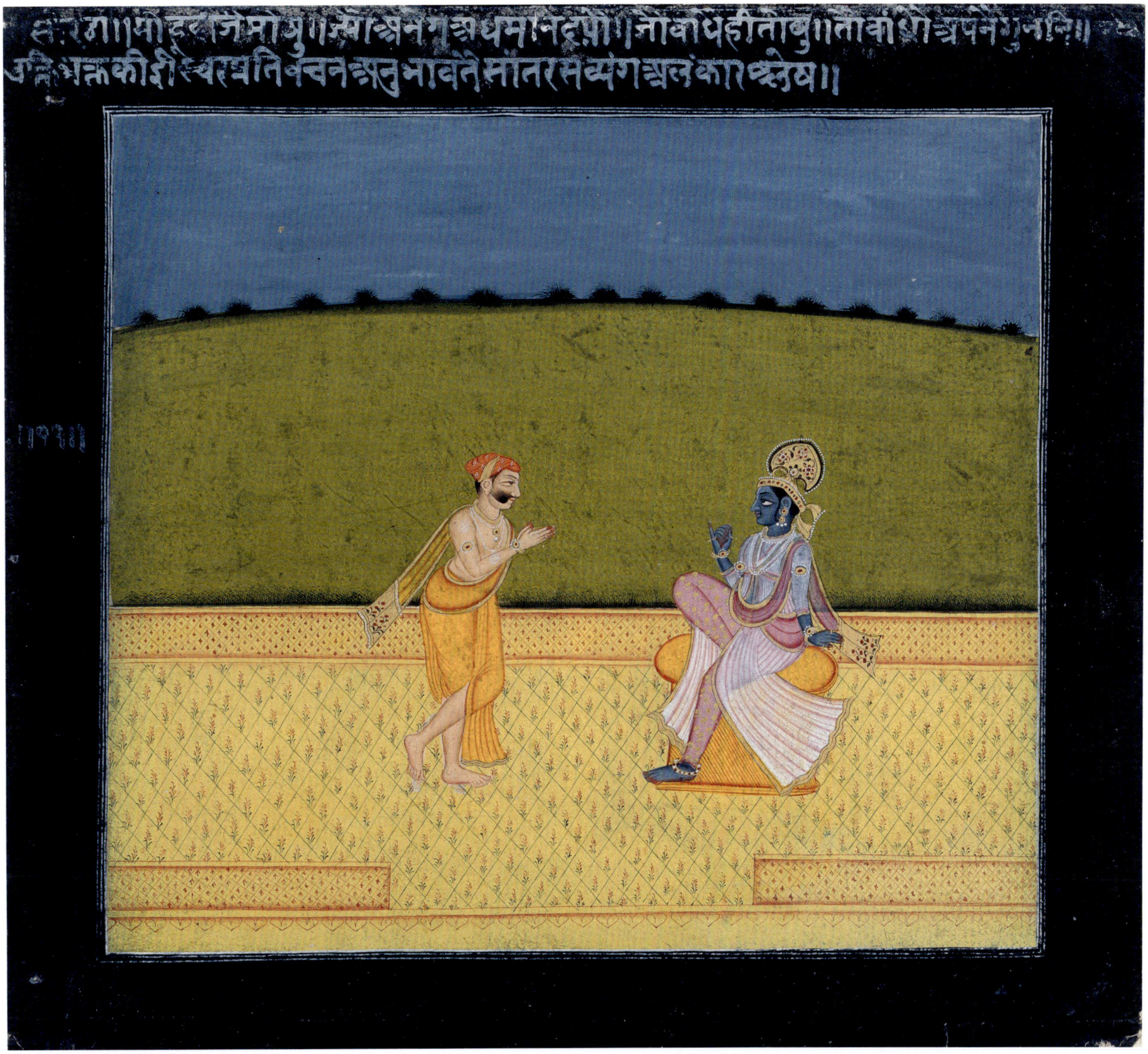

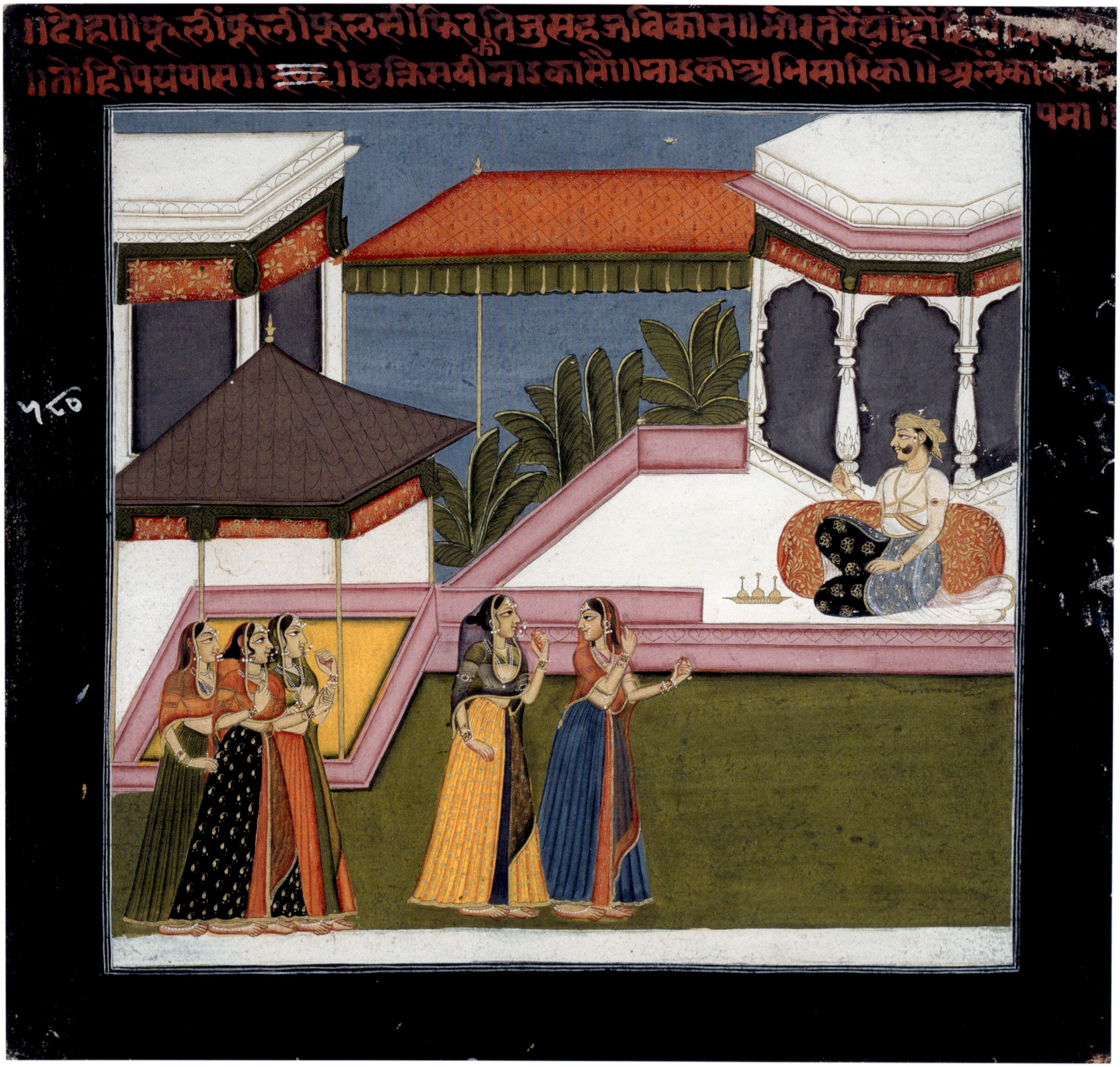

78 Young Prahlada converses with sages
79 Indra kills the demon Jambha

Folio 125(?) from the small Guler *Bhagavata Purana* series
Attributed to Manaku
Pahari, c. 1740
20.3 × 31.2 cm (folio)
Inscribed on top in Takri: *Indre Jambha maareya vajre kari*
("Indra (then) killed Jambha with his *vajra*-thunderbolt")
Museum Rietberg, Collection Danielle Porret, 2011.395

Folio 101 from the small Guler *Bhagavata Purana* series
Attributed to Manaku
Pahari, c. 1740
20 × 23.5 cm (folio)
Museum Rietberg, Collection Danielle Porret, 2011.397

The two drawings come from that great project which Manaku of Guler had embarked upon shortly after completing his famous *Gita Govinda* series of 1730: the illustration, in fact the envisioning, of that sacred text, the *Bhagavata Purana*, which devout Vaishnavas regard above everything else. The extent of the project is not possible to determine because of the wide dispersal of its folios – it might well have run into more than a thousand folios – but one does know that in the form of finished paintings, the series could be brought only up to a point after which, in close continuation, drawings take over.[1] Exactly at what point, or why the break came is impossible to establish but it would seem that some of the drawings that have surfaced or survived relate to the 7th *skandha* of the text and after.

Being given to dense narration as Manaku was, he seems to have dealt with each episode that he picked to draw with great care and in meticulous detail. In cat. no. 79 we pick up the narrative of the text at the point where Bali, the great demon king, has been felled in the battle with Indra, leader of the gods. But to Bali's aid jumps up instantly his great friend, the mighty *asura* Jambha, riding a fierce lion that was his mount. To begin with, he deals Indra heavy blows in the battle that ensues between them, striking his shoulder with his club and even mauling the god's elephant who fell to his knees. At this, Matali, Indra's chariot-driver, quickly brought his chariot, "drawn by one thousand horses" as the text says expansively. Indra climbed on to his resplendent chariot and even though Jambhasura was able to injure his driver, he rode on, "struck Jambhasura with his thunderbolt and severed his head from his body." The brief line inscribed in Takri on the top border precisely identifies the scene, for it reads: "*Indre Jambha maareya vajre kari*," meaning, "Indra (then) killed Jambha with his *vajra*-thunderbolt." One can imagine the drawings which must have preceded this one: the battle with and the felling of Bali, the attack on Indra and his elephant-mount by Jambha, the bringing in of the god's chariot by Matali. But none of these has surfaced. Here, however, one is at least able to see the climax of the battle.

Every detail is picked by Manaku with near perfection: the chariot with its many horses but without Matali, the driver, who had been injured; the manner in which Indra's hand is held high above his head for it is from that height that he has released his *vajra*-weapon; the multiple sharp points of the *vajra* which now lies embedded in Jambha's chest; the piteous manner in which the monster-headed, bird-toed *asura* now lies on the ground, dying; the cowering stance of the lion as it turns round and faces the advancing chariot of Indra. It is as if the painter were there as things happened.

As so often in folios of this extensive series of drawings, one notices that underneath the finished drawing are marks of an earlier version of the composition, the painter's initial thoughts as it were, made with a *basuti*-charcoal stick. Notice the legs of the horses, for instance, or the slight upward shifting of the figure of the lion. But one also notices that while the finished drawing is impeccable – the sheer brilliance with which the lion is seen and drawn, or the anger reflected in the raised eyebrow of Indra – the under-drawing is no less. It is just that Manaku must have reflected on the composition and modified it for his own reasons.

The theme of the second drawing (cat. no. 78) is not as easy to establish as the Indra–Jambha encounter, largely because the brief caption on the top border is now all but gone, owing to the folio being truncated. However, it is not unlikely that the scene represented is from the episode of the demon-king Hiranyakashipu and his son, Prahlada, who, much to the dislike of his father, was a devotee of Vishnu. Some other drawings have survived in which one sees Prahlada, who was a young boy at the time when he incurred his father's wrath, depicted as being much of the same age as here, and wearing the same kind of tall cap with its top edge serrated or consisting of folds. While in the other drawings one is able to see Prahlada's will being tested by his being put to torture or sought to be killed under his father's orders, the passage in this drawing seems to be of a quieter nature. Hiranyakashipu, as the episode goes, had tried to argue with his son, trying to convince him of the folly of his ways, but had failed. He even sent the boy to "the teachers of the demon race, Chanda and Marka"

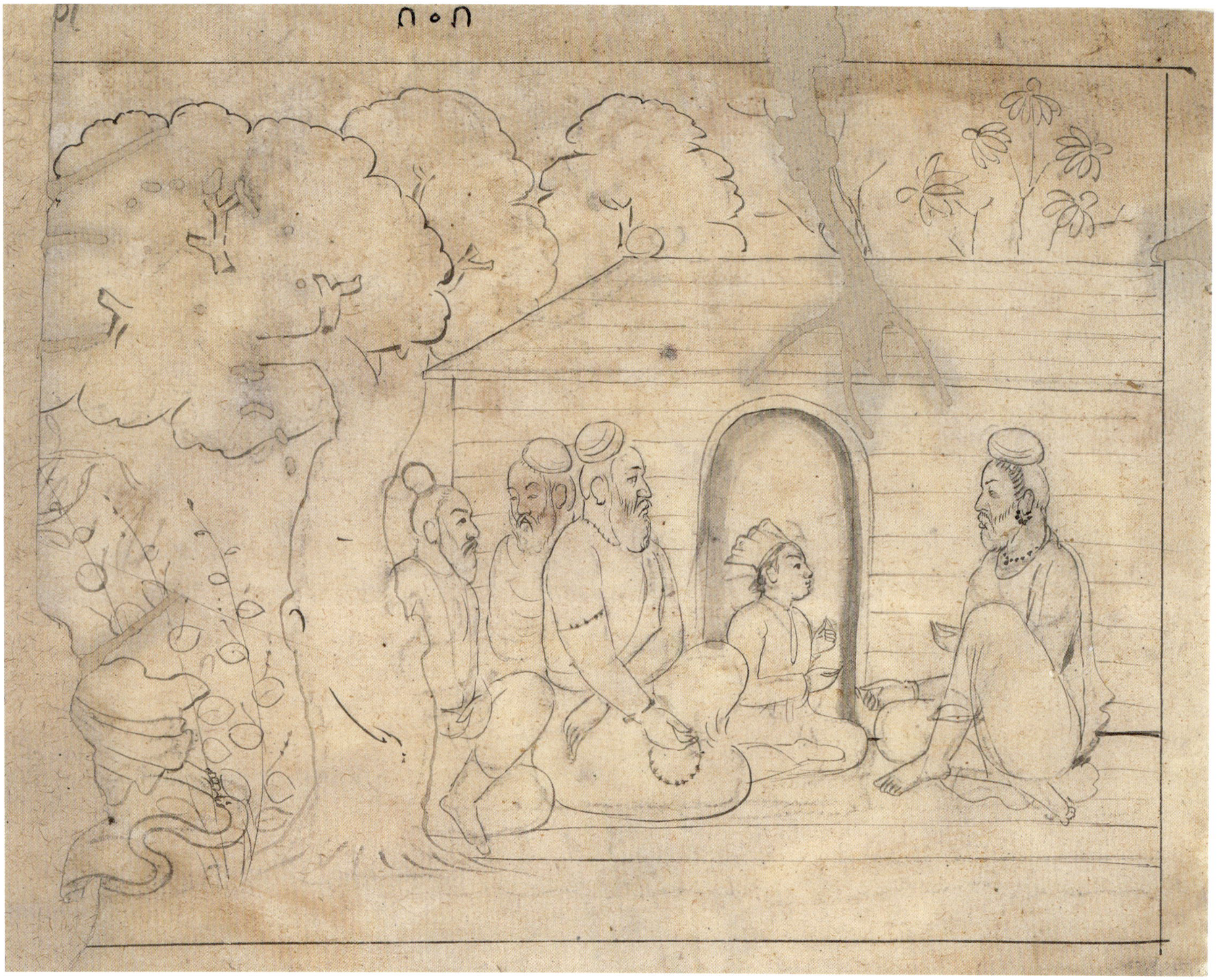

in the hope of reforming him, but to no avail. These teachers, even though there are no descriptions of them in the text, could easily have been sages; at least this is how – if one's identification of this scene is right – Manaku shows them, seated in a small group just outside their hut with young Prahlada in their midst, his hands held up in the gesture of explaining or arguing. One of the sages, whom he is addressing, also appears to be gesturing. A dialogue is clearly in progress.

The figures of all the older men emphatically follow the iconography of "sages" or learned men that Manaku had established for himself. One sees them again and again, not only in his drawings but also in his finished paintings from this series: calm demeanours, firm bodies, full beards rounded at the lower end, long hair piled up bun-like on the head, often with prayer-beads in hand. This is how one sees them here too, but that does not take away in the slightest from one's admiration for Manaku's remarkably firm hand, his understanding of and identification with the characters he created and his ability to evoke a sense of the space and of the occasion. With the lightest of hands, he suggests a grove of trees towering calmly above the sages' simple hut, but he also seems to have dealt with some turbulence in the damaged area of the drawing on the left. | BG

[1] For a list of published folios and drawings see Goswamy and Fischer 2011c, list no. 5.

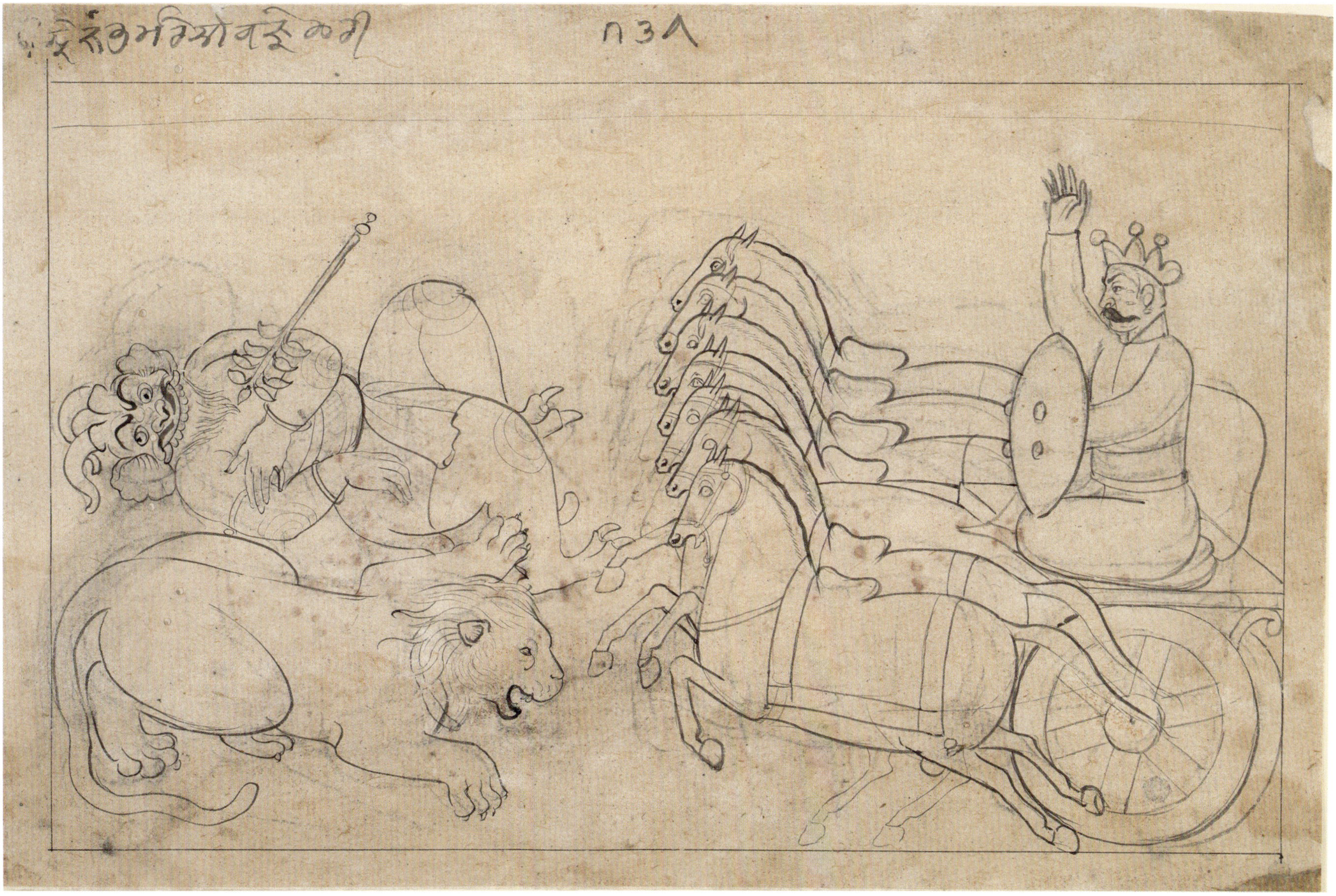

80 Vishnu seated on a lotus

Possibly the opening folio of a *Gita Govinda* series
Attributed to Nainsukh
Pahari, c. 1765–1775
15.6 × 24.7 cm (folio), 12.6 × 21.6 cm (painting)

At first sight, the figure raises thoughts of this being an icon, but clearly the suggestion by the painter – the marble terrace, the trees on either side – is that of a living presence. The great god, Vishnu, is seen seated on a full-blown lotus placed in the center of the cool terrace flanked by trees that peer in; he is four-armed, his face very youthful, the body remarkably slender. The upper part of the body is bare, revealing his glistening form "dark as a rain-cloud": the lower limbs are dressed in a *dhoti* in his favorite pita-yellow color; an *uttariya*-scarf is loosely draped over the shoulders, its long golden ends falling on either side and shown as scalloped so as to echo the sharp points of the lotus. As Vishnu crosses his legs, his knees merging with the curve of the pericarp, the gathers of his *dhoti* fall gracefully to the front, covering his feet and spreading out in a scalloped pattern. On his head is an elaborate gem-studded crown that fits like a skullcap topped by a finial that fans out like a peacock-feather *mukuta*. All four arms are bent at the elbow, the two upper hands holding a *gada*-mace and a lotus; the two lower hands bear a *shankha*-conch and a *chakra*-discus. These *ayudhas* – always associated with Vishnu – and emblematic of the four elements: fire, water, space and air are all made of gold studded with precious stones, save the lotus which looks freshly picked and is held aloft. There is rich jewelry on his body including the *kaustubh mani* on the chest and the *vanamala*-garland of wild flowers around the neck. Adding to the decoration are sacred caste-marks made with sandal-paste that adorn the forehead, shoulders, forearms, stomach, even the outer edges of the ears. But all these are not parts of a dry inventory of signs and symbols: the image, as Nainsukh has painted it, is felt and therefore moving.

The great Guler painter, one needs to recall, was familiar with this *rupa* of Vishnu, having certainly seen it in the *thakurdwara* at Jasrota and having painted it in the work in which Balwant Singh, his patron, is seen taking leave of his *ishta* deity at night while a *pandit* reads from a manuscript.[1] There are minor changes here, but that image might never have left Nainsukh's mind.

It is not unlikely that this leaf was conceived as the opening, perhaps even the invocatory, folio of a series that we, in our present state, know nothing about. There are other opening leaves, with the image of Ganesha, for instance, similarly seated on a terrace, which lead toward this thought.[2] The fact that the leaf bears marks of rubbing and creasing, especially on the trees, suggests this, for many opening leaves suffer from damage. The painting, one notices at the same time, is in part unfinished, as one can see from the incomplete state in which the marble terrace is left. If this was the opening leaf of a series that was being planned, it gives us some inkling, a glimmering, of the direction in which Nainsukh might have been heading at this time. The great phase of "recording", or conjuring up if one so likes, the life of Balwant Singh (1723–1763) was decidedly over by this time, and he had entered the service of a different patron, Amrit Pal of Basohli (b. c. 1745, r. c. 1757–1778), a man of religious inclination and possibly deeply interested in religious texts. A *Gita Govinda* series, perhaps?

A detail of some interest: the yellow border of this painting is unusual for Nainsukh. But then one recalls that the border of the painting he is seen as having just presented to Balwant Singh in that key painting of him with his patron, is also yellow of color.[3] | BG

1 Bharat Kala Bhavan, acc. no. 851, see Goswamy 1997, no. 76.
2 Museum Rietberg, permanent loan Barbara and Eberhard Fischer. Published in Beltz 2003, no. 37a.
3 Museum Rietberg, RVI 1551, see for instance Goswamy and Fischer 1992, no. 117.

Formerly in the George P. Bickford collection
Published: Goswamy 1997, no. 96; Goswamy and Fischer 1992, no. 129

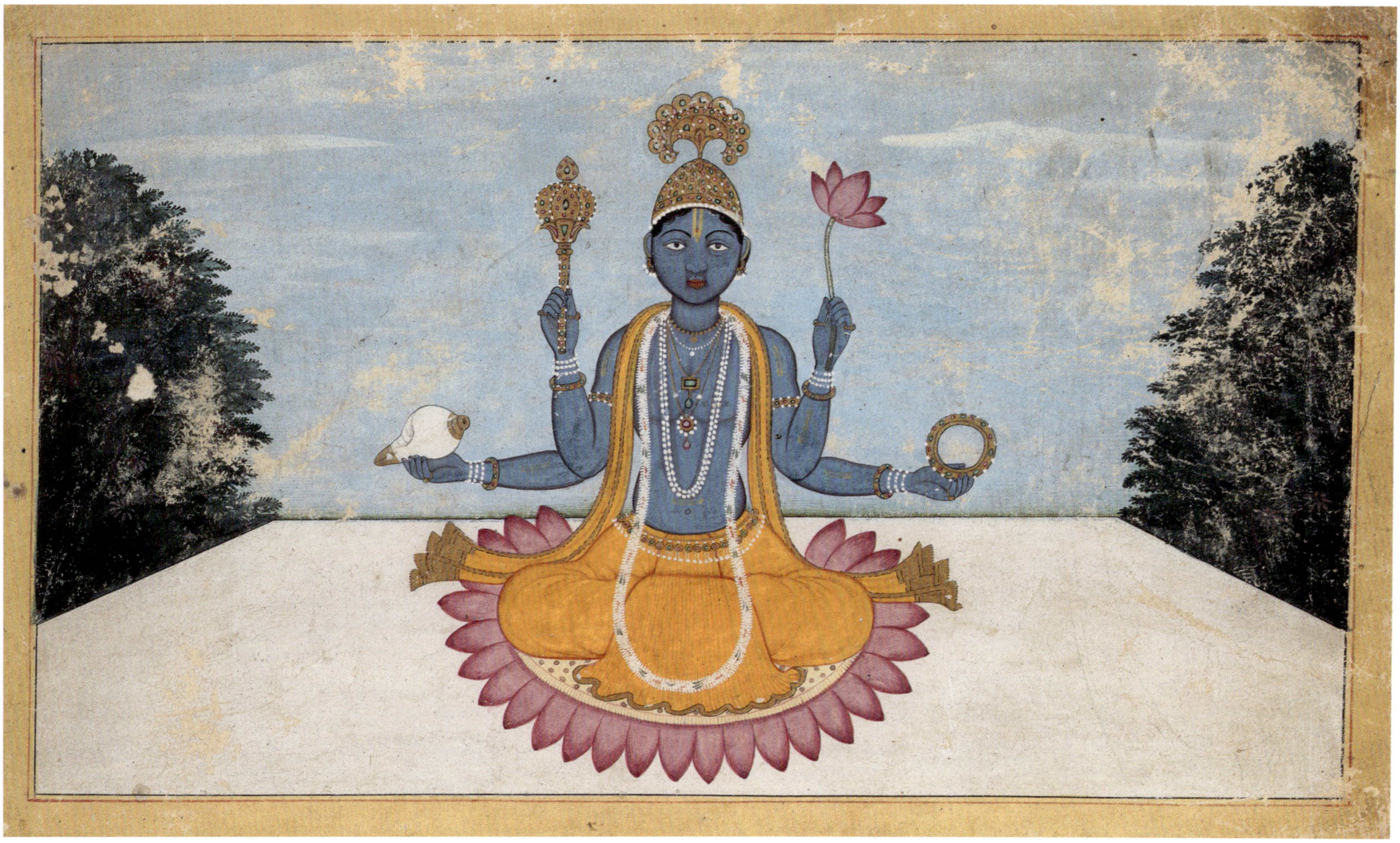

81 Bharata and Shatrughna return to Ayodhya

Folio from the (second) Guler *Ramayana* series
By a master of the first generation after Nainsukh of Guler
Pahari, c. 1780
24.8 × 35.5 cm (folio), 20 × 30.8 cm (painting)

The great *Ramayana* series to which this leaf belongs (see also cat. no. 82) carries no text, not even any captions. But the episode treated here by the painter is not difficult to identify. Devastated by the news of the death of their father, Dasharatha, and unable to bear the thought of Rama now living in exile in company with Sita and Lakshmana, the two brothers Bharata and Shatrughna set off, as the text says, toward the forest to try and bring Rama back to Ayodhya. And while they are gone, everyone waits anxiously for their return along with Rama: not only the three queens, headed by Kaushalya, the eldest, and the palace household, but the entire citizenry of Ayodhya. For who could live without Rama for fourteen years?

Bharata and Shatrughna look for Rama, Sita and Lakshmana in the forests everywhere, and do succeed in finding them leading the life of forest-dwellers. But all their attempts, all their entreaties and arguments, fail to persuade Rama to return. For, dearly as he loves his brothers, he tells them that he cannot even conceive of going back on the word he had given his father. "*Pran jaaye par vachan na jaayi*," as the popular saying, referring to this poignant situation, goes: "losing life is to be preferred to bringing dishonor by going back on a word given." The brothers return to Ayodhya, but empty-handed.

That is the moment, filled with sadness and failure, that the painter envisions here. The way he sets it up is sheer brilliance. From the left, the two brothers enter the space, both on foot, having left their chariots behind: Bharata the elder, identifiable through his darker, bluish skin like Rama's, goes ahead of Shatrughna. Heads downward inclined, eyes fixed on the ground as if unable to look up, they can be seen walking with leaden feet. Soldiers and retainers stand under the outer walls of the palace, watching. But they, especially the three guards standing close to the main entrance – the eyes of the one who clasps his shield to his chest are closed; another rests his sword on his shoulder in a gesture of resignation; the third simply looks away, unable to bear the sight as it were – can easily tell that the mission to bring Rama back has failed. Far above them in a window on the upper floor of the palace, partially hidden by the lattice-work balustrade, sits a lone figure – Kaushalya, one can be certain – peering down at the scene below. By this time, one can tell, she too knows about the two brothers having failed, but she waits. To learn of details, know what her noble son, Rama, said when asked to return?

What arrests attention above all, however, is the right part of the painting. The palace is completely bare here: not a soul stirs, no movement catches the eye, not even a stick of furniture or appointments is to be seen. It is as if the place has been abandoned. A feeling of complete desolation reigns, mirroring states of mind. A composition of Tulsidas, author of the celebrated Awadhi version of the *Ramayana*, the *Ramacharita-manasa*, inevitably comes to mind, especially as sung by Kumar Gandharva, the great classical singer: *aaj mohe raghubar ki sudh aayi*. Kaushalya sits in her lonesome palace, her mind constantly on her exiled son and what state he and his wife and brother must be in out in the wilderness. It is raining here, and the wind blows hard, she says to herself: what tree must be able to offer shelter to my children who are out there? And then: *Siya bina meri sooni rasoi, Lachhman bin thakurai*, she cries out aloud in that moving composition. There is no cheer in my kitchen with Sita gone; and the fraternity of the royal nobility is inconsolable, now that Lakshmana is not there.

These could not have been the words in the painter's mind, but something similar perhaps. Why else would he devote nearly two-fifths of the page at the right to this desolate, barren feeling? | BG

Published: Britschgi and Fischer 2008, no. 16

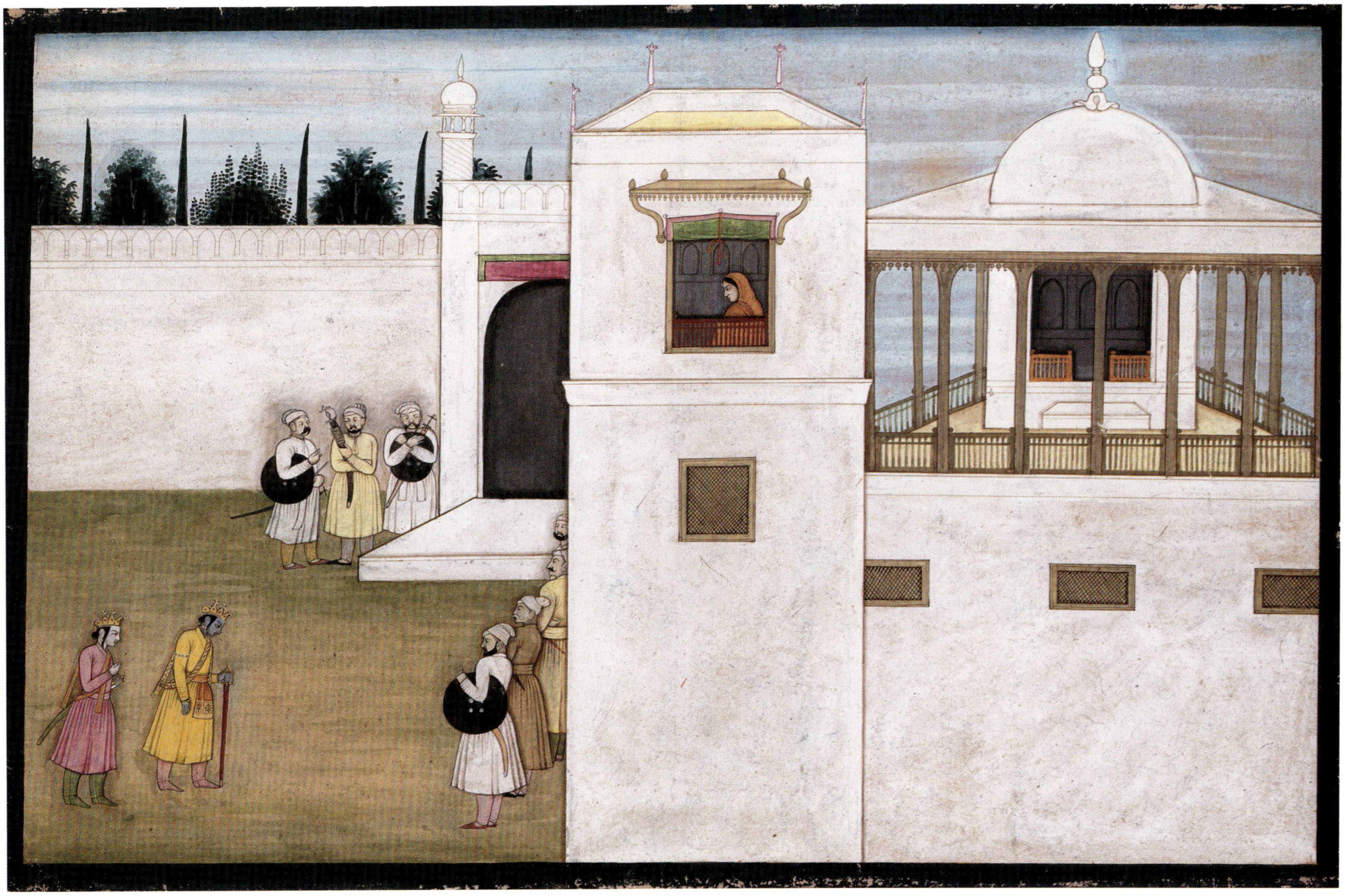

82 The ascetics of Chitrakuta ask Rama for protection

Folio from the (second) Guler *Ramayana* series
By a master of the first generation after Nainsukh of Guler
Pahari, c. 1780
25.2 × 35.5 cm (folio), 20.8 × 31 cm (painting)
Museum Rietberg, Collection Danielle Porret, 2011.2

The surroundings are sylvan: lush greenery everywhere, trees laden with fruit or festooned with flowering creepers, a stream flowing quietly by, a lake astir with lotuses in the far distance. It may not be a hermitage, but surely some *rishi* dwells here, all by himself. But there is in this setting some subdued sense of disquiet too perhaps. In front of the lone hut, directly under a tree, one sees the princely exiles: Rama and Sita, clad only in bark and leaves, sit on a deer-skin spread out for them by the *rishis* and forest-dwellers; Lakshmana stands close by, but at a slight distance from the group with his back turned even to his brother, attending to his quiver, his expression not that of a person at peace. Forefinger of his right hand raised, Rama is evidently addressing the small group, everyone in it seated on the ground in a semi-circle and listening. The theme of the conversation remains unclear. As told in the *Ramayana*, every so often Rama enters into philosophical discussions with learned sages while he is in the forest; at times, he seeks directions; at others he offers reassurance. But always in his supremely calm manner, for he sheds grace regardless of where he is or in what company. It would seem here however as if the *rishis* have told the prince in exile of their troubles: *rakshasas*, *nishacharas*, of all descriptions are a constant threat, now disturbing them in their meditations, now desecrating their *yajna* fires. And Rama speaks to them, in his "deep-as-the-rumbling-of-clouds" voice, as the text says, offering every possible help and protection. If this is the nature of the exchange, one can understand the agitation in the bearing of Lakshmana and his reaching out to his weapons: the quiver that holds his dreaded arrows to be followed by the bow that hangs from a branch above him. He is already beginning to prepare for encounters. The contrast between the calm aspect of Rama and the agitation of his irascible brother is superbly conveyed.

What is even more remarkable in this lush page is the manner in which the painter renders the different characters in the group sitting around Rama. The white-haired *rishi* seated closest to Rama, remarkably alert despite his years, is speaking with eloquent gestures; the matted-haired one next to him has withdrawn into himself, eyes closed, shoulders slightly hunched; by his side is another reclusive figure, wild hair thrown back, uncertain expression on his face, stroking his beard as if thinking; a younger man, wearing a priestly cap, with a disturbed expression on his face listens attentively as does the forest-dweller next to him. The one person that we do not see the face of is a young man, an acolyte, with his back toward us, a brass vessel by his side. The painter's grasp of attitudes and expressions in this group, his understanding of character, is astonishingly acute. This apart, however, as in so many leaves of this great series, there is rich, wonderful detail that makes the page come to life, bit by bit: the peacock that quietly moves towards the stream, untouched by all this; the enormously long bow that rests on Rama's shoulder but follows the curve of the door of the hut behind him; the flower garland that some welcoming forest dweller has put around Sita's neck; the thoughtful, almost disturbed gesture she makes as the threesome are on their way again – clearly we see them twice over in the same leaf, like we keep doing in countless works, and certainly in this one – assessing dangers, wondering what all this will come to. Meanwhile, some trees with their magnificent leafy crowns keep looking filled with space and amplitude while others stand there, denuded, forlorn, asking questions with their dried-up but finger-like branches. | BG

Published: Cran 1980, no. 83; Goswamy and Fischer 1992, no. 144; Britschgi and Fischer 2008, no. 23; Beach, Goswamy and Fischer 2011a, p. 704; Jahresbericht (Museum Rietberg) 2011, pp. 56–57

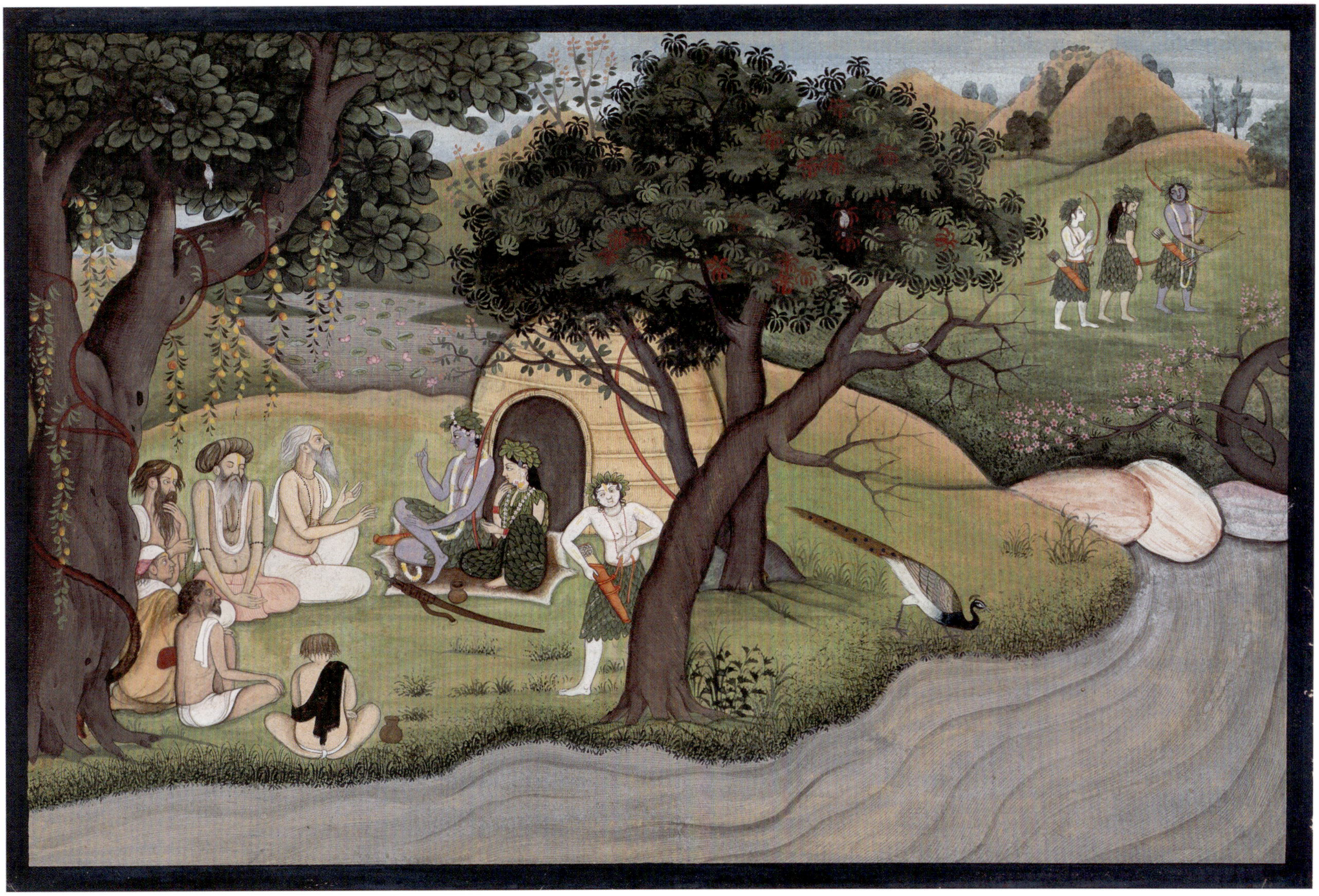

83 Ravidas, the cobbler saint

Folio from a series of *bhakti* saints
By a master of the first generation after Nainsukh of Guler
Pahari, c. 1790–1800
Inscribed on verso in Takri: *bhagat chamar ravidas*
21.5 × 15.9 cm (folio); 16.3 × 11.1 cm (painting)
Museum Rietberg, Collection Danielle Porret, 2011.338

It is a humble cobbler's abode that the painter shows us here, much like the simple village dwellings that he must have been so familiar with in his own Pahari surroundings: an unadorned single-room home with a thatched roof, a fence of rough wooden logs guarding the unpaved courtyard, a plantain tree with a conventional flower dangling from a branch, a niche in the smooth, neatly painted wall. But the man plying his trade as he sits in the courtyard, working on a piece of leather, cutting tool in hand, is no ordinary cobbler: he is Ravidas – also called Raidas sometimes – celebrated until today as one of the great saints which the *bhakti* age in medieval India was rich in. There were others like him, great devotees and saint-poets – Chhipa, a cloth-printer, for instance; Kabir, a weaver; Namdev, a tailor – who attained great celebrity too, despite the fact that they came from the lower, sometimes untouchable, segments of the society of those times. Winds of change had begun to blow then, mocking at the divisions that caste created and flouting the norms of an inequitable social order. It was the renowned purity of these men – all great devotees – and their noble, sometimes intensely poetic utterances, therefore that won them status and a place in people's hearts. A brief inscription in Takri on the verso of this folio identifies Ravidas clearly, but does not forget to mention that he was a *chamar* – lowly leather-worker or cobbler – for it reads: "*bhagat chamar ravidas*." Perhaps the whole series of which this folio is a part was meant to be seen as a tribute.[1]

Apart from the fact that it is beautifully drawn and painted, there is something quite moving about the image. Ravidas sits nearly unclothed save for a coarse white wrap draped around his slight frame – a simple cap on his head, *mala*-rosary round his neck – working but also listening to another person who sits facing him and is reading from a book, while gesturing with one hand. The staff lying by the man's side together with a small water vessel suggests that he is a visitor, someone who has just arrived perhaps. Who this man might be is left unstated, but there is a likelihood that the painter had the person of Kabir, the great weaver-saint-poet, in mind. The peacock feather stuck in his cap is almost a giveaway, for Kabir-*panthis* used to wear that routinely, and one knows of stories that speak of the two saints having met at least once, both of them coming from the environs of Benares as they did. One cannot be certain, but the thought of this being a "record" of their meeting is certainly intriguing.

There are details that are thoughtfully brought in: the basket in which other unworked leather pieces are lying; the awl close to Ravidas's feet; his own shoes that he had taken off before sitting down to work; an ewer of water that he must have needed in the midst of his hard labor. Everything is in place and in character. That Ravidas was a householder, not a recluse, is brought in by the painter introducing a woman, his wife apparently, who sits in the doorway of their room, concentrating on embroidering a pattern on a piece of leather: for a *jutti*-shoe, no doubt, that Ravidas will soon be working on. At one end of the bare courtyard grows the sacred *tulasi* plant and in the niche in the wall is drawn an image, that of a crowned deity: Vishnu perhaps?

The details of Ravidas's life are somewhat controversial. Some place his year of birth at 1376, others at 1399, still others in the early 15th century. That he was a *chamar* by birth and caste is established without doubt, but opinions differ about whether he was actually the preceptor of Mira Bai, the Chittor princess, who was a devotee of Krishna and a poet of great merit herself. Again, there are stories about his meetings with Guru Nanak, but the dates do not always match. One thing in this context is certain, however: that a number of Ravidas's compositions, as many as forty-one, found an honorable place in the great scripture of Sikhism, the *Adi Granth*.

But all this was nearly three hundred years before this painting was made. The painter only imagined Ravidas, but he imagined him well, and with deep feeling. | BG

1 Another folio from this series, showing the cloth-printer Chhipa, is in the collection of the Museum Rietberg (RVI 908).

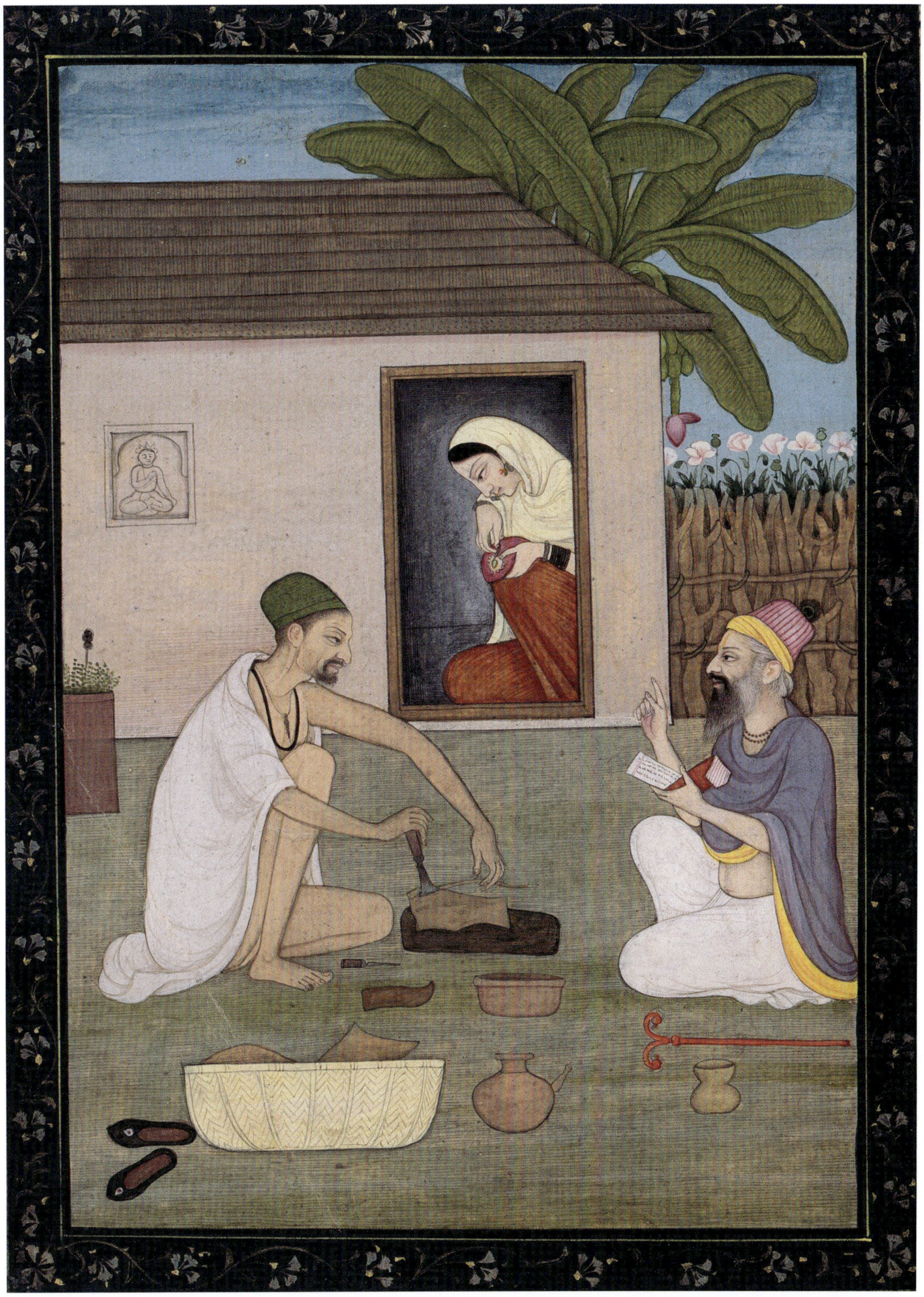

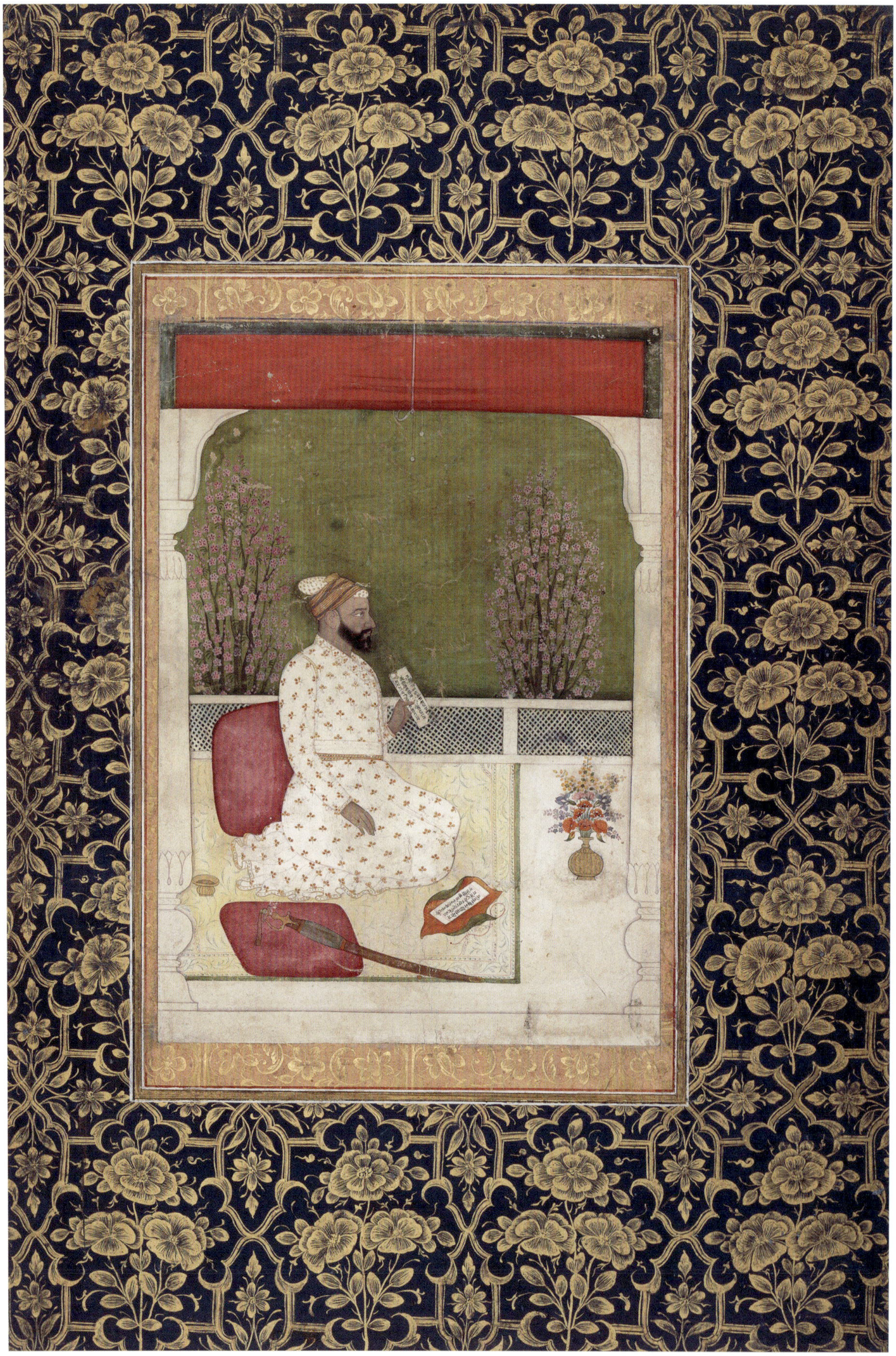

84 Portrait of a Pahari ruler

By an artist from the Seu-Nainsukh family workshop
Pahari, c. 1765
39.5 × 25 cm (folio), 20.5 × 14.3 cm (painting)

This elegant portrait seems now to put one in mind of one ruler or prince, and now of another, but it does not seem possible to precisely place it yet. Different names come swimming within one's ken: Brijraj Dev of Jammu, Ajit Singh of Jaswan, even Tegh Chand of Kangra in his younger years; and yet nothing quite seems to fit. There is no inscription that comes to one's aid. The only thing that can be said with certainty is that it is a Pahari ruler and that he or his painter wishes that he be seen as a devout man, possessed of princely dignity and appearance and yet not unaware of the higher things of life. For here, he sits holding a leaf – a *patra*, if one so likes, of the standard horizontal format – with a text of three lines written in Sanskrit in a minute hand, as if reading from it. Next to him on the carpet on which he himself is seated are other leaves obviously of the same text resting on a silken cloth wrap in which they were previously kept. One of those leaves has what appears to be a continuation of the leaf in his hand: also with three lines in Sanskrit text. Unfortunately the writing is so small and somewhat smudged now that it is difficult to read save for some words like *divyam* or *bhadram*, which only help to establish that the text is religious in character. What text it is is almost impossible to tell.

The setting is conventional: the prince is seen seated under an arch, the top part of which is covered by a cloth curtain now rolled up and tied. The terrace is of white marble with a lattice-work balustrade at the back, beyond which two beautiful plants rise in symmetry in full, colorful blossom. He himself is elegantly dressed as befits his status and regal bearing: a white *jama* with trefoil patterning in gold, and a neatly tied white turban to match with a crossband in gold and black going across it. There is no jewelry on his person save a ring on one finger, almost suggestive of the fact that it is a private, not a courtly, moment that is captured here. The look on the face is confident but not arrogant; there is no flamboyance in his attitude as he sits, legs tucked under, gaze directed in front. There are the usual signs of comfort and rank: a large scarlet colored cushion behind him, even though he does not lean against it, and another lying by the side on which a sword, his kingly weapon and symbol, rests. A small brass or gold vessel is next to him. What comes as a surprise however is the bouquet of flowers arranged in a golden vase that stands directly in front of the prince. It is oddly placed, for princes are rarely seen with flowers before them in this fashion. One cannot escape the feeling, however, that this vase is a late addition, possibly painted over a huqqa which the painter might routinely have placed there to begin with, and then been asked to remove, given the context.

The work is highly skilled: the drawing impeccable, the coloring rich but delicate. There is a high degree of finish and wonderful attention to detail. What adds decidedly to the impact the painting makes are the rich and broad floral borders in gold and blue within which it is set. It is as if the work had been meant for an album – the uneven width of the vertical borders is certainly suggestive of that – but one cannot be certain. | BG

Published: Cran 1980, no. 81

85 Vishnu as Vamana, the dwarf incarnation

Folio from a *Dasavatara* series
By an artist from the Seu-Nainsukh family workshop
Pahari, c. 1775
18.9 × 27.3 cm (folio); 15 × 23 cm (painting)
Museum Rietberg, Collection Danielle Porret, 2011.383

These were difficult times, the text says, not only for men but also for the gods. For, in the ongoing struggle between gods and demons, Bali, king of the *daitya*-demons, had asserted his power over all the three worlds and in fact taken control of *svarga* itself – the heavenly domain of the gods. It was therefore time for Vishnu to intervene, as the *Bhagavata Purana* says. He decided to incarnate himself yet again, and descended into the womb of Aditi, wife of the sage Kashyapa, eventually to be born as their son. The gods held their breath and when the Lord as baby was born there was great jubilation all around. Prayers were offered, conches were blown, big drums sounded and hymns of praise were sung, everyone participating: gods and sages and men. The Lord however had other plans. Soon after he was born, he transformed himself into "a dwarf Brahman boy," like a wonderfully skilled actor, even as his parents looked on. When his sacred thread ceremony was held, the sun-god Surya taught him the *Gayatri mantra*, the preceptor Brihaspati gave him the sacred thread, the Earth-goddess conferred upon him the skin of the black antelope, the heavens gave him an umbrella, Brahma presented him with a water pot, and so on.

Now ready to put his plan into action, Vishnu as the Dwarf – *Vamana* is the Sanskrit word – arrived at the door of Bali who was famed in all the three worlds for his generosity and for the gifts he could bestow upon Brahmanas. When Bali saw this young boy at his door, out of the respect he had for the learned, he went out to welcome him, and to wash his feet. What followed – Vamana asking the generous king for land that could be covered only by three steps; Bali agreeing readily to this and preparing to grant this trifle of a gift; Shukracharya, Bali's preceptor, trying to stop Bali from making the gift, having seen through Vamana's ruse – is all told in great detail in the text. But the moment chosen by the painter to visualize here is when the sacred gift is being sealed by the giver, in this case Bali, pouring water over the hand of the receiver, in this case Vamana.

What is of interest is the manner in which things are changed, and the text is departed from, even in respect of the iconography of Vamana. There is no narrative here and one sees only the moment of the gift being sealed, essentially because the painter is turning in a greatly simplified iconic image, much like in the case of the other *avatars* of Vishnu. It is the climactic moment, catching the essence of the *avatar*. All the same, the change in the iconography of Vamana is startling. When Bali saw him, Vamana appeared, the text says, as "a Brahman boy with the appearance of a *brahmachari* … with the zone of *munja*-grass tied round his waist and wearing as an upper garment a deer-skin in the manner of the sacred thread over his shoulder …" Vamana as we see him here is a dwarfish figure of course, but has the white-bearded aspect of a sage; he wears no antelope skin, nor a zone of *munja*-grass. But then there are other figures: Vindhyavali, Bali's royal consort, quietly watching; the preceptor Shukracharya with a wondering finger raised to his lips; and a demon attendant. A painter's way, to be sure, to ground the entire scene and the context. It is all very competently handled but one does get the feeling that this is not the first time the artist has painted this scene. | BG

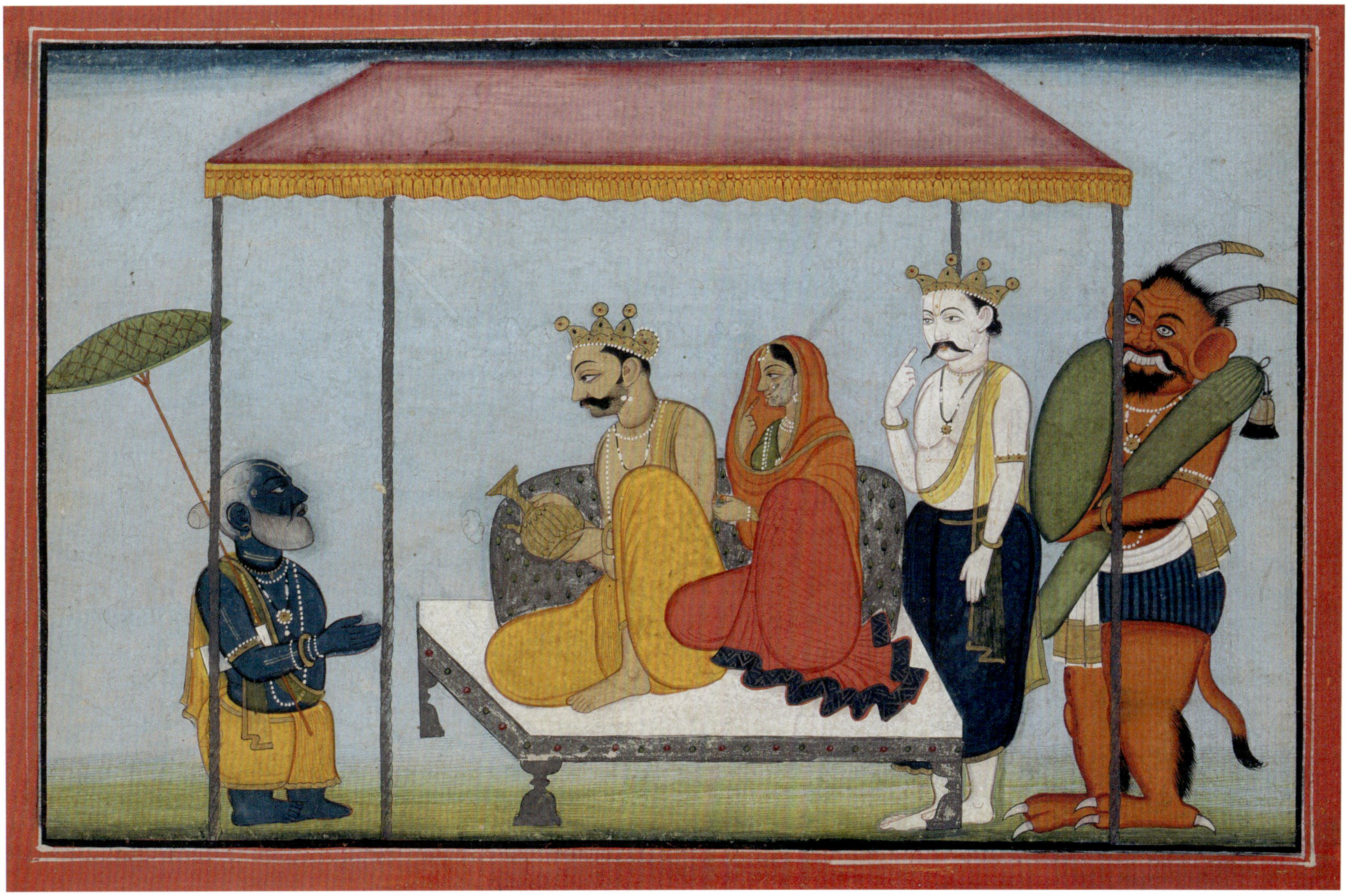

86 The Gods' hymn of praise for the Great Goddess

Folio 50 from a *Devi Mahatmya* series
From the family workshop of Seu-Nainsukh
Pahari, c. 1790
21.5 × 28.6 cm (folio); 18.3 × 25.2 cm (painting)
Inscribed on verso with eleven lines of the Sanskrit text in Devanagari
Museum Rietberg, Collection Danielle Porret, 2011.384

Another fierce battle is over. With the great demon chiefs Shumbha and Nishumbha slain and divine order now restored, the gods all appear again and stand here, singing another *stuti* – hymn of praise – for the Great Goddess. The text from the *Markandeya Purana* – called by different names: *Devi Mahatmya*, *Durga Saptashati*, *Chandi Path* – is all in glorification of the Great Goddess, but interspersed with descriptions of spirited action in which the Goddess takes on one great demon after another – Mahishasura, Dhumralochana, Raktabija, Chanda, Munda, Shumbha, Nishumbha among them. There are also quiet passages in it where the gods assemble, now to beg her to come to their aid, now to offer their own weapons to her, now to praise her. Here, after she has triumphed, the gods laud her as Narayani, an aspect of Vishnu-Narayan. But since the *shaktis* of the various gods had come to her aid on the fierce battlefield too and played such a part in the victory, they are likewise described, ending with the same words: *narayani namastu te*: "O Narayani, we bow to you."

In the image, which bears the number 50 on the top blue border – indicating that the series is moving towards its end, considering that so many Pahari series of the theme consisted of 57 folios – the seven *shaktis* and Shivaduti, here headed by the fearsome Kali stand at left while the gods stand facing them, humbly, all in a line – bodies slightly bent forward from the waist upwards, hands folded in obeisance, at right. It is not easy to identify all the gods, save for Indra with the many marks of the eyes on his body, and Surya and Chandra, their bodies painted a bright red and silvery white, respectively, but one understands that this group represents all the gods in heaven. The *shaktis*, on the other hand, can be clearly recognized: Brahmani on her swan mount, Maheshvari on a bull, Vaishnavi on the Garuda bird, Kaumari on a peacock, Aindri on the Airavata elephant, Varahi, Narasimhi and Shivaduti all standing. The *shlokas* go into detail about each one of the seven *matrikas* or *shaktis*, describing not only their mounts but also their *ayudhas* or weapons individually. At the head of the *saptamatrikas* of course stands the goddess Kali, a dread apparition: naked save for a loincloth, black of complexion, hair disheveled, holding weapons made of bones and her staff. The entire composition is neatly arranged against a flat orange ground – possibly hinting at the coming of a new age after all turmoil has ceased.

Several sets of the *Devi Mahatmya* were painted in the Pahari area, some of them by members of this very family of artists.[1] Not all of them are of equal merit and some show signs of less energy than others. Within the same family, of course, earlier compositions served as models that were followed with minor changes. Behind this folio, obviously, stood earlier works, but the execution remains skilled, the coloring is rich and precise, and the painter can be seen as having taken great care not only in getting the iconography of each *matrika/shakti* right, but also her character or inclination.

Evidently the series from which this folio comes was dispersed, pages having gone into different hands or public collections. A group of four folios of the *Devi Mahatmya* in the Metzger collection appears to be closely related to the present folio.[2] | BG

1 See Goswamy and Fischer 2011a, pp. 691–692.
2 See Bautze 1991, pp. 60–68 and Fischer 2005, nos. 47–50, 52.

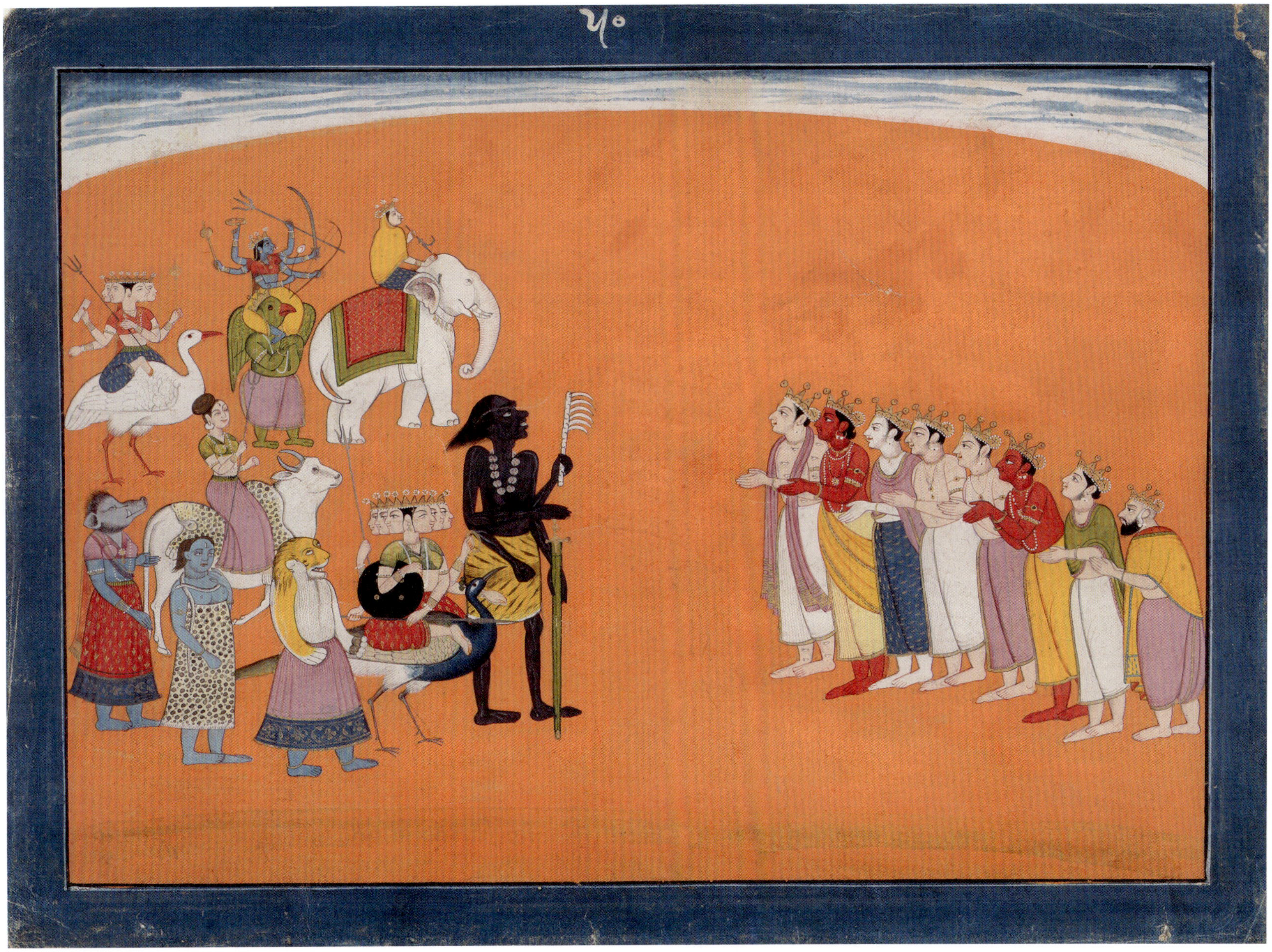
५०

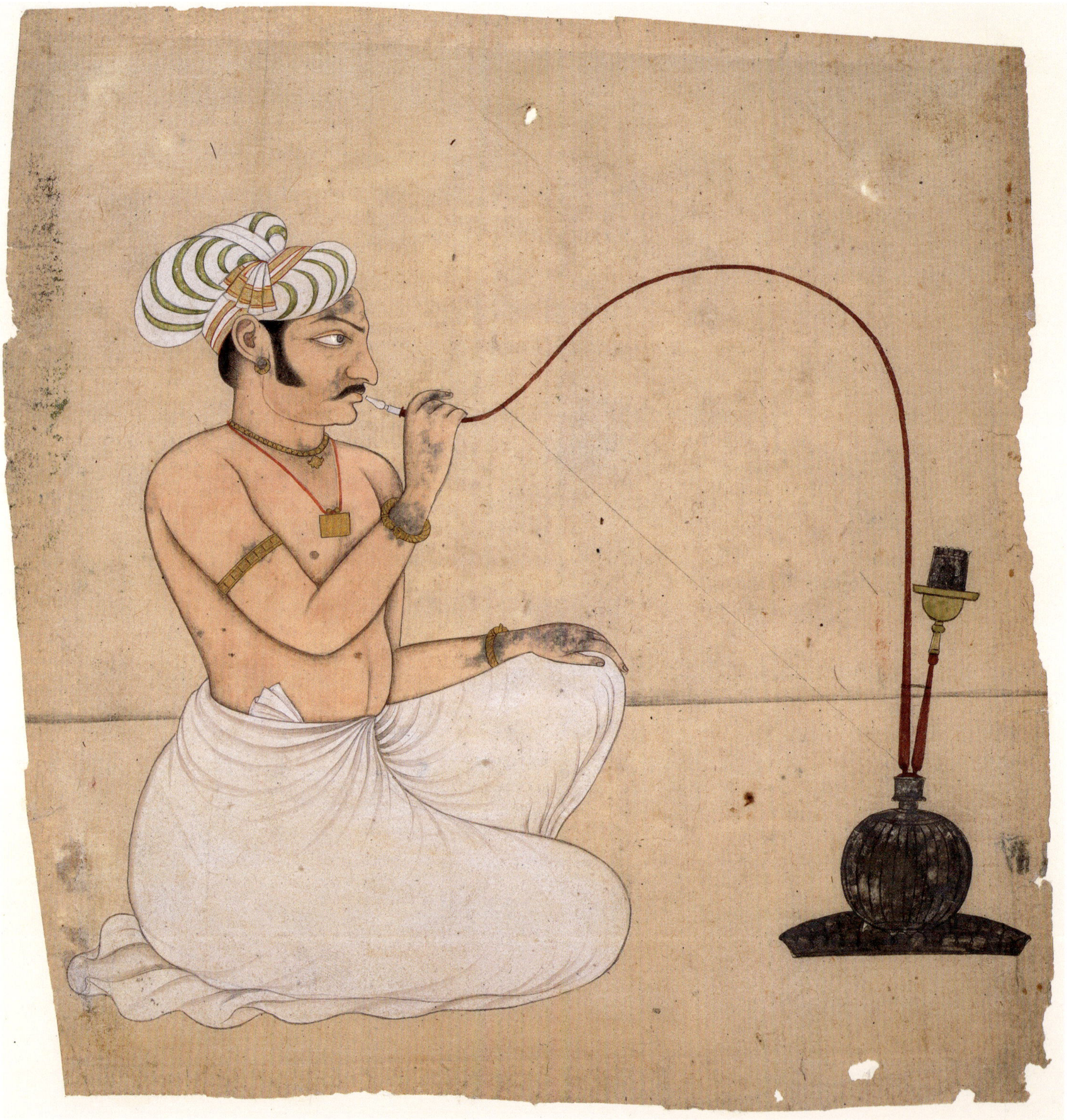

87 Raja Bhupat Pal of Basohli seated, smoking

From a Mankot workshop
Pahari, c. 1680
20.5 × 19 cm (average size of folio)

It is not unlikely that no contemporary portraits of this ruler, Bhupat Pal (c. 1598–1635), exist, but there was enough in the local imagination and legends for the painters to conjure up an image of him. Series of ancestral portraits, featuring kings long gone, were often made, but, wherever possible, the painters must have relied on what they heard. Bhupat Pal – it is almost certainly him that we see here, judging from other "inscribed" portraits of him that have come down[1] – was no ordinary figure. Between him and another powerful ruler, Jagat Singh of Nurpur – just across the river Ravi from Basohli – no love had ever been lost and, as a result of intrigue he was thrown into prison for some years by the emperor Jahangir. But he survived and worked himself into the entourage of Jahangir's successor, Shah Jahan, becoming for some time even a favorite at the Mughal court. His personal prowess was such that stories are still told of his having the strength to rub out the legend on a coin by pressing it between his thumb and forefinger.[2] What he ate, and how much of it, is told with relish in the old chronicles of Basohli. That he met a violent end – murdered by his old enemy, Jagat Singh – is known, but this was something greatly rued both in the Pahari region and at the Shajahani court.

A resplendent portrait of his in the Hodgkin collection, shows him in a conventional setting: seated on a floral carpet, a large bolster at the back, looking straight ahead of himself while smoking a straight-stemmed huqqa, the base of which is held by an attendant.[3] He is regally dressed there: a thin muslin *jama*, the upper part of which up to the short sleeve is gold-colored, worn over a striped *paijama*; long lappets of the *jama* tied under the left armpit stream down to the waist; a colorful striped *patka* in blue and black with floral end-panels featuring "Shahjahani herbals" secures his waist and on his head he wears a beautifully patterned turban, tightly tied with a small golden cross-band around it. The build is athletic and the face handsome, marked by long sideburns that end well below the ears. It is, however, the look in the eye that is truly arresting: sharp and alert and almost unforgiving.

This is very close to what we see in this brilliantly painted sketch. Here, however, the same personage – Bhupat Pal, as far as one can judge – is seen seated almost in a state of undress, upper part of the body completely bare, the lower part clad only in a *dhoti* wrinkled just below the waist where it is tied. The same kind of turban is however in place and so are gold armlets, bracelets, and a large amulet worn round the neck. The Raja is seen smoking a huqqa, the stem of which is still stiff and hard but rises in a curve toward the mouth. The features are markedly the same, chiefly the slightly hooked nose and the long sideburns. There is no attendant, no mark of state. But the regal bearing and the look in the eye convey exactly the same feeling as that seen in the Hodgkin portrait.

Questions do arise: why should so many rulers of Basohli, including this one, have been portrayed by members of the artist family that appears to have worked out of Mankot? Unless of course that family spread out from Mankot and its members took up work for patrons in nearby kingdoms. The more interesting question, however, is: if these portraits are not contemporary to the time of Bhupat Pal, why should, in addition to the formal portrait showing him seated in state – something which would not be out of the ordinary – a sketch of this kind have also been made? Idealized or imaginary portraits would seldom show a person in this informal a state, in virtual undress. There are no easy answers. | BG

1 Archer 1973, Mankot no. 12.
2 Archer 1973, I, p. 17.
3 Published: Topsfield and Beach 1991, no. 28 and Crill and Jariwala 2010, no. 43.

Published: Sotheby's, London, 5 July 1982, lot 65

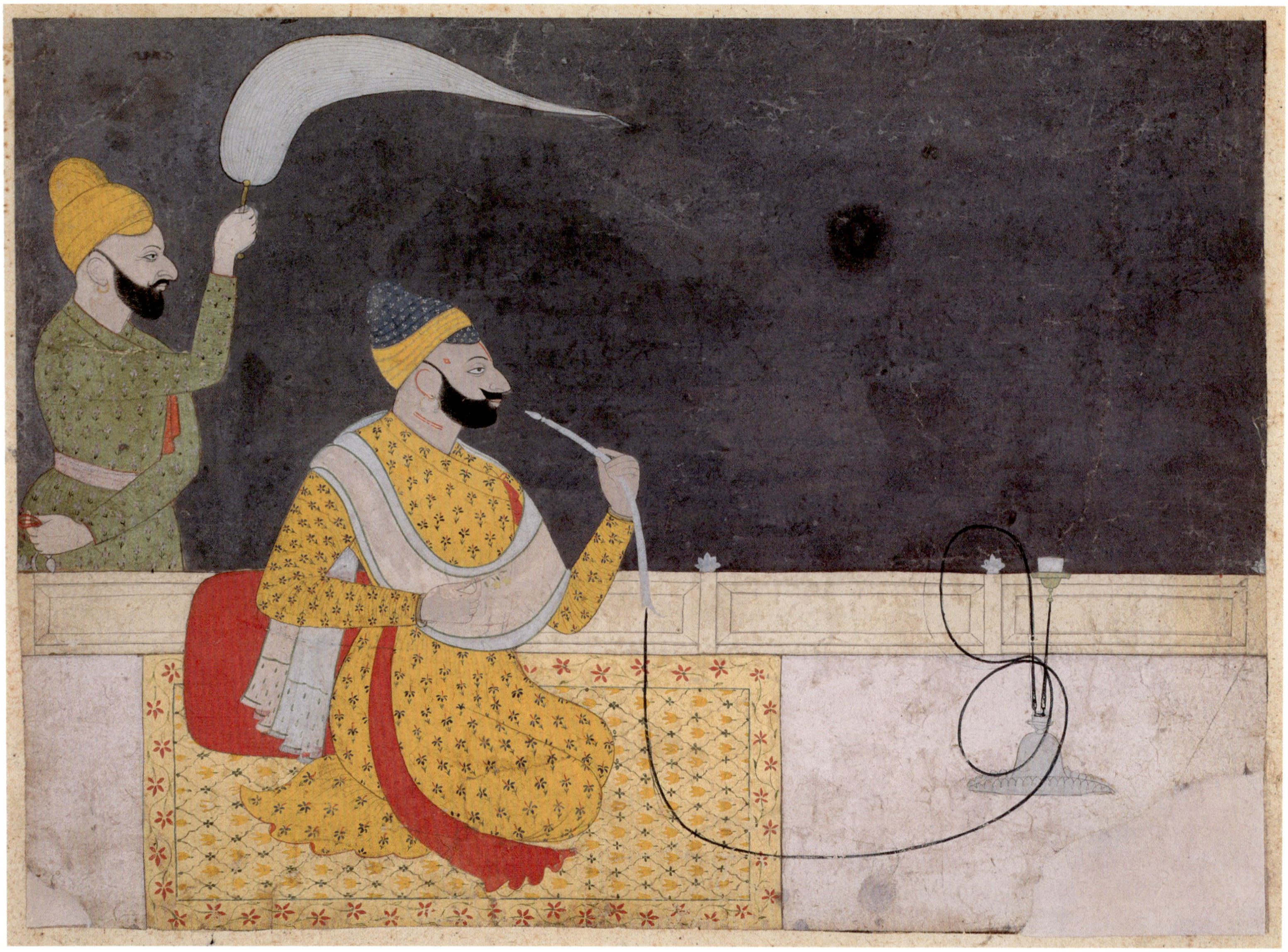

88 Raja Indra Dev of Bandralta seated, smoking

From a family workshop active at Bandralta
Pahari, c. 1750
20.2 × 27.3 cm (folio)
Museum Rietberg, Collection Danielle Porret, 2011.394

Remarkably little is known about this youthful ruler, fond of hunting and of flowers, among other things. The state he ruled over – Bandralta, now called Ramnagar – was very small, not far from Jammu and next door to Mankot, which had a flourishing atelier of artists. There is some uncertainty about the dates, although the best guess is that he was active between 1730 and 1760; but one knows for certain that he was a devout Vaishnava. The state of Bandralta was until recently referred to as a Narsinghi raj, meaning a state dedicated to Narasimha, fourth incarnation of Vishnu; and the fact that Indra Dev is referred to in some inscribed paintings as "Dewan" – rather than as a Raja – probably refers to his having dedicated his state to his deity, and himself acting as his deputy or "Dewan."[1] The practice was not unknown elsewhere in the Pahari area: consider for example the situation at Mandi where the state was dedicated to the deity Madho Rai, or at Kulu where the state was declared as the domain of Rama under the name Raghunath ji, with the ruler taking on the role of his deputy and ruling in his deity's name. We have a painting of Indra Dev seated in front of an image of his *ishta*, Vishnu; here in this portrait he prominently wears on his body – forehead, temple, neck – sacred marks proclaiming his devotion.[2]

Compared to some other paintings or drawings of Indra Dev, this image is relatively simple of composition: he is not seen in action, for instance, hunting and striking down an antelope, or being attended upon by courtiers other than a flywhisk bearer. Clearly however he is meant to be seen as seated in state: on a terrace ending in a balustrade at the back, a floral carpet under him, leaning against a bolster, smoking a huqqa with a long, curling pipe, the stem of which he holds regally in one hand. The dress is elegant: yellow, flowered *jama*, with a diaphanous wrap draped across the body. The painting is clearly iconic in character and reminds one strongly of another portrait of the Raja now in the Chhatrapati Shivaji Maharaj Vastu Sangrahalaya (formerly the Prince of Wales Museum) in Mumbai.[3] The athletic bearing is the same; the foppish curl of the mustache is similar; he wears the same turban turning somewhat conical at the top; even the *patka* at the waist trails in the same fashion along the thigh. Very similar is the stance of the flywhisk bearer, too, holding up as he is a summarily rendered *chauri*-flywhisk in his raised hand, with the left arm turning and disposed across the body. The man in the Mumbai painting bears the name mania rasal, but here he remains unnamed.

Indra Dev was a contemporary of Balwant Singh of Jasrota for whom the celebrated Nainsukh worked. Jasrota was not far from Bandralta and it is not unlikely that Indra Dev's painters had seen some of Nainsukh's work. The way in which – contrary to usual practice – the backgrounds of some of the paintings made for him are left bare and uncolored certainly brings that possibility to mind. | BG

1 See Archer 1973, I, pp. 11–12 (Bandralta nos. 2 and 3).
2 Khandalavala 1958, no. 76.
3 Archer 1973, Bandralta no. 4.

89 Gauda Malhari ragini

Folio from a *ragamala* series
From a family workshop active at Bilaspur
Pahari, c. 1740
22.2 × 15.4 cm (folio)

But for the fact that it is inscribed with the name of the *ragini*, it would not be easy to see this work as being from a *ragamala* series. The fact that the name given is Gauda Malhari makes it even more difficult to associate it with that musical mode, for that *ragini* relates, in the textual and the performative tradition, to the rainy season when *malhars* are sung and the skies are filled with clouds that roar and thunder. Here, two women sit, facing each other, both leaning against large bolster cushions, a narrow door filling the space between them. One might have thought of them as belonging to a *nayika-bheda* series, the heroine in love talking to a confidante. But then one knows that the names – as different from the ethos – of *ragas* and *raginis* were interpreted differently in different regions of India; this seems to be the Bilaspur painter's thoughts about that musical mode.

Regardless, one savors the painting for what it offers, all rubbing and tears included. The setting is elegant: large floral carpet filling nearly the entire lower half of the page; back wall dotted with niches of different shapes, each housing decoratively painted trays and vessels and vases; roof and eave featuring neatly articulated floral patterns; the split-bamboo screen covering the doorway with a tidily rolled-up screen close to the top. But the attention quickly moves away from these to the stances of the two young women, each bearing the aspect and air of princesses, and the possible subject of conversation between them. The maiden at right seems to be in a position slightly higher than that of her companion: the look in the eye and the more confident stance speak of that. What she holds in her raised left hand – a very thin, short applicator stick of the kind used for putting collyrium to the eyes – might be the clue to understanding exactly what the theme of the conversation might be, for surely there is reference here to some poetry to which we at this time do not have access. The lady seated facing her also has a similar stick in one hand which she is about to offer to her friend at right, while she holds a handkerchief in her right hand, ready for use as it were. Meanwhile, one takes in the elegant appearance of the two ladies: the thin blouses through which the outlines of their breasts clearly shimmer; the colorful skirts over which are draped flowered veils of gauze-like thinness; the jewelry – gold and pearls and precious stones – on their persons and the dainty painted marks on the foreheads. Are they, one wonders, speaking of the desire or the need to be at their elegant best as they wait for "him" to arrive in this season of rains? Or is there a reference to the rains having come and gone without his having arrived on promise and the consequent futility of decking themselves up now? The sky is certainly bare of clouds at this moment, only a trace remaining in the form of an arc. | BG

Published: Cran 1980, no. 80 (not illustrated)

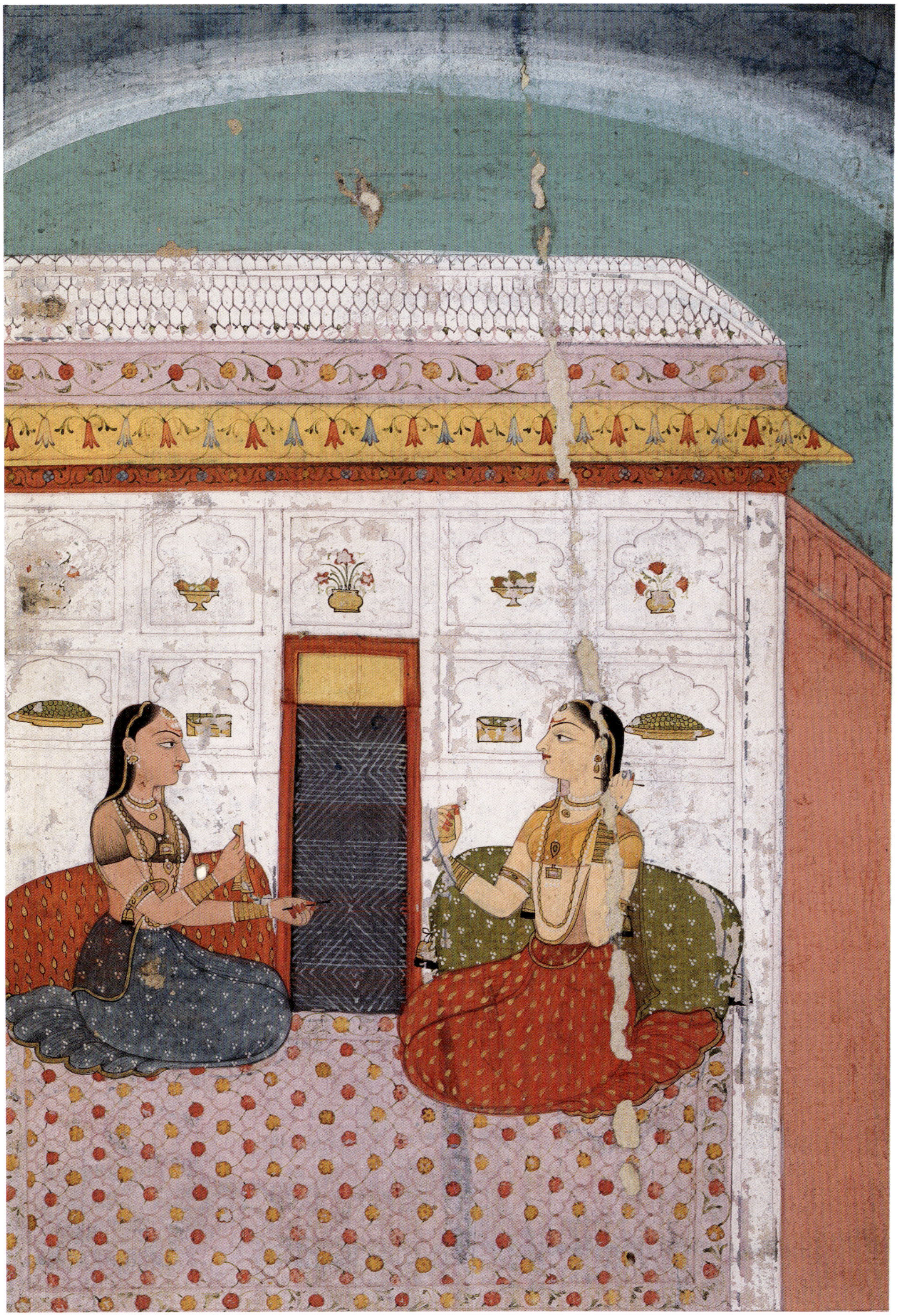

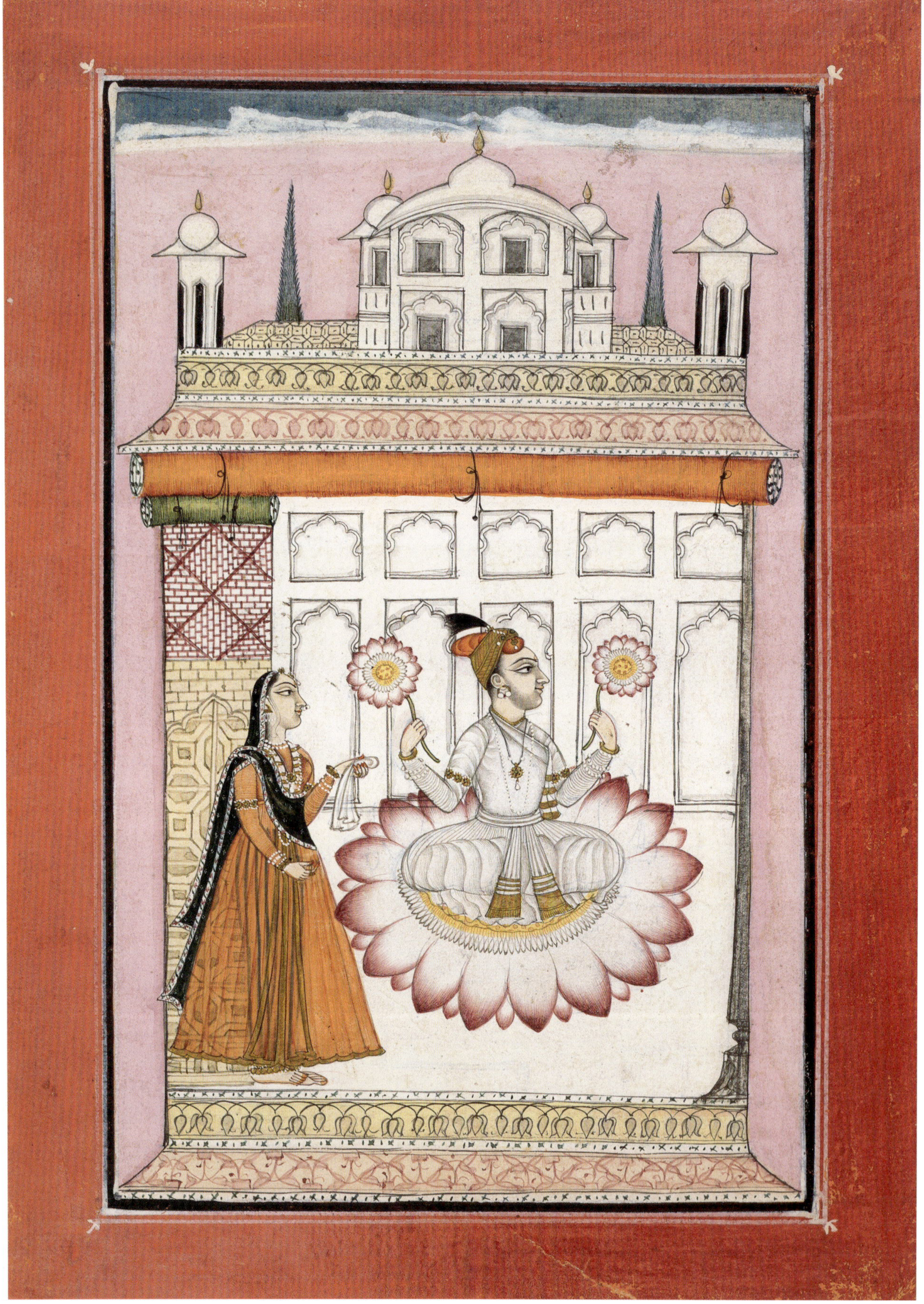

90 Kamala raga
91 Mevada raga

Folio from a *ragamala* series
From a workshop in Bilaspur
Pahari, mid-18th century
25.9 × 17.8 cm (folio), 20.7 × 12.8 cm (painting)
Inscribed on verso with two Takri and one Devanagari inscription
Museum Rietberg, Collection Danielle Porret, 2011.392

Folio from a *ragamala* series
From a workshop in Bilaspur
Pahari, mid-18th century
26.9 × 17.7 cm (folio), 21.5 × 12.6 cm (painting)
Inscribed on verso with one Takri and one Devanagari inscription
Museum Rietberg, Collection Danielle Porret, 2013.187

The relationship sought to be established between music and painting in what is generally referred to as *ragamala* painting opens up exciting vistas. The theme is of obvious interest, for it pulls many strands together, but also contentious, especially among practicing musicians who do not always see a correspondence between image and sound. Iconographies raise problems sometimes – for in different texts relating to music, many of them of great authority, the *dhyana*-images of different musical modes are very differently visualized – nomenclatures and classifications also do not always agree. And yet, most agreeably, the field remains rich. It is hard to think of a school or sub-style of painting in Rajasthan or in the Pahari area in which *ragamala* paintings were not made. Some brilliant works – visually engaging, emotionally affecting – belong to this genre, both painters and musicians sometimes posing a challenge to the viewer. It is a complex area, the difficulties compounded by the fact that not many *ragamala* series, intact in every way, have survived. But whatever has survived remains without doubt of interest.

The iconographies cause puzzlement sometimes, especially when one moves down from the six principal *ragas* to their "wives" – the *raginis* – but especially to their children – the *ragaputras* – even their numbers varying sometimes. Paintings are sometimes based upon false etymologies, especially in the Pahari area, where some names of *raginis* or *ragaputras* might have become known without their corresponding *dhyanas* having arrived from the "classical world" at the same time. Confronted with that situation, but determined to complete a series, painters sometimes fell back upon the literal meanings of the titles of the *ragaputras* and produced images that are completely at variance with the "image" or visualization intended in the texts. False etymologies were pressed into service at times. Scholars have struggled with the problem and some, for instance Klaus Ebeling, nearly gave up on Pahari *ragamalas*; all the same, the visual excitement offered by the images remains.

From the family workshops of painters active at Bilaspur have come a very large number of *ragamala* paintings, whole series having been painted there and analyzed later by Ernst and Rose L. Waldschmidt in their classic study.[1] These two paintings belong to one such workshop – ascribed sometimes to Chamba by other scholars – both paintings not devoted to any of the major *ragas*, or even to *ragini*, but to *ragaputras*. The paintings bear inscriptions at their back identifying the mode. On the verso of the leaf where a *ragaputra*, Kamala, is visualized (cat. no. 90), there are as many as three inscriptions, two of them in Takri, the script of the hills, and the third, possibly in a late hand, in Devanagari.[2] There are very minor variations in the inscribed texts, but each inscription identifies the *ragaputra* as Kamala, son of the *raga* Dipaka. The Devanagari inscription adds that this mode is the fourth son of *raga* Dipaka (*putra chautha*) and is the tenth leaf (of some series), while the "original" inscription in Takri, in a small, but somewhat inelegant, hand simply states that this is *dipake da putra raga kamala*, although this line is followed by a laconic addition, *pa. 4*, which could be expanded to read as *patra chautha*, meaning the fourth folio.

The name of the *ragaputra*, Kamala, being not difficult to interpret, the painter visualizes the musical mode as a young, smiling man seated cross-legged on a large blossoming lotus, holding in both his hands a lotus flower. As he looks towards the right, almost unaware of anyone else being close, a young woman, holding a handkerchief in one hand, stands in attendance. Behind the two rises the facade of a palatial structure with delicate ornamentation on the roof, the eave, the wall. There is no special emphasis on coloring or drawing but the air in the painting is generally pleasant.

The second painting (cat. no. 91) is similarly inscribed at the back – in Devanagari and Takri – but the texts are somewhat hard to interpret, in part because of damage and in part because of overwriting. The *raga* of which a *putra* depicted here is clearly mentioned; it is Malakauns – Malavakaushika in the Sanskrit original – but the name of the *ragaputra* does not appear as clearly. *Malakaushe da putra manjada duya, 2, patra 8,* reads the Devanagari inscription, while the Takri inscription in the small hand speaks of the *raga* being *mejada*, son of Malakauns. There being no *raga* – in the known classifications – by the name of "Manjada" or "Mejada," it is more than likely that the intention was to identify it as *raga* Mevada. That *ragaputra* is visualized as a musician playing, interestingly, on a bagpipe. That is exactly what one sees here.

Where this iconography comes from remains a matter for speculation, for a bagpipe is not known to be an Indian musical instrument. Here, the puzzlement is added to by the fact that the musician is dressed in uncommon habit: a hat on the head, the body covered in some kind of tunic and breeches. A European figure is perhaps what the painter had in mind, the impression added to by the fact that the man's hair is light colored, falls on the shoulders and is curly. As he plays – one also notices the uncommon panel with keys on which his fingers move having a carved female head at the top – a young woman, wearing a long dress held together with tie-cords at the chest, comes out of her chamber with a tray full of fruits which she seems to offer to the man. The model that the painter might have had in his mind is again a European woman, for one notices a different cut to the face and the light-brown, curly hair which falls to her shoulders.

The two figures remind one of paintings of European heads that one knows from Bundi or Mewar in Rajasthan, and it is not unlikely that the painter had access to some Rajasthani *ragamala* set from which he might have taken these. Nevertheless, on what the Rajasthani painter was basing his iconography would still remain a puzzle. One notices at the same time that the treatment of the palace facade, and the ornamentation that one sees in profusion remain grounded in the work of the workshop of this family based in Bilaspur or Chamba. | BG

1 Waldschmidt and Waldschmidt 1966.
2 Other folios from this series have likewise two Takri and one Devanagari inscriptions; see Bautze 1991, p. 127.

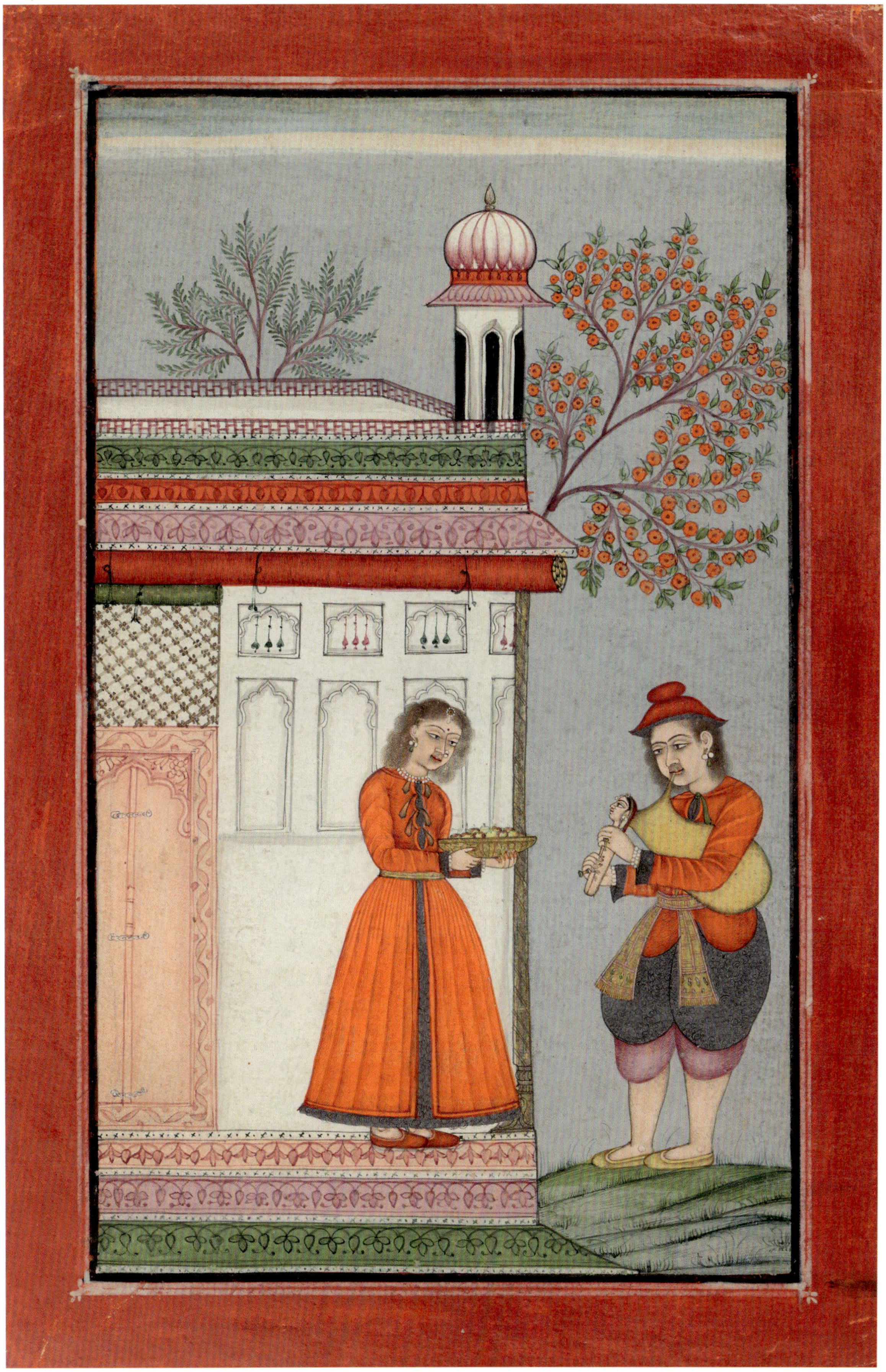

92 Krishna and Radha playing Holi

Possibly from a Nurpur workshop
Pahari, c. 1770
28.8 × 20.8 cm (folio), 23.6 × 15.9 cm (painting)

In the literature of India, especially in the north, there are countless references to, and descriptions of, Krishna and Radha playing Holi – that boisterous, colorful festival that comes every year in the Hindi month of Phalguna – even if the *Bhagavata Purana* barely mentions it. In the late 16th-century text, the *Rasikapriya* of Keshavadasa, the poet speaks of everyone getting drenched in color, as men and women throw, sprinkle and smear color, and this becoming an occasion for Krishna to seize upon and "attack" bevies of girls, among them of course, Radha. In a 19th-century poem, the poet simply takes off and speaks – sings might be a better term – of one color followed by another that the two lovers throw upon each other: *baingani, kiramchi, surmayi, piazi, kapoori,* and the like. It turns into a riot. At times, in texts that treat the love between Krishna and Radha as a "secret," the lovers keep inventing pretexts under which they can come together without provoking too much comment. Holi provides the perfect occasion. This is the way it goes on, poets celebrating and painters taking off from them.

Here, Krishna has arrived at Radha's "palatial" home in the company of three of his *gopa* friends. Two of them carry colored powder – *gulal* – in pouches they have made of their *uttariya*-scarves, but Krishna has equipped himself with a *pichkari*-jet syringe with which he can throw and sprinkle colored water some distance, knowing that Radha might not come down from her balcony. "*Mat maaro shyam pichkari*," as the song has it, says Radha in mock protest, asking him to desist, but of course it has no effect on Krishna. Retaliating from where she stands up there, Radha, with a fistful of colored powder in her hand, throws it down. It has not reached Krishna yet, but that is not the intention of the painter. He simply turns it into a theatrical moment, a masque as it were. The eyes of the lovers are locked and they seem to be unaware of anyone else's presence. In any case, no one else is moving, neither the *gopas* nor the girl companions of Radha who peep from behind a pillar at this playful exchange. Interestingly, the lone *gopa* standing in the entrance gate to Radha's courtyard is seen making a gesture with one hand toward his face as if asking for colored powder to descend upon him too. It is all hilarity, a *dol utsav* as everyone calls it.

There are signs of the painting waiting to be finished. All the architectural details that one expects to see – the decoration on the pillar and the gate, the patterning on the floor, for instance – are not there. The spandrels in the four corners are clearly not meant to be bare: they are simply unfinished. Despite that, the painting, sparsely peopled as it is compared to those elaborate Holi scenes that so many Pahari painters have left behind, makes an impact. Because of its reticence, its simplicity perhaps?

The figures are all uncommonly tall and slim, and the faces of the *gopa* boys look a bit pinched. Radha, with a demure face, is, like everyone else, tall and long-legged. Krishna, as the painter renders him, however occupies the central space: slim and blue-skinned, he wears his usual *pita-vastra dhoti* on the lower limbs and a crown, his *mora-mukuta*, that almost defines him: glistening gold, with five points, topped by a peacock feather. The work was once assigned by Archer to Nurpur,[1] but it is difficult to be certain. | BG

[1] See Czuma 1975, no. 107.

Formerly in the George P. Bickford Collection
Published: Czuma 1975, no. 107; Cran 1980, no. 85 (not illustrated)

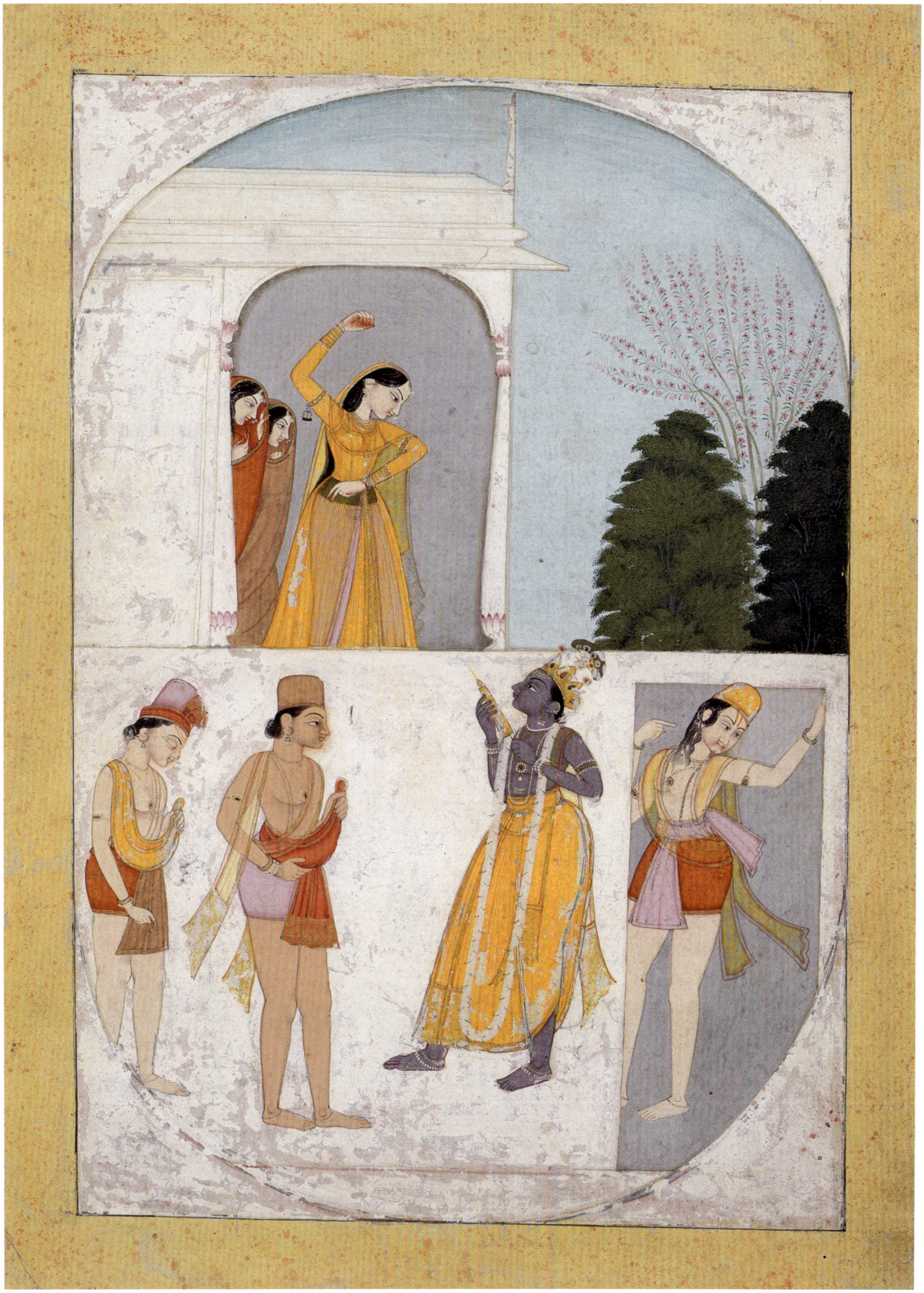

93 Krishna pretending to milk a cow

From a workshop at Jammu
Pahari, c. 1770
24.2 × 18.6 cm (folio), 19.6 × 14.8 cm (painting)

He is a cowherd of course, having been born in the house of Nanda, chief of that village of cowherds – the texts never tire of saying this – but Krishna does not go around milking cows, and certainly not in people's homes. If he is here, then, in Radha's home – she is the one holding a calf from his rope – it is part of a ruse. Among the many pretexts he keeps inventing just to be able to meet or be with Radha, his beloved – feigning sickness so that she can come visiting him like others; throwing a protective blanket over her as it begins to rain in the fields; going to listen to a religious discourse where "everyone" would gather, and so on – is the one when he comes in the early hours of the morning under the guise of a milker of cows. There are different versions of this ruse: thus, Radha's parents have gone away and she alone is in charge of the cows; it is still dark in the wee hours of the morning, and he would not be recognized. But here he is in full light – the painter's reluctance to depict the dark comes in the way, perhaps – crouching on the ground and beginning to milk the cow, not even casting a glance for the moment at Radha as she stands, trying to look intently at this man. Of course he can be recognized, certainly by us, dressed as he is as usual – yellow *dhoti*, golden crown topped by peacock feathers, dark body bejeweled – but Radha is not meant to know this. Disbelief is to be willingly suspended.

The theme and the scene established, there are delightful touches that the painter would have wanted us to see. For instance, the manner in which Krishna is only going through the preparatory motions of milking. His eyes are clearly not on the job at hand but almost beginning slyly to look back, without turning his head, to see Radha. On her part, Radha – elegantly dressed in a reddish skirt, a blue *orhani*-veil that is tied at the waist and a yellow *choli*-blouse – has, one realizes, a hint of suspicion in her eyes as she bends her head to look. It is the stance of the brilliantly drawn cow, however, that is the most endearing. While her young one is moving friskily toward her udders, her eyes are not on him but on Krishna, for her head is completely turned towards him, her Lord as he is of everyone. After all, as the texts keeps reminding the reader, he is *gopala*: master and protector of cows.

Very engagingly, the painter leaves the background bare: a light green with an irregular band of white high on the horizon. No setting is established, neither home nor hearth. It is on the lovers and their furtive love, that the painter wishes to concentrate. The figures are drawn with a very sure hand and the coloring is delicate. Radha's face reminds one of a number of paintings that have been assigned to Jammu by Archer.[1] The skilled workmanship puts one in mind of the Seu-Nainsukh family, but we do not at this point of time know which family workshop was active in that area. | BG

1 For example Archer 1973, Jammu no. 71.

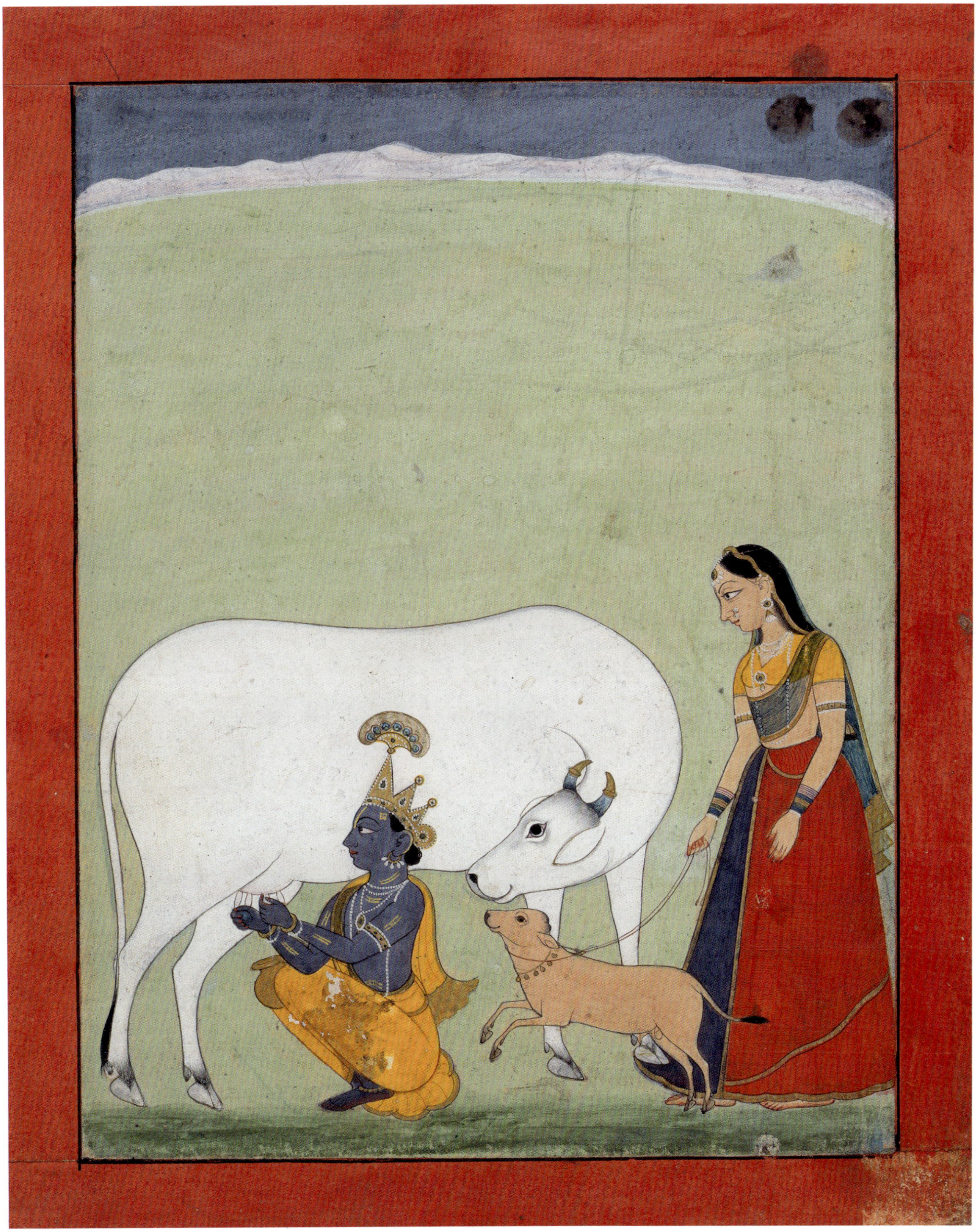

94 Lovers in a garden

From the family workshop of Sajnu of Mandi, possibly by Muhammadi Pahari, c. 1810
24.5 × 18.8 cm (folio), 23.2 × 17.2 cm (painting)

There is a feeling of complete leisure in the air, and of togetherness. A handsome young prince with his consort, arm lovingly draped around her shoulder, is taking a walk in the garden of his palace. But the two are not completely by themselves, a maid/confidante walks a couple of steps behind them, carrying a huqqa one end of the smoking stem of which is – interestingly – not in his hand, but hers. A flower held sportingly in one hand, he turns to gaze at her lovely face, but one senses a brief element of surprise on his face too, and one wonders about that. Is it because, playfully, she has suddenly "snatched" the huqqa stem away from him to make as if she wants to share his indulgence in the habit, or at least have a brief taste of it? There are hints of this playfulness in the painting that one needs to pick up. The near warning gesture she is making to the maid with her right hand, almost on the sly, is meaningful: it is as if she is telling her not to speak even a word about it, to make no comment at all. The bevy of four women standing at the door – evidently confidantes, palace ladies – clearly registers surprise, each in her own fashion: the one ahead of the others, dressed in a lilac *peshwaz*, extends a hand with fingers spread as if, her head turned toward them, asking the others just to look at this; another raises a wondering finger to her lips, equally surprised. For them to see the couple taking a walk in the garden could not have been an unusual sight, but this? It is not as if women did not smoke huqqas in the Pahari region – there are paintings with princesses seated by themselves and smoking – but for her smoking in the presence of her husband, especially when he himself is not, would have been an unusual sight. Is it one of the games that lovers play and poets write about, one wonders? Or is it that one is overreading the painting?

There is elegance in this painting, reflected as much in the cool marble architecture and the well laid out garden with its parterres of flowers, its walking paths and a water-channel at the back, as in the attires that one sees. The prince cuts a graceful figure, dressed as he is in a patterned white *jama* that trails along the floor and a neatly tied turban with a golden cross-band reminiscent of the turbans in paintings of the Sansar Chand (r. 1775–1823) period. The tastefully colored *peshwaz* that the women wear – mauve-pink, saffron-yellow, lilac – brushing the ground and rising at a slight angle at the back, make a very pleasant impression too. One notices that there is far more jewelry, including a bejeweled belt that is slung low below the waist, on the person of the princess rather than on the other women, but none of them is completely bereft of it.

It is not unlikely that this painting was done by the painter at the asking of a princess who wished to recall her lover's presence while he is far away. We know of paintings that came from the royal collection of Guler in which there are inscriptions to this effect: clear records of *virahini* women's longings to be joined to their lovers in paintings if not in real life.

At first sight the suggestion that comes to mind is that the work is in the hand of a member of the Seu-Nainsukh family, but it is far more likely that it comes from the workshop of Sajnu of Mandi. It may not be in that painter's own hand, but that of Muhammadi, a follower and disciple. At least two things lead to that thought: the relatively short stature of the women and the cuts of their faces. | BG

Published: Cran 1980, no. 87 (not illustrated)

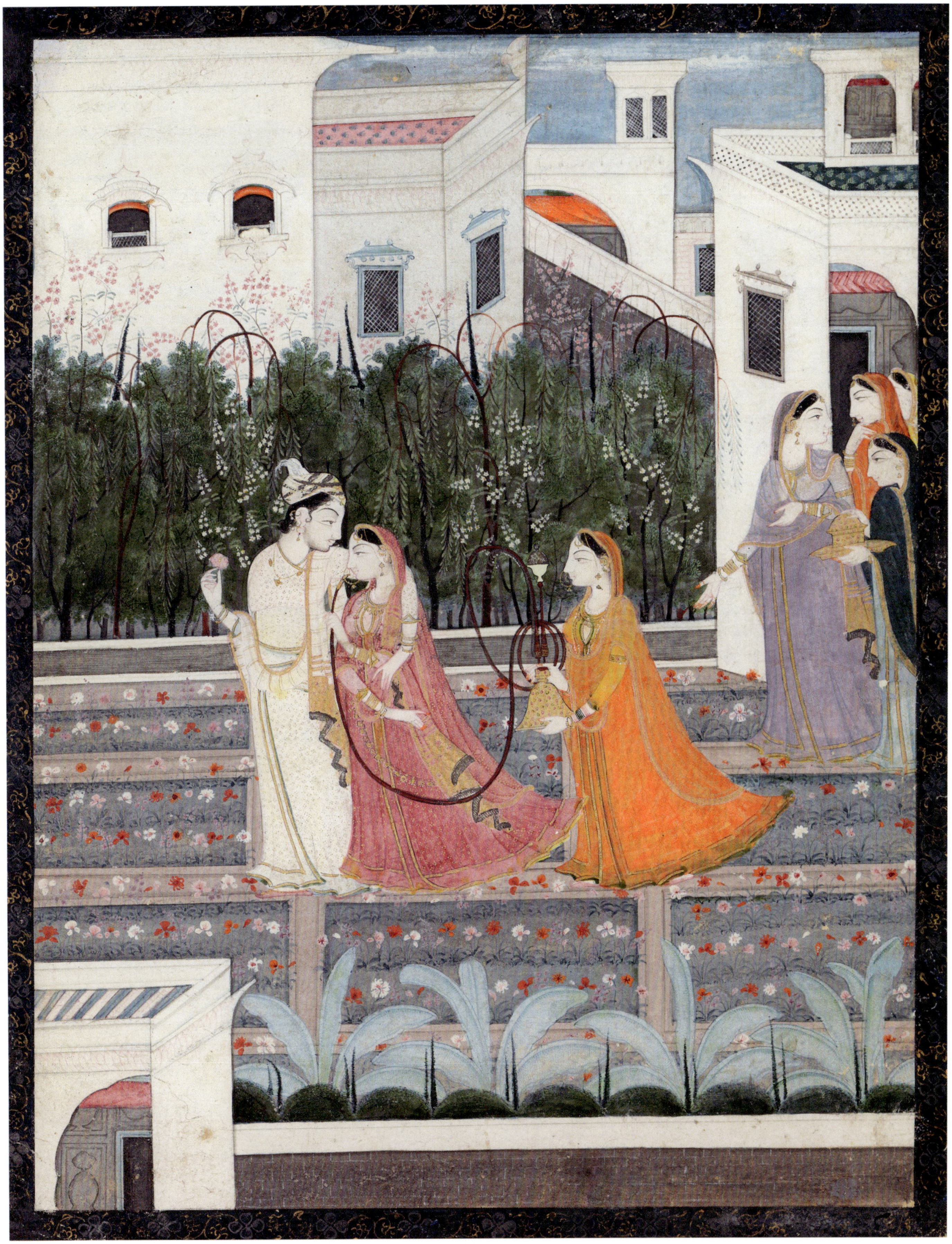

95 A seated Sikh warrior

From a series of portraits of Sikh nobles
From the family workshop of Purkhu of Kangra
Pahari, c. 1825
13.2 × 10.25 cm (painting)

The portrait is uninscribed, but the name that comes to mind is that of Gurmukh Singh Lamma (b. 1772), a brave soldier who joined the service of Maharaja Ranjit Singh. This, because of the evidently tall stature of the man – *lamma*, Punjabi for *lamba*, means tall – something that the painter is keen to emphasize here. It is known that Gurmukh Singh, who figures in the chronicles of the Maharaja's times, was not very tall himself, and he might have inherited the sobriquet from the armed contingent of Mohar Singh Lamma, who is certainly spoken of as having been exceptionally tall.[1] But oral descriptions and "titles" like this helped painters to visualize, apart from observe, the men they were asked to paint. While Mohar Singh barely finds mention in contemporary records, Gurmukh Singh's name emerges with prominence for he commanded a part of the Maharaja's armies. The emphasis in the portrait is also on the soldierly aspect of the man: hilt of a long sword resting in his lap, a large shield fastened to the back. The identification that comes to mind therefore might not be off the mark.

To pursue the career of Gurmukh Singh a bit: having joined as a young boy the camp of Maha Singh Sukerchakkia, Ranjit Singh's grandfather, Gurmukh Singh grew up as a childhood companion of the future Maharaja. When Lahore was captured by Ranjit Singh in 1799, Gurmukh Singh was by his side. Later, his name became associated with several campaigns: Kasur, Attock, Kashmir and the one against the Gurkhas in 1809. Severely wounded in battle, not once but many times, his valor stood out and honors at the hand of the Maharaja came his way, mostly in the form of large *jagirs* of land. If he did not rise beyond a certain level, it was due to the intrigues of the Dogra brothers, as family records say.

Whoever he is – whether Gurmukh Singh Lamma or not – the man we see in the portrait has, for all the simplicity in which he is dressed – *kurta*, *paijama*, *patka*, brief turban, all in pure white – an almost regal bearing. There is a sense of inner calm and of discipline in the face, and the attitude, with hands almost clasped and placed in the lap, is one of humility. But one also gets the feeling that he could spring into action any moment. There is skill in the rendering, a lack of fussiness that impresses. One is aware of several portraits of this kind, unfinished in part as they appear – quickly finished as it were against a white primed ground – that members of the family of Purkhu of Kangra painted for the Maharaja and those in the royal circle. A scrap of a letter written by Purkhu to his elder brother, now published,[2] establishes his own connection with Lahore in any case. But the impression of being relatively quickly done is belied by the fineness of detail that one sees here: the treatment of the beard, the few strands of loose hair on the back of the neck, the neatness with which the loops and turns of the straps and belt are treated. | BG

1 See Griffin 1865, pp. 540–542.
2 Goswamy and Fischer 2011b, p. 722 and fig. 1b.

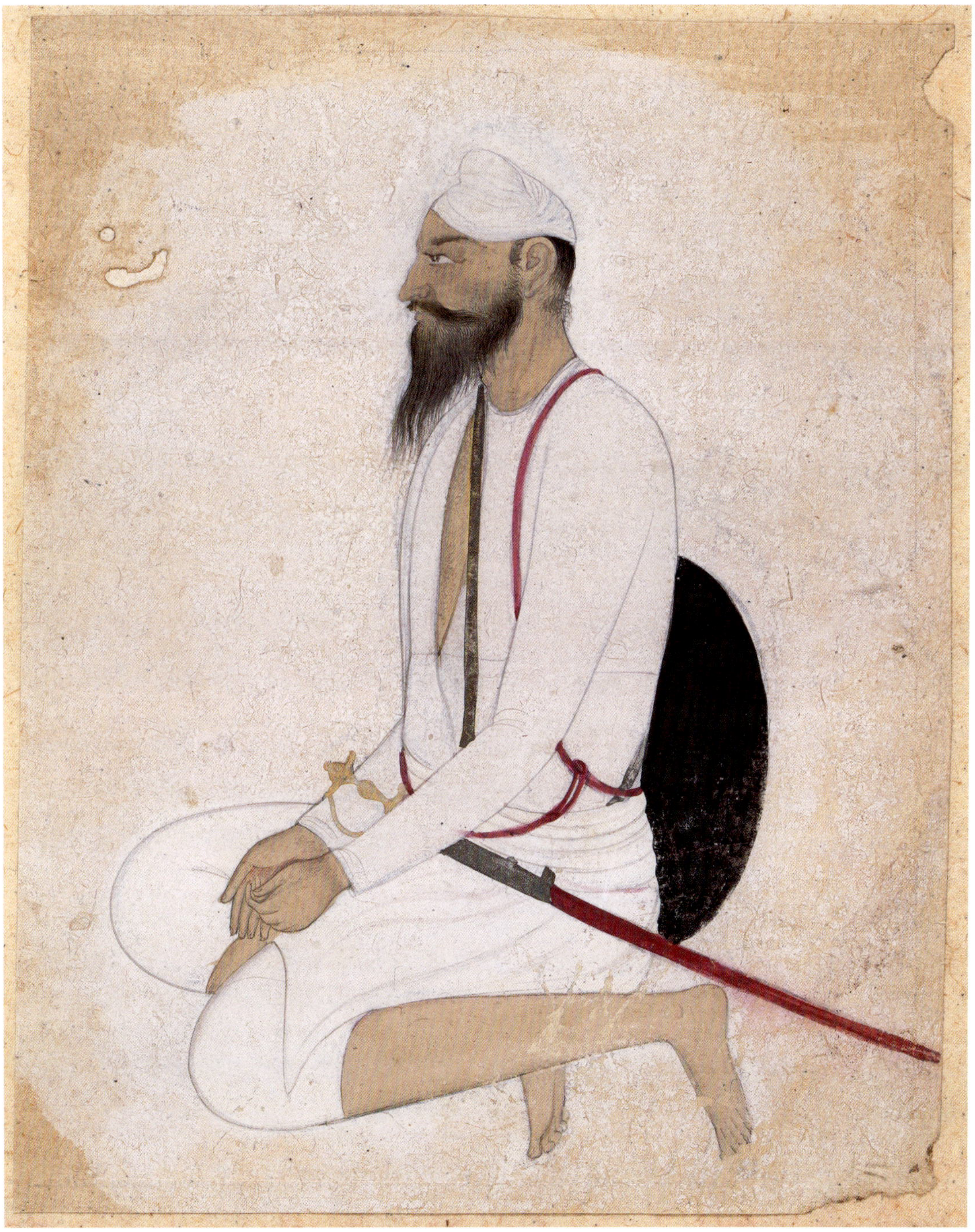

96 Ravana, devotee of Shiva

From a late Kangra workshop
Pahari, c. 1830
27 × 17.5 cm (folio), 24.8 × 15.3 cm (painting)

From the countless tales that speak of the devotion of Ravana, lord of Lanka, to Shiva – some based on sacred texts, others that hover about in the air in the form of folk stories – the painter here picks, surprisingly, an uncommon one. In one of those tales one reads about Ravana's pride being humbled when he, in a fit of anger at being stopped from crossing over Mt. Kailasha where Shiva is in dalliance with his consort Parvati, begins to shake the mountain itself using his mighty arms: the mountain shakes but only for a brief moment, for Shiva just presses it down with the toe of his foot, and it all turns completely still. In another story, Ravana turns one of his heads into a gourd and his entrails into the strings of the *rudra vina* as he begins to sing a *stotra*-hymn in honor of his *ishta*. No sacrifice is too big for him, no penance enough. Whatever the context, the king always emerges as utterly devoted to Shiva; incessantly he worships him in the hope of being granted the boon of immortality. Here he stands just below the lofty mountain, looking up, feet lightly crossed in the mode of submission and prayer, holding in his hands a blooming lotus and several *mala*-rosaries, but also one of his own heads that he has cut off as an offering to the deity. Looking up, one sees that there is another cut-off head that already lies at the feet of Shiva close to the fire that burns there. If his ten heads – he is after all *dashanana, dashagriva* – are still intact, it is because the story is that as soon as one head is cut off another would spring up in its place.

Up there, on the top of the mountain, under the lone tree, Shiva, the eternal recluse, clad only in a tiger skin, with Parvati by his side holding a lotus in her hand, is seen seated on a leopard skin, with a benign look in his eyes. The two children of the divine couple, Ganesha and Karttikeya, look on while a Brahmin stands facing Shiva as if speaking to him. The great bull Nandi, Shiva's *vahana*, his skin dappled and his back covered with a wrap to keep the cold away, casts a quiet gaze at the spectacle.

There is decided feeling in the page, even if it does not have the quality of the great paintings that emerged from the painters' workshops at Kangra. The sombre brown background, the sharp angle at which the crystalline rocks rise toward the top, the atmosphere of a hermitage and deer moving about in peace down below, are all brought in with clear intent. The detail of an ass's head atop the ten "normal" heads of Ravana also deserves to be noticed, for not always does one see this feature, leaving the question open as to when exactly it started being brought in. There is firmness of drawing in the figures of Ravana and the Brahmin, but, oddly, the figures of Shiva and Parvati are not drawn with the same degree of intensity. | BG

Published: Cran 1980, no. 90 (not illustrated)

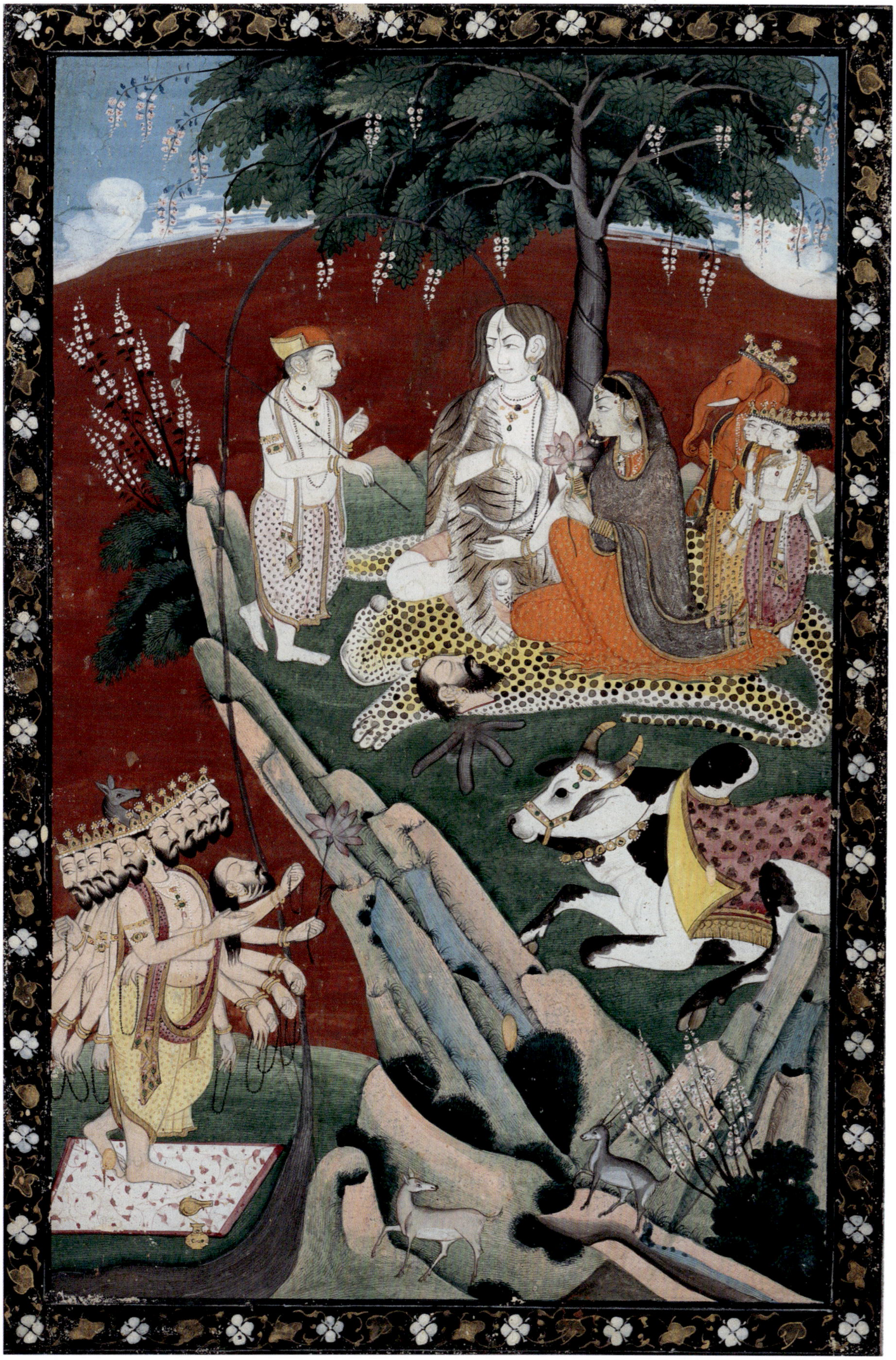

97 Go-Dhuli, the hour of cowdust

Possibly a folio from a *Bhagavata Purana* series
From a late Kangra workshop
Pahari, c. 1830
25.5 × 29.6 cm (folio), 19.8 × 24 cm (painting)

"Krishna, whose eyes were large like lotus-petals, and the [mere] hearing and singing of whose glory brings merit, entered Vraja with his elder brother Balarama, in company of his cowherd followers who were singing his praises," runs a passage from the Tenth Book of the *Bhagavata Purana*, among the most sacred of works for the devotees of Krishna. "The cowherd women rushed out in crowds to welcome and see with eager eyes, Lord Krishna, looking charming with sylvan flowers and peacock feathers adorning his curly locks of hair, overlaid with dust raised by [the hoofs of] cows, of beautiful eyes and bewitching smiles, but playing on his flute while followed by cowherds singing his glory."

This specific passage follows the description of a miraculous feat of Krishna, the killing of yet another powerful demon, but captures something of the excitement of the everyday event of his returning home with his herd of cows after having grazed them all day long together with his *gopa* friends. Descriptions of this nature are scattered over the pages of the text but again and again one reads of "the damsels of Vraja, drinking with their black-bee-like eyes the honey in the lotus-like countenance of Krishna" and through that bringing "the fever of separation from him during the day time." The hour of his return is of course the *go-dhuli vela*, the "hour of cowdust," considered especially auspicious: till today, in villages in northern India, men and women walk behind the cows as they return, simply to be able to "bathe" in the sacred dust their feet raise.

Some great paintings of this theme, as painted by Pahari painters, have come down, one of them published by Coomaraswamy[1] and others inspiring painted textiles – *pichhavais* – from Nathdwara in Rajasthan, that great center of Krishna worship. And even if this is a late work, unequal in quality to those earlier ones, it holds interest because of the feeling that inheres in it. The painter brings in a number of little vignettes of great interest. Consider, for instance, the women who stand in their balconies – having waited all day long for this hour – excitedly pointing with their fingers to Krishna as he returns. One notices also the shy sweetness in the group of four women outside the main gate of the village, who appear to have just set out, pitchers in hand, to fetch water from the river when they see the herd coming and, with it, "their Krishna." The merriment in the group of *gopas* returning with Krishna is caught well in the figures that dance and play on drums even as Krishna plays upon his flute. The group of cows, skin colors varying from one to the other, one of them even dappled, is a delight to see, for their responses to the moment are so varied. Some of them, separated from their young ones, are moving in haste so as to go through the main gate; the hind part of one of them that is already past the gate shows; and there is one that is turning her head back as if more interested in gazing at Krishna and hearing the sweet notes of his flute than in rushing toward the gate.

There are frailties in the line that the painter commanded, some figures not coming across with conviction, and the coloring tends to be on the edge of being a bit loud, especially when it comes to the broad mauve border. But there are compensations in the joyousness of the occasion that the painter captures here. | BG

1 Coomaraswamy 1926, CCXXXIII (pl. LXXII).

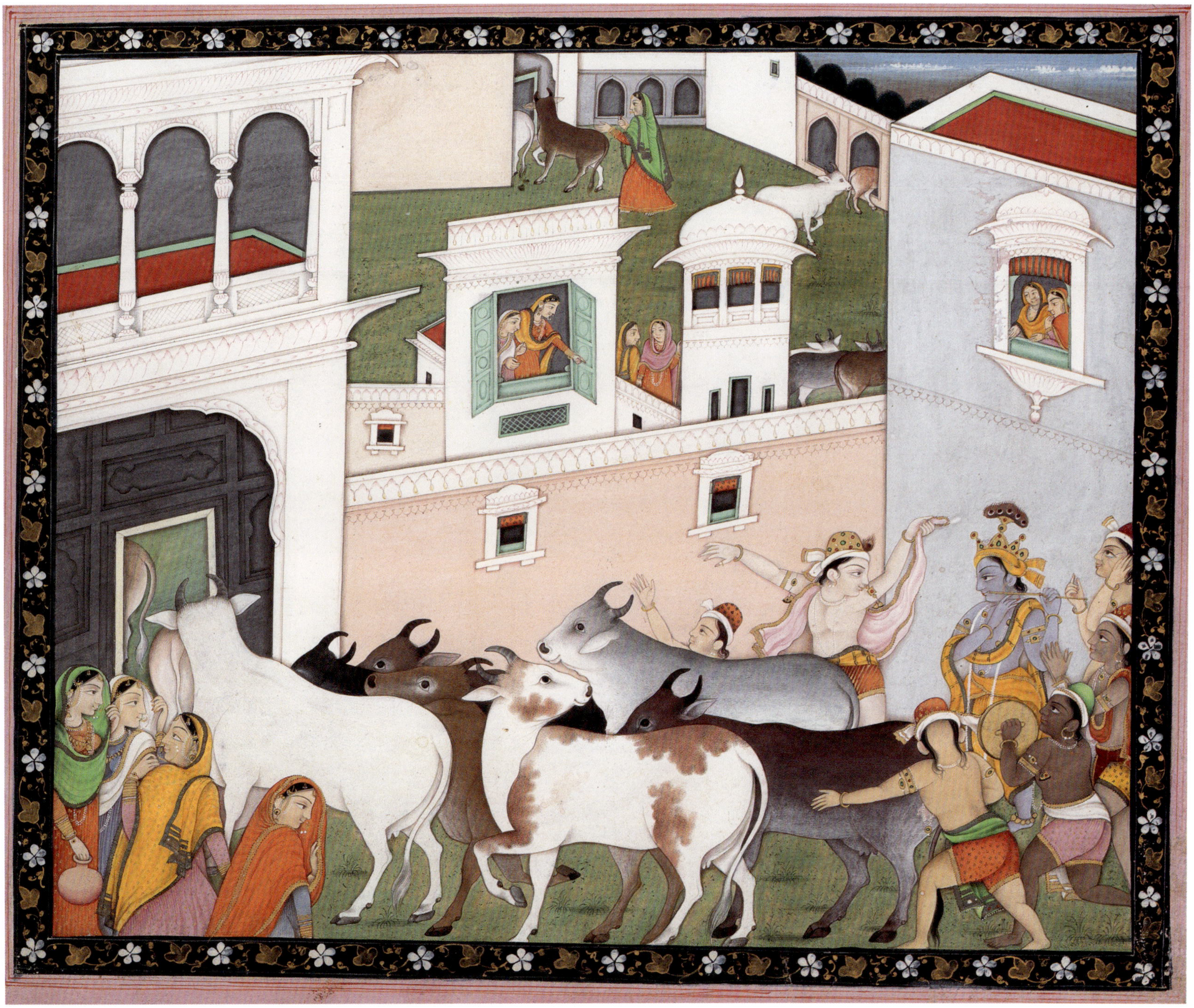

98 Study of a horse and his groom

Possibly by a second generation artist of the Seu-Nainsukh family
Punjab plains, c. 1825
16.6 × 20.9 cm (folio)

The question that crosses the mind is – considering that the groom who holds the horse's reins is a Sikh by his looks – whether the animal is none other than Leili, Maharaja Ranjit Singh's much-loved horse. The Maharaja's acquisition of the horse is quite a story: how it belonged to an Afghan chief of the Yusufzai tribe; how he denied the Maharaja the horse using every possible means including deceit; how the Maharaja eventually had to send a strong force to subdue the chief and get the horse for himself. There are more or less contemporary accounts, by chroniclers and foreign travelers, of the appearance of the horse, but they somehow differ. The name, Leili – "dark as the night" – suggests both the color of the animal and its being a mare rather than a horse. That the animal in this painting obviously is not. One description of Leili is that, being the finest of the horses belonging to the Maharaja, "[...] round his knees he has gold bangles: he is a dark grey, with black legs, thirteen years old, and full sixteen hands high."[1] That description again does not fit this image. One concludes reluctantly therefore, that Leili is not what one is looking at.

Another thought that comes to mind is whether the image of the horse is from a series based on that highly regarded ancient text, *Shalihotra Samhita* – "a treatise on horses" – of which illustrated copies were often made for royalty. But since this is an isolated folio, one cannot be certain. All that one can say, therefore, is that the painting is of a handsome, well-groomed animal – softly spotted, with a smooth grayish-blue coat – tastefully accoutred and saddled and ready to spring into action. Who it belonged to cannot be guessed except that, the Sikhs in general being a valiant and martial people, the horse was probably owned by a member of the royalty or the nobility. The presence of a groom – simply dressed in a blue *dhoti*, white *kurta* and waistcloth, wearing a turban on his head that was in fashion at the Maharaja's court – who stands facing left, flywhisk resting on his shoulder, as if waiting for the master to appear, further strengthens that impression.

The workmanship is skilled, the drawing of the horse impeccable. The Lahore painter Imam Bakhsh made several drawings of horses, many of them uncolored and in pencil, but this does not seem to be his work.[2] In general, it reminds one of the hand of the Seu-Nainsukh family in the second generation after Nainsukh, members of which had taken up employment in the plains after patronage in the hills had dried up and worked both for the Maharaja and the powerful Sandhanwalia *sardars*. In some respects, the work is of a summary nature since the painter takes no interest in establishing a setting, or showing any interest in the background. But that might well be for the reason that the "points" of a horse are best seen against a flat, clear background. To recall: there are paintings from the Pahari area that show a newly brought in horse being examined by a ruler, with a large spotless white sheet being held by servants behind the horse for the "points" to stand out against it.[3] | BG

1 von Hügel 1845, p. 334.
2 For a discussion of Imam Bakhsh see Lafont and Schmitz 2002.
3 See, for example, Goswamy 1997, no. 16.

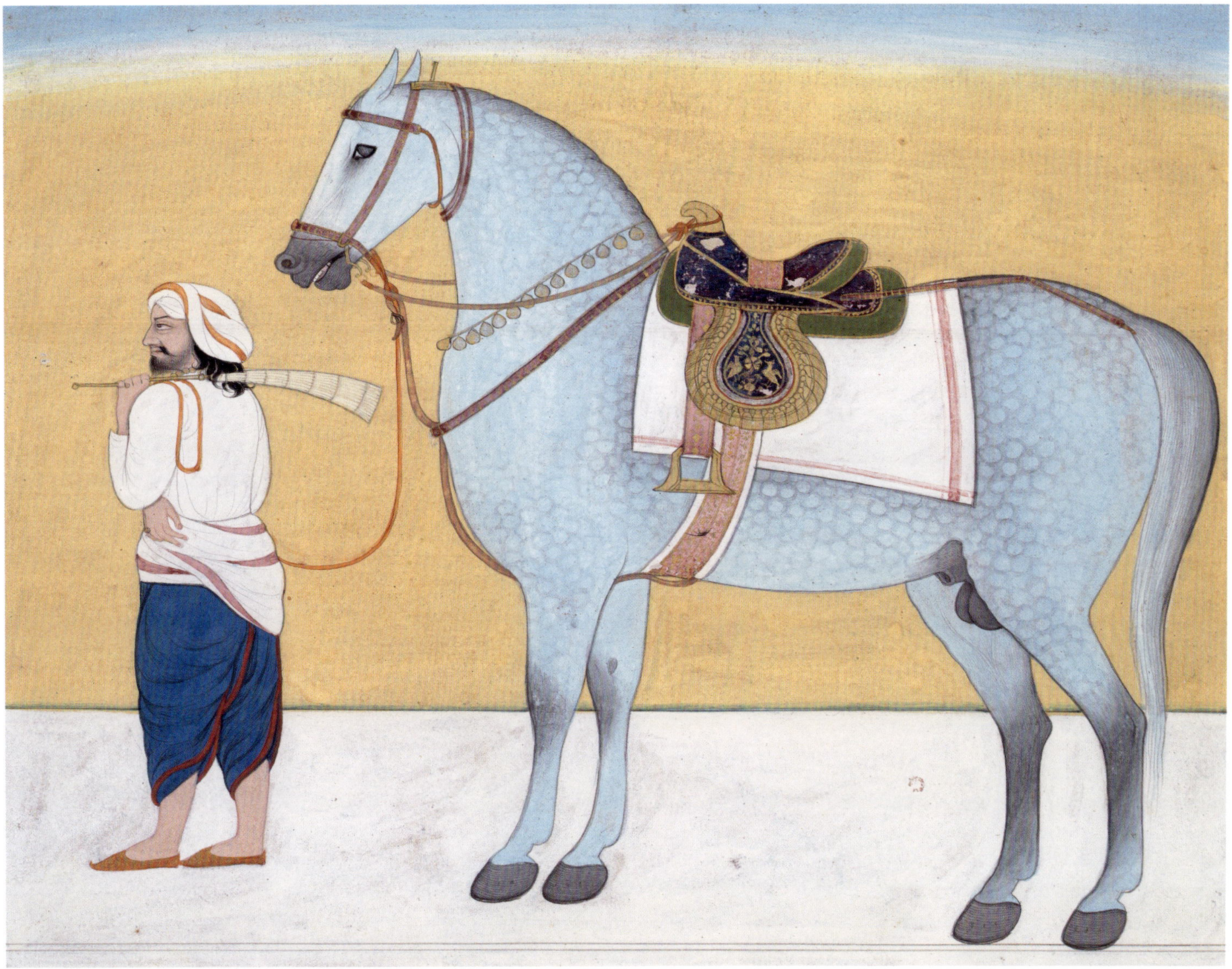

99 Seated courtier

Folio from a series of portraits
Attributed to Chhajju, grandson of Nainsukh
Pahari/Punjab plains, Lahore, series dated 1847–1848
19 × 15.2 cm (folio), 13.2 × 10.25 cm (painting)
Inscribed on verso with two Devanagari and one Persian inscriptions and several numerals (see main text)

The inscribed notes and caption on the verso of this painting tell us a few things about it. There are three inscriptions, two in Devanagari and one, in a pencilled hand, in Persian. The main inscription, written in fairly bold and confident Devanagari characters reads: *pandat prem narain muradabad ke kaul*, meaning, "[the likeness of] Pandit Prem Narayan of Muradabad, Kaul [by family name]." The other Devanagari inscription at the bottom of the page – but, oddly, placed upside down – is in a far neater hand and in relatively small characters. It gives essentially the same information – *pandat prem narain muradabad ke* – but omits the family name Kaul. The third inscription, written with a pencil in Persian characters, only confirms the information one already has from the other two, for it reads: *prem narain ji sahib … kaul*. Here the Brahmin honorific "Pandit" is dropped but the tone is more respectful, the words *ji sahib* having been added, leading one almost to the thought that it might have been put in at a late date by some member of the same family, a descendant perhaps.

There are then the different numbers that appear on the same side of the folio. Almost at the very top is the number 59 in Takri numerals, suggesting that a Pahari hand must have been at work; there is then the same number 59 in Persian numerals just below it. Toward the top left is another number 52 also in Persian numerals and finally the number 1 at top right. The suggestion that all these numbers raise is that this painting comes from a fairly extensive series; also that it was part of an official record; and that there is some Pahari association with the image.

Almost certainly the portrait comes from a series that was painted at the court of Maharaja Ranjit Singh of Lahore (r. 1801–1831). A number of portraits in a similar setting – a person of some rank or status seated all by himself with or without a bolster or cushion, under an arch, on a floral carpet, with a low balustrade at the back – have come down.[1] Each person in that series is named and often his profession or calling is suggested by a meaningful object that sits close to him: manuscripts, pen and inkwell, a scroll, etc. One sees a *jyotishi*-astrologer, a *vaidya*-physician, a poet, a calligrapher, and so on. No drawn-up lists of men who were members of the court of the Maharaja are available even though countless names are scattered over the pages of the chronicle of the Lahore court by Sohan Lal Suri, the *Umdat-ut Tawarikh*. It would seem, however, that the task of preparing likenesses of all notables was assigned to the court painter/s. That these notables were drawn to the court of the Sikh Maharaja is well established; the fact that this Pandit, of the Kaul family, came from Muradabad is therefore no surprise.

On a dated colophon page of this series, now lost, the name of the painter, Chhajju (c. 1775–1850), appeared.[2] That name is significant, for Chhajju came from the family of Pandit Seu of Guler, being a grandson of Nainsukh, and we know from other sources that he, together with his two brothers Harkhu and Gokul, had moved to the Punjab plains after patronage from the Pahari rulers had started drying up in the hills.[3] The Takri number 59 makes sense in this connection, and it might well have been in Chhajju's hand.

This is not a great portrait. The pandit's face is captured well but there is no penetration of character, no psychological insight that Chhajju provides. But it is part of a useful, courtly record. There is competence in the work even if it is simply a straightforward likeness – face, dress, the muslin cap on the head, all in place – as it was possibly meant to be. The light blue background, the rolled-up striped curtain at the top, the bolster, one gets the feeling, are parts of the iconography of a series. | BG

1 For a discussion of four folios from this series see Atal 1973. For other portraits from the same set see Christie's, London, July 1978, lot 90 (pl. 16) and Christie's, London, April 1979, lot 129 (pl. 23).
2 The inscription on the verso of the portrait of Pandit Durga Parshad Kaul is reproduced in Atal 1973, p. 28. The series – according to the inscription – was said to contain 88 paintings and was dated to 1847–1848.
3 Goswamy and Fischer 1992, p. 310, and Goswamy 1999.

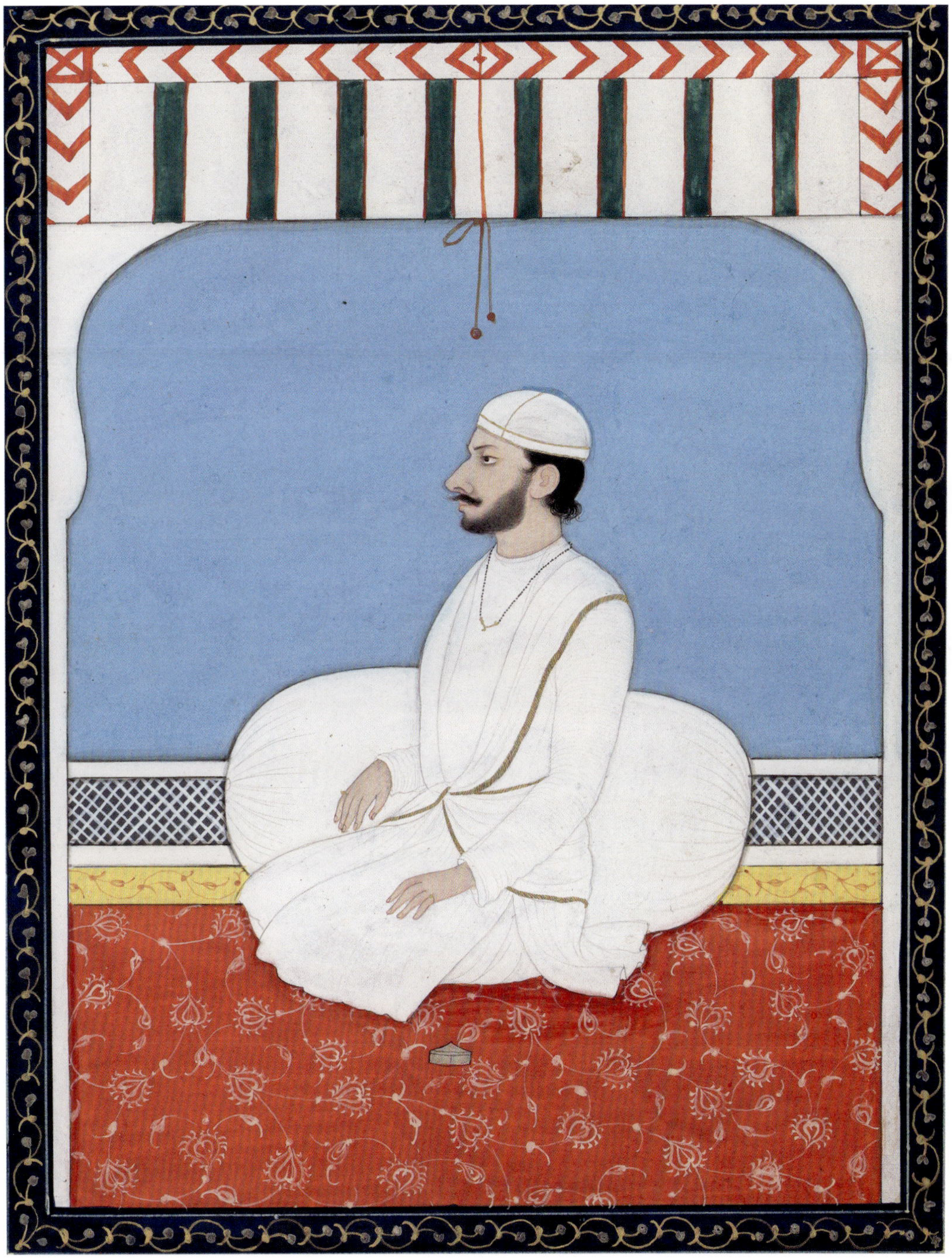

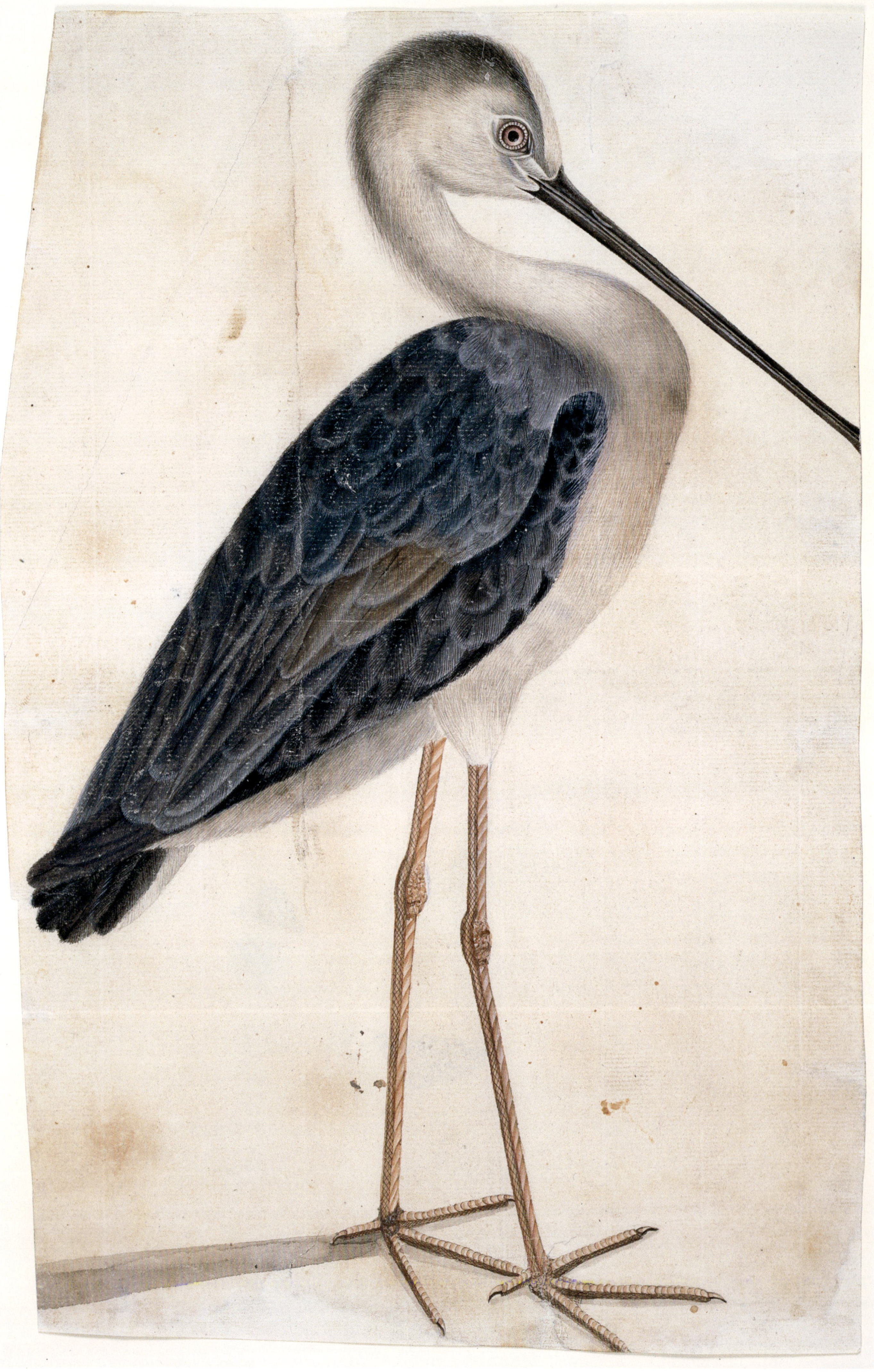

100 A young crane

Folio, possibly from an album of bird studies
Company style, c. 1800
35.5 × 24 cm (average folio size)

The revival of interest in studies of flora and fauna that came in with some of the senior-most British civil servants in India reminds one almost of the great interest that the emperor Jahangir took in these themes a hundred and fifty or so years before them. Studies such as the "turkey cock" which had come in from another land, or the "zebra" which some Turks brought with them from African lands come readily to mind. But there were countless others, of course.

Here, in the lands controlled by the East India Company from the latter part of the 18th century onwards, there emerged major patrons of this genre of painting: Sir Elijah Impey, the Chief Justice and his wife, Lady Impey, for instance; or Marquis Wellesley, the Governor General. Interest in flora and fauna which seemed to have disappeared or lain dormant suddenly came to life again, evidently in response to the patrons' needs. One knows that enormous albums were prepared, the one for Marquis Wellesley alone consisting of 2,660 folios of natural history paintings, showing plants, birds, mammals, insects and fish.[1] The interest of the British was evidently inspired by natural curiosity about their freshly acquired dominions on the one hand, and by the spirit of scientific inquiry on the other. The question however was where to find the painters for taking up these jobs. Artists from their own land sometimes found this kind of work "too elaborate, decorative and expensive." Local talent had therefore to be tapped. Fortunately, for them, the search did not have to extend too far. For, close by, in Patna, a group of painters had already turned to this kind of work, and names of talented men like Bhavanidas and Ramdas surface from there. Among the most gifted perhaps was Shaikh Zayn-al Din whose name appears on some paintings of exceptional quality. One can imagine that it might not have been easy for these painters, for it meant coming to terms with the new way of doing things. There were new materials to be negotiated, among them the English paper that the patrons provided for the preparation of these albums but which had a surface that the painters were not used to painting on. Again the colors to be used were European watercolors even if they were mixed with the white that painters working in the Indian tradition knew all too well. But it was their own prodigious powers of observation, and their application, which must have come to their aid in performing the tasks assigned to them.

This young bird, with its long beak and its feathers of delicate, festive colors, bears, as the artist renders it, a knowing look in its eyes. Whether the look is of curiosity or of caution it is not easy to determine, but there is clear expression in it. The detailing of the texture and the colors of the feathers is crisp as are the markings on the long, thin legs that throw a customary shadow on the ground. There is delicacy in the treatment, reminding one of the description of this class of work in which are captured "the lustre of a feather, the roughness of an animal's coat, the velvet texture of a petal, or the rough and leathery surface of a leaf." | BG

[1] Archer M. 1983.

101 Unidentified fish
102 The Sowlee
103 The Mahi

From an album with 28 watercolors of fish, crustaceans, amphibians and a turtle
By Shaikh 'Abdullah
Company style, Calcutta, c. 1800
32.5 × 34 cm (average folio size)

In her book *Natural History Drawings in the India Office Library*, Mildred Archer draws pointed attention to two almost opposed views that were constantly being aired in the writings of the servants of the East India Company. Dr. Benjamin Heyne, the Company's botanist in the Carnatic region, writing in 1804 in his "Minute on Natural History," held this view: "To facilitate and promote all enquiries which may be calculated to enlarge the boundaries of general science, is a duty imposed on the British Government in India in its presented exalted situation." He went on to add: "And the discharge of that duty is in a more especial manner required from us, when any material addition can be made to the public stock of useful knowledge without involving considerable expense."[1] On the other hand Dr. George Finlayson – surgeon in the service of the Company, and not a professional botanist – wrote this: "The curiosity that is gratified with inquiring into the laws implanted in organized beings, or into the general phenomena which characterize the material world at large, admits of, and is usually attended by, gratification as permanent as it is unmixed; every step is attended with unalloyed pleasure, every new acquisition leads and stimulates to further discovery."[2]

Somewhere it seems, between the commitment to professional "duty" and amateur enthusiasm, a very sizeable amount of material about the natural world came to be collected in those relatively early years of the British presence in India. Whole albums were commissioned by enlightened and interested civil servants, the work entrusted to Indian painters many of whom, sensing the change that was coming about in taste, were increasingly shifting their attention to recording phenomena, whether from the world of flora or fauna. These three studies of fish, acutely observed and sharply rendered, are apparently in the hand of the painter whose name appears on them as "Shaikh 'Abdulla." There is some information that he lived near "the Colingy bazaar" – Chowringhee bazaar? – in Calcutta,[3] but not much more is known about him. Whether he was related to the highly gifted "Shaikh Zain-al Din," in whose hand some superb studies of birds have survived, can only remain a matter of speculation.

It is clear that Sheikh 'Abdullah had mastered the art of painting in watercolor. Much like the painter families from Patna that had boldly taken to this medium, the painter knew exactly of the need to move with speed but was also aware of the demands of precision. The sharpness with which every scale of the fish, every changing look in the eyes, every gauze-like filament, is caught by him in these studies elicits true admiration. The names of the fish as recorded are evidently anglicized versions of local names: "mahi" having turned into "mowhee," for instance.

The series once belonged to "Henry Plowden" whose name is recorded.[4] In Charles Prinsep's *Record of Services* two Plowdens are listed: Richard Chincheley Plowden and William Henry Chincheley Plowden.[5] The former served in the Company from 1803 to 1829 and the latter from 1841 to 1853. It is not unlikely that these two were father and son, and Henry Plowden, who might well have been in Calcutta as a young man, might have commissioned this series while there, for that is where there was a concentration of painters working in this style. | BG

1 Archer M. 1962, p. 29.
2 Archer M. 1962, p. 49.
3 Sotheby's, London, 12 October 1982, lot 68.
4 In the lot notes in Sotheby's, London, 12 October 1982, lot 68 it is furthermore mentioned that an artist's receipt inside the cover of the album is dated 30th of May, 1800.
5 Prinsep 1885.

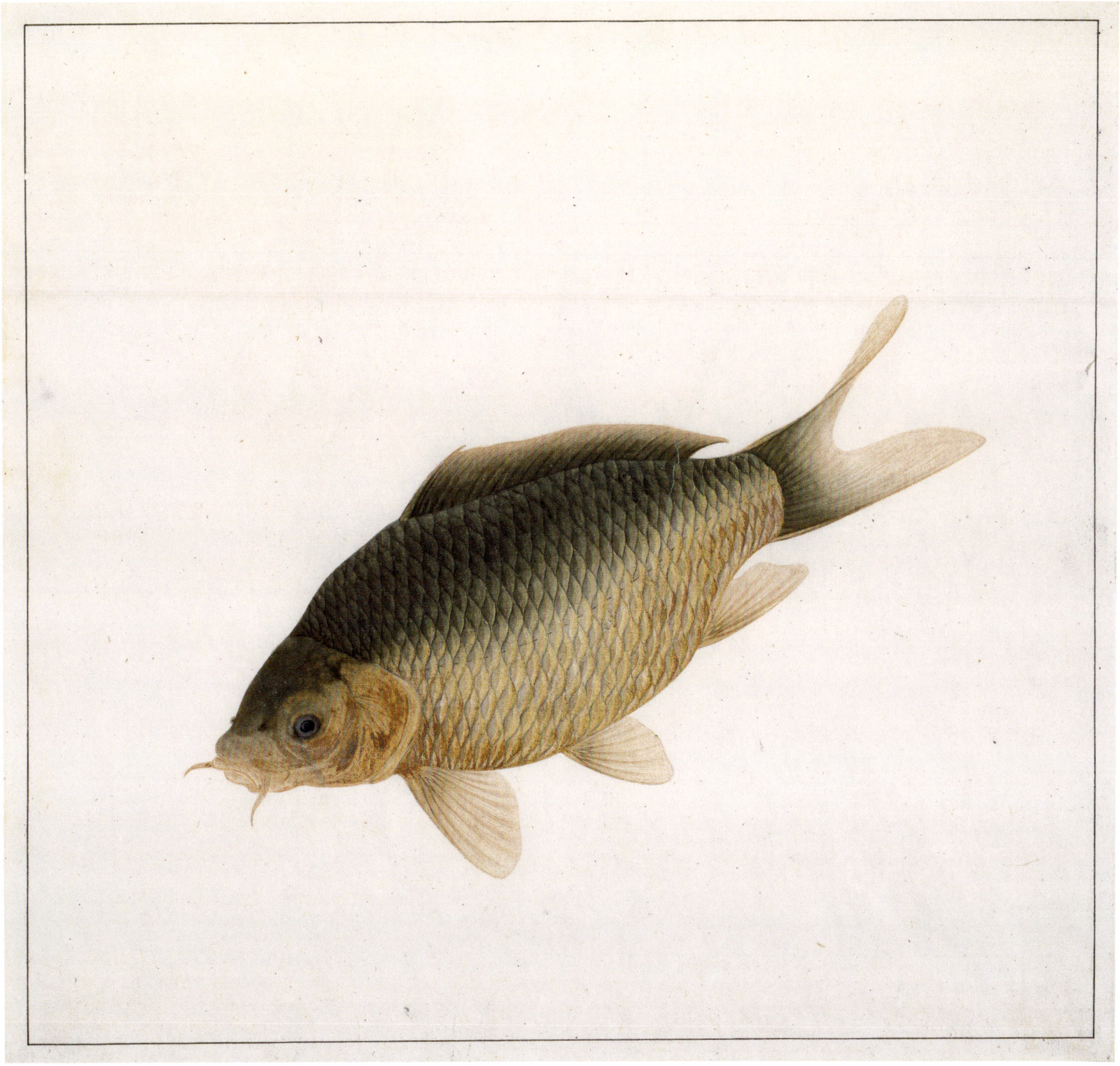

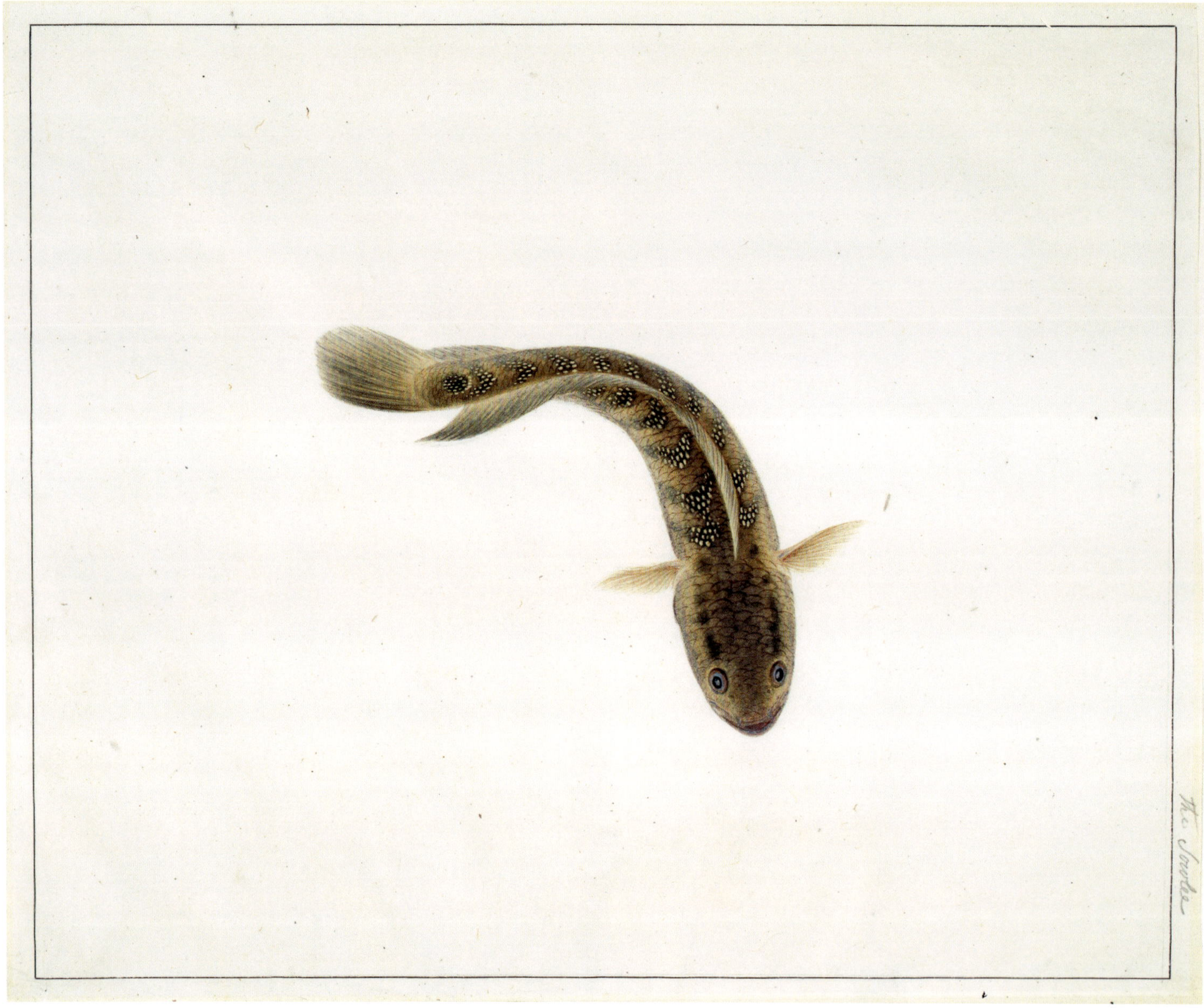

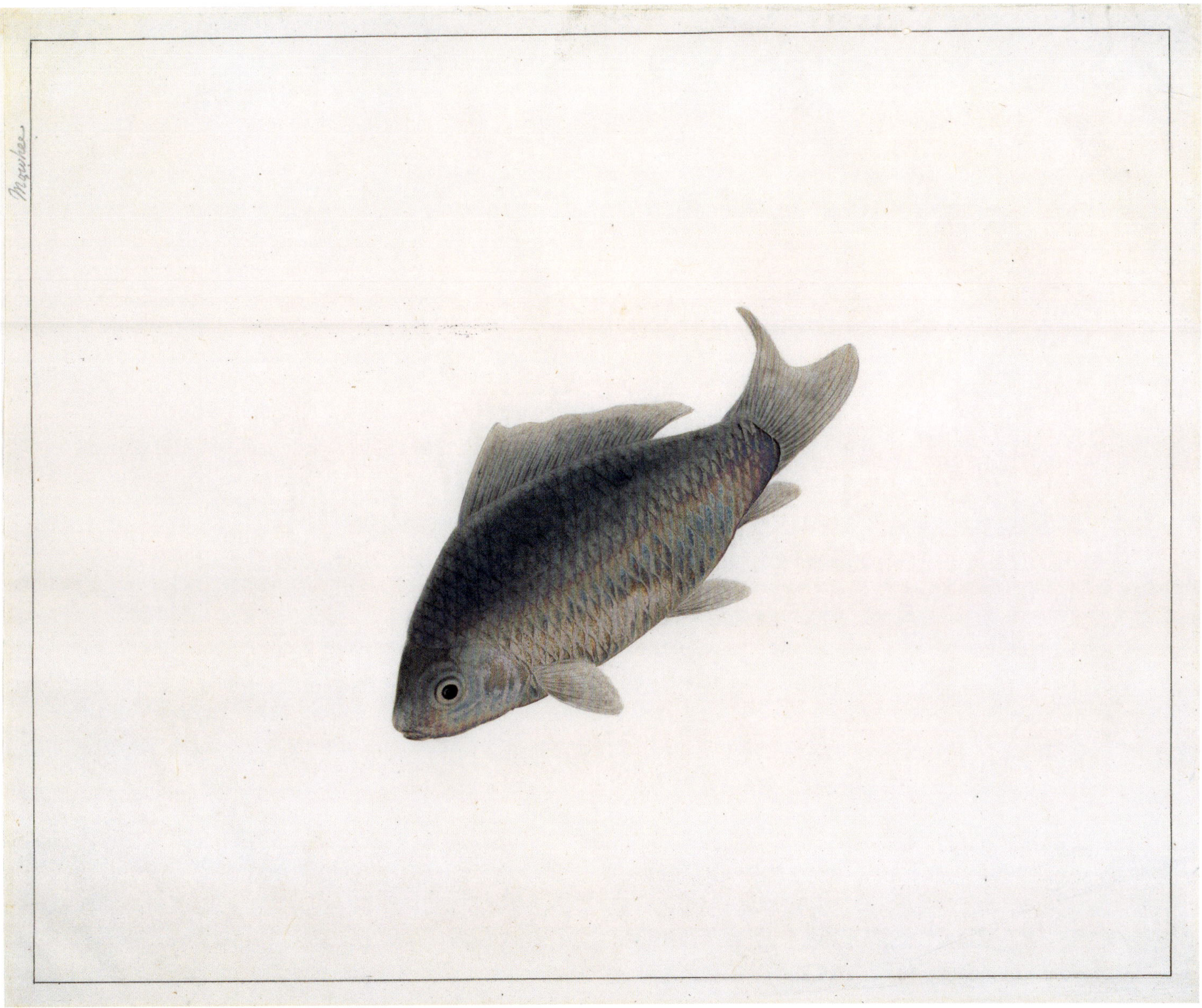

104 Raja Udit Narain Singh of Benares

Patna, c. 1830
28.3 × 20.9 cm (folio)

Raja Udit Narain Singh of Benares (r. 1795–1830) sits in comfort with one foot raised up on an elaborately carved seat, with his right hand holding a huqqa snake and his left his sword.

Benares had previously been a *jagir* in the province of Awadh, but successive zamindars who called themselves rajas managed to extract it from Awadh and achieve a kind of independence before 1775, when control was passed to the East India Company's government in Calcutta. Warren Hastings's attempts to deal with the rebellion of Raja Chait Singh of Benares in 1781 were one of the chief causes of his impeachment by the British parliament. Chait Singh's nephew Mahip Narain Singh was then placed on the *gaddi* until his death in 1795 when his son Udit Narain Singh succeeded at the age of fifteen. He ruled until 1835, but being judged a bad administrator, his lands were confiscated by the Company and placed under direct rule in return for a stipend. They were not returned to the Raja's rule for half a century. The palace in the fort at Ramnagar, just upstream on the Ganges from Benares proper, was built by Raja Balwant Singh in the middle of the 18th century.

The Rajas of Benares fulfilled a religious as well as a temporal role in their capacity as *Kashi Naresh* or Lords of Kashi or Benares and their presence was and still is essential for the correct performance of big religious ceremonies. The family is Brahmin and they have traditionally been patrons of Sanskrit and Sanskritic culture as well as often being considerable scholars in their own right. Ramnagar became one of the great centers of Hindu culture in Benares and under Udit Narain Singh the great *Ramlila* festival at Ramnagar was initiated. This is one of the most elaborate of the *Ramlila* stagings in India, extending over 31 days instead of the usual ten, and is staged over the entire town of Ramnagar.

Raja Udit Narain Singh was often portrayed in the early 19th century seated in comfort and smoking his huqqa. A drawing dated to 1818–1819 shows him sitting among cushions, a huqqa snake in his hand, and a distinctively wide turban on his head, in three-quarter view, looking out at the viewer.[1] This was printed around 1830 by Sir Charles D'Oyly, the amateur artist and lithographic printer and the Company's Opium Agent at Patna, but in mirror reverse, and is found in some of the miscellaneous scrapbooks of productions from the Behar Amateur Lithographic Press.[2] A fully painted version appeared at auction.[3] A version painted on ivory is in the Victoria and Albert Museum.[4] The Governor-General, the Marquess of Hastings, was received by the Raja with great dignity in September 1814 and Bishop Heber met him in 1824: "I received a visit from the Raja of Benares, a middle-aged man, very corpulent, with more approach to color in his cheeks than is usually seen in Asiatics, and a countenance and appearance not unlike an English farmer." | JL

1 British Library (Add.Or.5464).
2 British Library (P2481, f. 60).
3 Christie's, South Kensington, 2 May 2003, lot 65.
4 Archer M. 1992, no. 246.

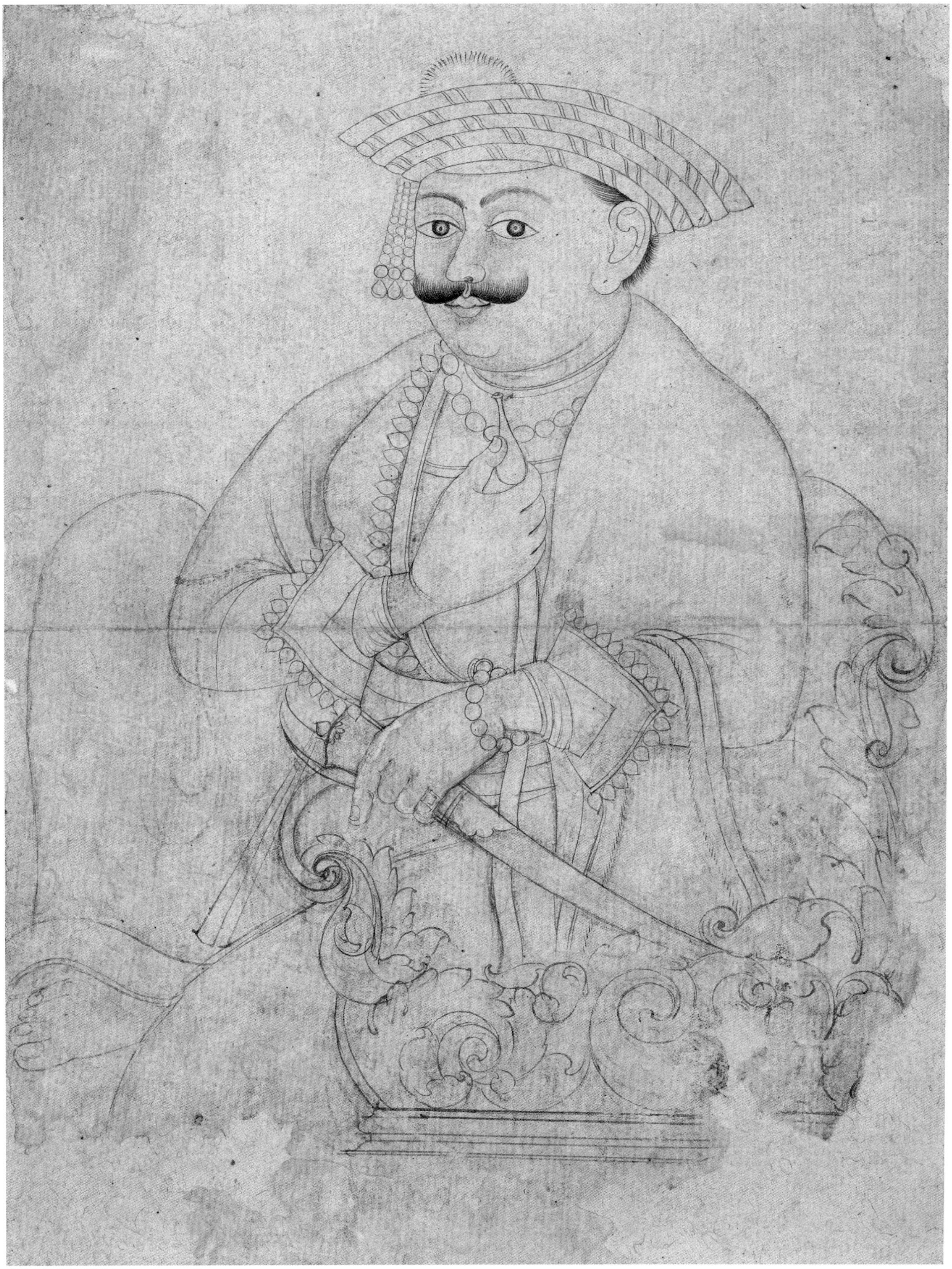

105 Krishna triumphing over Kaliya

Folio, possibly from a *Krishna Lila* series
South India, probably Mysore, 18th century
27 × 18.6 (folio); 25.7 × 17.6 cm (painting)

So many paintings of this series keep reminding one of the celebrated composition of that great Krishna devotee, Vallabhacharya – founder of the Vallabha *sampradaya* – the *Madhurashtakam*: "Eight verses filled with Sweetness." *Adharam madhuram, vadanam madhuram, nayanam madhuram, hasitam madhuram,* it opens. "Enticingly sweet are his lips, enticing his face, enticing his eyes, enticing his smile." Each of the stanzas of this composition ends with the words: *madhuradhipate akhilam madhuram*: "everything about the Lord of Sweetness is sweet." As *bala gopala*, the "boy cowherd" – some paintings are inscribed with a different name: *bala mukunda* – Krishna wins every single heart.

Among his countless *lilas* is the one in which he triumphs over the Naga-serpent Kaliya who had poisoned the waters of the Yamuna with its noxious fumes. Knowing that he has to subdue him, and regardless of the danger involved, Krishna jumped into the waters of the river; a fierce contest between the great serpent and the "boy cowherd" ensued; when he was about to kill the serpent, his many wives, the *naginis*, pleaded with him to spare the life of their lord; and when the contest ended, to the surprise and the joy of everyone, Krishna emerged from the waters triumphant, dancing over the hoods of the serpent. Another demon had been defeated; another threat over.

This is the moment, climactic and suffused with joy, that the painter renders. Butterball still in one hand, the other holding up the tail of the serpent, Krishna dances: a slow, cadenced dance, while on either side of him stands a *nagini*, each wearing a tall *mukuta*-crown, hands folded, eyes filled with pleading. All around the richly bejeweled form of Krishna lotuses appear, as much to suggest the waters from which he has emerged as to point to his divine, detached nature. Nothing has disturbed the Lord of Sweetness, neither the danger, nor the struggle. The smile had not left his lips even for a moment, the painter seems to say. It is after all a part of his *lila*. Painting after painting from this joyous series conveys the same feeling, the same message as it were.[1] Nearly each time, the figure of Krishna, filling the entire page, is placed inside an arch at the back, suggestive of being an icon, occupying its proper space in a niche.

There is extraordinary stylization in the work, exaggerations and distortions all an integral part of it. The heavy bulging figure, as if still possessed of baby fat, the strongly modeled areas where joints and protuberances are shown, the thick contours, the emphasis on features such as the eyes and the mouth, both treated with the noble artificiality of a dancer's mask, all appear a little strange at first, but one realizes that they exert a powerful pull. The intense coloring of the bluish-black figure of Krishna leaves an impression upon the mind. The decoration attracts as much as the rhythms and the easy, fluid flow of the work. One knows that everything here is *alaukika*, – "not of this world." | BG

[1] For other folios see Leach 1986, figs. 101i and 101ii.

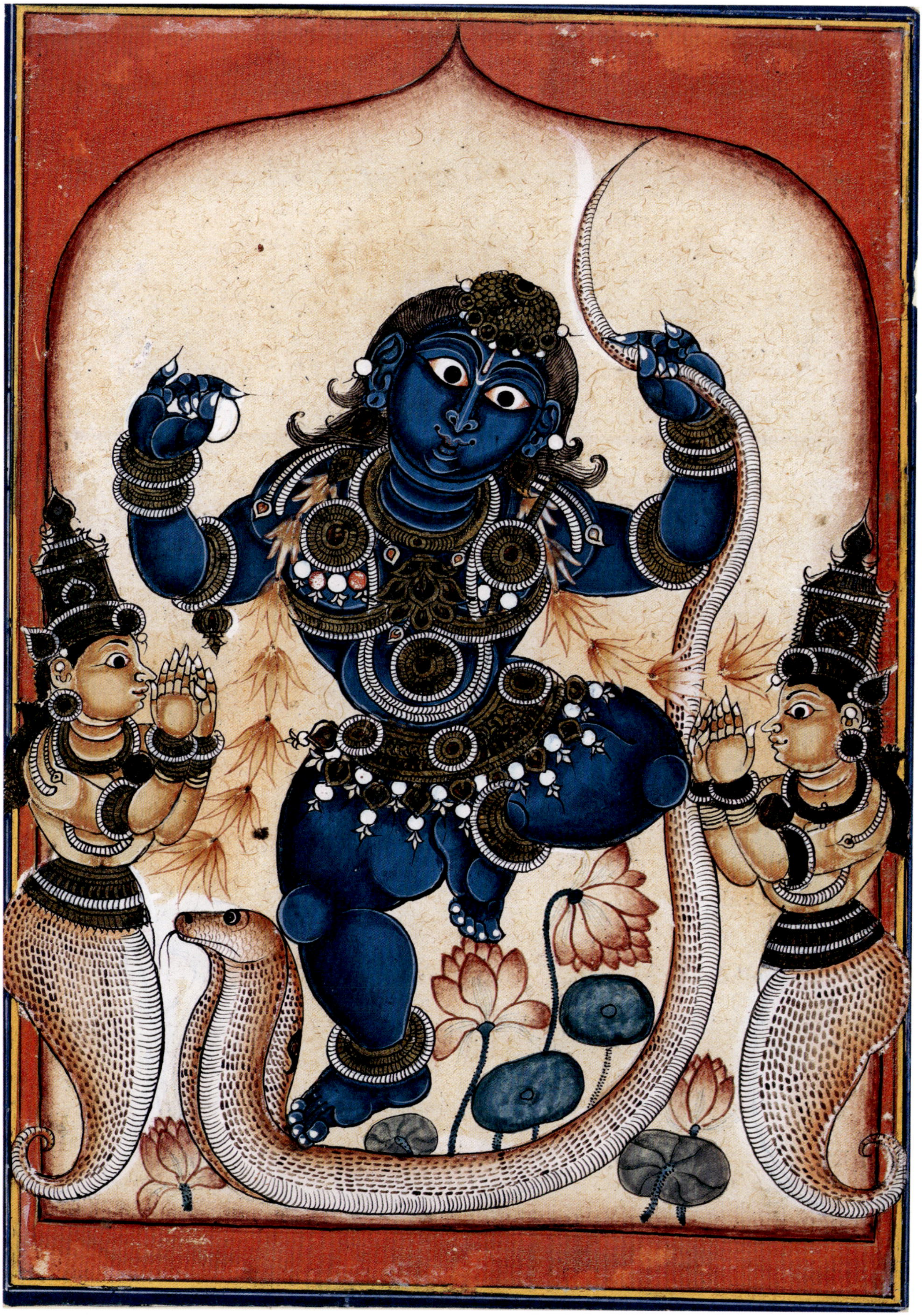

bibliography

Ahluwalia 2008
Ahluwalia, R. *Rajput Painting: Romantic, Divine and Courtly Love from India.* London: British Museum Press.

Aitken 2010
Aitken, Molly Emma. *The Intelligence of Tradition in Rajput Court Painting.* New Haven and London: Yale University Press.

Aitken 2011
Aitken, Molly Emma. "Sahib Ram." In *Masters of Indian Painting: 1100–1900*, ed. Milo C. Beach, Eberhard Fischer and B.N. Goswamy. Zürich: Artibus Asiae Publishers, 623–640.

Ambalal 1987
Ambalal, Amit. *Krishna as Srinathji: Rajasthani Paintings from Nathdvara.* Ahmedabad: Mapin.

Andhare 1972
Andhare, S.K. "A dated Amber Ragamala and the Problem of Provenance of the Eighteenth Century Jaipuri Painting." *Lalit Kala* 15: 47–51.

Andhare 1987
Andhare, S.K. *Chronology of Mewar Painting.* Delhi: Agam Kala Prakashan.

Archer 1959
Archer, W.G. *Indian Painting in Bundi and Kotah.* London: HMSO.

Archer 1963
Archer, W.G. *Indian Miniatures from the Collection of Mildred and W. G. Archer.* Washington, D. C.: Smithsonian Institution.

Archer 1973
Archer, W.G. *Indian Paintings from the Punjab Hills; a Survey and History of Pahari Painting.* London and New York: Sotheby Parke Bernet.

Archer M. 1962
Archer, Mildred. *Natural History Drawings in the India Office Library.* London: Her Majesty's Stationery Office.

Archer M. 1983
Archer, Mildred. *The Marquis Wellesley Collection: Indian Artists Under British Patronage.* London: Alfalak and Scorpion Communications.

Archer M. 1992
Archer, Mildred. *Company Paintings: Indian Paintings of the British Period.* London: Victoria and Albert Museum.

Archer and Falk 1989
Archer, Mildred and Toby Falk. *India Revealed: the Art and Adventures of James and William Fraser 1801–35.* London: Cassell.

Atal 1973
Atal, Chand Kumar. "Some Miniature Portrait Paintings of the Sikh Period." *Roopa-Lekha* 44/1–2: 26–29.

Bahadur 1972
Bahadur, K.P. *Rasikapriya of Keshavadasa.* Delhi: Motilal Banarsidass.

Bailey and Gombrich 2005
Bailey, Greg and Richard Gombrich. *Love Lyrics, by Amaru & Bhartrhari & by Bilhana.* New York: New York University Press, JJC Foundation.

Bautze 1987a
Bautze, Joachim. *Drei Bundi "Ragamalas": Ein Beitrag zur Geschichte der rajputischen Wandmalerei.* Stuttgart: Franz Steiner Verlag.

Bautze 1987b
Bautze, Joachim. *Indian Miniature Paintings, c. 1590–c. 1850.* Amsterdam: Galerie Saundarya Lahari.

Bautze 1987c
Bautze, Joachim. "Zur Darstellung der Hauptgottheiten Kotas in der Malerei der zweiten Hälfte des 18. und der ersten Hälfte des 19. Jahrhunderts." *Berliner Indologische Studien* 3: 253–279.

Bautze 1991
Bautze, Joachim. *Lotosmond und Löwenritt: Indische Malerei.* Stuttgart: Linden-Museum.

Bautze 2000
Bautze, Joachim. "Scenes of Devotion and Court Life: Painting under Maharao Ram Singh of Kota." In *Court Painting in Rajasthan*, ed. Andrew Topsfield. Bombay: Marg Publications, 123–138.

Beach 1974
Beach, Milo Cleveland. *Rajput Painting at Bundi and Kotah.* Ascona: Artibus Asiae.

Beach 1992
Beach, Milo Cleveland. *Mughal and Rajput Painting.* Cambridge: Cambridge University Press.

Beach 2011a
Beach, Milo C. "Masters of Early Kota Painting." In *Masters of Indian Painting: 1100–1900*, ed. Milo C. Beach, Eberhard Fischer and B.N. Goswamy. Zürich: Artibus Asiae Publishers, 459–478.

Beach 2011b
Beach, Milo C. "The Sirohi Master." In *Masters of Indian Painting: 1100–1900*, ed. Milo C. Beach, Eberhard Fischer and B.N. Goswamy. Zürich: Artibus Asiae Publishers, 479–490.

Beach and Singh 2005
Beach, Milo Cleveland and Rawat Nahar Singh. *Bagta and Chokha: Master Artists at Devgarh.* Zürich: Artibus Asiae.

Beltz 2003
Beltz, Johannes. *Ganesha: Der Gott mit dem Elefantenkopf.* Zürich: Museum Rietberg Zürich.

Binney 1973
Binney, Edwin 3rd. *Indian Miniature Painting from the Collection of Edwin Binney, 3rd. The Mughal and Deccani Schools.* Portland, Oregon: Portland Art Museum.

Binney 1981
Binney, Edwin 3rd. "Sultanate Painting from the Collection of Edwin Binney, 3rd." In *Chhavi–2. Rai Krishnadasa Felicitation Volume*, ed. Anand Krishna. Banaras: Bharat Kala Bhavan, 25–31.

Binney and Archer 1968
Binney, E., 3rd and W.G. Archer. *Rajput Miniatures from the Collection of Edwin Binney, 3rd.* Portland: Portland Art Museum.

Brac de la Perrière 2008
Brac de la Perrière, Éloïse. *L'Art du livre dans l'Inde des sultanats.* Paris: Presses de l'Université Paris-Sorbonne.

Britschgi and Fischer 2008
Britschgi, Jorrit and Eberhard Fischer. *Rama und Sita. Das Ramayana in der Malerei Indiens*. Zürich: Museum Rietberg.

Chandra M. 1957
Chandra, Moti. *Mewar Painting in the Seventeenth Century*. New Delhi: Lalit Kala Akademi.

Chandra M. 1971
Chandra, Moti. *Mewar Painting*. New Delhi: Lalit Kala Akademi.

Chandra P. 1971
Chandra, Pramod. *Indian Miniature Painting: The Earnest C. and Jane Werner Watson Collection*. Madison: University of Wisconsin.

Cimino 1985
Cimino, Rosa Maria. *Life at Court in Rajasthan: Indian Miniatures from the Seventeenth to the Nineteenth Century*. Firenze: Mario Luca Giusti.

Cimino 1987
Cimino, Rosa Maria. "Spazio e Tempo nella Miniatura del Mewar." *Rivista degli Studi Orientali* 61: 115–188.

Colnaghi 1976
Colnaghi, P & D. *Persian and Mughal Art*. London: P & D Colnaghi Co. Ltd

Colnaghi 1978
Colnaghi, P & D. *Indian Painting: Mughal and Rajput and a Sultanate Manuscript*. London: Colnaghi.

Coomaraswamy 1926
Coomaraswamy, Ananda K. *Catalogue of Indian Collections in the Museum of Fine Arts, Boston, Part V, Rajput Painting*. Cambridge, MA: Harvard University Press.

Cran 1980
Cran, R. *Miniatures indiennes*. Neuchâtel: Musée d'ethnographie.

Crill 2000
Crill, Rosemary. *Marwar Painting. A History of the Jodhpur Style*. Mumbai/Jodhpur: India Book House and Mehrangarh Publishers.

Crill and Jariwala 2010
Crill, Rosemary and Kapil Jariwala, eds. *The Indian Portrait, 1560–1860*. London: National Portrait Gallery.

Czuma 1975
Czuma, Stanislaw. *Indian Art from the George P. Bickford Collection*. Cleveland: Cleveland Museum of Art.

Del Bontà 1999
Del Bontà, Robert. "Reinventing Nature: Mughal Composite Animal Paintings." In *Flora and Fauna in Mughal Art*, ed. Som Prakash Verma. Mumbai: Marg Publications, 69–82.

Dalrymple and Sharma 2012
Dalrymple, William and Yuthika Sharma, eds. *Princes and Painters in Mughal Delhi, 1707–1857*. New Haven and London: Asia Society Museum in association with Yale University Press.

Das 1986
Das, A.K. *Treasures of Amber Painting, Series Five: Amber Jaipur Painting*. Jaipur: Maharaja Sawai Man Singh II Museum Trust.

Diamond, Glynn and Jasol 2008
Diamond, Debra, Catherine Glynn and K.S. Jasol. *Garden & Cosmos: the Royal Paintings of Jodhpur*. London: Thames & Hudson.

Dickinson and Khandalavala 1959
Dickinson, Eric and Karl J. Khandalavala. *Kishangarh Painting*. New Delhi: Lalit Kala Akademi.

Doshi 1972
Doshi, Saryu. "An Illustrated Manuscript from Aurangabad." *Lalit Kala* 15: 15–28.

Doshi 1995
Doshi, Saryu, ed. *The Royal Bequest. Art Treasures of the Baroda Museum and Picture Gallery*. Bombay: India Book House Limited.

Dye 2001
Dye, J.M., III. *The Art of India, Virginia Museum of Fine Arts*. Richmond, VA and London: Virginia Museum of Fine Arts/Philip Wilson Publishers.

Ebeling 1973
Ebeling, Klaus. *Ragamala Painting*. Basel: Ravi Kumar.

Ehnbom 1985
Ehnbom, Daniel J. *Indian Miniatures. The Ehrenfeld Collection*. New York: Hudson Hills Press.

Ehnbom 2011
Ehnbom, Daniel. "The Masters of the Dispersed *Bhagavata Purana*." In *Masters of Indian Painting: 1100–1900*, ed. Milo C. Beach, Eberhard Fischer and B.N. Goswamy. Zürich: Artibus Asiae Publishers, 77–96.

Ehnbom and Topsfield 1987
Ehnbom, Daniel J. and Andrew Topsfield. *Indian Miniature Painting*. London: Spinks.

Falk and Archer 1981
Falk, Toby and Mildred Archer. *Indian Miniatures in the India Office Library*. London: Sotheby Parke Bernet.

Falk and Digby 1979
Falk, Toby and Simon Digby. *Mughal India*. London: Colnaghi.

Findly 1981
Findly, Ellison Banks. *From the Courts of India: Indian Miniatures in the Collection of the Worcester Art Museum*. Worcester, Mass.: Worcester Art Museum.

Fischer 2005
Fischer, Eberhard. *Göttinnen. Indische Bilder im Museum Rietberg*. Zürich: Museum Rietberg.

Fogg 2000
Islamic Manuscripts, cat. 22. London: Sam Fogg.

Gahlin 1991
Gahlin, Sven. *The Courts of India: Indian Miniatures from the Collection of the Foundation Custodia, Paris*. Zwolle: Waanders.

Gahlin 2002
Gahlin, Sven. *Couleurs de l'Inde: nouvelles acquisitions de la Collection Frits Lugt*. Paris: Fondation Custodia.

Glynn, Skelton and Dallapiccola 2011
Glynn, Catherine, Robert Skelton and Anna Dallapiccola. *Ragamala Paintings from India from the Claudio Moscatelli Collection.* London: Philip Wilson.

Goetz 1950
Goetz, Hermann. *The Art and Architecture of Bikaner State.* Oxford: Bruno Cassirer.

Goswamy 1997
Goswamy, B.N. *Nainsukh of Guler, a Great Indian Painter from a Small Hill State.* Zürich: Artibus Asiae Publishers.

Goswamy 1999
Goswamy, B.N. *Painters at the Sikh Court: A Study Based on Twenty Documents.* New Delhi: Aryan Books.

Goswamy and Bhatia 1999
Goswamy, B.N. and Usha Bhatia. *Painted Visions, the Goenka Collection of Indian Paintings.* New Dehli: Lalit Kala Akademi.

Goswamy and Fischer 1987
Goswamy, B.N. and Eberhard Fischer. *Wonders of a Golden Age. Painting at the Court of the Great Mughals: Indian Art of the 16th and 17th Centuries from Collections in Switzerland.* Zürich: Museum Rietberg.

Goswamy and Fischer 1992
Goswamy, B.N. and Eberhard Fischer. *Pahari Masters – Court Painters of Northern India.* Zürich: Artibus Asiae Publishers.

Goswamy and Fischer 2011a
Goswamy, B.N. and Eberhard Fischer. "The First Generation after Manaku and Nainsukh of Guler." In *Masters of Indian Painting: 1100–1900*, ed. Milo C. Beach, Eberhard Fischer and B.N. Goswamy. Zürich: Artibus Asiae Publishers, 687–718.

Goswamy and Fischer 2011b
Goswamy, B.N. and Eberhard Fischer. "Purkhu of Kangra." In *Masters of Indian Painting: 1100–1900*, ed. Milo C. Beach, Eberhard Fischer and B.N. Goswamy. Zürich: Artibus Asiae Publishers, 719–732.

Goswamy and Fischer 2011c
Goswamy, B.N. and Eberhard Fischer. "Manaku." In *Masters of Indian Painting: 1100–1900*, ed. Milo C. Beach, Eberhard Fischer and B.N. Goswamy. Zürich: Artibus Asiae Publishers, 641–658.

Goswamy and Smith 2005
Goswamy, B.N. and Caron Smith. *Domains of Wonder: Selected Masterworks of Indian Painting.* San Diego: San Diego Museum of Art.

Griffin 1865
Griffin, Sir Lepel H. *The Panjab Chiefs. Historical and Biographical Notices of the Principal Families in the Territories under the Panjab Government.* Lahore: T.C. McCartney-Chronicle Press.

Gupta 1990
Gupta, B.D. "Bundelkhand through the Ages." In *A Panorama of Indian Culture: Professor A. Sreedhara Menon Felicitation Volume*, ed. K.K. Kusuman. New Delhi: Mittal Publications, 150–160.

Habighorst, Reichart and Sharma 2007
Habighorst, Ludwig, Peter A. Reichart and Vijay Sharma. *Love for Pleasure. Betel, Tobacco, Wine and Drugs in Indian Miniatures.* Koblenz: Ragaputra Edition.

Haidar 1995
Haidar, Navina. *The Kishangarh School of Painting, c. 1680–1850.* Ph.D. thesis. Oxford: University of Oxford.

Haidar 2000
Haidar, Navina. "Satire and Humour in Kishangarh Painting." In *Court Painting in Rajasthan*, ed. Andrew Topsfield. Bombay: Marg Publications, 78–91.

Haidar 2011
Haidar, Navina. "Nihal Chand." In *Masters of Indian Painting: 1100–1900*, ed. Milo C. Beach, Eberhard Fischer and B.N. Goswamy. Zürich: Artibus Asiae Publishers, 595–606.

Heeramaneck 1984
Heeramaneck, Alice. *Masterpieces of Indian Painting: from the Former Collections of Nasli M. Heeramaneck.* S.l.: Alice Heeramaneck.

Hickmann and Enderlein 1979
Hickmann, Regina and Volkmar Enderlein. *Indische Albumblätter, Miniaturen und Kalligraphien aus der Zeit der Moghul-Kaiser.* Leipzig: Gustav Kiepenheuer Verlag.

Isacco and Dallapiccola 1982
Isacco, Enrico and Anna Dallapiccola, eds. *Krishna the Divine Lover.* New York: C.H.P. Editions.

Jackson and Jaffer 2009
Jackson, Anna and Amin Jaffer. *Maharaja: the Splendour of India's Royal Courts.* London: V & A Publishing.

Jahresbericht (Museum Rietberg) 2011
Museum Rietberg. *Jahresbericht 2011.* Zürich: Museum Rietberg.

Khan 1979–80
Khan, Faiyaz Ali. "The Painters of Kishangarh." *Roopa-Lekha* 51/1–2: 61–69.

Khandalavala 1950
Khandalavala, Karl. "Leaves from Rajasthan." *Marg* 4/3: 2–24, 49–56.

Khandalavala 1958
Khandalavala, Karl. *Pahari Miniature Painting.* Bombay: New Book Co.

Khandalavala 1987
Khandalavala, Karl J. "Facets of Indian Miniature Painting." In *A Collector's Dream. Indian Art in the Collection of Basant Kumar and Saraladevi Birla and the Birla Academy of Art and Culture*, ed. Karl J. Khandalavala and Saryu Doshi. Bombay: Marg Publications, 67–164.

Khandalavala and Chandra 1965
Khandalavala, Karl and Moti Chandra. *Miniatures and Sculptures from the Collection of the Late Sir Cowasji Jehangir, Bart.* Bombay: Trustees of the Prince of Wales Museum.

Khandalavala, Chandra and Chandra 1960
Khandalavala, Karl; Moti Chandra and Pramod Chandra. *Miniature Paintings from the Sri Motichand Khajanchi Collection.* New Delhi: Lalit Kala Akademi.

Krishna A. 1963
Krishna, Anand. *Malwa Painting.* Varanasi: Bharat Kala Bhavan.

Krishna N. 1985
Krishna, Naval. "Bikaneri Miniature Painting Workshops of Ruknuddin, Ibrahim and Nathu." *Lalit Kala* 21: 23–27.

Lafont and Schmitz 2002
Lafont, Jean-Marie and Barbara Schmitz. "The Painter Imam Bakhsh of Lahore." In *After the Great Mughals: Painting in Delhi and Regional Courts in the 18th and 19th Centuries*, ed. Barbara Schmitz. Mumbai: Marg Publications, 74–99.

Leach 1986
Leach, Linda York. *Indian Miniature Paintings and Drawings*. Cleveland: The Cleveland Museum of Art.

Leach 1995
Leach, Linda York. *Mughal and Other Indian Paintings from the Chester Beatty Library*. London: Scorpion Cavendish.

Leach 1998
Leach, Linda York. *Paintings from India. The Nasser D. Khalili Collection of Islamic Art*. Vol. VIII. Oxford: The Nour Foundation in association with Oxford University Press.

Lerner 1974
Lerner, Michael. *Indian Miniatures: From the Jeffrey Paley Collection*. New York: Metropolitan Museum of Art.

Losty 1995
Losty, Jeremiah P. "Aurangabad or Mewar? The Influence of the Deccan on Rana Jagat Singh's Ramayana of 1649–53." In *Indian Painting: Essays in Honour of Karl J. Khandalavala*, ed. B.N. Goswamy. New Delhi: Lalit Kala Akademi, 290–315.

Losty 2000
Losty, Jeremiah P. "A Hitopadesha Manuscript of 1761–62 from Uniara." In *Court Painting in Rajasthan*, ed. Andrew Topsfield. Bombay: Marg Publications, 109–122.

Losty 2002
Losty, Jeremiah P. "Towards a New Naturalism: Portraiture in Murshidabad and Avadh, 1750–80." In *After the Great Mughals: Painting in Delhi and Regional Courts in the* 18th and 19th Centuries, ed. Barbara Schmitz. Mumbai: Marg Publications, 34–55.

Losty 2008
Losty, Jeremiah P. *The Ramayana: Love and Valour in India's Great Epic – the Mewar Ramayana Manuscripts*. London: British Library.

Losty 2010
Losty, Jeremiah P. *Indian Miniatures from the James Ivory Collection*. London: Francesca Galloway.

Losty 2011
Losty, Jeremiah P. *Indian Miniature Paintings from the Lloyd Collection*. London: Oliver Forge and Brendan Lynch.

Losty 2013
Losty, Jeremiah P. *Indian Painting 1580–1850*, Exhibition New York. London: Oliver Forge and Brendan Lynch.

Losty [forthcoming]
Losty, Jeremiah P. "The Carpet at the Window: a European Motif in the Mughal *Jharokha* Portrait." In *Indian Painting: Themes, History and Interpretations; Essays in Honour of B N Goswamy*, ed. M. Sharma and P. Kaimal. Ahmedabad: Mapin Publishing.

Losty and Galloway 2007
Losty, Jeremiah P. and Francesca Galloway. *Sringar: An Exhibition Celebrating Divine and Erotic Love*. London: Francesca Galloway.

Losty and Leach 1998
Losty, Jeremiah P. and Linda York Leach. *Mughal Paintings from the British Library*. London: Indar Pasricha Arts.

Losty and Roy 2012
Losty, Jeremiah P. and Malini Roy. *Mughal India: Art, Culture and Empire*. London: The British Library.

Mason 2001
Mason, Darielle. *Intimate Worlds: Indian Paintings from the Alvin O. Bellak Collection*. Philadelphia: Philadelphia Museum of Art.

McInerney 2011
McInerney, Terence. "Dalchand." In *Masters of Indian Painting: 1100–1900*, ed. Milo C. Beach, Eberhard Fischer and B.N. Goswamy. Zürich: Artibus Asiae Publishers, 563–578.

Mehta 1926
Mehta, N.C. *Studies in Indian Painting; a Survey of some New Material Ranging from the Commencement of the VIIth Century to circa 1870 A.D.* Bombay: D.B. Taraporevala Sons.

Mehta 1935
Mehta, N.C. "A Note on *Ragamala*." *Journal of the Indian Society of Oriental Art* 3: 145–147.

Michell, Lampert and Holland 1982
Michell, George; Catherine Lampert and Tristram Holland, eds. *In the Image of Man. The Indian Perception of the Universe through 2000 Years of Painting and Sculpture*. London: Arts Council of Great Britain.

Mittal 1963
Mittal, Jagdish. "Painting of the Hyderabad School." *Marg* 16/2: 43–56.

Okada and Richard 1986
Okada, Amina and Francis Richard. *À la cour du Grand Moghol*. Paris: Bibliothèque Nationale.

Pal 1978
Pal, Pratapaditya. *The Classical Tradition in Rajput Painting from the Paul F. Walter Collection*. New York: The Pierpont Morgan Library/ The Gallery Association of New York State.

Pal 1983
Pal, Pratapaditya. *Court Paintings of India, 16th–19th Centuries*. New York: Navin Kumar.

Pal 2004
Pal, Pratapaditya. *Painted Poems. Rajput Paintings from the Ramesh and Urmil Kapoor Collection*. Ahmedabad: Mapin Publishing/Norton Simon Museum.

Pal et al. 1989
Pal, Pratapaditya, Janice Leoshko, Joseph M. Dye, III, and Stephen Markel. *Romance of the Taj Mahal*. Los Angeles and London: Los Angeles County Museum of Art and Thames and Hudson Ltd.

Poster et al. 1994
Poster, Amy G., Sheila Canby, Pramod Chanda and Joan Cummings. *Realms of Heroism: Indian Paintings at the Brooklyn Museum*. New York: The Brooklyn Museum.

Prinsep 1885
Prinsep, Charles Campbell. *Record of Services of the Honourable East India Company's Civil Servants in the Madras Presidency from 1741 to 1858. Compiled and Edited from Records in the Possession of the Secretary of State for India*. London: Trübner & Co.

Pratap 1996
Pratap, Rita. *The Panorama of Jaipur Paintings*. New Delhi: D.K. Printworld.

Roy 2008
Roy, Malini. *50× India: the 50 Most Beautiful Miniatures from the Rijksmuseum*. Amsterdam: Rijksmuseum.

Schmitz 2002
Schmitz, Barbara. "After the Great Mughals." *After the Great Mughals. Painting in Delhi and the Regional Courts in the 18th and 19th Centuries*, ed. Barbara Schmitz. Mumbai: Marg Publications, 1–11.

Seyller 1999
Seyller, John. *Workshop and Patron: The Freer* Ramayana *and Other Illustrated Manuscripts of 'Abd al-Rahim*. Zürich: Artibus Asiae Publishers.

Seyller 2010
Seyller, John. "Two Mughal Mirror Cases." *Journal of the David Collection* 3: 130–159.

Seyller 2011
Seyller, John. "Manohar." In *Masters of Indian Painting: 1100–1900*, ed. Milo C. Beach, Eberhard Fischer and B.N. Goswamy. Zürich: Artibus Asiae Publishers, 135–152.

Seyller with Seitz 2010
Seyller, John with Konrad Seitz. *The Eva and Konrad Seitz Collection of Indian Miniatures. Vol. 1: Mughal and Deccani Paintings*. Zürich: Museum Rietberg.

Sharma 1974
Sharma, O.P. *Indian Miniature Painting: Exhibition Compiled from the Collection of the National Museum, New Delhi*. Brussels: Bibliothèque Royale.

Skelton 1973
Skelton, Robert. *Rajasthani Temple Hangings of the Krishna Cult*. New York: American Federation of the Arts.

Skelton 1981
Skelton, Robert. "Shaykh Phul and the Origins of Bundi Painting." In *Chhavi-2. Rai Krishnadasa Felicitation Volume*, ed. by Anand Krishna. Benares: Bharat Kala Bhavan, 123–129.

Smart and Walker 1985
Smart, Ellen S. and Daniel S. Walker. *Pride of the Princes: Indian Art of the Mughal Era in the Cincinnati Art Museum*. Cincinnati: Cincinnati Art Museum.

Sodhi 1999
Sodhi, J. *A Study of Bundi School of Painting: From the Collection of the National Museum, New Delhi*. New Delhi: Abhinav.

Spink 1982
Spink & Son. *Two Thousand Years of Indian Art*. London: Spink & Son.

Spink 1987
Spink & Son. *Indian Miniature Painting*. London: Spink & Son.

Stronge 1999
Stronge, Susan, ed. *The Arts of the Sikh Kingdoms*. London: V&A Publications.

Tod 1920
Tod, James. *Annals and Antiquities of Rajasthan*, ed. W. Crooke. London: Humphrey Milford.

Tooth & Sons 1974
Tooth, Arthur & Sons. *Indian Paintings from the 17th to 19th Centuries: Including Examples from Rajasthan, the Punjab Hills, Deccan and Other Areas*. London: Waddington and Tooth Galleries II.

Tooth & Sons 1977
Tooth, Arthur & Sons. *Indian Paintings from the 17th to 19th Centuries: Including Examples from Rajasthan, the Punjab Hills, Deccan and Other Areas*. London: Waddington and Tooth Galleries II.

Topsfield 1980
Topsfield, Andrew. *Paintings from Rajasthan in the National Gallery of Victoria*. Melbourne: National Gallery of Victoria.

Topsfield 1994
Topsfield, Andrew. *Indian Paintings from Oxford Collections*. Oxford: Asmolean Museum in association with the Bodleian Library.

Topsfield 2002
Topsfield, Andrew. *Court Painting at Udaipur: Art under the Patronage of the Maharanas of Mewar*. Zürich: Artibus Asiae Publishers.

Topsfield 2004
Topsfield, Andrew, ed. *In the Realm of Gods and Kings*. London: Philip Wilson Publishers.

Topsfield 2012
Topsfield, Andrew. *Visions of Mughal India. The Collection of Howard Hodgkin*. Oxford: Ashmolean Museum.

Topsfield and Beach 1991
Topsfield, Andrew and Milo Cleveland Beach. *Indian Paintings and Drawings from the Collection of Howard Hodgkin*. London: Thames and Hudson.

Tuli 1999
Tuli, Neville. *Intuitive Logic, the Next Step: Auctions of Indian Art*. New Delhi and Mumbai: Heart in association with Mapin Publishing.

von Hügel 1845
von Hügel, Charles. *Travels in Kashmir and the Panjab, containing a Particular Account of the Government and Character of the Sikhs*. London: John Petheram.

Waldschmidt and Waldschmidt 1966
Waldschmidt, Ernst and Rose Leonore Waldschmidt. *Musikinspirierte Miniaturen aus der Sammlung des Museums für Indische Kunst Berlin. Teil 1: Ragamala-Bilder aus dem westlichen Himalaya-Gebiet*. Berlin und Wiesbaden: Museum für Indische Kunst, Harrassowitz.

Waldschmidt and Waldschmidt 1975
Waldschmidt, Ernst and Rose Leonore Waldschmidt. *Miniatures of Musical Inspiration in the Collection of the Berlin Museum of Indian Art, Part II, Ragamala Pictures from Northern India and the Deccan.* Berlin: Museum für Indische Kunst.

Welch 1976
Welch, Stuart Cary. *Indian Drawings and Painted Sketches.* New York: The Asia Society.

Welch 1978
Welch, Stuart Cary. *Room for Wonder: Indian Painting During the British Period.* New York: American Federation of Arts.

Welch and Beach 1965
Welch, Stuart Cary and Milo Cleveland Beach. *Gods, Thrones, and Peacocks. Northern Indian Painting from Two Traditions: Fifteenth to Nineteenth Centuries.* New York: Asia House Gallery.

Welch et al. 1987
Welch, Stuart Cary, Annemarie Schimmel, Marie L. Swietochowski and Wheeler M. Thackston. *The Emperors' Album. Images of Mughal India.* New York: The Metropolitan Museum of Art.

Welch et al. 1997
Welch, Stuart Cary et al. *Gods, Kings and Tigers: the Art of Kotah.* Munich and New York: Prestel.

Wright 2008
Wright, Elaine, ed. *Muraqqa'. Imperial Mughal Albums from the Chester Beatty Library.* Alexandria, VA: Art Services International.

Zebrowski 1983
Zebrowski, Mark. *Deccani Painting.* London: Sotheby's.

Imprint

This publication accompanies the exhibition

A Secret Garden – Indian Paintings from a Private Collection

held at the Museum Rietberg Zürich from March 18 until June 29, 2014.

Editor
Jorrit Britschgi,
Museum Rietberg Zürich

Copy-editing
Julie Pickard, London

Graphic design
Elizabeth Hefti, Winterthur

Typesetting
Elizabeth Hefti, Claudia Rossi

Lithographs
Albert Walker, Winterthur

Proofreading
Lisa Schons, Konstanz

Printing and binding
freiburger graphische betriebe,
Freiburg i.Brsg.

Front cover
Lovers in a garden, possibly by Muhammadi, Mandi, c. 1810 (cat. 94)

ISBN 978-3-85881-750-1

Verlag Scheidegger & Spiess AG
Niederdorfstrasse 54
CH-8001 Zürich
Switzerland

www.scheidegger-spiess.ch